ISBN 978-1-334-71398-9
PIBN 10643256

For support please visit www.forgottenbooks.com

1 MONTH OF
FREE
READING

at

www.ForgottenBooks.com

By purchasing this book you are eligible for one month membership to ForgottenBooks.com, giving you unlimited access to our entire collection of over 1,000,000 titles via our web site and mobile apps.

To claim your free month visit:

www.forgottenbooks.com/free643256

English
Français
Deutsche
Italiano
Español
Português

www.forgottenbooks.com

Mythology Photography **Fiction**
Fishing Christianity **Art** Cooking
Essays Buddhism Freemasonry
Medicine **Biology** Music **Ancient
Egypt** Evolution Carpentry Physics
Dance Geology **Mathematics** Fitness
Shakespeare **Folklore** Yoga Marketing
Confidence Immortality Biographies
Poetry **Psychology** Witchcraft
Electronics Chemistry History **Law**
Accounting **Philosophy** Anthropology
Alchemy Drama Quantum Mechanics
Atheism Sexual Health **Ancient History**
Entrepreneurship Languages Sport
Paleontology Needlework Islam
Metaphysics Investment Archaeology
Parenting Statistics Criminology
Motivational

REPORT ON THE SANITARY CONDITION OF THE
LABOURING POPULATION OF GREAT BRITAIN.

A

SUPPLEMENTARY REPORT

ON THE RESULTS OF A SPIECAL INQUIRY INTO

THE

PRACTICE OF INTERMENT IN TOWNS.

MADE

AT THE REQUEST OF HER MAJESTY'S PRINCIPAL SECRETARY OF STATE
FOR THE HOME DEPARTMENT,

BY

EDWIN CHADWICK, Esq.

BARRISTER AT LAW.

Presented to both Houses of Parliament, by Command of Her Majesty.

LONDON:
PRINTED BY W. CLOWES AND SONS, STAMFORD STREET,
FOR HER MAJESTY'S STATIONERY OFFICE.

1843.

CONTENTS.

CONTENTS.

APPENDIX.

SANITARY REPORT.—SUPPLEMENT.

INTERMENTS IN TOWNS.

To the Right Honourable Sir James Graham, Bart.,
&c., &c., &c.

SIR,

In compliance with the request which I have had the honour to receive from you, that I would examine the evidence on the practice of interment, and the means of its improvement, and prepare for consideration a Report thereon, I now submit the facts and conclusions following :—

It has been remarked, as a defect in the General Report on the evidence as to the sanitary condition of the labouring population, that it did not comprise any examination of the evidence as to the effects produced on the public health, by the practice of interring the dead amidst the habitations of the town population. I wish here to explain that the omission arose from the subject being too great in its extent, and too special in its nature, to allow of the completion at that time, of any satisfactory investigation in relation to it even if it had not then been under examination by a Committee of the House of Commons, whose Report is now before the public.

To obtain the information on which the following report is founded, I have consulted, as extensively as the time allowed and my opportunities would permit, ministers of religion who are called upon to perform funereal rites in the poorer districts : I have made inquiries of persons of the labouring classes, and of secretaries and officers of benefit societies and burial clubs, in the metropolis and in several provincial towns in the United Kingdom, on the practice of interments in relation to those classes, and on the alterations and improvements that would be most in accordance with their feelings : I have questioned persons following the occupation of undertaker, and more especially those who are chiefly engaged in the interment of the dead of the labouring classes, on the improvements which they deem practicable in the modes of performing that service : I have consulted foreigners resident in the metropolis, on the various modes of interment in their own countries : I have

B

examined the chief administrative regulations thereon in Germany, France, and the United States : and I have consulted several eminent physiologists as to the effects produced on the health of the living, by emanations from human remains in a state of decomposition.   I need scarcely premise that the moral as well as the physical facts developed in the course of this inquiry are often exceedingly loathsome ; but general conclusions can only be distinctly made out from the various classes of particular facts, and the object being the suggestion of remedies and preventives, it were obviously as unbecoming to yield to disgusts or to evade the examination and calm consideration of those facts, as it would be in the physician or the surgeon, in the performance of his duty with the like object, to shrink from the investigation of the most offensive manifestations of disease.

§ 1. It appears that the necessity of removing interments from the midst of towns is very generally admitted on various considerations, independently of those founded on the presumed injurious effects arising from the practice to the public health. I believe an alteration of the practice is strongly desired by many clergymen of the established church, whose incomes, even with the probable compensation for the loss of burial dues, might be expected to be diminished by the discontinuance of *intra-mural* interments. Exemptions from a general prohibition of such interments are, however, claimed in favour of particular burial-grounds, situate within populous districts, of which grounds it is stated that they are not over-crowded with bodies, and of which it is further alleged that they have not been known, and cannot be proved, to be injurious to the public health.

The statements as to the innocuousness of particular graveyards are supported by reference to the general testimony of a number of medical witnesses of high professional position, by whom it is alleged that the emanations from decomposing human remains do not produce specific disease, and, further, that they are not generally injurious.   The practical consequences of these doctrines extend beyond the present question, and are so important in their effects on the sanitary economy of all towns, as apparently to require that no opportunity should be lost of examining the statements of facts on which they are founded.

The medical evidence of this class has generally been given in answer to complaints made by the public, of the offensiveness, and the danger to health which arises from the practice of dissection in schools of anatomy amidst crowded populations.   The chief fact alleged to prove the innocuousness of emanations from the dead is, that professors of anatomy experience no injury from them.   Thus, Dr. Warren, of Boston, in a paper cited by M. Parent Duchâtelet, states, that he has been accustomed all his life to dissecting-rooms, in which he has been engaged night and day.   " It has sometimes happened to me," he observes, "after having dissected bodies in a state of putrefaction, to have experienced a sort of weakness and the loss of appetite ; but the phenomena were never otherwise than transient. During the year 1829, the weather being excessively hot, decomposition advanced with a degree of rapidity such as I have rarely witnessed: at that season the emanations became so irritating, that they paralyzed the hands, producing small pustules and an excessive · itching, and yet my general health was in nowise affected."

· Again, whilst it is stated by M. Duchâtelet that students who attend the dissecting-rooms are sometimes seriously injured, and even killed by pricks and cuts with the instruments of dissection, yet it is denied that they are subject to any illness from · the emanations from the remains "other than a nausea and a dysentery for two or three days at the commencement of their studies." Fevers the students of medicine are confessedly liable to, but he says it is only when they are in attendance on the living patients in the fever wards.

Sir Benjamin Brodie pointed out to me, that from the precautions taken, by the removal of such portions of the viscera as might be in an advanced state of decomposition, and from the ventilation of dissecting-rooms being much improved, the emanations from the bodies dissected are not so great as might be supposed; nevertheless, he observes:—

There is no doubt that there are few persons who during the anatomical season are engaged for many hours daily in a dissecting-room for a considerable time, whose health is not affected in a greater or less degree ; and there are some whose health suffers considerably. I have known several young men who have not been able to prosecute their studies in the dissecting-room for more than three or four weeks at a time, without being compelled to leave them and go into the country. The great majority, however, do not suffer to that extent, nor in such a way as to cause interruption to their studies ; and, altogether, the evil is not on a sufficiently large scale to attract much notice, even among the students themselves.

A writer on public health, Dr. Dunglison, maintains that "we have no satisfactory proof that malaria ever arises from animal putrefaction singly;" and as evidence of this position he adduces the alleged fact of the numbers of students who pass through their education without injury ; yet he admits—

In stating the opinion that putrefaction singly does not occasion malarious disease, we do not mean to affirm that air highly charged with putrid miasmata may not, in some cases, powerfully impress the nervous system so as to induce syncope and high nervous disorder; or that, when such miasmata are absorbed by the lungs in a concentrated state, they may not excite putrid disorders, or dispose the frame to unhealthy erysipelatous affections. On the contrary, experiment seems to have shown that they are deleterious when injected; and cases are detailed in which, when exhaled from the dead body, they have excited serious mischief in those exposed to their action. According to Percy, a Dr. Chambon was required by the Dean of the Faculté de Medicine of Paris to demonstrate the liver and its appendages before the faculty on applying for his licence. The decomposition of the subject given him for the demonstration was so far advanced, that Chambon drew the attention of the Dean to it, but he was required to go on. One of the four candidates, Corion, struck by the putrid emanations which escaped from the body as soon as it was opened, fainted, was carried home, and died in seventy hours; another, the celebrated Fourcroy, was attacked with a burning exanthematous eruption; and two others, Laguerenne and Dufresnoy, remained a long time feeble, and the latter never completely recovered. " As for Chambon," says M. Londe, "indignant at the obstinacy of the Dean, he remained firm in his place, finished his lecture in the midst of the Commissioners, who inundated their handkerchiefs with essences, and, doubtless, owed his safety to his cerebral excitement, which during the night, after a slight febrile attack, gave occasion to a profuse cutaneous exhalation."

An eminent surgeon, who expressed to me his belief that no injury resulted from emanations from decomposing remains, for *he* had suffered none, mentioned an instance where he had conducted the post mortem examination of the corpse of a person of celebrity which was in a dreadful state of decomposition, without sustaining any injury; yet he admitted, as a casual incident which did not strike him as militating against the conclusion, that his assistant was immediately after taken ill, and had an exanthematous eruption, and had been compelled to go to the sea side, but had not yet recovered. Another surgeon who had lived for many years near a churchyard in the metropolis, and had never observed any effluvia from it, neither did *he* perceive any effects of such emanations at church or anywhere else; yet he admitted that his wife perceived the openings of vaults when she went to the church to which the graveyard belonged, and after respiring the air there, would say, "they have opened a vault," and on inquiry, the fact proved to be so. He admitted also, that formerly in the school of anatomy which he attended, pupils were sometimes attacked with fever, which was called " the dissecting-room fever," which, since better regulations were adopted, was now unknown.

§ 2. In proof of the position that the emanations from decomposing remains are not injurious to health at any time, reference is commonly made to the statements in the papers of Parent Duchâtelet, wherein he cites instances of the exhumation of bodies in an advanced stage of decomposition without any injurious consequences being experienced by the persons engaged in conducting them.

At the conclusion of this inquiry, and whilst engaged in the preparation of the report, I was favoured by Dr. Forbes with the copy of a report by Dr. V. A. Riecke, of Stuttgart, "On the Influence of Putrefactive Emanations on the Health of Man," &c., in which the medical evidence of this class is closely investigated. In reference to the statements of Parent Duchâtelet on this question, Dr. Riecke observes—

When Parent Duchâtelet appeals to and gives such prominence to the instance of the disinterments from the churchyard of St. Innocens, and states that they took place without any injurious consequences, although at last all precautions in the mode of disinterring were thrown aside, and that it occurred during the hottest season of the year, and therefore that the putrid emanations might be believed to be in their most powerful and injurious state, I would reply to this by asking the simple question, what occasion was there for the disinterment? Parent Duchâtelet maintains complete silence on this point; but to me the following notices appear worthy of attention. In the year 1554, Houlier and Fernel, and in the year 1738, Lemery, Geoffroy, and Hunaud, raised many complaints of this churchyard; and the two first had asserted that, during the plague, the disease had lingered longest in the neighbourhood of the Cimetière de la Trinité, and that there the greatest number had fallen a sacrifice. In the years 1737 and 1746 the inhabitants of the houses round the churchyard of St. Innocens complained loudly of the revolting stench to which they were exposed. In the year 1755 the matter again came into notice : the inspector who was intrusted with the inquiry, himself saw the vapour rising from a large common grave, and convinced himself of the injurious effects of this vapour on the inhabitants of the neighbouring house.* "Often," says the author of a paper which we have before often alluded to, "the complexions of the young people who remain in this neighbourhood grow pale. Meat sooner becomes putrid there than elsewhere, and many persons cannot get accustomed to these houses." In the year 1779, in a cemetery which yearly received from 2000 to 3000 corpses, they dug an immense common grave near to that part of the cemetery which touches upon the Rue de la Lingerie. The grave was 50 feet deep, and made to receive from 1500 to 1600 bodies. But in February, 1780, the whole of the cellars in the street were no longer fit to use. Candles were extinguished by the air in these cellars; and those who only approached the apertures were immediately seized with the most alarming attacks. The evil was only diminished on the bodies being covered with half a foot of lime, and all further interments forbidden. But even that must have been found insufficient, as, after some years, the great work of disinterring the bodies from this churchyard was determined upon. This undertaking, according to Thouret's report, was carried on from December, 1785, to May, 1786; from December, 1786, to February, 1787; and in August and October of the same year: and it is not unimportant to quote this passage, as it clearly shows how little correct Parent Duchâtelet was in his general statement, that those disinterments took place in the hottest seasons of the year. It is very clear that it was exactly the coldest seasons of the year which were chosen for the work; and though in the year 1787 there occurs the exception of the work having been again begun in August, I think it may be assumed that the weather of this month was unusually cold, and it was therefore thought the work might be carried on without injurious effects. It does not, however, appear to have been considered safe to continue the work at that season, since the report goes on to state that the operations were again discontinued in September.

Against those statements of Parent Duchâtelet, as to the innocuousness

---

* According to a memoir on this subject, read at the Royal Academy of Sciences, by M. Cadet de Vaux, in the year 1781, " Le méphetisme qui s'etoit dégagé d'une des fosses voisines du cimetière, avoit infecté toutes les caves: on comparait aux *poisons* les plus subtils, à ceux dont les sauvages impregnant leur flèches meurtrières, la terrible activité de cette émanation. Les murs baignés de l'humidité dont elles les pénétroit, pouvoit communiquer, disoit on par le seul attouchement les accidens les plus redoutable." See Mémoires de la Societé Royale de Médecine, tom. viii. p. 242 ; also Annales de Chimie, tom. v. p. 158. As an instance of the state of the cellars around the grave-yard, it is stated, that a workman being engaged in one of them put his hand on the wet wall. He was warned that the moisture on the walls was poisonous, and was requested to wash the hand in vinegar. He merely dried his hand on his apron: at the end of three days the whole arm became numb, then the hand and lower arm swelled with great pain, blisters came out on the skin, and the epidermis came off.

of the frequent disinterments in Père La Chaise, statements which are supported by the testimony of Orfila and Ollivier, in regard to their experience of disinterments, I would here place positive facts, which are not to be rejected. "I," also remarks Duvergie, " have undertaken judicial disinterments, and must declare that, during one of these disinterments at which M. Piedagnel was present with me, we were attacked with an illness, although it was conducted under the shade of a tent, through which there was passing a strong current of wind, and although we used chloride of lime in abundance. M. Piedagnel was confined to his room for six weeks." Apparently, Duvergie is not far wrong when he states his opinion that Orfila had allowed himself to be misled by his praiseworthy zeal for the more general recognition of the use of disinterments for judicial purposes, to understate the dangers attending them, as doubtless he had used all the precautions during the disinterments which such researches demand; and to these precautions (which Orfila himself recommended) may be attributed the few injurious effects of these disinterments. It, however, deserves mentioning, that, if Orfila did undertake disinterments during the heat of summer, it must have been only very rarely; at least, amongst the numerous special cases which he gives, we find only two which took place in July or August, most of the cases occurred in the coldest season of the year. I cannot refrain from giving, also, the information which Fourcroy gained from the grave-diggers of the churchyard of St. Innocens. Generally they did not seem to rate the danger of displacing the corpses very high: they remarked, however, that some days after the disinterment of the corpses the abdomen would swell, owing to the great development of gas; and that if an opening forced itself at the navel, or anywhere in the region of the belly, there issued forth the most horribly smelling liquid and a mephitic gas; and of the latter they had the greatest fear, as it produced sudden insensibility and faintings. Fourcroy wished much to make further researches into the nature of this gas, but he could not find any grave-digger who could be induced by an offered reward to assist him by finding a body which was in a fit state to produce the gas. They stated, that, at a certain distance, this gas only produced a slight giddiness, a feeling of nausea, languor, and debility. These attacks lasted several hours, and were followed by loss of appetite, weakness, and trembling. "Is it not very probable," says Fourcroy, "that a poison so terrible that when in a concentrated state, it produced sudden death, should, even when diluted and diffused through the atmosphere, still possess a power sufficient to produce depression of the nervous energy and an entire disorder of their functions? Let any one witness the terror of these grave-diggers, and also see the cadaverous appearance of the greatest number, and all the other signs of the influence of a slow poison, and they will no longer doubt of the dangerous effects of the air from churchyards on the inmates of neighbouring houses."

After having strenuously asserted the general innocuousness of such emanations, and the absence of foundation for the complaints against the anatomical schools, Parent Duchâtelet concludes by an admission of their offensiveness, and a recommendation in the following terms :—

" Instead of retaining the ' debris' of dissection near the theatres of anatomy, it would certainly be better to remove them every day : but as that is often impracticable, there ought, on a good system of ' assainisse-ment,' to be considered the mode of retaining them without incurring the risk of suffering from their infection."

After describing the mode of removing the " debris," he concludes—

" Thus will this part of the work be freed from the inconveniences which accompanied and formed one of the widest sources of ' infection,' and of the disgust which were complained of in the theatres of anatomy."

§ 3. The statements of M. Duchâtelet respecting the innocuous-ness of ' emanations from decomposing animal and vegetable remains, observed by him at the *chantiers d'equarissage,* or receptacle for dead horses, and the *depôts de vidange,* or re-ceptacle of night soil, &c., at Montfaucon, near Paris, are cited in this country, and on the continent, as leading evidence to sustain the general doctrine ; but as it is with his statements of the direct effects of the emanations from the grave-yards, so it is with relation to his statements as to the effects of similar emanations on the health of the population ; the facts appear to have been imperfectly observed by him even in his own field of observation. In the Medical Review, conducted by Dr. Forbes, reference is made to the accounts given by Caillard of the epidemic which occurred in the vicinity of the Canal de l'Ourcq near Paris in 1810 and subsequent years :—

In the route from Paris to Pantin (says he), exposed on the one side to the miasmatic emanations of the canal, and on the other, to the putrid efflu-via of the *voiries*, the diseases were numerous, almost all serious and obsti-nate. This disastrous effect of the union of putrid effluvia with marsh miasmata, was especially evident in one part of this route, termed the Petit Pont hamlet, inhabited by a currier and a gut-spinner, the putrid waters from whose operations are prevented from escaping by the banks of the canal, and exposed before the draining to the emanations of a large marsh. This hamlet was so unhealthy, that of five-and-twenty or thirty inhabitants I visited about twenty were seriously affected, of whom five died.

In the carefully prepared report on the progress of cholera at Paris, made by the commission of medical men, of which Parent Duchâtelet was a member, it is mentioned, as a singular incident, that in those places where putrid emanations prevailed, " le cholera ne s'est montré ni plus redoutable ni plus meurtrier que dans autres localities." Yet the testimony cited as to this point is that of the Maire, " whose zeal equalled his intelligence," and he alleges the occurrence of the fact of the liability to fevers which M. Duchâtelet elsewhere denies.

" I have also made some observations which seem to destroy the opinions received at this time, as to the sanitary effect of these kinds of receptacles ; for,

" 1st. The inhabitants of the houses situated the nearest to the depôt, and which are sometimes *tormented* with fevers, have never felt any indis-position."

§ 4. To prove the innocuousness of emanations from human re-mains on the general health, evidence of another class is adduced, consisting of instances of persons acting as keepers of dissecting rooms, and grave-diggers, and the undertakers' men, who it is stated have pursued their occupations for long periods, and have never-theless maintained robust health.

The examination of persons engaged in processes exposed to

miasma from decomposing animal remains in general only shows that habit combined with associations of profit often prevents or blunts the perceptions of the most offensive remains. Men with shrunken figures, and the appearance of premature age, and a peculiar cadaverous aspect, have attended as witnesses to attest their own perfectly sound condition, as evidence of the salubrity of their particular occupations. Generally, however, men with robust figures and the hue of health are singled out and presented as examples of the general innocuousness of the offensive miasma generated in the process in which they are engaged. Professor Owen mentions an instance of a witness of this class, a very robust man, the keeper of a dissecting room, who appeared to be in florid health (which however proved not to be so sound as he himself conceived), who professed perfect unconsciousness of having sustained any injury from the occupation, and there was no reason to doubt that he really was unconscious of having sustained or observed any ; but it turned out, on inquiry, that he had always had the most offensive and dangerous work done by an inferior assistant; and that within his time he had had no less than eight assistants, and that every one had died, and some of these had been dissected in the theatre where they had served. So, frequently, the sextons of graveyards, who are robust men, attest the salubrity of the place; but on examining the inferiors, the grave-diggers, it appears, where there is much to do, and even in some of the new cemeteries, that as a class they are unhealthy and cadaverous, and, notwithstanding precautions, often suffer severely on re-opening graves, and that their lives are frequently cut short by the work.* There are very florid and robust undertakers ; but, as a class, and with all the precautions they use, they are unhealthy ; and a master undertaker, of considerable business in the metropolis, states, that " in nine cases out of ten the undertaker who has much to do with the corpse is a person of cadaverous hue, and you may almost always tell him whenever you see him." Fellmongers, tanners, or the workmen employed in the preparation of hides, have been instanced by several medical writers as a class who, being exposed to emanations from the skins when in a state of putrefaction, enjoy good health ; but it appears that all the workmen are not engaged in the process when the skins are in that state, and that those of them who are, as a class, do experience the common consequences. The whole class of butchers, who are much in the open air and have very active exercise, and who are generally robust and have florid health, are commonly mentioned as instances in proof of the innocuousness of the emanations from the remains in slaughter-houses ; but master butchers admit that the men exclusively

---

* Vide also, Traité des Maladies des Artisans, par Patissier, d'apres Ramazzini, 8vo. Paris, 1822, p. 151, sur les Fossoyeurs : "Le sort des fossoyeurs est tres deplorable, leur face est livide, leur aspect triste : je n'en ai vu aucun devenir vieux." Also pp. 108-9, 137, 144.

engaged in the slaughter-houses, in which perfect cleanliness and due ventilation are neglected, are of a cadaverous aspect, and suffer proportionately in their health.

Medical papers have been written in this country and on the continent to show that the exposure of workmen to putrid emanations in the employment of sewer cleansing has no effect on the general health; and when the employers of the labourers engaged in such occupations are questioned on the subject, their general reply is, that their men " have nothing the matter with them :" yet when the *class* of men who have been engaged in the work during any length of time are assembled; when they are compared with classes of men of the same age and country, and of the like periods of service in other employments free from such emanations, or still more when they are compared with men of the same age coming from the purer atmosphere of a rural district, the fallacy is visible in the class, in their more pallid and shrunken aspect—the evidence of languid circulation and reduced "tone," and even of vitality—and there is then little doubt of the approximation given me by an engineer who has observed different classes of workmen being correct, that employment under such a mephitic influence as that in question ordinarily entails a loss of at least one-third of the natural duration of life and working ability.

The usual comment of the employers on the admitted facts of the ill-health and general brevity of life of the inferior workmen engaged in such occupations is, " But they drink—they are a drunken set;" and such appears frequently, yet by no means invariably, to be the case. On further examination it appears that the exposure to the emanations is productive of nervous depression, which is constantly urged by the workmen as necessitating the stimulus of spirituous or fermented liquors. The inference that the whole of the effects are ascribable to the habitual indulgence in such stimuli is rebutted by the facts elicited on examination of other classes of workmen who indulge as much or more, but who nevertheless enjoy better health, and a much greater average duration of life. It is apt to be overlooked that the weakly rarely engage in such occupations, or soon quit them ; and that, in general, the men are of the most robust classes, and have high wages and rather short hours of work, as well as stimulating food. A French physician, M. Labarraque, states in respect to the tanners, that, notwithstanding the constant exposure to the emanations from putrid fermentations; it has not been "remarked" of the workmen of this class that they are more subject to illness than others. A tanner, in a manual written for the use of the trade, without admitting the correctness of this statement, observes : "Whatever may be the opinion of M. Labarraque on this point, we do not hesitate to declare the fact that this species of labour cannot be borne by weakly, scrofulous, or lymphatic subjects.*

* Manuel du Tanneur et Corroyeur. Paris, 1833, p. 325.

§ 5. So far as observations have been made on the point (and the more those reported upon it are scrutinized, the less trustworthy they appear to be), workmen so exposed do not appear to be peculiarly subject to epidemics; many, indeed, appear to be exempted from them to such an extent as to raise a presumption that such emanations have on those "acclimated" to them an unexplained preservative effect analogous to vaccination. That one miasma may exclude, or neutralize, or modify the influence of another, would appear to be *primâ facie* probable. But it is now becoming more extensively apparent that the same cause is productive of very different effects on different persons, and on the same persons at different times; as in the case mentioned by Dr. Arnott of the school badly drained at Clarendon Square, Somers' Town, where every year, while the nuisance was at its height, and until it was removed by drainage, the malaria caused some remarkable form of disease; one year, extraordinary nervous affection, exhibiting rigid spasms, and then convulsions of the limbs, such as occur on taking various poisons into the stomach; another year, typhoid fever; in another, ophthalmia; in another, extraordinary constipation of the bowels, affecting similar numbers of the pupils. Such cases as the one before cited with respect to the depôt for animal matter in Paris, where the workmen suffered very little, whilst the people living near the depôt were "tormented with fevers," are common. The effects of such miasma are manifested immediately on all surrounding human life (and there is evidence to believe they are manifest in their degree on animal life[*]), in proportion to the relative strength of the destructive agents and the relative strength or weakness of

* In the course of some inquiries which I made with Professor Owen, when examining a slaughterman as to the effects of the effluvia of animal remains on himself and family, some other facts were elicited illustrative of the effects of such effluvia on still more delicate life. The man had lived in Bear-yard, near Clare-market, which was exposed to the combined effluvia from a slaughter-house and a tripe factory. He was a bird-fancier, but he found that he could not rear his birds in this place. He had known a bird fresh caught in summer-time die there in a week. He particularly noted as having a fatal influence on the birds, the stench raised by boiling down the fat from the tripe offal. He said, "You may hang the cage out of the garret window in any house round Bear-yard, and if it be a fresh bird, it will be dead in a week." He had previously lived for a time in the same neighbourhood in a room over a crowded burial-ground in Portugal-street; at times in the morning he had seen a mist rise from the ground, and the smell was offensive. That place was equally fatal to his birds. He had removed to another dwelling in Vere-street, Clare-market, which is beyond the smells from those particular places, and he was now enabled to keep his birds. In town, however, the ordinary singing-birds did not, usually, live more than about 18 months; in cages in the country, such birds were known to live as long as nine years or more on the same food. When he particularly wished to preserve a pet bird, he sent it for a time into the country; and by repeating this removal he preserved them much longer. The fact of the pernicious effect of offensive smells on the small graminivorous birds, and the short duration of their life in close rooms and districts, was attested by a bird-dealer. In respect to cattle, the slaughterman gave decided reasons for the conclusion, that whilst in the slaughter-house they lost their appetites and refused food from the effect of the effluvium of the place, and not, as was popularly supposed, from any presentiment of their impending fate. *Vide* General Sanitary Report, p. 103, note, and p. 106,

the beings exposed to them; the effects are seen first on infants; then on children in the order of their age and strength; then on females, or on the sickly, the aged, and feeble ; last of all, on the robust workmen, and on them it appears on those parts of the body that have been previously weakened by excess or by illness. Whilst M. Parent Duchâtelet was looking for immediate appearances of acute disease on the robust workmen living amidst the decomposing animal effluvium of the Montfaucon, I have the authority of Dr. Henry Bennett for stating that he might have found that the influ-ence of that effluvium was observable on the sick at half a mile dis-tant. "When I was house surgeon at St. Louis," says Dr. Bennett, " I several times remarked, that whenever the wind was from the direction of the Montfaucon, the wounds and sores under my care assumed a foul aspect. M. Jobert, the surgeon of the hospital, has told me that he has repeatedly seen hospital gangrene manifest itself in the wards apparently under the same influence. It is a fact known to all who are acquainted with St. Louis, that the above malady is more frequent at that hospital than at any other in Paris, although it is the most airy and least crowded of any. This, I think, can only be attributed to the proximity of the Montfaucon. Indeed, when the wind blows from that direction, which it often does for several months in the year, the effluvium is most odious." As an instance of a similar influence of another species of effluvium, not observed by the healthy inhabitants of a district, it is stated that at a large infirmary in this country, when the piece of orna-mental water, which was formerly stagnant in front of the edifice, had a greenish scum upon it, some descriptions of surgical operations were not so successful as at other times, and a flow of fresh water has been introduced into the reservoir to prevent the miasma.

The immediate contrasts of the apparent immunity of adults to conspicuous attacks of epidemics, may perhaps account for the persuasion which masters and workmen sometimes express, that they owe an immunity from epidemics to their occu-pation, and that the stenches to which they are exposed actually "purify" the atmosphere. Numbers of such witnesses have heretofore been ready to attest their conviction of the pre-servative effect, and even the positive advantages to health, of the effluvia generated by the decomposition of animal or of vegetable matter, or of the fumes of minerals, of smoke, soot, and coal gas. But though they do not peculiarly suffer from epidemics, it is usually found that they are not exempted. In a recent return of the state of health of some workmen engaged in cleansing sewers, whilst it appeared that very few had suffered any attack from fever, nearly all suffered bowel attacks and violent intestinal derange-ment. If the effects of such emanations invariably appeared in the form of acute disease, large masses of the population who have lived under their influence must have been exterminated. In general the poison appears only to be generated in a sufficient degree of intensity to create acute disease under such a conjunction

of circumstances, as a degree of moisture sufficient to facilitate de
composition, a hot sun, a stagnant atmosphere, and a languid
population.   The injurious effects of diluted emanations are constantly traceable, not in constitutional disturbance at any one time ;
they have their effect even on the strong, perceptible over a space
of time in a general depression of health and a shortened period
of existence.   This or that individual may have the florid hue of
health, and may live under constant exposure to noxious influences
to his sixtieth or his seventieth year; but had he not been so
exposed he might have lived in equal or greater vigour to his
eightieth or his ninetieth year.   A cause common to a whole
class is often, however, not manifest in particular individuals, but
is yet visible in the pallor and the reduced sum of vitality of the
whole class, or in the average duration of life in that class, as
compared with the average duration of life of another class similarly situated, in all respects except in the exposure to that one
cause.*   The effects of a cause of depression on a class are sometimes visible in the greater fatality of common accidents.   An
excess of mortality to a class is almost always found, on examination, to be traceable to an adequate cause.   From the external
circumstances of a class of the population, a confident expectation
may be formed of the sum of vitality of the class, though nothing
could be separately predicated of a single individual of it.   If the
former vulgar notions were correct as to the salubrity of the
stenches which prevail in towns, the separate as well as the combined results of these several supposed causes of salubrity must
be to expel fevers and epidemics from the most crowded manufacturing districts, and to advance the general health of the inhabitants above that of the poorer rural population; but all such
fallacies are dissipated by the dreadful facts on the face of the
mortuary records showing a frequency of deaths, and a reduction
of the mean duration of life, in proportion to the constancy and the
intensity of the combined operation of these same causes.†
    § 6. The observations of the effects of such emanations on the

---

    * On the evidence of individual cases the innocuousness of many poisons and dis-
eases might be proved.   Individuals are sometimes found to resist inoculation.   It
is a singular, and as yet unexplained fact, that centenarians are often found in the
greatest proportion in times and places where the average duration of life of the
whole population is very low.   It has been shown from an accurate registration of
centuries in Geneva, that as the average duration of life amongst the whole community advanced, the proportion of extreme cases of centenarians diminished.   According to the bills of mortality there were nearly three times as many centenarians
in London a century ago than at present.   Out of 141,720 deaths within the bills of
mortality during the five years ended 1742, the deaths of 58 persons alone of 100
years and upwards of age are recorded; whilst out of 139,876 deaths which occurred in the metropolis as returned by the registrar-general, during the three years
which ended 30th June, 1841, only 22 deaths of 100 years of age and upwards are
recorded.   The average age of death of all who died was then 24 years ; it is now,
judging from an enumeration made from the returns of 1839, about 27 years; and
there appears to have been a considerable improvement in all periods of life up to
90 years.
    † Vide Appendix of the district returns of the Mortuary Registration.

general health of classes of human beings have been corroborated by experiments on animals.

§ 7. Another doctrine more extensively entertained than that above noticed, is, that although putrid emanations are_productive of injury, they are not productive of specific disease, such as typhus. The medical witnesses say, that they were exposed to such emanations in dissecting-rooms, where bodies of persons who have died of small-pox, typhus, scarlatina, and every species of disease, are brought ; that they pursued their studies in such places, and were unaware of typhus or other disease having been taken by the students in them, though that disease was frequently caught by students whilst attending the living in the fever wards.*

The strongest of this class of negative evidence appears to be that of undertakers, all of whom that I have seen state that neither specific disease nor the propagation of any disease was known to occur amongst them, from their employment. Neither the men who handle, or who "coffin," the remains; nor the barbers who are called in to shave † the corpses of the adult males; nor the bearers of the coffins, although, when the remains are in an advanced state of decomposition, the liquid matter from the corpse frequently escapes from the coffin, and runs down over their clothes, are observed to catch any specific disease from it, either in their noviciate, or at any other time. When decomposition is very far advanced, and the smell is very offensive, the men engaged in putting the corpse into the coffin smoke tobacco ; and all have recourse to the stimulus of spirituous liquor. But it is not known that by their infected clothes they ever propagate specific disease in their families, or elsewhere. Neither does this appear to be observed amongst the medical men themselves.‡

§ 8. On the other hand, the undertakers observe such instances, as will be stated in their own words in a subsequent part of the

---

* In the medical profession examples are not rare of the attainment of extreme old age ; yet as a class they bear the visible marks of health below the average. The registration of one year may be an imperfect index ; but the mortuary registration for the year 1839 having been examined, to ascertain what was the average age of death of persons of the three professions, it appears that the average age of the clergymen who died in London during that year was 59; of the legal profession 50, and of the medical profession 45. Only one medical student was included in the registration : had the deaths of those who died in their noviciate been included, the average age of death of the medical profession would have been much lower.

† An instance in exception of a barber having caught fever is subsequently stated.

‡ Two days in the week the London Fever Hospital is open to the friends of the patients, who often spend a considerable time in the wards, sometimes sitting on the beds of the sick ; yet these visitors never take fever themselves, nor are they ever known to convey it by their clothes to persons out of the hospital. In like manner the persons employed to convey the clothes of the fever-patients from the wards of the hospital do not take fever, nor is there any evidence whatever that typhus fever is, or can be, propagated merely by the clothes ; yet it is remarkable that the laundresses who wash the clothes, which often contain excrementious matters from the patients, or from the dead, of an amount perceptible to the senses, rarely if ever escape fever. It is inferred, that in this case the poison is by the heat put in a state of vapour, which is inhaled, and being sufficient in quantity, produces the disease.

report, where others have caught fever and small-pox, apparently from the remains of the dead, and they mention instances of persons coming from a distance to attend funerals, who have shortly afterwards become affected with the disease of which the person buried had died. Of the undertakers it is observed, that being adults, they were likely to have had small-pox. Dr. Williams, in a work stated to be of good authority, on the effects of morbid poisons, relates the case of four students infected with small-pox by the dead body of a man who had died of this disease, that was brought into the Windmill-street Theatre, in London, for dissection. One of them saw the body, but did not approach it; another was near it, but did not touch it; a third, accustomed to make sketches from dead bodies, saw this subject, but did not touch it; the fourth alone touched it with both his hands; yet all the four caught the disease. Sir Benjamin Brodie mentions cases which occurred within his own knowledge, of pupils who caught small-pox after exposure to the emanations in the dissecting-room from the bodies of persons who had died of that disease.

Dr. Copeland, in his evidence before the Committee of the House of Commons, adduced the following remarkable case, stated to be of fever communicated after death:—

About two years ago (says he) I was called, in the course of my profession, to see a gentleman, advanced in life, well known to many members in this house and intimately known to the Speaker. This gentleman one Sunday went into a dissenting chapel, where the principal part of the hearers, as they died, were buried in the ground or vaults underneath. I was called to him on Tuesday evening, and I found him labouring under symptoms of malignant fever; either on that visit or the visit immediately following, on questioning him on the circumstances which could have given rise to this very malignant form of fever, for it was then so malignant that its fatal issue was evident, he said that he had gone on the Sunday before (this being on the Tuesday afternoon) to this dissenting chapel, and on going up the steps to the chapel he felt a rush of foul air issuing from the grated openings existing on each side of the steps; the effect upon him was instantaneous; it produced a feeling of sinking, with nausea, and so great debility, that he scarcely could get into the chapel. He remained a short time, and finding this feeling increase he went out, went home, was obliged to go to bed, and there he remained. When I saw him he had, up to the time of my ascertaining the origin of his complaint, slept with his wife; he died eight days afterwards; his wife caught the disease and died in eight days also, having experienced the same symptoms. These two instances illustrated the form of fever arising from those particular causes. Means of counteraction were used, and the fever did not extend to any other members of the family.

Assuming that that individual had gone into a crowded hospital with that fever, it probably would have become a contagious fever. The disease would have propagated itself most likely to others, provided those others exposed to the infection were pre-disposed to the infection, or if the apartments where they were confined were not fully ventilated, but in most cases where the emanations from the sick are duly diluted by fresh air, they are rendered innocuous. It is rarely that I have found the effects from dead animal matter so very decisive as in this case, because in the usual circumstances of burying in towns the fetid or foul air exhaled from the dead is generally so diluted and scattered by the wind, as to produce only a general ill effect upon those predisposed; it affects the health of the community by lowering the vital powers, weakening the digestive processes, but without producing any prominent or specific disease.

Mr. Barnett, surgeon, one of the medical officers of the Stepney Union, who has observed the symptoms observable in those persons who are exposed to the emanations from a crowded grave-yard, thus describes them :—

They are characterized by more or less disturbance of the whole system, with evident depression of the vital force, as evinced throughout the vascular and nervous systems, by the feeble action of the heart and arteries, and lowness of the spirits, &c. These maladies, I doubt not, if surrounded by other causes, would terminate in fever of the worst description. The cleanliness, &c., of the surrounding neighbourhood, perhaps, prevents this actually taking place.

Some years since a vault was opened in the church-yard (Stepney), and shortly after one of the coffins contained therein burst with so loud a report that hundreds flocked to the place to ascertain the cause. So intense was the poisonous nature of the effluvia arising therefrom, that a great number were attacked with sudden sickness and fainting, many of whom were a considerable period before they recovered their health.

The vaults and burial ground attached to Brunswick chapel, Lime-house, are much crowded with dead, and from the accounts of individuals residing in the adjoining houses, it would appear that the stench arising therefrom, particularly when a grave happens to be opened during the summer months, is most noxious. In one case it is described to have pro-duced instant nausea and vomiting, and attacks of illness are frequently imputed to it. Some say they have never had a day's good health since they have resided so near the chapel-ground, which, I may remark, is about five feet above the level of the surrounding yards, and very muddy—so much so, that pumps are frequently used to expel the water from the vaults into the streets.

The bursting of leaden coffins in the vaults of cemeteries, unless they are watched and "tapped" to allow the mephitic vapour to escape, appears to be not unfrequent. In cases of rapid decomposition, such instances occur in private houses before the entombment. An undertaker of considerable experience states :—

"I have known coffins to explode, like the report of a small gun, in the house. I was once called up at midnight by the people, who were in great alarm, and who stated that the coffin had burst in the night, as they described it, with 'a report like the report of a cannon.' On proceeding to the house I found in that case, which was one of dropsy, very rapid decomposition had occurred, and the lead was forced up. Two other cases have occurred within my experience of coffins bursting in this manner. I have heard of similar cases from other undertakers. The bursting of lead coffins without noise is more frequent. Of course it is never told to the family unless they have heard it, as they would attribute the bursting to some defective construction of the coffins."

The occurrence of cases of instant death to grave-diggers, from accidentally inhaling the concentrated miasma which escapes from coffins, is undeniable. Slower deaths from exposure to such miasma are designated as "low fevers," and whether or not the constitu-tional disturbances attendant on the exposure to the influence of such miasma be or not the true typhus, it suffices as a case requiring a remedy, that the exposure to that influence is apt to produce grievous and fatal injuries amongst the public.

§ 9. Undertakers state that they sometimes experience, in particularly crowded grave-yards, a sensation of faintness and nausea without perceiving any offensive smell. Dr. Riecke appears to conclude, from various instances which are given, that emanations from putrid remains operate in two ways,—one set of effects being produced through the lungs by impurity of the air from the mixture of irrespirable gases; the other set, through the olfactory nerves by powerful, penetrating, and offensive smells. On the whole, the evidence tends to establish the general conclusion that offensive smells are true warnings of sanitary evils to the population. The fact of the general offensiveness of such emanations is adduced by Dr. Riecke also as evidence of their injurious quality.

Another circumstance which must awaken in us distrust of putrid emanations, is the powerful impression they make on the sense of smell. It certainly cannot be far from the truth to call the organ of smell the truest sentinel of the human frame. "Many animals," observes Rudolphi, "are entirely dependent on their sense of smell for finding out food that is not injurious; where their smell is injured they are easily deceived, and have often fallen a sacrifice to the consequent mistakes." Amongst all known smells, there is, perhaps, no one which is so universally, and to such a degree revolting to man, as the smell of animal decomposition. The roughest savage, as well as the most civilized European, fly with equal disgust from a place where the air is infected by it. If an instinct ever can be traced in man, certainly it is in the present case: and is instinct a superfluous monitor exactly in this one case? Can instinct mislead just in this one circumstance? Can it ever be, that the air which fills us with the greatest disgust, is the finest elixir of life, as Dumoulins had the boldness to maintain in one of his official reports. Hippolyte Cloquet, in his Osphrestologie has attempted to throw some light on the effect of smell on the human frame, and though we must entirely disregard many of the anecdotes which he has blended into his inquiry, yet the result remains firmly proved that odours in general exert a very powerful influence on the health of men, and that all very acutely impressing smells are highly to be suspected of possessing injurious properties.

§ 10. I beg leave on this particular topic to submit the facts and opinions contained in communications from two gentlemen who have paid close and comprehensive attention to the subject.

Dr. Southwood Smith, who, as physician to the London Fever Hospital, and from having been engaged in several investigations as to the effects of putrid emanations on the public health, must have had extensive means of observation, states as follows :—

1. That the introduction of dead animal matter under certain conditions into the living body is capable of producing disease, and even death, is universally known and admitted. This morbific animal matter may be the product either of secretion during life or of decomposition after death. Familiar instances of morbific animal matter, the result of secretion during life, are the poisons of small-pox and cow-pox, and the vitiated fluids formed in certain acute diseases, such as acute inflammations, and particularly of the membranes that line the chest and abdomen. On the examina-

tion of the body a short time after death from such inflammations, the fluids are found so extremely acrid, that even when the skin is entirely sound, they make the hands of the examiner smart; and if there should happen to be the slightest scratch on the finger, or the minutest point not covered by cuticle, violent inflammation is often produced, ending, sometimes within forty-eight hours, in death. It is remarkable, and it is a proof that in these cases the poison absorbed is not putrid matter, that the most dangerous period for the examination of the bodies of persons who die of such diseases is from four to five hours after the fatal event, and while the body is yet warm.

That the direct introduction into the system of decomposing and putrescent animal matter is capable of producing fevers and inflammations, the intensity and malignity of which may be varied at will, according to the putrescency of the matter and the quantity of it that is introduced, is proved by numerous experiments on animals; while the instances in which human beings are seized with severe and fatal affections from the application of the fluids of a dead animal body to a wounded, punctured, or abraded surface, sometimes when the aperture is so minute as to be invisible without the aid of a lens, are of daily occurrence. Though this fact is now well known, and is among the few that are disputed by no one, it may be worth while to cite a few examples of it, as specimens of the manner in which the poison of animal matter, when absorbed in this way, acts; a volume might be filled with similar instances.

The following case is recorded by Sir Astley Cooper:—Mr. Elcock, student of anatomy, slightly punctured his finger in opening the body of a hospital patient about twelve o'clock at noon, and in the evening of the same day, finding the wound painful, showed it to Sir Astley Cooper after his surgical lecture. During the night the pain increased to extremity, and symptoms of high constitutional irritation presented themselves on the ensuing morning. No trace of inflammation was apparent beyond a slight redness of the spot at which the wound had been inflicted, which was a mere puncture. In the evening he was visited by Dr. Babington, in conjunction with Dr. Haighton and Sir Astley Cooper; still no local change was to be discovered, but the nervous system was agitated in a most violent and alarming degree, the symptoms nearly resembling the universal excitation of hydrophobia, and in this state he expired within the period of forty-eight hours from the injury.

The late Dr. Pett, of Hackney, being present at the examination of the body of a lady who had died of peritoneal inflammation after her confinement, handled the diseased parts. In the evening of the same day, while at a party, he felt some pain in one of his fingers, on which there was a slight blush, but no wound was visible at that time. The pain increasing, the finger was examined in a stronger light, when, by the aid of a lens, a minute opening in the cuticle was observed. During the night the pain increased to agony, and in the morning his appearance was extremely altered; his countenance was suffused with redness, his eyes were hollow and ferrety; there was a peculiarity in his breathing, which never left him during his illness; his manner, usually gay and playful, was now torpid, like that of a person who had taken an excessive dose of opium, he described himself as having suffered intensely, and said that he was completely knocked down and had not the strength of a child, and he sunk exhausted on the fifth day from the examination of the body.

George Higinbottom, an undertaker, was employed to remove in a shell the corpse of a woman who had died of typhus fever in the London Fever Hospital. In conveying the body from the shell into the coffin, he observed that his left hand was besmeared with a moisture which had oozed from it. He had a recent scratch on his thumb. The following morning this scratch was inflamed; in the evening of the same day he was attacked with a cold shivering and pain in his head and limbs, followed the next by other symptoms of severe fever; on the fourth day there was soreness in the top of the shoulder and fulness in the axilla; on the fifth the breast became swollen and effloresceent; on the seventh delirium supervened, succeeded by extreme prostration and coma, and death took place on the tenth day.

A lady in the country received a basket of fish from London which had become putrid on the road. In opening the basket she pricked her finger, and she slightly handled the fish. On the evening of this day inflammation came on in the finger, followed by such severe constitutional symptoms as to endanger life, and it was six months before the effects of this wound subsided and her health was restored.

Among many other cases, Mr. Travers gives the following, as displaying well the minor degrees of irritation, local and constitutional, to which cooks and others, in handling putrid animal matter with chapped and scratched fingers, are exposed:—A cook-maid practised herself on a stale hare, for the purpose of learning the mode of boning them, in spite of being strongly cautioned against it. A few days afterwards two slight scratches, which she remembered to have received at the time, began to inflame; one was situated on the fore-finger and the other on the ring-finger. This inflammation was accompanied with a dull pain and feeling of numbness, and an occasional darting pain along the inside of the fore-arm. The next day she was attacked with excruciating pain at the point of the fore-finger, which throbbed so violently as to give her the sensation of its being about to burst at every pulsation. The following morning constitutional symptoms came on; her tongue was white and dry; she had no appetite; there was great dejection of spirits and languor, and a weak and unsteady pulse. After suffering greatly from severe pain in the finger, hand, and arm, and great constitutional derangement and debility, the local inflammation disappeared in about three weeks, and she then began to recover her appetite and strength.

2. It is proved by indubitable evidence that this morbific matter is as capable of entering the system when minute particles of it are diffused in the atmosphere as when it is directly introduced into the blood-vessels by a wound. When diffused in the air, these noxious particles are conveyed into the system through the thin and delicate walls of the air vesicles of the lungs in the act of respiration. The mode in which the air vesicles are formed and disposed is such as to give to the human lungs an almost incredible extent of absorbing surface, while at every point of this surface there is a vascular tube ready to receive any substance imbibed by it and to carry it at once into the current of the circulation. Hence the instantaneousness and the dreadful energy with which certain poisons act upon the system when brought into contact with the pulmonary surface. A single inspiration of the concentrated prussic acid, for example, is capable of killing with the rapidity of a stroke of lightning. So rapidly does this poison affect the system, and so deadly is its nature, that more than one physiologist has lost his life by incautiously inhaling it while using it for the purpose of experiment. If the nose of an animal be slowly passed over a bottle containing this poison, and the animal happen to inspire during the moment of the passage, it drops down dead instantaneously, just as when the poison is applied in the form of a liquid to the tongue or the stomach. On the other hand, the vapour of chlorine possesses the property of arresting the poisonous effects of prussic acid; and hence when an animal is all but dead from the effects of this acid, it is sometimes suddenly restored to life by holding its mouth over the vapour of chlorine.

During every moment of life in natural respiration a portion of the air of the atmosphere passes through the air vesicles of the lungs into the blood, while a quantity of carbonic acid gas is given off from the blood, and is transmitted through the walls of these vesicles into the atmosphere. Now that substances mixed with or suspended in atmospheric air may be conveyed with it to the lungs and immediately enter into the circulating mass, any one may satisfy himself merely by passing through a recently painted chamber. The vapour of turpentine diffused through the chamber is transmitted to the lungs with the air which is breathed, and passing into the current of the circulation through the walls of the air vesicles, exhibits its effects in some of the fluid excretions of the body, even more rapidly than if it had been taken into the stomach.

Facts such as these help us to understand the production and propagation of disease through the medium of an infected atmosphere, whether on a large scale, as in the case of an epidemic which rapidly extends over a nation or a continent, or on a small scale, in the sick chamber, the dissecting room, the church, and the church-yard.

Thus it is universally known that, when the atmosphere is infected with the matter of small-pox, this disease is produced with the same and even with greater certainty than when the matter of small-pox is introduced by the lancet directly into a blood-vessel in inoculation.

It is equally well known that, when the air is infected by particles of decomposing vegetable and animal matter, fevers are produced of various types and different degrees of intensity; that the exhalations arising from marshes, bogs, and other uncultivated and undrained places, constitute a poison chiefly of a vegetable nature, which produces principally fevers of an intermittent or remittent type; and that exhalations accumulated in close, ill-ventilated, and crowded apartments in the confined situations of densely-populated cities, where little attention is paid to the removal of putrefying and excrementitious matters, constitute a poison chiefly of an animal nature, which produces continued fever of the typhoid character. There are situations in which these putrefying matters, aided by heat and other peculiarities of climate, generate a poison so intense and deadly, that a single inspiration of the air in which they are diffused is capable of producing almost instantaneous death; and there are other situations in which a less highly concentrated poison accumulates, the inspiration of which for a few minutes produces a fever capable of destroying life in from two to twelve hours. In dirty and neglected ships, in damp, crowded, and filthy gaols, in the crowded wards of ill-ventilated hospitals filled with persons labouring under malignant surgical diseases or bad forms of fever, an atmosphere is generated which cannot be breathed long, even by the most healthy and robust, without producing highly dangerous fever.

. 3. The evidence is just as indubitable that exhalations arise from the bodies of the dead, which are capable of producing disease and death. Many instances are recorded of the communication of small-pox from the corpse of a person who has died of small-pox. This has happened not only in the dwelling-house before interment, but even in the dissecting room. Some years ago five students of anatomy, at the Webb-street school, Southwark, who were pursuing their studies under Mr. Grainger, were seized with small-pox, communicated from a subject on the dissecting-table, though it does not appear that all who were attacked were actually engaged in dissecting this body. One of these young men died. There is reason to believe that emanations from the bodies of persons who have died of other forms of fever have proved injurious and even fatal to individuals who have been much in the same room with the corpse.

The exhalations arising from dead bodies in the dissecting room are in general so much diluted by admixture with atmospheric air, through the ventilation which is kept up, that they do not commonly affect the health in a very striking or marked manner; and by great attention to ventilation, it is no doubt possible to pursue the study of anatomy with tolerable impunity. Yet few teachers of anatomy deny that without this precaution this pursuit is very apt to injure the health, and that, with all the precaution that can be taken, it sometimes produces such a degree of diarrhœa, and at other times such a general derangement of the digestive organs, as imperatively to require an absence for a time from the dissecting room and a residence in the pure air of the country. The same statements are uniformly made by the professors of Veterinary anatomy in this country. The result of inquiries which I have personally made into the state of the health of persons licensed to slaughter horses, called knackers, is, that though they maintain their health apparently unimpaired for some time, yet that after a time the functions of the nutritive organs become impaired, they begin to emaciate, and present a cadaverous appearance, slight wounds fester and become difficult to heal, and that upon the whole they are a short-lived race.

The exhalations arising from dead bodies interred in the vaults of churches, and in church-yards, are also so much diluted with the air of the atmosphere, that they do not commonly affect the health in so immediate and direct a manner as plainly to indicate the source of these noxious influences. It is only when some accidental circumstances have favoured their accumulation or concentration in an unusual degree, that the effects become so sensible as obviously to declare their cause. Every now and then, however, such a concurrence of circumstances does happen, of which there are many instances on record; but it may suffice for the present to mention one, the particulars of which I have received from a gentleman who is known to me, and on the accuracy of whose statements I can rely.

Mr. Hutchinson, surgeon, Farringdon-street, was called on Monday morning, the 15th March, 1841, to attend a girl, aged 14, who was labouring under typhus fever of a highly malignant character. This girl was the daughter of a pew-opener in one of the large city churches, situated in the centre of a small burial ground, which had been used for the interment of the dead for centuries, the ground of which was raised much above its natural level, and was saturated with the remains of the bodies of the dead. There were vaults beneath the church, in which it was still the custom, as it had long been, to bury the dead. The girl in question had recently returned from the country, where she had been at school. On the preceding Friday, that is, on the fourth day before Mr. Hutchinson saw her, she had assisted her mother during three hours and on the Saturday during one hour, in shaking and cleansing the matting of the aisles and pews of the church. The mother stated, that this work was generally done once in six weeks; that the dust and effluvia which arose, always had a peculiarly fœtid and offensive odour, very unlike the dust which collects in private houses; that it invariably made her (the mother) ill for at least a day afterwards; and that it used to make the grandmother of the present patient so unwell, that she was compelled to hire a person to perform this part of her duty. On the afternoon of the same day on which the young person now ill had been engaged in her employment, she was seized with shivering, severe pain in the head, back, and limbs, and other symptoms of commencing fever. On the following day all these symptoms were aggravated, and in two days afterwards, when Mr. Hutchinson first saw her, malignant fever was fully developed, the skin being burning hot, the tongue dry and covered with a dark brown fur, the thirst urgent, the pain of the head, back, and extremities severe, attended with hurried and oppressed breathing, great restlessness and prostration, anxiety of countenance, low muttering delirium, and a pulse of 130 in the minute.

In this case it is probable that particles of noxious animal matter progressively accumulated in the matting during the intervals between the cleansing of it; and that being set free by this operation and diffused in the atmosphere, while they were powerful enough always sensibly to affect even those who were accustomed to inhale them, were sufficiently concentrated to produce actual fever in one wholly unaccustomed to them, and rendered increasingly susceptible to their influence by recent residence in the pure air of the country; for it is remarkable that miasms sometimes act with the greatest intensity on those who habitually breathe the purest air.

The miasms arising from church-yards are in general too much diluted by the surrounding air to strike the neighbouring inhabitants with sudden and severe disease, yet they may materially injure the health, and the evidence appears to me to be decisive that they often do so. Among others who sometimes obviously suffer from this cause, are the families of clergymen, when, as occasionally happens, the vicarage or rectory is situated very close to a full church-yard. I myself know one such clergyman's family, whose dwelling-house is so close to an extremely full churchyard, that a very disagreeable smell from the graves is always perceptible in some of the sitting and sleeping rooms. The mother of this family states that she has never had a day's health since she has resided in this house, and that her children are always ailing; and their ill health is attributed, both by the family and their medical friends, to the offensive exhalations from the church-yard.

Dr. Lyon Playfair states as follows in his communication—

There are two kinds of changes which animal and vegetable matters undergo, when exposed to certain influences. These are known by the terms of "decay" and "putrefaction." Decay, properly so called, is a union of the elements of organic matter with the oxygen of the air; while putrefaction, although generally commencing with decay, is a change or transformation of the elements of the organic body itself, without any necessary union with the oxygen of the air. When decay proceeds in a body without putrefaction, offensive smells are not generated; but if the air in contact with the decaying matter be in any way deficient, the decay passes into putrefaction, and putrid smells arise. Putrid smells are rarely if ever evolved from substances destitute of the element nitrogen.

Both decaying and putrefying matters are capable of communicating their own state of putrefaction or of decay to any organic matter with which they may come in contact. To take the simplest case, a piece of decayed wood, a decaying orange, or a piece of tainted flesh is capable of causing similar decay or putrefaction in another piece of wood, orange, or flesh. In a similar manner the decaying gases evolved from sewers occasion the putrescence of meat or of vegetables hung in the vicinity of the place from which they escape. But this communication of putrefaction is not confined to dead matter. When tainted meat or putrescent blood-puddings are taken as food, their state of putrefaction is frequently communicated to the bodies of the persons who have used them as food. A disease analogous to rot ensues, and generally terminates fatally. Happily this disease is little known among us, but it is of very frequent occurrence in Germany.

The decay or putrefaction communicated by putrid gases or by decaying matters does not always assume one form, but varies according to the organs to which their peculiar state is imparted. If communicated to the blood it might possibly happen that fever may arise; if to the intestines, dysentery or diarrhœa might result; and I think it might even be a question worthy of consideration, whether consumption may not arise from such exposure. Certainly it seems to do so among cattle. The men who are employed in cleaning out drains are very liable to the attacks of dysentery and of diarrhœa; and I recollect instances of similar diseases occurring among some fellow-students, when I attended the dissecting-rooms.

The effects produced by decaying emanations will vary according to the state of putrefaction or decay in which these emanations are, as well as according to their intensity and concentration. Thus it occurs frequently that persons susceptible to contagion may be in the vicinity of a fever patient without acquiring the disease. I know one celebrated medical man who attends his own patients in fever without danger, but who has never been able to take charge of the fever-wards in an infirmary, from the circumstance of his being unable to resist the influence of the contagion under such circumstances. This gentleman has had fever several times. This shows that the contagion of fever requires a certain degree of *concentration* before it is able to produce its immediate effects. A knowledge of this circumstance has induced several infirmaries (the Bristol infirmary, for example) to abolish altogether fever-wards and to scatter the fever cases indiscriminately through the medical wards. Owing to this distribution, cases in which fever is communicated to other patients or nurses in the infirmary are very unfrequent, although they are far from being so in those hospitals where the fever cases are grouped together.

I consider that the want of attention to the circumstance of the concentration of decaying emanations is a great reason that the effects of miasmata in producing fever is still a *questio vexata*. Thus there may be many church-yards and sewers evolving decaying matter, and yet no fever may occur in the locality. Some other more modified effect may be produced, according to the degree of concentration of the decaying matter, such as diarrhœa or even dysentery; or there may be no perceptible effects produced, although the blood may still be thrown into a diseased state which will render it susceptible to any specific contagion that approaches. It must be remembered that decaying exhalations will not always produce similar effects, but that these will vary not only according to the concentration, but also according to the state of decomposition in which the decaying matters are.

The rennet for making cheese is in a peculiar state of decay, or rather is capable of a series of states of decay, and the flavour of the cheese manufactured by means of it varies also according to the state of the rennet. Just so with the diseases produced by the peculiar state or concentration of decaying matters or of specific contagious. When the Asiatic cholera visited this country many of the towns were afflicted with dysentery before the cholera appeared in an unquestionable form. In like manner the miasmata evolved from church-yards may produce injurious effects which may not be sufficiently marked to call attention until they assume a more serious form by becoming more concentrated. But notwithstanding the absence of marked effects, it is extremely probable that constant exposure to miasmata may produce a diseased state of the blood. Thus I had occasion to visit and report upon, amongst other matters, the state of slaughter-houses in Bristol. These are generally situated in courts, very inefficiently ventilated, as all courts are. I remarked that the men employed in the slaughter-houses had a remarkably cadaverous hue, and this was participated in a greater or less degree by the inhabitants of the court. So much was this the case, that in a court where the smells from the slaughter-house were so offensive that my companion had immediately to retire from sickness, I immediately singled out one person as not belonging to the court from a number of people who ran out of their houses to inquire the object of my visit. The person who attracted my attention from her healthy appearance compared with the others, had entered this court to pay a visit to a neighbour.

§ 11. That conclusions respecting such immensely important effects can only be established by reasonings on facts frequently so scattered over distant times and places as to require much research to bring them together; that those conclusions are still open to controversy, and have hitherto been maintained only by references to statements of distant observations, whilst regularly sustained examinations of the events occurring daily in our large towns might have placed them beyond a doubt; may be submitted as showing the necessity of some public arrangements to ensure constant attention, and complete information on these sub-jects, as the basis of complete measures of prevention.

§ 12. The conclusions, however, which appear to be firmly esta-blished by the evidence, and the preponderant medical testimony, are on every point, as to the essential character of the physical evils connected with the practice of interment, so closely coincident with the conclusions deduced from observation on the continent, that from Dr. Riecke's report (and to which a prize was awarded by an eminent medical association), in which the preponderant medical opinions are set forth, they may be stated in the following terms :—

" The general conclusions from the foregoing report may be given as follows :

" The injurious effect of the exhalations from the decomposi-tion in question upon the health and life of man is proved by a sufficient number of trustworthy facts ;

" That this injurious influence is by no means constant, and de-pends on varying and not yet sufficiently explained circumstances ;

" That this injurious influence is manifest in proportion to the degree of concentration of putrid emanations, especially in con-fined spaces ; and in such cases of concentration the injurious in-fluence is manifest in the production of asphyxia and the sudden and entire extinction of life ;

" That, in a state less concentrated, putrid emanations produce various effects on the nerves of less importance, as fainting, nausea, head-ache, languor ;

" These emanations, however, if their effect is often repeated, or if the emanations be long applied, produce nervous and putrid fevers ; or impart to fevers, which have arisen from other causes, a typhoid or putrid character ;

" Apparently they furnish the principal cause of the most deve-loped form of typhus, that is to say, the plague (*Der Bubonenpest*). Besides the products of decomposition, the contagious material may also be active in the emanations arising from dead bodies."

§ 13. Such being the nature of the emanations from human remains in a state of decomposition, or in a state of cor-ruption, the obtainment of any definite or proximate evidence of the extent of the operation of those emanations on the health of the population nevertheless appears to be hopeless in crowded districts. In such districts the effects of an invisible fluid have not been observed, amidst a complication of other causes, each of a nature ascertained to produce an injurious effect upon the public health, but undistinguished, except when it accidentally becomes predominant. The sense of smell in the majority of inhabitants seems to be destroyed, and having no perception even of stenches which are insupportable to strangers, they must be unable to note the excessive escapes of miasma as antecedents to disease. Occasionally, however, some medical witnesses, who have been accustomed to the smell of the dissecting-room, detect the smell of human remains from the grave-yards, in crowded districts ; and other witnesses have stated that they can distinguish what is called the "dead man's smell," when no one else can, and can distinguish it from the miasma of the sewers.

In the case of the predominance of the smell from the grave-yard, the immediate consequence ordinarily noted is a head-ache. A military officer stated to me that when his men occupied as a barrack a building which opened over a crowded burial-ground in Liverpool, the smell from the ground was at times exceedingly offensive, and that he and his men suffered from dysentery. A gentleman who had resided near that same ground, stated to me that he was convinced that his own health, and the health of his children had suffered from it, and that he had removed, to avoid further injury. The following testimony of a lady, respecting the miasma which escaped from one burial-ground at Manchester, is adduced as an example of the more specific testimony as to the perception of its effects. This testimony also brings to view the circumstance that in the towns it is not only in surface emanations from the grave-yards alone that the morbific matter escapes.

You resided formerly in the house immediately contiguous to the bury-ing-ground of ——— chapel, did you not ?—Yes I did, but I was obliged to leave it.

Why were you so obliged ?—When the wind was west, the smell was dreadful. There is a main sewer runs through the burying-ground, and the smell of the dead bodies came through this sewer up our drain, and until we got that trapped, it was quite unbearable.

Do you not think the smell arose from the emanations of the sewer, and not from the burying-ground ?—I am sure they came from the burying-ground; the smell coming from the drain was exactly the same as that which reached us when the wind was west, and blew upon us from the burying-ground. The smell was very peculiar ; it exactly resembled the smell which clothes have when they are removed from a dead body. My servants would not remain in the house on account of it, and I had several cooks who removed on this account.

Did you observe any effects on your health when the smells were bad ?—Yes, I am liable to head-aches, and these were always bad when the smells were so also. They were often accompanied by diarrhœa in this house. Before I went there, and since I left, my head-aches have been very trifling.

Were any of the other inmates of the house afflicted with illness ?—I had often to send for the surgeon to my servants, who were liable to ulcer-ated sore throats.

And your children, were they also affected ?—My youngest child was very delicate, and we thought he could not have survived; since he came here he has become quite strong and healthy, but I have no right to say the burying-ground had any connexion with his health.

§ 14. In the course of an examination of the Chairman and Sur-veyor of the Holborn and Finsbury Division of Sewers, on the general management of sewers in London, the following passage occurs :—

"You do not believe that the nuisance arises in all cases from the main sewers? (Mr. Roe)—Not always from the main sewers. (Mr. Mills)—Connected with this point, I would mention, that where the sewers came in contact with church-yards, the exudation is most offensive.

" Have you noticed that in more than one case?—Yes.

" In those cases have you had any opportunities of tracing in what manner the exudation from the church-yards passed to the sewer?—It must have been through the sides of the sewers.

"Then, if that be the case, the sewer itself must have given way?—No; I apprehend even if you use concrete, it is impossible but that the adjacent waters would find their way even through cement; it is the natural consequence. The wells of the houses adjacent to the sewers all get dry whenever the sewers are lowered.

"You are perfectly satisfied that in the course of time exudations very often do, to a certain extent, pass through the brick-work?—Yes; it is impossible to prevent it.

"Have you ever happened to notice whether there was putrid matter in all cases where the sewer passed through a burial-ground?—The last church-yard I passed by was in the parish of St. Pancras, when the sewer was constructing. I observed that the exudation from it into the sewer was peculiarly offensive, and was known to arise from the decomposition of the bodies.

"At what distance was the sewer from the church-yard where you found that?—Thirty feet.'

Mr. Roe subsequently stated—

" Mr. Jacob Post, living at the corner of Church-street, Lower Road, Islington, stated to our clerk of the works, when we were building a sewer opposite Mr. Post's house, that he had a pump, the water from the well attached to which had been very good, and used for domestic purposes; but that, since a burying-ground was formed above his house, the water in his well had become of so disagreeable a flavour as to prevent its being used as heretofore: and he was in hopes that the extra depth of our sewer would relieve him from the drainage of the burying-ground, to which he attributed the spoiling of his water."

Professor Brande states that he has " frequently found the well-water of London contaminated by organic matters and ammoniacal salts," and refers to an instance of one well near a church-yard, " the water of which had not only acquired odour but colour from the soil;" and mentions other instances of which he has heard, as justifying the opinion, that as " very many of these wells are adjacent to church-yards, the accumulating soil of which has been so heaped up by the succession of dead bodies and coffins, and the products of their decomposition, as to form a filtering apparatus, by which all *superficial* springs must of course be more or less affected." Some of the best springs in the metropolis are, fortunately, of a depth not likely to be considerably affected by such filtration. In Leicester, and other places, I have been informed of the disuse of wells near church-yards, on account of the perception of a taint in them. The difficulty of distinguishing by any analysis the qualities of the morbific matter when held in solution or suspension in water, in combination with other matters in towns, and the consequent importance of the separate examination already given to those qualities, may be appreciated from such cases as the following, which are by no means unfrequent. In the instance of the water of one well in the metropolis, which had ceased to be used, in consequence of an offensive taste (contracted, as was suspected, from the drainage of an adjacent church-yard), it was doubted whether it could be determined by analysis what portion of the pollution arose from that source, what from the leakage of adjacent cess-pools, and what from the leakage of coal-gas from adjacent gas-pipes. In most cases of such complications, the parties responsible for any one contributing source of injury are apt to challenge, as they may safely do, distinct proof of the separate effect produced by that one. Popular perceptions, as well as chemical analysis, are at present equally baffled by the combination, and complaints of separate injuries are rarely made. If, therefore, the combined evil is to remain until complaints are made of the separate causes, and their specific effects on the health, and until they can be supported by demonstration, perpetual immunity would be ensured to the most noxious combinations.

The effects of unguarded interments have, however, as will subsequently be noticed, been observed with greater care on the continent, and the proximity of wells to burial-grounds has been reported to be injurious. Thus it is stated in a collection of reports concerning the cemeteries of the town of Versailles, that the water of the wells which lie *below* the church-yard of St. Louis could not be used on account of its stench. In consequence of various investigations in France, a law was passed, prohibiting the opening of wells within 100 metres of any place of burial; but this distance is now stated to be insufficient for deep wells, which have been found on examination to be polluted at a distance of from 150 to 200 metres. In some parts of Germany, the opening of wells nearer than 300 feet has been prohibited.

§ 15. Where the one deleterious cause is less complicated with others, as in open plains after the burial of the dead in fields of battle, the effects are perceived in the offensiveness of the surface emanations, and also in the pollution of the water, followed by disease, which compels the survivors to change their encampments.

The fact is thus adduced in the evidence of Dr. Copeland:—

"It is fully ascertained and well recognized that the alluvial soil, or whatever soil that receives the exuviæ of animal matter, or the bodies of dead animals, will become rich in general; it will abound in animal matter; and the water that percolates through the soil thus enriched will thus become injurious to the health of the individuals using it: that has been proved on many occasions, and especially in warm climates, and several remarkable facts illustrative of it occurred in the peninsular campaigns. It was found, for instance, at Ciudad Rodrigo, where, as Sir J. Macgregor states in his account of the health of the army, there were 20,000 dead bodies put into the ground within the space of two or three months, that this circumstance appeared to influence the health of the troops, inasmuch as for some months afterwards all those exposed to the emanations from the soil, as well as obliged to drink the water from the sunk wells, were affected by malignant and low fevers and dysentery, or fevers frequently putting on a dysenteric character."

§ 16. In the metropolis, on spaces of ground which do not exceed 203 acres, closely surrounded by the abodes of the living, layer upon layer, each consisting of a population numerically equivalent to a large army of 20,000 adults, and nearly 30,000 youths and children, is every year imperfectly interred. Within the period of the existence of the present generation, upwards of a million of dead must have been interred in those same spaces.

§ 17. A layer of bodies is stated to be about seven years in decaying in the metropolis : to the extent that this is so, the decay must be by the conversion of the remains into a gas, and its escape, as a miasma, of many times the bulk of the body that has disappeared.

§ 18. In some of the populous parishes, where, from the nature of the soil, the decomposition has not been so rapid as the interments, the place of burial has risen in height; and the height of many of them must have greatly increased but for surreptitious modes of diminishing it by removal, which, it must be confessed, has diminished the sanitary evil, though by the creation of another and most serious evil, in the mental pain and apprehensions of the survivors and feelings of abhorrence of the population, caused by the suspicion and knowledge of the disrespect and desecration of the remains of the persons interred.

§ 19. The claims to exemption in favour of burial-grounds which it is stated are not overcrowded would perhaps be most favourably considered by the examination of the practice of interment in the new cemeteries, where the proportion of interments to the space is much less.

§ 20. I have visited and questioned persons connected with several of these cemeteries in town and country, and I have caused the practice of interments in others of them to be examined by more competent persons. The inquiry brought forward instances of the bursting of some leaden coffins and the escape of mephitic vapour in the catacombs; the tapping of others to prevent similar casualties ; injuries sustained by grave-diggers from the escapes of miasma on the re-opening of graves, and an instance was stated to me by the architect of one cemetery, of two labourers having been injured, apparently by digging amidst some impure water which drained from some graves. No precedent examination of the evils affecting the public health, that are incident to the practice of interment, appears to have been made, no precedent scientific or impartial investigation appears to have been thought necessary by the joint-stock companies, or by the Committees of the House of Commons, at whose instance privileges were conferred upon the shareholders: no new precautionary measures or improvements, such as are in use abroad, appear consequently to have been introduced in them; the practice of burial has in general been simply removed to better looking, and in general, better situated places. The conclusion, however, from the examination of these places (which will subsequently be reverted to) is, that if most of the cemeteries themselves were in the midst of the population, they would, even in their present state, often contribute to the combination of causes of ill health in the metropolis, and several of the larger towns.

§ 21. It has been considered that all danger from interments in towns would be obviated if no burials were allowed except at a depth of five feet. But bodies buried much deeper are found to decay; and so certain as a body has wasted or disappeared is the fact that a deleterious gas has escaped. In the towns where the graveyards and streets are paved, the morbific matter must be diffused more widely through the sub-soil, and escape with the drainage. If the interments be so deep as to impede escapes at the surface, there is only the greater danger of escape by deep drainage and the pollution of springs.

Dr. Reid detected the escape of deleterious miasma from graves of more than 20 feet deep. He states—

In some churchyards I have noticed the ground to be absolutely saturated with carbonic acid gas, so that whenever a deep grave was dug it was filled in some hours afterwards with such an amount of carbonic acid gas that the workmen could not descend without danger. Deaths have, indeed, occurred occasionally in some churchyards from this cause, and in a series of experiments made in one of the churchyards at Manchester, where deep graves are made, each capable of receiving from 20 to 30 bodies, I found in general that a grave covered on the top at night was more or less loaded with carbonic acid in the morning, and that it was essential, accordingly, to ventilate these grave-pits before it was safe to descend.

This I effected on some occasions by means of a small chauffer placed at the top, and at one end of the grave a tube or hose being let down from it to the bottom of the grave. The fire was sustained by the admission of a small portion of fresh air at the top, and the air from the bottom of the grave was gradually removed as the upper stratum was heated by the fire around which it was conveyed; and when it had been once emptied in this manner a small fire was found sufficient to sustain a perpetual renewal of air, and prevent the men at work in the grave pits from being subject to the extreme oppression to which they are otherwise liable, even when there may be no immediate danger. A mechanical power might be used for the same purpose; and chemical agents, as a quantity of newly slaked lime, are frequently employed, as they absorb the carbonic acid. From different circumstances that have since occurred, it appears to me probable that numerous examples of strata or superficial soil containing carbonic acid may be more frequently met with than is generally suspected, and that while in churchyards the presence of large quantities of carbonic acid may be frequently anticipated, its presence must not always be attributed solely to the result of the decomposition of the human body.

The amount of carbonic acid that collects within a given time in a deep grave pit intended to receive 20 or 30 bodies, is much influenced by the nature of the ground in which it is dug. In the case referred to, the porous texture of the earth allowed a comparatively free aerial communication below the surface of the ground throughout its whole extent. It was, in reality, loaded with carbonic acid in the same manner as other places are loaded with water; it was only necessary to sink a pit, and a well of carbonic acid was formed, into which a constant stream of the same gas continued perpetually to filter from the adjacent earth, according to the extent to which it was removed. From whatever source, however, the carbonic acid may arise, it is not the less prone to mingle with the surrounding air, and where the level of the floor of the church is below the level of the churchyard, there the carbonic acid is prone to accumulate, as, though it may be ultimately dispersed by diffusion, it may be considered as flowing in the same manner in the first instance as water, where the quantity is considerable.

Again, where the drainage of the district in which the church may be placed is of an inferior description, and liable to be impeded periodically by the state of the tide, as in the vicinity of the Houses of Parliament, where all the drains are closed at high water, the atmosphere is frequently of the most inferior quality. I am fully satisfied, for instance, not only from my own observation, but from different statements that have reached me, and also from the observations of parties who have repeatedly examined the subject at my request, that the state of the burying-ground around St. Margaret's church is prejudicial to the air supplied at the Houses of Parliament, and also to the whole neighbourhood. One of them, indeed, stated to me lately that he had avoided the churchyard for the last six months, in consequence of the effects he experienced the last time he visited it. These offensive emanations have been noticed at all hours of the night and morning; and even during the day the smell of the churchyard has been considered to have reached the vaults in the House of Commons, and traced to sewers in its immediate vicinity. When the barometer is low, the surface of the ground slightly moist, the tide full, and the temperature considerable—all which circumstances tend to favour the evolution of effluvia both from the grave-pits and the drains—the most injurious influence upon the air is observed. In some places not far from this churchyard fresh meat is frequently tainted in a single night, on the ground-floor, in situations where at a higher level it may be kept without injury for a much longer period. In some cases, in private houses as well as at the Houses of Parliament, I have had to make use of ventilating shafts, or of preparations of chlorine, to neutralize the offensive and deleterious effects which the exhalations produced, while, on other occasions, their injurious influence has been abundantly manifested by the change induced in individuals subjected to their influence on removing to another atmosphere. No grievance, perhaps, entails greater physical evils upon any district than the conjoined influence of bad drainage and crowded churchyards; and until the drainage of air from drains shall be secured by the process adverted to in another part of this work, or some equivalent measures, they cannot be regarded as free from a very important defect.

The drainage of air from drains is, indeed, desirable under any circumstances; but when the usual contaminations of the drain are increased by the emanations from a loaded churchyard, it becomes doubly imperative to introduce such measures; and if any one should desire to trace the progress of reaction by which the grave-yards are continually tending to free themselves of their contents, a very brief inquiry will give him abundant evidence on this point. My attention was first directed to this matter in London ten years ago, when a glass of water handed to me at an hotel, in another district, presented a peculiar film on its surface, which led me to set it aside; and after numerous inquiries, I was fully satisfied that the appearance which had attracted my attention arose from the coffins in a churchyard immediately adjoining the well where the water had been drawn. Defective as our information is as to the precise qualities of the various products from drains, church-yards, and other similar places, I think I have seen enough to satisfy me that in all such situations the fluids of the living system imbibe materials which, though they do not always produce great severity of disease, speedily induce a morbid condition, which, while it renders the body more prone to attacks of fever, is more especially indicated by the facility with which all the fluids pass to a state of putrefaction, and the rapidity with which the slightest wound or cut is apt to pass into a sore.

Mr. Leigh, surgeon and lecturer of chemistry at Manchester, confirms the researches made by Dr. Reid in that town, and observes on this subject—

But the decomposition of animal bodies is remarkably modified by external circumstances where the bodies are immersed in or surrounded by water, and particularly, if the water undergo frequent change, the solid tissues become converted into adipocire, a fatty spermaceti-like substance, not very prone to decomposition, and this change is effected without much gaseous exhalation. Under such circumstances nothing injurious could arise, but under ordinary conditions slow decomposition would take place, with the usual products of the decomposition of animal matters, and here the nature of the soil becomes of much interest. If the burial-ground be in damp dense compact clay, with much water, the water will collect round the body, and there will be a disposition to the formation of adipocire, whilst the clay will effectually prevent the escape of gaseous matter. If on the other hand the bodies be laid in sand or gravel, decomposition will readily take place, the gases will easily permeate the superjacent soil and escape into the atmosphere, and this with a facility which may be judged of when the fact is stated, that under a pressure of only three-fourths of an inch of water, coal gas will escape by any leakage in the conduit pipes through a stratum of sand or gravel of three feet in thickness in an exceedingly short space of time. The three feet of soil seems to oppose scarcely any resistance to its passage to the surface; but if the joints of the pipes be enveloped by a thin layer of clay, the escape is effectually prevented.

If bodies were interred eight or ten feet deep in sandy or gravelly soils, I am convinced little would be gained by it; the gases would find a ready exit from almost any practicable depth.

§ 22. He also expresses an opinion concurrent with that of other physiologists, that the effects of these escapes in an otherwise salubrious locality, soon attract notice, but their influence in obedience to the laws of gaseous diffusion, developed by Dalton and Graham, is not the less when scattered over a town, because in a multitude of scents they escape observation. In open rural districts these gases soon intermix with the circumambient air, and become so vastly diluted that their injurious tendency is less potent.

Other physical facts which it is necessary to develope in respect to the practice of interment may be the most conveniently considered in a subsequent portion of this report, where it is necessary to adduce the information possessed, as to the sites of places of burial, and the sanitary precautions necessary in respect to them.

§ 23. From what has already been adduced, it may here be stated as a conclusion,

That inasmuch as there appear to be no cases in which the emanations from human remains in an advanced stage of decomposition are not of a deleterious nature, so there is no case in which the liability to danger should be incurred either by interment (or by entombment in vaults, which is the most dangerous) amidst the dwellings of the living, it being established as a general conclusion in respect to the physical circumstances of interment, from which no adequate grounds of exception have been established ;—

That all interments in towns, where bodies decompose, contribute to the mass of atmospheric impurity which is injurious to the public health.

Injuries to the Health of Survivors occasioned by the delay of Interments.

In order to understand the state of feeling of the labouring classes, and the general influence upon them, and even the effects on their health, of the practice of interment, it will be necessary to submit for consideration those circumstances which immediately precede the interment, namely, the most common circumstances of the death.

§ 24. In a large proportion of cases in the metropolis, and in some of the manufacturing districts, one room serves for one family of the labouring classes : it is their bed-room, their kitchen, their wash-house, their sitting room, their dining room ; and, when they do not follow any out-door occupation, it is frequently their work room and their shop. In this one room they are born, and live, and sleep, and die amidst the other inmates.

§ 25. Their common condition in large towns has been developed by various inquiries, more completely than by the census. As an instance, the results may be given of an inquiry lately made, at the instance and expense of Lord Sandon, by Mr. Weld, the secretary of the Statistical Society, as to the condition of the working classes resident in the inner ward of St. George's, Hanover Square, and in the immediate vicinity of some of the most opulent residences in the metropolis. It appeared that 1465 families of the labouring classes had for their residence 2175 rooms, and 2510 beds. The distribution of rooms and beds was as follows :—

DWELLINGS.	Number of Families.	BEDS.	Number of Families.
Single rooms for each family	929	One bed to each family .	623
Two ,, ,,	408	Two ,, ,,	638
Three ,, ,,	94	Three ,, ,,	154
Four ,, ,,	17	Four ,, ,,	21
Five ,, ,,	8	Five ,, ,,	8
Six ,, ,,	4	Six ,, ,,	3
Seven ,, ,:	1	Seven ,, ,,	1
Eight ,, ,,	1	Dwellings without a bed .	7
Not ascertained	3	Not ascertained	10
Total . .	1,465	Total . .	1,465

Out of 5945 persons 839 were found to be ill, and yet the season was not unhealthy.   One family in 11 had a third room (and that not unoccupied) in which to place a corpse.   This, however, appears to be a favourable specimen.   From an examination made by a committee of the Statistical Society into the condition of the poorer classes in the borough of Marylebone, it appeared that the distribution of rooms amongst the portion of population examined showed that not more than one family in a hundred had a third room.

No. occupying part of a room, 159 families, and 196 single persons.

„	one room .	382	„	56	„
	two rooms	61	„	2	
„	three rooms	5	„	7	„
„	four rooms	1	„	0	„

§ 26. Mr. Leonard, surgeon and medical officer of the parish of St. Martin's-in-the-Fields, gives the following instances of the circumstances in which the poorest class of inhabitants die, which may be adduced as exemplifications of the dreadful state of circumstances in which the survivors are placed for the want of adequate accommodation for the remains immediately after death, and previous to the interment :—

There are some houses in my district that have from 45 to 60 persons of all ages under one roof, and in the event of death, the body often occupies the only bed till they raise money to pay for a coffin, which is often several days.   They are crowded together in houses situate in Off-alley, the courts and alleys opening from Bedfordbury, Rose-street, Angel-court, courts and alleys opening from Drury-lane and the Strand, and even in places fitted up under the Adelphi arches; even the unventilated and damp underground kitchens are tenanted.   Of course the tenants are never free from fevers and diarrhœa, and the mortality is great.   The last class live, for the most part, in lodging-rooms, where shelter is obtained, with a bed or straw, for from 2d. to 4d. per night, and where this is not obtainable, the arches under the Adelphi afford a shelter.   In the lodging-rooms I have seen the beds placed so close together as not to allow room to pass between them, and occupied by both sexes indiscriminately.   I have known six people sleep in a room about nine feet square, with only one small window, about fifteen inches by twelve inches; and there are some sleeping-rooms in this district in which you cannot scarcely see your hand at noon-day.

How long is the dead body retained in the room beside the living?—If the person has subscribed to a club, or the friends are in circumstances to afford the expense of the funeral, it takes place, generally, on the following Sunday, if the death has occurred early in the week; but if towards the end of the week, then it is sometimes postponed till the Sunday week after, if the weather permit; in one case it was twelve days.   In the other cases I have known much opposition to removal till after a subscription had been collected from the affluent neighbours; and in some instances, after keeping the body several days, I have been applied to to present the case to the relieving officer, that it might be buried by the parish.   Amongst the Irish it is retained till after the wake, which "*is open to all comers*" as long as there is anything *dacent to drink or smoke*; but I must bear witness, also, to the frequent exhibition, in a large majority of the poor, of those affectionate attentions to the mortal remains of their relatives, which all are anxious to bestow, and which, notwithstanding the danger and want of accommodation, make them loth to part with them.

In what condition is the corpse usually, or frequently, retained?—Amongst the Irish, it does not signify of what disease the person may have died, it is retained often for many days, laid out upon the only bed, perhaps, and adorned with the best they can bestow upon it, until the *coronach* has been performed. Thus fevers and other contagious diseases are fearfully propagated. I remember a case of a body being brought from the Fever Hospital to Bullin-court, and the consequences were dreadful; and this spring I removed a girl, named Wilson, to the infirmary of the workhouse, from a room in the same court. I could not remain two minutes in it; the horrible stench arose from a corpse which had died of phthisis twelve days before, and the coffin stood across the foot of the bed, within eighteen inches of it. This was in a small room not above ten feet by twelve feet square, and a fire always in it, being (as in most cases of a like kind) the only one for sleeping, living, and cooking in. I mention these as being particular cases, from which most marked consequences followed; but I have very many others, in which the retention of the body has been fraught with serious results to the survivors.

Will you describe the consequences of such retention?—Upon the 9th of March, 1840, M—— was taken to the Fever Hospital. He died there, and without my knowledge the body was brought back to his own room. The usual practice, in such cases, is to receive them into a lock-up-room, set apart for that purpose in the workhouse. I find that upon the 12th his step-son was taken ill. He was removed immediately to the Fever Hospital. Upon the 18th the barber who shaved the corpse was taken ill, and died in the Fever Hospital, and upon the 27th another step-son was taken ill, and removed also.

Upon the 18th of December, 1840, I—— and her infant were brought, ill with fever, to her father's room in Eagle-court, which was ten feet square, with a small window of four panes; the infant soon died. Upon the 15th of January, 1841, the grandmother was taken ill; upon the 2nd of February the grandfather also. There was but one bedstead in the room. They resisted every offer to remove them, and I had no power to compel removal. The corpse of the grandmother lay beside her husband upon the same bed, and it was only when he became delirious and incapable of resistance that I ordered the removal of the body to the dead-room, and him to the Fever Hospital. He died there, but the evil did not stop here: two children, who followed their father's body to the grave, were, the one within a week and the other within ten days, also victims to the same disease. In short, five out of six died.

In October, 1841, a fine girl, C——, died of cynanche maligna: her body was retained in a small back room. Upon the 1st of November another child was taken ill, and upon the 4th two others were also seized with the same disease.

Upon the 2nd of February, 1843, H——, in Heathcock-court, died of fever. I recommended the immediate removal of the body from the attic room of small dimensions, but it was retained about ten days, the widow not consenting to have it buried by the parish, and not being able to collect funds sooner: their only child was seized with fever, and was several weeks ill.

Upon the 3rd of March, 1843, B—— died of a fever in Lemontree-yard; the body was retained some days, in expectation of friends burying it, but in the mean time a child of B——, and one of a lodger in the same house, were infected.

Upon the 13th March, 1843, I saw a family in Hervey's-buildings, which is more open, and the rooms of a better class than those in some other situations. I found there the corpse of a person who had died of a fever; the father and mother were just taken ill, and a child was taken ill soon after. The foot of the coffin was within ten inches of the father's head as he lay upon his pillow. I caused it to be removed as soon as possible, and the three cases terminated favourably. In the case in Bullin-court, mentioned before, the girl Wilson was affected with nausea vertigo, general prostration of strength, and trembling, the usual symptoms in these cases. Soon after her removal, the mother of the deceased was seized with typhus, and is now only so far recovered as scarcely to be able to go about and attend to another son, who is at present ill of the same disease. These are a few cases only in which serious evils followed on retention of the body. I could multiply them, if necessary; but they will suffice to show that there should be power of removal to some recognized place of safety given to the district medical officer for the benefit of the individuals concerned and the public at large. The rooms are often most wretched in which these cases occur; the neighbourhood is badly ventilated and drained, or often not drained at all, and if the medical officer were responsible for his acts, and bound to report regularly, there would be a sufficient guarantee that no unnecessary harshness would be exercised in the performance of a duty absolutely required for the preservation of the public health, and the safety of those dearest to the sufferers themselves.

Comparing the effects of the practice of retaining the bodies before interment, with the effects of emanations from the dead after interment, when buried in crowded districts, which appears to you to be the most pernicious practice?—When a body is retained in a small room, badly ventilated, and often with a fire in it, the noxious gases evolved in the process of decomposition are presented to persons exposed to them in a highly concentrated form, and if their health is in a certain state favourable to receive the contagion, the effect is immediate. In crowded burial-grounds in which I have never seen a body at a less depth than three feet from the surface (allowing for the artificial building up of the ground to give apparent depth to the grave), the gases having this thickness of earth to penetrate, arrive at the surface in a divided state, and by small quantities at a time mix so gradually with the atmosphere, that it becomes comparatively harmless by dilution, and is scarcely perceptible. In confined situations, where the ground is limited in extent, the long continuance of gradual evolutions of noxious matter would, doubtless, be a cause of debility to surrounding inhabitants; but such instances, I think, are rare. I have made inquiry in the immediate neighbourhood of grave-yards, and I form my opinion from the result. There can be no doubt whatever as to the propriety of burial beyond the limits of towns, and if the corpse of the poor man could be deposited at a distance, without entailing a greater expense upon him, I think it would improve the health of our large towns very much; but I believe the retention of the corpse in the room with the living is fraught with greater danger than that produced by the emanations from even crowded grave-yards.

§ 27. The condition in which the remains are often found on the occurrence of a death at the eastern part of the metropolis are thus described by Mr. John Liddle, the medical officer of the Whitechapel district of the Whitechapel Union.

What is the class of poor persons whom you, as medical officer, are called upon to attend to?—The dock labourers, navigators, bricklayers' labourers, and the general description of labourers inhabiting Whitechapel and lower Aldgate.

On the occurrence of a death amongst this description of labourers, what do you find to be the general condition of the family, in relation to the remains. How is the corpse dealt with?—Nearly the whole of the labouring population there have only one room. The corpse is therefore kept in that room where the inmates sleep and have their meals. Sometimes the corpse is stretched on the bed, and the bed and bed-clothes are taken off, and the wife and family lie on the floor. Sometimes a board is got on which the corpse is stretched, and that is sustained on tressels or on chairs.

Sometimes it is stretched out on chairs. When children die, they are frequently laid out on the table. The poor Irish, if they can afford it, form a canopy of white calico over the corpse, and buy candles to burn by it, and place a black cross at the head of the corpse. They commonly raise the money to do this by subscriptions amongst themselves and at the public-houses which they frequent.

What is the usual length of time that the corpse is so kept?—The time varies according to the day of the death. Sunday is the day usually chosen for the day of burial. But if a man die on the Wednesday, the burial will not take place till the Sunday week following. Bodies are almost always kept for a full week, frequently longer.

What proportion of these cases may be positively contagious?—It appears from the Registrar-General's Report (which, however, cannot be depended on for perfect accuracy, as the registrar's returns are very incorrect,—I do not think I have been required to give a certificate of death upon more than three occasions), that in the year 1839, there were 747 deaths from epidemic diseases which formed about one-fifth of the whole of the deaths in the Whitechapel Union.

Have you had occasion to represent as injurious this practice of retaining the corpse amidst the living?—I have represented in several communications in answer to sanitary inquiries from the Poor Law Commission Office, that it must be and is highly injurious. It was only three or four days ago that an instance of this occurred in my own practice, which I will mention. A widow's son, who was about 15 years of age, was taken ill of fever. Finding the room small, in which there was a family of five persons living, I advised his immediate removal. This was not done, and the two other sons were shortly afterwards attacked, and both died. When fever was epidemic, deaths following the first death in the same family were of frequent occurrence. In cases where the survivors escape, their general health must be deteriorated by the practice of keeping the dead in the same room.

Do you observe any peculiarity of habit amongst the lower classes accompanying this familiarity with the remains of the dead?—What I observe when I first visit the room is a degree of indifference to the presence of the corpse: the family is found eating or drinking or pursuing their usual callings, and the children playing. Amongst the middle classes, where there is an opportunity of putting the corpse by itself, there are greater marks of respect and decency. Amongst that class no one would think of doing anything in the room where the corpse was lying, still less of allowing children there.

Mr. Byles, surgeon, of Spitalfields, states, that the above description is generally applicable to the condition of the dwellings of the labouring classes, and to the circumstances under which the survivors are placed on the occurrence of a death in that district. He observes, moreover—

In the more malignant form of fever, especially scarlatina, the instances of death following the first case of death are frequent. The same holds good in respect to measles, and in respect to small-pox in families where vaccination has been neglected. I have also known instances of children who had been vaccinated becoming the subject of fever apparently from the effluvia of the body of a child who had died of the small-pox. I have often had occasion urgently to represent to the parish and union officers the necessity of a forcible interference to remove bodies. Coffins have been sent and the bodies removed and placed in a vault under the church until interment, and the rooms limewashed at the expense of the parish.

Were such removals resisted?—Not generally; they were in some few instances.

§ 28. Mr. Bestow, a relieving officer of the adjacent district of Bethnal Green, who is called upon to visit the abodes of those persons of the labouring classes, who on the occurrence of death fall into a state of destitution, thus exemplifies the common consequences of the retention of the corpse in the living and working rooms of the family :—

Is the corpse generally kept in the living or in the working room?—In the majority of cases the weavers live and work in the same room ; the children generally sleep on a bed pushed under the loom.   Before a coffin is obtained, the corpse is generally stretched on the bed where the adults have slept.   It is a very serious evil in our district, the length of time during which bodies have been kept under such circumstances.   I have frequently had to make complaint of it.   We are very often complained to by neighbours of the length of time during which the bodies are kept.   We have very often had disease occasioned by it.   I have known, in one case, as many as eight deaths, from typhus fever, follow one death ; there were five children and two or three visitors whose illness and deaths were ascribed to the circumstance.

In January, 1837, a man named Clark, in George Gardens, in this parish, having been kept a considerable length of time unburied (I was informed beyond a fortnight), I was directed to visit the case, and I found the house consisted of two small rooms, wherein resided his wife and seven children.   I remonstrated with them upon the impropriety of keeping the body so long, and offered either to bury, or to remove it, as it was then becoming very offensive.   I was informed it would be buried on the following Sunday, as it would not be convenient for the whole of the relatives to attend the funeral earlier, and I understood a very great number did attend. I find that on the 30th of the same month (January) I was called again to visit Ann Clark, one of the family, in the same miserable abode, who was lying upon some rags, very ill of fever.   I had her removed, but she ultimately died ; and I again remonstrated with the family remaining in the same house, and offered to take them into the workhouse, which was declined, stating, it was their intention to remove in a few days to another house.   And on the 20th of February, my attention was called to the same family, who had then removed to No. 3, Granby Row, not far from their former abode, and here I found the mother and the whole of the children (as I had predicted to them, if they persisted in their habits), all ill of fever without much hopes of their recovery.   I had five removed to the London Fever Hospital immediately ; but out of seven who were affected, two died. My attention was shortly afterwards directed to Henry Clark, of Barnet Street, who was a relative, and had taken fever (it was stated) by having attended the funeral of his friend ; he, it seems, communicated it to his wife and two children, one of whom died ; next followed Stephen Clark, of Edward Street, who, having visited the above-named relative, and attended the funeral of their infant shortly afterwards, had fever ; also his wife and three children, one of whom died also.   In August, 1837, I was called to visit the case of Sarah Masterton, No. 11, Suffolk Street, whose husband lay dead of fever ; she was with two children in the same room, and the corpse not in a coffin.   They were in the most deplorable condition, and so bad with fever that none of the neighbours would venture to enter the room with me.   I had the dead body removed in a shell to our dead-house, and the woman and children to the infirmary in the workhouse. Two of them ultimately recovered ; one died.   In the same house, and in the upper room, I next found Robert Crisp, with a wife and child, upon whom I could not prevail to leave the place, and my urgent entreaties were treated with contempt and bad language.   Ultimately, however, his child died, and not until then could I persuade him to get another place, neither would he have the infant removed, or come into the workhouse himself.

William Procktor, residing in a miserable hut in Camden's Gardens, of only one room, with a wife and two children, when visited, was found badly affected with fever, of which the wife died, and the body was kept in the same place wherein all the family resided and slept, for more than a week. The man was next attacked, and then the children; and for a considerable time they were attended by our medical officer, but I believe they all ultimately recovered.

His report book contained frequent instances of cases of the like description.

§ 29. Mr. T. Abraham, surgeon, one of the Registrars for the City of London, who has had much practice as a parochial medical officer, was asked upon this subject—

In the course of your practice, have you had occasion to believe that evil effects are produced by the retention of the corpse in the house?— Yes; I can give an instance of a man, his wife, and six children, living in one room in Draper's Buildings. The mother and all the children successively fell ill of typhus fever: the mother died; the body remained in the room. I wished it to be removed the next day, and I also wished the children to be removed, being afraid that the fever would extend. The children were apparently well at the time of the death of the mother. The recommendation was not attended to: the body was kept five days in the only room which this family of eight had to live and sleep in. The eldest daughter was attacked about a week after the mother had been removed, and, after three days' illness, that daughter died. The corpse of this child was only kept three days, as we determined that it should positively be removed. In about nine days after the death of the girl, the youngest child was attacked, and it died in about nine days. Then the second one was taken ill; he lay twenty-three days, and died. Then another boy died. The two other children recovered.

By the immediate removal of the corpse, and the use of proper preventive means, how many deaths do you believe might have been prevented?—I think it probable that the one took it from the other, and that, if the corpse of the first had been removed, the rest would have escaped, although I, of course, admit that the same cause which produced the disease in the mother might also have produced it in the children. I believe that, in cases of typhus, scarlatina, and other infectious diseases, it frequently happens that the living are attacked by the same disease from the retention of the body.

Mr. Blencarn, surgeon, one of the medical officers of the City of London Union, was asked—

Have you observed any evil effects following the practice of the long retention of the corpse in the house amidst the living?—Yes; I have observed effects follow, but I cannot say produced by them, though they were perhaps increased by them. In those cases which I have had, where there has been a succession of cases of fever in the same family, after a death it has generally occurred that the parties affected have complained two or three days before that they felt very unwell. Generally this has been the case. I have in such instances ordered them medicine immediately. Since the Union has been established, we have immediately removed all fever cases to the fever hospital.

The retention of the corpse amidst the living, under such circumstances, must aggravate the mortality, must it not?—There cannot be a moment's doubt about it.

§ 30. Mr. Barnett, surgeon, one of the medical officers of the Stepney Union, thus exemplifies the effects of the practice in his own district. After speaking of the prevalence of nervous depression, ascribable to the contiguity to a crowded grave-yard, he says :—

Similar symptoms are observable when the dead are kept any length of time in crowded apartments. I well recollect a child dying, during the summer months, of scarlet fever, and the parents persisted in keeping the corpse for a considerable period, notwithstanding the intreaties of the rest of the inmates to the contrary, all of whom complained of being ill therefrom. The result was the production of several cases of typhoid fever and much distress. A short time ago, I was requested to attend a family consisting of five persons ; they resided in a room containing about 500 cubic feet, with but little light and much less ventilation. One child was suffering from small-pox, and died in a day or two : the corpse was allowed to remain in the room. The two other children were soon attacked by the disease, as well as a child belonging to a person residing in the same house, who was imprudent enough to bring it into this apartment, though cautioned not to do so. The stench arising from the living and dead was so intolerable that it produced in myself severe head-ache, and my friend, who accompanied me, complained of sudden nervousness. The parents of these children (one of whom is since dead) are suffering great debility.

The similarity of symptoms produced in these cases might perhaps lead us to the conclusion that the cause was probably the same in all ; consequently, whether this poison be diluted or concentrated, it should, at all times, be carefully avoided. For this purpose, I should recommend the early removal of the dead from such apartments, and a check to be put to the baneful practice of burying the dead so near the surface in crowded districts.

§ 31. The accounts given by the medical practitioners and persons who are chiefly in attendance on the parties before death, are corroborated by the evidence of undertakers and others engaged in providing goods and services for the performance of the last rites for artisans of a condition to defray the funeral expenses.

Mr. Wild, an undertaker, residing in the Blackfriars Road, London, who inters between 500 and 600 bodies annually, of which about 350 are of the working classes, states, that the time during which the corpse is kept in the house varies from five to twelve days.

The greater proportion of the working men in London live and sleep in one room only, do they not ?—Three-fourths of the rooms we have to visit are single rooms ; the one room is the only room the poor people have.

When you visit the room, in what condition do you find the corpse ? How is it laid out ?—Generally speaking, we only find one bed in the room, and that occupied by a corpse. It frequently happens that there is no sacking to the bedding ; when they borrow a board or a shutter from a neighbour, in order to lay out the corpse upon it ; they have also to borrow other convenient articles necessary, such as a sheet. The corpse of a child is usually laid out on the table. The Irish poor have a peculiar mode of arranging the corpse ; they place candles around the bed, and they have a black cross placed at the head of the bed.

Is the practice of keeping bodies in the place of abode for a long time much altered in cases where the death has occurred from fever or any contagious disease ?—Very seldom ; they would keep them much longer if it were not for the undertaker, who urges them to bury them. In cases of rapid decomposition of persons dying in full habit there is much liquid ; and the coffin is tapped to let it out. I have known them to keep the corpse after the coffin had been tapped twice, which has, of course, produced a disagreeable effluvium.   This liquid generates animal life very rapidly; and within six hours after a coffin has been tapped, if the liquid escapes, maggots, or a sort of animalculæ, are seen crawling about.   I have frequently seen them crawling about the floor of a room inhabited by the labouring classes, and about the tressels on which the tapped coffin is sustained.   In such rooms the children are frequently left whilst the widow is out making arrangements connected with the funeral.   And the widow herself lives there with the children.   I frequently find them altogether in a small room with a large fire.

Have you known instances of the spread of disease amongst the members of the family residing in the same room where the corpse is kept?—Some medical men have said that corpses of persons who have contagious diseases are not dangerous; but my belief is, that in cases of small-pox and scarlatina it is dangerous; and only the other day a case of this nature occurred,—a little boy, who died of the small-pox.   Soon after he died, his sister, a little girl who had been playing in the same room, was attacked with small-pox and died.   The medical attendant said, the child must have touched the corpse. A poor woman, a neighbour, went over to see one of these bodies, and was much afflicted and frightened, and I believe touched the body.   She was certainly attacked with the small-pox, and, after lingering some time, died a few days since.   The other day at Lambeth, the eldest child, of a person died of scarlet fever.   The child was about four years old; it had been ill a week.   There were two other children, one was three years old and the other sixteen months.   When the first child died there were no symptoms of illness for three days afterwards, the corpse of the eldest was kept in the house; here it was in a separate room, but the medical man recommended early interment, and it was buried on the fourth day.   The youngest child had been taken by the servant into the room where the corpse was, to see it, and this child was taken ill just before the burial and died in about a week.   The corpse of this child was retained in the house three weeks.   It is supposed that the other child had also been taken into the room to see the corpse and touch it, and at the end of the three weeks it also died. · The medical attendant was clearly of opinion that had the first child been early removed, it would have been saved.   The undertaker's men who have to put into coffins the corpses of persons who have died from any contagious disease, are sometimes sick and compelled to take instantly gin or brandy; and they will feel sickly for some hours after, but they are not known to catch the disease.   I have often heard the men say on the morning following, "I have been able to take no breakfast to-day," and have complained of want of appetite for some time after.

Mr. Jeffereys, an undertaker, residing in Whitechapel, gives a similar account of the dreadful effects of this practice.

It is stated that the practice of keeping the body in the house is a very great evil; how long have you known bodies to be kept in the house before interment?—I have known them to be kept three weeks : we every week see them kept until the bodies are nearly putrid: sometimes they have run away almost through the coffin, and the poor people, women and children, are living and sleeping in the same room at the same time.   In some cases there is superstition about the interments, but it is not very frequent.   Then when the corpse is uncovered, or the coffin is open, females will hang over it.   A widow who hung over the body of her husband, caught the disease of which he died.   The doctor told her he knew she must have kissed or touched the body : she died, leaving seven orphans, of whom four are now in an orphan asylum.   A young man died not long since, and his body rapidly decomposed.   His sister, a fine healthy girl, hung over the corpse and kissed it; in three weeks after she died also.

§ 32. The descriptions given by the labouring classes themselves of the circumstances precedent to the removal of the body for interment, are similar to those in the instances above cited. They are thus described by John Downing, one of several respectable mechanics examined :—

You, as secretary [of a burial society] are called upon to attend the funeral; are you not?—Yes, I am. It is part of our rules, also, that the secretary shall see the body and identify it. When old members, whom I have known, have been sick, I have visited them, although I am not obliged to do it.

What in the case of death is the condition in which you generally find the corpse ?—It is generally stretched out on a shutter, with a sheet over it. Children are generally laid out on the table.

In how many cases do you find that those whom you visit, who may perhaps be considered to be of the class of respectable mechanics, do you find them occupying more than one room ?—About one case in six.

Have you observed any effects from the long retention of the body in the same room as the family ?—Yes, I have known children to have taken the disease and die ; I have also known the widow who has hung over the body and kissed it, become ill and die through it. I have known other cases where there has been severe illness. I have myself been made ill by visiting them ; I have felt giddy in the head and very sick, and have gone to the nearest house of refreshment to get some brandy. I have felt the effects for two or three days.

§ 33. The next class of witnesses, who receive the remains at the place of burial, attest the fact that the smell from the coffin is frequently powerfully offensive, and that it is by no means an uncommon occurrence that the decomposing matter escapes from it, and in the streets, and in the church, and in the church-yard, runs down over the shoulders of the bearers.

§ 34. So far as the inquiry has proceeded in the provincial towns, it appears that the practice of keeping the corpse in the crowded living rooms does not differ essentially from the practice in the metropolis. Mr. R. Craven, a surgeon residing at Leeds, who has had great experience amongst that population, states—

The Irish almost universally live huddled together in great numbers in a small space. I have often known as many as twenty human beings lodged and fed in a dirty filthy cottage with only two rooms. Great many live in cellar dwellings. I have frequently seen a cellar dwelling lodge a family of seven to ten persons, and that in close confined yards. I have seen a cellar dwelling in one of the most densely-populated districts of Leeds in which were living seven persons, with one corner fenced off and a pig in it ; a ridge of clay being placed round the fence to prevent the wet from the pigsty running all over the floor, and to this cellar there was no drainage.

I believe that a much larger proportion of the Irish attacked by fever, die, than of English. Children they do not make so much parade of, as here is greater difficulty of obtaining the funds for their burial. It is no uncommon thing to see a corpse laid out in a room where eight to twelve persons have to sleep, and sometimes even both sleep and eat.

He also states also that—

Amongst the handloom weavers there is some difference. They generally live in cottages consisting of two small rooms or cellar dwellings; these have always a large space occupied by the loom ; and in cottages of two rooms I have frequently seen two families residing having in the upper room two looms. When deaths occur in this class the corpse cannot be laid out without occupying the space where the family have to work (the father or mother weaving, and children winding or rendering other assistance), or in the room where they live and eat. This, I am of opinion, has a very debasing effect on the morals of this class of the community, making especially the rising generation so familiar with death that their feelings are not hurt by it : it has also a very injurious physical effect, frequently propagating disease in a rapid manner and to an immense extent.

§ 35. Mr. Christopher Fountaine Browne, one of the parochial surgeons of Leeds, whose district comprehends a population of 45,000 persons, chiefly of the working classes, states that:—

The people amongst whom I practise generally occupy one room where they live in, and a bedroom above ; but I have known many instances of a family, say a man, his wife, and from three to six children, having only one bed and one apartment for all purposes. But a great many dwellings there consist of only one room, and in many of the lodging-houses I have seen five or six beds in one small room, in which it has been acknowledged that from 12 to 14 persons have passed the night, and the air has been so bad that I have been compelled to stand at the window whilst visiting the patient.

He also states, that—

He has seen many deaths take place in such houses when the body remains in the bed where it died ; and I have known it remain two or three nights before interment. In Irish cases they keep them longer. I have seen a child lie in a down-stairs room in a corner, dead of small-pox, and another dying, and the house full of lodgers eating their meals. The length of time that a corpse is kept varies very much according to the disposition of the relatives and the means of procuring a burial, as there are no restrictions as to the length of time bodies are to be kept.

I have observed, that in cases of small-pox disease frequently follows in rapid succession on different members of the same family. I have frequently known cases of a low typhoid character arise where many persons sleep in the same room : the addition of a death from any such cause of course increases the danger to the living.

In Manchester and in several northern districts, it appears that by custom the corpse seldom remains unburied more than three or four days, but during that time it remains in the crowded rooms of the living of the labouring classes. Every day's retention of the corpse is to be considered an aggravation of the evil ; but the evidence is to be borne in mind that the miasma from the dead is more dangerous immediately after death, or during the first and second day, than towards the end of the week. In a proportion of cases decomposition has commenced before the vital functions have ceased ; immediately after death decomposition often proceeds with excessive rapidity in the crowded rooms, which have then commonly larger fires than usual.

§ 36. It is observed by some of the witnesses that usually, and except by accident, and in few cases, the miasma from the remains of the dead in grave-yards can only reach the living in a state of diffusion and dilution ; and that large proportions of it probably escape without producing any immediately appreciable evil. The practice, however, of the retention of the remains in the one room of the living brings the effluvium to bear directly upon the survivors when it is most dangerous, when they are usually exhausted bodily by watching, and depressed mentally by anxiety and grief—circumstances which it is well known greatly increase the danger of contagion. The males of the working-classes in general die earlier than the females, and in the greater number of cases the last duties fall to the widow ; and the prevalence of fatal disease chiefly amongst the children is frequently attributed to the circumstance, that she is aroused from the stunning effect of the bereavement by the necessity of going abroad and seeking pecuniary aid, and making arrangements for the funeral, whilst the children are left at home in the house with the corpse.

In Scotland, from an aversion to sleeping in the presence of the corpse, it is the practice to sit up with it, and there is then much drinking of ardent spirits.   Mr. W. Dyce Guthrie speaks strongly of the evils attendant upon the practice of the unguarded retention of the body under such circumstances, and of the instances known by himself where persons have come from a distance to attend the funeral of a departed friend, and have returned infected with a disease similar to that which terminated the friend's existence.   The concurrent and decided opinion of himself and a number of other medical witnesses is, that the public health is much more affected by the pestiferous influence of the corpse during the interval of time that occurs from the moment of death, up to the hour of the funeral, than it commonly is or can be after interment.

§ 37. Of the deaths which take place in the metropolis, it will be seen that more than one-half are the deaths of the labouring classes. The following table, taken from the Mortuary Registries during the year 1839, shows the numbers of deaths amongst the chief classes of society, and the proportions of deaths from epidemic diseases.   At least four out of five of the deaths of the labouring classes, it will be remembered, are stated to occur in the single living and sleeping room, that is to say, upwards of 20,000 annually.

	Number of Deaths of each Class.			Ratio of Deaths of Children to Total Deaths.	Number of Deaths from Epidemic, Endemic, and Contagious Diseases.	Ratio of Deaths from Epidemic, Endemic, and Contagious Diseases to Total Deaths.	Average Age at Death of the whole Class, including Children.
	Adults.	Children under 10 Years.	Total.				
Gentry, Professional Persons, & their Families	1,724	529	2,253	1 in 4$\frac{8}{10}$	210	1 in 10$\frac{7}{10}$	44
Tradesmen, Clerks, & their Families . .	3,979	3,703	7,682	1 in 2$\frac{1}{10}$	1,428	1 in 5$\frac{4}{10}$	25
Undescribed . .	2,996	2,761	5,757	1 in 2$\frac{1}{10}$	1,051	1 in 5$\frac{5}{10}$	28
Labourers and their Families.	12,045	13,885	25,930	1 in 1$\frac{8}{10}$	5,469	1 in 4$\frac{8}{10}$	22
Paupers . . .	3,062	593	3,655	1 in 6$\frac{2}{10}$	557	1 in 6$\frac{6}{10}$	49
Total . .	23,806	21,471	45,277	1 in 2$\frac{1}{10}$	8,715	1 in 5$\frac{2}{10}$	27

In making up this table, all who were not distinguished as master tradesmen were entered as mechanics. This circumstance would give to the labouring classes an appearance of a higher average age of death than is gained by them. On the other hand, some of the labouring classes will be found to have died in the workhouse, which would perhaps keep the average where it now stands, whilst if the registration were more accurate, the average age of death of the middle classes might be found to be about 27. The average age of death of 27 given for the whole metropolis is not made as an average of the averages, but from the average of the whole. The apparent high average of the age of death of paupers arises from the smaller proportion of children amongst them : and the larger proportion of aged adults who seek refuge in the workhouse.*

§ 38. The deaths registered from epidemic, endemic, and contagious diseases during the year 1839, which was by no means an unhealthy year, were as follows in Liverpool, Manchester, Leeds, and Birmingham :— .

	Total Number of Deaths.	Deaths from Epidemic, Endemic, and Contagious Diseases.	Ratio of Deaths from Epidemic Disease to the Total Number of Deaths.
Liverpool . . .	7,435	1,844	1 in 4
Manchester . .	6,774	2,006	1 in $3\frac{4}{10}$
Leeds	4,388	965	1 in $4\frac{5}{10}$
Birmingham . .	3,639	747	1 in $4\frac{9}{10}$

The numbers of deaths which occurred during that year amongst the labouring classes are not distinguished, but they were for the next year as follows. And in the three first-named towns, I conceive that the proportion of cases of deaths amongst those classes where the corpse is kept in the living room, is in all probability as great as in the metropolis.

Liverpool . . . 5,597			Leeds 3,395		
Manchester . . 4,629			Birmingham . . 2,715		

I am unaware of any data existing in the towns in Scotland from which any estimate can be made of the extent to which the evils in question are prevalent there. In the recent Report on the Census, sufficient is shown of the condition of the labouring population in the towns in Ireland to prove, that in them, the evils must fall with at least as great severity as they are described to occur in the worst conditioned districts in England.†

§ 39. If the returns and the statements of witnesses acquainted with the crowded districts be correct, that four out of five families of the labouring classes have each but one room, then

---

* In the Appendix will be found further particulars and exemplifications of the facts, deducible from the mortuary registers, together with the returns from the several registration districts in the metropolis, of which the above is a summary.

†. Vide Appendix.—Paper on the Mortuary Returns.

every unit of upwards of 20,000 deaths per annum which occur in the metropolis, every unit of 4600 deaths of the labouring classes which occur annually at Liverpool, must be taken as representing a horrible scene of the retention of the corpse amidst the family in the manner described in the testimony of those who have witnessed it;—and every unit of some 4000 deaths from epidemics in the metropolis, and every third or fourth recorded death in other towns, and even in crowded villages, represents a distressing scene, and moreover a case of peculiar danger and probable permanent injury to the survivors amongst whom it takes place. Great, however, as may be the physical evils to them, the evidence of the mental pain and moral evil generally attendant on the practice of the long retention of the body in the rooms in use and amidst the living, though only noticed incidentally, is yet more deplorable.

§ 40. The duty which attaches to male relations, or which a benevolent pastor, if there were the accommodation, would exercise on the occurrence of the calamity of death to any member of a family, is to remove the sensitive and the weakly from the spectacle, which is a perpetual stimulus to excessive grief, and commonly a source of painful associations and visible images of the changes wrought in death, to haunt the imagination in after-life. When the dissolution has taken place under circumstances such as those described, it is not a few minutes' look after the last duties are performed and the body is composed in death and left in repose, that is given to this class of survivors, but the spectacle is protracted hour after hour through the day and night, and day after day, and night after night, thus aggravating the mental pains under varied circumstances, and increasing the dangers of permanent bodily injury. The sufferings of the survivors, especially of the widow of the labouring classes, are often protracted to a fatal extent. To the very young children, the greatest danger is of infection in cases of deaths from contagious and infectious disease. To the elder children and members of the family and inmates, the moral evil created by the retention of the body in their presence beyond the short term during which sorrow and depression of spirits may be said to be natural to them is, that familiarity soon succeeds, and respect disappears. These consequences are revealed by the frequency of the statements of witnesses, that the deaths of children immediately following, of the same disease of which the parent had died, had been accounted for by "the doctor," or the neighbours, in the probability that the child had caught the disease by touching the corpse or the coffin, whilst playing about the room in the absence of the mother. Dr. Reicke, in the course of his dissertation on the physical dangers from exposure to emanations from the remains, mentions an instance where a little child having struck the body of the parent which had died of a malignant disease, the hand and arm of the child was dangerously inflamed with malignant pustules in conse-quence. The mental effects on the elder children or members of the family of the retention of the body in the living room, day after day, and during meal times, until familiarity is induced,—retained, as the body commonly is, during all this time in the *sordes* of disease, the progress of change and decomposition dis-figuring the remains and adding disgust to familiarity,—are attested to be of the most demoralizing character. Such deaths occur sooner or later in various forms in every poor family ; and in neighbourhoods where there are no sanitary regulations, where they are ravaged by epidemics, such scenes are doubly familiar to the whole population.

§ 41. Astonishment is frequently excited by the cases which abound in our penal records indicative of the prevalence of habits of savage brutality and carelessness of life amongst the labouring population ; but crimes, like sores, will commonly be found to be the result of wider influences than are externally manifest ; and the reasons for such astonishment, will be diminished in proportion as those circumstances are examined, which influence the minds and habits of the population more powerfully than precepts or book education. Among these demoralizing circumstances, which appear to be preventible or removable, are those which the present inquiry brings to light. Disrespect for the human form under suffering, indifference or carelessness at death,—or at that destruction which follows as an effect of suffering—is rarely found amongst the uneducated, unconnected with a callousness to others' pain, and a recklessness about life itself. A known effect on uneducated survivors of the frequency of death amongst youth or persons in the vigour of life, is to create a reckless avidity for immediate enjoyment. Some examples of the demoralization attendant on such circumstances cannot but be apparent in the evidence arising in the course of this inquiry into other practices connected with interments.

§ 42. On submitting the above to a friend, a clergyman, whose benevolence has carried him to alleviate the sufferings in several hundred death-bed scenes in the abodes of the labouring classes, and who has been present, perhaps, at every death in his own flock, in a wretchedly crowded parish, he writes in the following terms his confirmation :—

" The whole of this I can testify, from personal knowledge, to be just. With the upper classes, a corpse excites feelings of awe and respect ; with the lower orders, in these districts, it is often treated with as little ceremony as the carcase in a butcher's shop. Nothing can exceed their desire for an imposing funeral ; nothing can surpass their efforts to obtain it ; but the deceased's remains share none of the reverence which this anxiety for their becoming burial would seem to indicate. The inconsistency is entirely, or at least in great part, to be attributed to a single circumstance—that the body is never absent from their sight—eating, drinking, or sleeping, it is still by their side; mixed up with all the ordinary functions of daily life, till it becomes as familiar to them as when it lived and moved in the family circle. From familiarity it is a short step to desecration. The body, stretched out upon two chairs, is pulled about by the children, made to serve as a resting-place for any article that is in the way, and is not seldom the hiding-place for the beer-bottle or the gin if any visitor arrives inopportunely. Viewed as an outrage upon human feeling, this is bad enough; but who does not see that when the respect for the dead, that is, for the human form in its most awful stage, is gone, the whole mass of social sympathies must be weakened—perhaps blighted and destroyed? At any rate, it removes that wholesome fear of death which is the last hold upon a hardened conscience. They have gazed upon it so perpetually, they have grown so intimate with its terrors, that they no longer dread it, even when it attacks themselves, and the heart which vice has deadened to every appeal of religion is at last rendered callous to the natural instinct of fear."

That it is possible by legislative means to stay the progress of this dreadful demoralization, which must, if no further heed be taken of it, go on with the increased crowding of an increasing population; that it is possible to abate the mental and physical suffering; to extend to the depressed urban districts an acceptable and benign and elevating influence on such impressive occasions; may be confidently affirmed, and will in a subsequent stage of this Report be endeavoured to be shown by reference to actual examples of successful measures.

Expenses of Funerals and their effects on the Living.

§ 43. The practice of the long retention of the dead before burial being the one from which the greatest evil accrues, the circumstances by which the practice is chiefly influenced are the first submitted for consideration.

The causes which influence this practice amongst the greatest number of the population appear to be, first, the expense of funerals—next, the delay in making arrangements for the funeral,—the natural reluctance to part with the remains of the deceased, and occasionally a feeling of apprehension, sometimes expressed on the part of the survivors, against premature interment.

The expense of interments, though it falls with the greatest severity on the poorest classes, acts as a most severe infliction on the middle classes of society, and governs so powerfully the questions in respect to the present and future administrative arrangements, and involves so many other evils, as to require as complete an exposition as possible of its extent and operation.

The testimony of witnesses of the most extensive experience is of the following tenor in London and the crowded town districts of England. Mr. Byles, the surgeon, of Spitalfields, in reference to the delay of interments, states—

.The difficulty of raising the subscription to bury the dead, is I apprehend one chief cause of the delay. When, in the instance of the death of a child, I ask why it cannot be interred earlier, the usual reply is, we cannot raise the money earlier.

Mr. Wild, the undertaker, states—

The time varies from five to twelve days. This arises from the difficulty of procuring the means of making arrangements with the undertaker, and the difficulty of getting mourners to attend the funeral. They have a great number to attend, neighbours, fellow-workmen, as well as relations. The mourners with them vary from five to eight couple; it is always an agreement for five couple at the least.

One of the witnesses of the labouring classes, who had acted as secretary to an extensive burial society, gives the following account of the causes which operate to produce the delay.

What is the average length of time they remain unburied?—Never less than a week. If they die in the middle of the week they are generally kept until the Sunday week. I have known instances, however, where they have been kept as long as a fortnight.

What have been the causes of this retention of the body?—In general it has been the want of money to defray the dues. In some cases, however, the widow has been reluctant to part with the corpse.

In what proportion of cases has this occurred?—It may have been in one case in thirty, as far as I can recollect.

§ 44. Mr. Baker, the coroner, stated to me that he has met with some cases where inquests have been promoted in consequence of suspicions excited amongst neighbours on account of the delay of interments; it turned out that the deaths had been natural, and that the delay had arisen from the difficulty of procuring money to defray the funeral expenses. Mr. Bell, who for several years acted as clerk to Mr. Stirling, the late coroner for Middlesex, even cites several dreadful cases of children found dead in the metropolis, in which, on inquiry, it was proved that the deaths were natural, but that the bodies had been actually abandoned in consequence of the difficulty of raising the money for interment, and the reluctance to apply for parochial aid.

§ 45. The nature of the expenses of interments in London, and their operation on the whole practice, are most fully developed in the examination of Mr. Wild.

Supposing the expenses of interment reduced, and the conveniences increased, do you think that there would be much or any reluctance to early interment, on account of any general feeling of dislike on the part of the survivors to earlier removals or interments?— No, I do not think there would be any reluctance.

In cases where the obstacles arising from the expense and the inconvenience preventing the attendance of friends do not exist, is there a frequent reluctance expressed to early interment?—It is not frequent. Sometimes, but very seldom, the deceased may have expressed a wish not to be hurried out of the house soon after he was dead.

Do you find that there is less delay amongst the higher and middle classes?

—There is certainly much less delay amongst them; but with them the corpses are early placed either in lead or in double coffins, and the delay is of less consequence.

Amongst the poorer classes, is not the widow often made ill during the protracted delay of the burial?—Yes, very often. They have come to me in tears, and begged for accommodation, which I have given them. On observing to them, you seem very ill; a common reply is, "Yes, I feel very ill. I am very much harassed, and I have no one to assist me." I infer from such expressions that the mental anxiety occasioned by the expense, and want of means to obtain the money, is the frequent cause of their illness. My opinion is, that unless the undertaker gave two-thirds of them time or accommodation for payment, they would not be able to bury the dead at all.

Do you consider that funerals in general are made unnecessarily expensive? —Yes, they are, even under their present system unnecessarily expensive. The average price of funerals amongst the working classes for adults will be about 4*l*. This sum generally provides a good strong elm coffin, bearers to carry the corpse to the grave, pall and fittings for mourners. For children the average cost is 30*s*., but these charges do not include ground and burial fees.

Are they so even when the funerals are provided by burial societies, and made the subject of special attention?—In benefit societies and burial clubs there is generally a certain sum set aside for the burial, which sum is, I consider, frequently most extravagantly expended. This arises from the secretary, or some other officer of the club being an undertaker. When a death takes place the club money is not paid directly: it is usually paid on the club or quarterly night following. The member dying seldom leaves any money beyond the provision in his club to bury him, consequently the widow or nominee makes application to the secretary, who tells her that he cannot give any money to purchase mourning for herself and family until the committee meets; this may be three months after the death; but, says the secretary, "give me the funeral, I will advance you a few pounds upon my own account;" so that the widow is obliged to submit to any charge he may think fit to make. I do not mean to be understood that this is always the case—I am sorry to say it is of frequent occurrence.

In general, are not the expenses of burial in the Dissenters' burial-grounds less than those of burial in the grounds belonging to the Established Church?—On the average one-third less.‡

On the occasion of burial in Dissenters' burial-grounds, is any question ever raised as to whether the deceased was a subscribing member of the community to which the grounds belong?—No question is ever asked.

Of corpses of the labouring classes whom you yourself have buried in the burial-grounds of Dissenters, how many will have been of subscribing members of the community to which the grounds belong?—Not one in twenty.

Then the preference arises from the greater cheapness of the burial in those grounds?—Yes, and the greater convenience. The burial, instead of being fixed at one particular hour, as in cases of burials in the Church, may be had within a range of three hours. This convenience has a great influence on the choice of places of burial.

Have burials in the Dissenters' grounds been increasing of late?—Very much: their places of burial are in general no better; they are, indeed, in some instances worse than the grounds belonging to the parish churches, but they would, probably, have enlarged and improved them, and, at the rate at which they have proceeded, they would soon have three-fourths of all the burials;—chiefly on account of the increased cheapness and accommodation attendant on their burials.

Are the ordinary expenses and inconveniences of funerals generally severely oppressive to persons of the middle classes?—Very generally: it often occurs that a poor widow is crippled in her means through life by the expense of a funeral. An ordinary funeral, burial fees and all, will cost from 50*l.* to 70*l.*, which will deprive her of 5*l.* a year from ten to fourteen years, besides the interest.

Without any deductions of the solemnity, for how much less might such a funeral be performed?—For about 50 per cent. less. Indeed, I have proved that practically for some time past.

Is not much of the accompaniments of funerals which, as at present conducted, are deemed part of the solemnity, questionable in its effect as well as appropriateness? Is it not the effect of custom, rather than any choice or wish of the parties?—Merely customary : the term used in giving orders is, "provide what is customary."

Are you aware that the array of funerals, commonly made by undertakers, is strictly the heraldic array of a baronial funeral, the two men who stand at the doors being supposed to be the two porters of the castle, with their staves, in black; the man who heads the procession, wearing a scarf, being a representative of a herald-at-arms; the man who carries a plume of feathers on his head being an esquire, who bears the shield and casque, with its plume of feathers ; the pall-bearers, with batons, being representatives of knights-companions-at-arms; the men walking with wands being supposed to represent gentlemen-ushers, with their wands :—are you aware that this is said to be the origin and type of the common array usually provided by those who undertake to perform funerals?—No; I am not aware of it.

It may be presumed that those who order funerals are equally unaware of the incongruity for which such expense is incurred?—Undoubtedly they are.

What is the cost of porters, the men who bear staves covered with black?—The cost of the mutes varies from 18*s.* to 30*s.* In some cases of respectable persons, where silk scarfs or fittings, including hat-bands and gloves, are used, 5*l.* 5*s.* is charged to families for those fittings. To parties in moderate circumstances, two guineas would be charged for the fittings and the pay.

What is the charge for the person who walks with a scarf?—The usual charge to a respectable family would be a guinea, besides fittings, scarfs, gloves, and hat-bands, which would altogether amount to about two guineas and a half for this man.

What is the charge for the plume of feathers borne on the head before the hearse?—The charge for the feathers would be about two guineas; then there is the man's gloves, scarf, and fittings, which make it about three guineas and a-half.

What is the charge per man bearing batons?—The charge, including silk fittings, will be about 22*s.* each man.

What is the charge for each man bearing a wand?—About the same price.

How many men of this description would be required for what is deemed a respectable funeral?—About twenty men; for if the coffin be a leaden one it would require about eight men to bear it.

What other charges are there of the same kind?—There are velvets attached to the hearse, including feathers, and feathers to the horses, which makes from ten to fifteen guineas more.

What is charged for the pall?—From one to four guineas would be charged for the use of the pall.

What is it usual to give to the clergyman?—A silk scarf of three yards and a half, a silk hatband, and black kid gloves.

What may be the expense of this?—About two guineas to the parties.

Is anything usually given to the clerk?—Yes, the same as to the minister.

Is anything given to the sexton?—Yes, they do in respectable families, or rather the undertaker does so, for his own gain. The cost of the whole,—minister, sexton, and undertaker, will be about seven guineas to a respectable family, but it is usual to compound the matter by giving them money; I generally give the minister 18*s.*, and the clerk 15*s.*, and the sexton, perhaps, 15*s.*

Is such an array as that described adopted in the case of the funerals of

E

tradesmen as well as of other classes?—They have frequently the same number of men.

A clergyman's widow, who has solicited aid for her sons, whom she has found it difficult to educate, states that the expenses of her husband's funeral were upwards of 110*l.* On being asked how she could incur such an expense, she states that she considered it her duty to have a respectable funeral, and ordered the undertaker to provide what was respectable; that she knew not what she ordered in that condition, and merely gave general orders. Now is not this a frequent case, and is not the undertaker's usual interpretation of respectability that which is expensive, the parties knowing little about it?—Yes, that is frequently so.

In the case of funerals of persons of moderate respectability costing, say about 60*l.*, how many of such men as those described would there be attending it?—About fourteen.

For a curate, or person of that condition, would there be that number and array?—Yes.

What would be the expense of the funeral of a person of the condition of an attorney?—From 60*l.* to 100*l.*; but this would not include the expense of tomb or monument, or burial-fees.

If a person of such a condition were buried, would it be of about twenty attendants, with such an array as that described?—Yes; for such a person the cost would be about 100 guineas, exclusive of the burial-fees.

There would then be the same number of attendants as those mentioned, about twenty men?—Yes, about twenty men.

The funeral being ordered of an upholsterer, is it not usually provided by an undertaker?—Yes.

In how many cases of funerals will there be "the second profit?"—In nearly two-thirds of the cases of burial in the upper classes.

Is the same observation applicable to the funerals amongst the middle classes?—Yes; I think in nearly the same proportion.

How much of the profit will be the profit of the upholsterer?—Nearly half: if the funeral costs 50*l.* to the upholsterer from the undertaker, it will cost about 100*l.* from the undertaker to the family.

Is there much credit given in the business to respectable families?—Not much; for as soon as letters of administration are taken out the funeral expenses are discharged.

The average expense of the funeral of an adult of the labouring class being about 4*l.*, exclusive of the burial fees, and that of a child about 30*s.*, what may be stated to be the ordinary expense of the funeral of a tradesman of the lowest class, as ordinarily conducted?—Of the very lowest class—of a class in condition not much beyond that of a mechanic, the funeral expenses might be from 10*l.* to 12*l.*

What would be the ordinary expense for the funeral of a child of a person of this class?—The ordinary expense would be about 5*l.*

What would be the ordinary expense of the funeral of a tradesman of a better class?—From 70*l.* to 100*l.*

What do you consider would be a low average for the ordinary expense of the whole class of tradesmen's funerals?—About 50*l.* would, I consider be a low average for the whole class.

What may be considered the average of ordinary expenses of the funerals of children of the class dying below 10 years of age?—About 14*l.*

Might 100*l.* be taken as the average expense of the funeral of a person of the condition of a gentleman?—No; they range from 200*l* to 1,000*l.* I think that 150*l.* would be a low average.

What may be considered the ordinary expense of the funeral of a child of this class?—About 30*l.* would be the average.

What may be the ordinary expense of the funerals of persons of rank or title?—The expense varies from 500*l.* to 1500*l.* A large part of this expense has, however, commonly been for the removal of the remains from town to the family vault by a long cavalcade moving by very slow stages ; but the conveyance by railway makes as much as 500*l.* difference in the expense of a funeral of this class.

What may be the average expense of the funeral of a child of this class ? —About 50*l.*

Do you believe it to be practicable, by proper regulations, greatly to reduce the existing charges of interments ?—Yes; a very great reduction indeed may be made, at least 50 per cent.

May it be confidently stated that under such reductions, whatever of respectability in exterior is now attached to the trappings, or to the mode of the ceremony, might be preserved ?—Oh, yes ; I should say it might, and that they could scarcely fail to be increased.

§ 46. Mr. Dix, an undertaker, who inters from 800 to 1000 persons annually, of whom about 300 are of the class of independent labourers, being questioned on this topic, stated as follows :—

The lowest average expense of a poor man's burial, from extensive evidence, is stated to be about 5*l.*; but that is where it is done, as it usually is, second or third hand. I frequently perform funerals three deep : that is, I do it for one person, who does it for another who does it for the relatives of the deceased, he being the first person applied to.

The people then generally apply to the nearest person ?—Yes, they do. Everybody calls himself an undertaker. The numerous men employed as bearers become undertakers, although they have never done anything until they have got the job. I have known one of these men get a new suit of clothes out of the funeral of one decent mechanic.

§ 47. The conclusions in respect to the unnecessary expense of funerals appear to be applicable, with little variation, to the most populous provincial towns. In the rural districts the expense of funerals of the class of gentry appears to be even more expensive. In most of the provincial towns the expense of the funerals of the more respectable class of tradesmen does not appear to be much less than in London. In Scotland, the expenses of the funerals of persons of the middle classes appear, from a communication from Mr. Chambers, to vary from 12*l.* to 25*l.* In Glasgow the expenses of funerals of persons of the middle class appear to vary from 12*l.* to 50*l.*

§ 48. To persons of the condition of the widows of officers in the army or navy, or of the legal profession, or of persons of the rank of gentry who have but limited incomes, the expenses of the funerals often subject them to severe privations during the remainder of their lives. The widow is frequently compelled to beg pecuniary assistance for the education of her children, which the superfluous expenses of the funerals of the adult members of the family would have supplied ; and these expenses are incurred often in utter disregard of express requests of the dying, that the funerals should be plain, and divested of unnecessary expense. The expenses are often incurred equally against the wishes of the survivors. The cause of this appears to be that the funeral arrangements, and the determination of what is proper, and what customs shall be maintained, fall, as shown by the evidence, to those who have a direct interest,—and when the nature of their separate establish-

ments are considered, are commonly acting under a strong necessity,—in maintaining a system of profuse expenditure. The
circumstances·of the death do not admit of any effective competition or any precedent examination of the charges of different undertakers, or any comparison and consideration of their
supplies; there is no time to change them for others that are less
expensive, and more in conformity to the taste and circumstances
of the parties. An executor who had ordered a coffin and
service of the " most simple description," conformably to the
intentions of the deceased, expecting the coffin to cost not more
than five pounds, having, under peculiar circumstances, occasion
to call for the bill previously to the interment, found, to his surprise, that instead of five the charge for the coffin amounted to
nearly twenty pounds. "What," he says, " could be done? we
could not turn the body out of the coffin: I would have paid
double rather than have disturbed the peace of the house on that
solemn occasion, by a dispute, or by an objection either to
that charge, or to the disgusting frippery with which those who
attended the dead were covered against their tastes." The
survivors, however, are seldom in a state to perform any
office of every-day life; and they are at the mercy of the first
comer. The supplies of the funeral goods and services, are,
therefore, a multiform monopoly, not apparently on the parts of
the chief undertakers, or original and real preparers of the
funeral materials and services, but of second or third parties
living in the immediate neighbourhood,—persons who assume
the business of an undertaker, and who obtain the ·first orders.
The reason why the charges are seldom or ever disputed after
interment is that, however severe or extortionate they may be,
it would be more severe for the widow, or survivor, or friends,
to scrutinise the items, or resist the payment of the total
amount. Nor can it be expected of any individual to break
through such customs, however generally they may be disliked.
All isolated efforts to simplify the supplies and use of the goods
and *materiel,*—all objections to the demands for them are exposed to the calumny that proper respect to the deceased is be-
grudged. A late right reverend bishop, who thought it a moral
duty to resist an extortionate charge for such service, and he did
so even in a court of law,—the well-intended, but isolated effort,
was fruitless. Another reason for the impunity of the extortion is,
that much of the funeral expenses are from trust-funds of the
higher and middle classes, who influence the practice of the lower
classes; and the trustees have but weak motives and means to de-
fend them. In so far as the funeral expenses are concerned, such
funds, as will appear in respect to the funds raised for burial
amongst the labouring classes, are an exposed prey.

§ 49. If there be any sort of service, which principles of civic
polity, and motives of ordinary benevolence and charity, require

to be placed under public regulation, for the protection of the private individual who is helpless, it is surely this, at the time of extreme misery and helplessness of the means of decent interment. On inspecting the condition of the whole class of persons engaged in the performance of the service of undertakers, it may be confidently stated that the class who only act as agents, could not suffer, and must gain morally and socially, and ultimately pecuniarily by a change that would be beneficial to the public. No class can be otherwise than benefited by change, from an occupation in which they are kept waiting and dependent on profits which fall to them at wide and irregular intervals. Notwithstanding the immensely disproportionate profits of these persons in some cases, and the immense aggregate expenditure to the public, there appear to be very few wealthy undertakers. They are described by one of them, " as being some few of them very respectable, but the great majority as men mostly in a small grubbing way of business." In this trade we have now the means of knowing to an unit, from the mortuary registration, the amount of service required ; and we have some means of obtaining a proximate estimate of the number of persons engaged in its performance.

§ 50. The number of deaths per diem in the metropolis (inclusive of the death of those who die in the workhouses, whose interment being provided for by the parish and union officers, are not cases for every-day competition) is on an average of three years 114. The number of persons whose sole business is that of undertakers, whose names are enumerated in the Post-office Directory for the year 1843 for the metropolis is 275. Besides these there are 258 " undertakers and carpenters," 34 " undertakers and upholsterers," 56 "undertakers and cabinet-makers," 51 "undertakers and builders," 25 "undertakers and appraisers," 19 "undertakers and auctioneers," 7 "undertakers and house-agents," 3 " undertakers and fancy cabinet-makers," 2 " undertakers and packing-case makers ;" making in all no less than 730 persons for the 114 deaths, or between six and seven undertakers waiting for the chance of every private funeral. But these are masters who, whether they act as agents or principals, have shops and establishments, and the list does not include the whole of them, as the Directory is not understood to include all the masters residing in bye-streets and places. Some have two and three funerals per diem, and some eight or ten; and it is apparent, even under the existing imperfect arrangements, the undertaker's service might be better performed by forty or fifty than by the 275 principals, who have no other occupation, and whose establishments and expenses, as well as the cost of their own maintenance, must, if the business be equally distributed, be charged on little more than two funerals a-week. If the business be not equally distributed, and a minority have (as will have been perceived) a much larger share of the funerals than the rest, the majority will be the more severely driven, as they are in fact, to charge their expenses on a much smaller number of funerals.   When the additional number of tradesmen of mixed occupations are brought as waiters for the chances of employment, the number of burials distributed amongst them all is reduced to 10 funerals to every master in 11 weeks, or less than one a-week each.   It is stated, that much larger numbers than are named in the Directory retain the insignia of undertakers in their shop-windows, for the sake of the profits of one or two funerals a-year.   They merely transmit the orders to the furnishing undertaker, who supplies materials and men at a comparatively low rate; and it is stated that the real service is rendered by about sixty tradesmen of this class, who compete with each other in furnishing the supplies to a multitude of inferior tradesmen, probably exceeding 1000, amongst whom the excessive profits arising from extortionate charges are thus irregularly distributed.   The profits of these agents or second parties are often, however, divided with others by the system (which pursues the head of the family to the last) of corrupting servants for their "good word" or influence by bribes or allowances, against which the only effectual defence is care to secure purchases at prices so low as to preclude them.   Physicians of great eminence have expressed their horror at the facts of which they have been informed, of large sums of money having been promised and given to head servants to secure to the particular tradesman the performance of the funeral.   The undertakers who were questioned on the subject admitted explicitly that such is "an occasional but not an universal practice," and that such sums as 10*l.*, 20*l.*, and even 50*l.*, have been known to have been given for such orders, according to the scale of expense and profit of the funeral.   One undertaker stated that whenever a medical man took the trouble to bring him an order for a funeral, he always, as a matter of course, paid him a fee ; and he believed it was a common practice.   It was, however, only the inferior practitioners who brought these orders.   Physicians usually carefully abstain from giving any recommendations of tradesmen in such cases.

§ 51.   Such being the state of the service as respects the multitude of principals ; the state of the service as respects the inferior dependents is, that as at present conducted it is, as far as it goes, demoralizing. The journeymen, who form the superfluous retinue of attendants for whom so much expense is incurred, gain very little by their extravagant pay.   "They are," says one master undertaker, "kept long waiting, and are taken away to a distance from their homes, and are put to great expense in drinking at public-houses, and acquiring very bad habits." The accounts given by undertakers themselves of the conduct of the men composing the hired retinue of funerals, as at present conducted, are corroborative of the following instance

given by a gentleman who was a witness of the scene described :—

If the relatives of one who has been honoured with what is called a
respectable funeral could witness the scenes which commonly ensue, even
at the very place where the last ceremony has been performed, they would
be scandalized at the mockery of solemnity which has preceded the disgusting indecency exhibited at the instant when the mourners are removed.
An empty hearse, returning at a quick pace from a funeral, with half a
dozen red-faced fellows sitting with their legs across the pegs which held
the feathers, is a common exhibition. But let the relatives see what has
preceded the ride home of the undertaker's men. In the spring of 1842,
two friends walked into a village inn about twelve miles from London, for
the purpose of dining. One had recently sustained a severe domestic
calamity. The inn is generally distinguished for its neatness and quiet.
All now seemed confusion. The travellers were shown up stairs to a com-
fortable room. But the shouts,.the laughing, the rapping the tables, the
ringing the bells, in an adjoining room were beyond endurance ; and when
the landlady appeared with her bill of fare, she apologized for what was so
different from the ordinary habit of her guests. "Is it a club feast?"
" Oh, no, gentlemen ; they are the undertaker's men—blackguards I should
say. They have been burying poor Lord ———— ; he was much beloved here. Shame on them. But they will soon go back to town, for
they are nearly drunk." The travellers left the house till it was cleared of
these harpies."

§ 52. Men of the class who are every day to be seen stopping
in parties at public houses on their return from the places of
burial, are intrusted without care or selection to perform what
may be shown to be important sanitary and civil ministrations of
enshrouding and preparing the body for burial. The impressions
created by the bearing of these coarse, unknown, unrespected,
irresponsible hands, add to the revolting popular associations with
death.

The extent of the public interests affected by so much of the
practice of interment, as the undertaker's service embraces, will be
better appreciated in a subsequent stage of this report, and after
the consideration of the facts unfolded in the course of an examination of the influence of the expenses of funerals specifically on
the states of mind, social habits and economy of the labouring
classes in towns of England.

Specific Effects of the Expenses of Funerals, and Associations to defray them amongst the Labouring Classes.

§ 53. The desire to secure respectful interment of themselves and
their relations is, perhaps, the strongest and most widely-diffused
feeling amongst the labouring classes of the population. Subscriptions may be obtained from large classes of them for their
burial when it can be obtained neither for their own relief in
sickness, nor for the education of their children, nor for any
other object. The amount of the twenty-four millions of deposits in the savings' banks of the United Kingdom is 29*l.* each

depositor. Judging from particular investigations, it would appear that upwards of 5*l.* of each deposit may be considered a sum devoted to defray the expenses of burial, and about as much more to provide mourning and other expenses. From six to eight millions of savings may be considered as devoted to these objects.

§ 54. The following is an answer to some inquiries on the subject from the secretary of the St. Martin's Lane Provident Institution, an institution in which the deposits amount to 1,168,850*l.*, and the depositors, amounting to upwards of 32,000, comprehend some of the most frugal and respectable of the labouring classes :—

As you wished me to mention any facts within my knowledge, arising out of this institution and its concerns, bearing upon the question of *sepulture,* I would first state, that the average *annual number* of deaths occurring amongst our depositors (now about 32,000 in number) in the course of the last nine years, has been 231 ; these, taking the last of such years for an example, are divisible under the classes shown by the subjoined statement. By reference to this statement it will be seen how large a class of our depositors consists of individuals of the poorer or labouring population ; and amongst that class, in regard to the question of *sepulture,* from the opportunity afforded me of inspecting the charges made for funerals, I should say that the expenses incurred for the funeral and interment alone are seldom so little as 4*l.*, generally amount to 5*l.* and upwards, and not unfrequently exceed 6*l.*

It is, I may observe, no uncommon practice for parties to leave deposits in their names, about the amount I have stated, for the very purpose of providing for the expenses of their interment, so as to ensure for themselves, under any change of circumstances, a decent burial; this feeling has prevailed so strongly in instances within my own knowledge, that, upon the happening of the death, the party has been found to have died at last an inmate of a poor house, and destitute of every kind of property, save only the little fund appropriated for the purpose I have stated. This feeling is not confined solely to the poorest class of our depositors: an instance lately occurred in which a depositor to the amount of 32*l.*, made a special request that 20*l.* of this money might, in the event of her death, be paid only to *her undertaker* on production of his account and of *her burial certificate,* and the balance to be paid to her relatives. The depositor died in the following year, and her wishes were accordingly carried into effect, with the concurrence of a relative, to whom it appeared she had communicated the arrangement she had thus made in regard to her money deposited with this institution.

Total Number of Deaths in the Year ending 31st March, 1842.	Total Effects of such deceased Depositors, certified as under the following Amounts, viz:—							
	£50	£100	£200	£300	£400	£450	£600	£800	Amount to £1000 and upwards
232	133	32	23	10	1	5	6	6	16

Occurrences such as those above alluded to are not unfrequent. Those who, as paupers, have led a life of dissipation, and have saved nothing for other objects, have yet reserved and concealed a small hoard to provide interment in a mode agreeable to their feelings. Besides the immense amount of money reserved for this purpose in the savings' banks, it forms the great object of the benefit clubs: in most large towns there are burial clubs instituted for no other purpose. In the town of Preston nearly 30,000 persons, men, women, and children, are associated in six large societies for the purpose of burial; the chief of these clubs comprehends 15,164 members, and has since its commencement expended upwards of 1,000*l.* per annum, raised in weekly contributions, from a half-penny and a penny to three-halfpence and two-pence per week. A benevolent officer, in giving an account of this club, expresses a hope that it may be practicable, in connexion with it, to get up some provision for the living, in the shape of medical attendance for the sick, an object which appears to have been entirely lost sight of in these societies. Besides the burial societies, of which the funds are deposited in the savings' banks, there are others in which the funds are placed out in the hands of private persons, traders, who pay interest upon them.

§ 55. As an example of the allowances in the provincial clubs, it may be mentioned, that on an examination of the rules of 90 friendly societies at present existing in the borough and town of Walsall, comprising upwards of 5000 members, it appeared that the allowances insured for funerals were as follows:—that

For the Funeral of the Husband.			For the Funeral of the Wife.	
22 societies	. pay £10		36 societies	. pay £3
12	 8		16	 5
8	 7		14	 4
3	 16		9	 8
			3	 6
			3	 7

The burial allowances in the others were not specified.

§ 56. It must be premised, that it appears to be a serious error to regard the arrangements of all of this class of clubs as the arrangements of the poor people themselves; the arrangements are evidence only of the intensity of their feelings on the subject of interment, of their ignorance and their extensive need of information and trustworthy guidance.

There are, for example, in Westminster, Marylebone, Finsbury, the City, and the Tower Hamlets, districts of the metropolis, about 200 of such societies, composed chiefly of the labouring classes, comprising from 100 to 800 members each, possessing aggregate amounts of deposits of from 90*l.* to 1000*l.* each; raised in contributions of from three-halfpence to two-pence per week, and paying on the death of a member from 5*l.* to 10*l.* Besides these, there are clubs of a higher description, mostly amongst the smallest class of tradesmen, where the sums insured extend to sums as high as 200*l.*, payable at the member's death, and are understood to be chiefly devoted to the payment of the funeral expenses. The burial clubs for the labouring classes are generally got up by an undertaker and by the publican at whose house the club is held. The state of feeling addressed in the formation of these societies is denoted by the terms of the placards issued at the joint expense of the publican or of the undertaker, or rather of some mechanic or person of another trade, who gets the business done by an undertaker. These placards are frequently headed " In the midst of life we are in death;" and the addresses are in such terms as the following, which is taken from " The United Brothers' and Sisters' Burial Society," held at the Old Duke William public house, Ratcliffe Highway :—

" In contemplating the many vicissitudes and changes incident to all persons of every station in life, and the many anxieties that crowd about our advancing years, more particularly the labouring class, through the uncertainty of employment, by long illness, or for want of friends reduced to extreme distress, and after a long and miserable life, and in expectation of that awful change which we must one time or other undergo, without ever providing for a decent interment, it will be some alleviation to our sufferings to remember that we bring no pecuniary burthen on our commiserating friends and relations, that at least we have divested our suffering families of that anxiety respecting our mortal remains which would add another pang to their already lacerated hearts : it too frequently occurs to the sorrow of many a feeling heart, who mourns over the deplorable loss of a beloved husband, wife, or friend ; to obtain this desirable object, this society offers to the public, on easy terms, advantages worthy the consideration of persons in all stations of life."

The terms of insurance are—

" That to defray the necessary expenses of printing books, bills, &c., that members of the first class, if under the age of 55 years, shall pay 1s. entrance, and contribute 1s. per month to the box and 2d. per quarter to the secretary ; and members of the second class, under the age of 55 years, shall pay 6d. entrance, and 6d. per month to the box, and 2d. per quarter to the secretary ; and every person above the age of 55 years, and members of the first class, to pay 2s. entrance, and contribute 1s. 6d. per month to the box, and 2d. per quarter to the secretary ; and every member of the second class to pay 1s. entrance, and contribute 1s. per month to the box, and 2d. per quarter to the secretary. No more than 20 members will be admitted above the age of 60 years. They to be free in 12 months ; nor shall any article that may be hereafter made exclude them."

The benefits insured are to be—

" That at the death of a free member, immediate notice shall be given to T. Scotcher, undertaker, who shall perform the funeral, and he shall inform one of the committee, and the first meeting night after the burial, his or her relation, next of kin, or nominee, on producing satisfactory evidence, will be entitled (if a member of the first class) to the sum of 10l.; if a member of the second class, and above seven years, to 5l. ; if under the age of seven years, to 3l. ; but when the stock of this society amounts to 150l. in the public funds, if a member in the first class admitted ten years, 12l. will be allowed ; and if a member admitted ten years in the second class, 6l. will be allowed, deducting all arrears on the books ; and for the credit of the society, the committee shall see the undertaker's bill discharged."

The publican is secured by a provision that the box shall not be removed to any other public house; and the office of "J. Scotcher, undertaker and founder of the Society," is made permanent. An arbitrary rule, in such terms as the following, is so couched (the officers being judges) as to suppress complaint. This rule is common to other societies:—

That if any member charge the committee, or any member thereof, or trustees, or secretary, with any improper practice in the management of the society, and cannot make it appear just, he or she shall be fined 5s., or be excluded.

It is to be observed that the high and exclusive spirit of some of the rules would seem to show how little the body of the members are consulted in the preparation of them. Thus, in the "Ancient Friendly Society," it is provided that " if any man sits down to drink with the stewards to pay sixpence, whether a member or not." It is provided in the rules of the " Loyal United Friends," that " if any person sit down to drink with the committee he is to pay sixpence;" and it is the same with a large proportion of the others.

In what is called an " improved burial society," of the date of 1841, called the East London Burial Society, held at the Swan public house, Bethnal Green, the terms are :—

That the members of this society shall pay their contributions weekly or monthly, and shall pay 1d. per quarter extra, to defray other expenses attending the society. Every member shall pay 1d. per week for the first class, from two to fifty-five years; the second class, from ten to fifty-five years, 2d. per week; the third class, from ten to fifty-five years, shall pay 3d. per week.

Richard Crafer appears to be the president, and William Duggan secretary; then Richard Crafer afterwards appears as the undertaker. With respect to him the following is inserted as a fundamental rule of the society :—

That Richard Crafer, being the founder of this Society, shall be the undertaker, and no future articles shall remove him, so long as he gives general satisfaction to the society, and in case of his death, his eldest son shall claim the same for the benefit of the widow, and at her decease the same shall devolve on the eldest son living.

Mr. William Duggan is appointed secretary, and for his attendance and services he shall be allowed the sum of 1d. per quarter, for as many members as there are on the society's books : he will assist the society with his best advice, and register good and healthy members, and post the books. He shall be allowed 3d. each for all notices he may deliver on the society's business, but not obliged to go more than two miles from the club-house.

This is preceded by the usual rule, that—

Any member *coming* to the society's meeting house in liquor, so as to disturb the proceedings, shall be fined 1s., and ordered to leave the room; and should any member charge the committee, secretary, president, trustees, or landlord with any unjust proceedings relative to the society, and cannot substantiate the same, he or she shall pay a fine not exceeding 10s. to the stock, or be excluded.

In the society of " United Brewers and Draymen," of which J. Guy is secretary and undertaker, one of the fundamental rules is, that—

At the funeral of a member, the secretary shall provide fittings for porters and six pall beareirs, for which he shall be allowed 1*l.*, whether they are used or not, provided such member dies and is interred within three miles of any meeting-house.

The particulars of the provision commonly held out, is stated in the following rule of the General Burial Society :—

That the landlord for the time being shall be treasurer, and when there is sufficient cash, above what is necessary to supply the exigencies of the society, the same shall be vested in the public funds, in the names of the trustees appointed by the committee.   The landlord, as treasurer, &c., shall give proper security for the due performance of his offices.

An evil entailed beyond the excessive amount of subscriptions paid for an object that is but poorly obtained, is the impulse given by it to the vice of drinking ; to the destruction of real friendly sympathy amongst the working classes, by making the announcement of the death to be received as the demoralizing announcement of a coming carousal.   Such expenses can only be incurred in the absence of proper feeling, in the face of destitute orphan children.   The secretary of one of the better ordered burial clubs, a working man, thus speaks of the regulations which tend to drinking.   He was asked—

What number of members have you ?—Two hundred, who pay sixpence per month.

What is the publican's advantage out of this?—The allowance is sixpence spending-money from each committee-man.   I do not like this, and have wanted to change the place of meeting to a coffee-house, for the members frequently add a shilling to the sixpence spending-money, and are then not in a condition to begin business ; but I find it is part of the rules of this, as well as of the other societies, that they shall be held at public houses.

On the occasion of the funeral is there no drinking ?—Yes, there is ; that is another great evil, and I wish there was a way of remedying it.   The family provide themselves with drink, and the friends coming also drink.   I have known this to be to such excess, that the undertaker's men, who always take whatever drink is given them, are frequently unfit to perform their duty, and have reeled in carrying the coffin.   At these times it is very distressing.   The men who stand as mutes at the door, as they stand out in the cold, are supposed to require most drink, and receive it most liberally.   I have seen these men reel about the road, and after the burial we have been obliged to put these mutes and their staves into the interior of the hearse and drive them home, as they were incapable of walking.   After the return from the funeral, the mourners commonly have drink again at the house.   This drinking at the funeral is a very great evil.

Besides the regulations of meeting which lead to expenditure for drinking, besides express regulations for allowances of drink, the "funeral allowances" are sometimes read by the publican to mean "expenditure" with him.   The officers of a club in Liverpool having been summoned before Mr. Rushton, the magistrate, for the non-payment of a sum allowed by the rules, for funeral expenses, the steward of the club attended, and in answer to the claim, stated that the complainant had refused to take 4s. worth of whiskey at the house where the club meetings were held, a quantity which had been used and allowed in that and other clubs, as forming part of the " funeral expenses." Notwithstanding the usage, the magistrate refused to sanction the steward's reading of the term ; and decided that the whole of the payment of expenses must be in money and not in whiskey.

It is difficult to ascertain the amount spent in drink, but it appears from the amount cited of the expenditure in the 90 societies at Walsall, that the required allowance was 2d. per month, in others 3d., and the aggregate sum spent in those clubs (if it were only limited to the rule), must have amounted to 981l. 13s. 4d. ; but besides these prescribed portions of drink, there are prescribed annual feasts, at from 2s. 3d. to 3s. 6d. per member, amounting to an annual sum of 257l. 10s., making a total of 1239l. 3s. 4d. per annum, expended in such expenses. Besides these, there are decoration expenses, in which one society alone expended between 70l. and 80l. Seventeen of the societies had lost 1500l.; and one of them 600l., through various causes (such as the defalcations of secretaries), either directly or indirectly, attributable to an inefficient system of management. If the one year's expenditure on drink, feast, and decoration money, were placed out in the savings' bank, at interest, together with the amount of losses from mismanagement, the amount due to the contributors, to this small group of societies, would, at the end of 10 years, have amounted to the sum of 5328l. 19s. 3d.

§ 57. To prevent frauds, some of the rules provide that the secretary shall see the body. For this service, in the society called the " Frugal Society," where 7l. is allowed for the interment, a fee of 2s. 6d. is allowed to him, and 4s. if he have to go from two to five miles for the purpose. It is to be observed, that this is the usual fee provided by such societies for any inspection of the body.

The publican is generally made the treasurer, and usually the money is placed by him into the hands of his brewer, by whom from four to five per cent. interest is paid for its use as capital. In other instances it forms a capital for the publican himself; in some instances it is lent to other tradesmen. Though failures of societies have occurred from the failure of those to whom their funds have been lent, they do not appear to have been so frequent as the failures from the erroneous bases in respect to insurance on which they are generally founded.

§ 58. Believing that if the sums insured for burial in most of the burial clubs were received in money, the premiums paid by the members of these clubs are excessive, as compared with the premiums paid in the higher classes of insurance offices, I have submitted a number of their regulations, which may be considered specimens of the common terms of assurance, to Mr. Jenkin Jones, the actuary of the National Mercantile Life Assurance Society. His conclusions, which are confirmed by Mr. Griffith Davies, the actuary of the Guardian Office, show that for a risk, for which, if the Northampton tables were taken as the basis of the assurance, that in the large society at Preston, where an annual premium of 3s. 9d. would be taken for one risk by an assurance office, 7s. 10d. is taken from the contributors by the club. The General Friendly Society, for a risk for which 3s. 9d. would suffice on the Northampton table, receives 11s. 5d. Instead of an average premium of 5s. 2d., the " Friendly Society" takes 11s. 1d. If we add 25 per cent., to the premium that would be charged according to the Northampton rate (which is supposed to represent a higher mortality than the average) for expenses of management, including books, stationery, &c., and to cover the loss of interest occasioned by weekly or monthly contributions, instead of annual premiums payable at the beginning of each year, in nearly all these clubs the poor man pays an excess for burial of, at least, one-third,—besides the expense of liquor more than he would otherwise drink, which he is induced to take at the time of his multiplied attendances to pay his weekly subscriptions. There are various causes (which it would require a long report to specify) for the failure of these clubs, and for the loss of the savings devoted to their objects. The chief manager, the undertaker, has commonly an immediate interest in the admission of bad lives, which bring him quick funerals. The younger members often begin to perceive that they are subjected to unduly heavy charges, and when they are in the majority, they break up the society and divide the stock among them equally, and the older members who have contributed from the commencement are mercilessly deprived of the consolation for which they have during a great part of their lives made the most constant sacrifices. Independently of the excessive rates charged by these societies, the principle upon which the charges are made is a very unjust one, viz.—that of charging the same rate to each member, without reference to age.

§ 59. It will be seen from the following table that the " Friendly" Society's premium (11s. 1d.) is rather more than double the average of the Northampton (5s. 2d.), and the premium by the Northampton rates for ages 15 and 45 are 3s. 10d., and 7s. 9d ; the premiums of the " Friendly" Society, therefore, according to their own average, ought not to be more for these ages than about twice these amounts, or for age 15, 7s. 8d.; age 45, 15s. 6d.; but members between these ages pay alike (11s. 1d.), the younger member therefore pays 3*s.* 5*d. more* than he ought, and the older member 4*s.* 5*d.* less than he ought.

Age.	"Friendly" Society Premium.	Average Premium according to the Northampton Rate.	Premium according to the Northampton Rate.
	s. d.	*s. d.*	*s. d.*
7—45	11 1	5 2	..
15	..	..	3 10
45	..	..	7 9

And by the Northampton rate (upon the principle adopted by the society), the younger member would have to pay 1*s.* 4*d.* more and the elder member 2*s.* 7*d.* less than he ought. As an exemplification of the instability of such societies, Mr. Tidd Pratt mentioned to me that at a recent election of a poor man to a vacancy in the Metropolitan Benefit Societies' Asylum, a condition of which is that the candidate must be above sixty years of age, and have been a member of a benefit society more than ten years, there were 32 candidates, from whose documents it appeared that the societies of no less than 14 out of the 32 had been dissolved, and that some of them had belonged to two societies, and that both had failed them. Such societies are nevertheless constantly renewed on the old and unsafe foundations; and so intense is the prevalent feeling on the subject of respectful interment, that to secure it, a large proportion of the working population pay the same extravagant premiums to several of these clubs, in the hope that one, at least, may at the last avail them. On the death of a mechanic, the first business of an experienced undertaker is to ascertain of how many societies the deceased was a member, and to arrange the funeral accordingly. I am informed that it is not unfrequent that such sums as fifteen, twenty, thirty, and even forty pounds' expenses are incurred for a mechanic's funeral under these circumstances. When two or three of the undertakers of different clubs meet on the same search, and when they cannot agree to "settle" between them their shares in the performance of the funerals, very complex questions arise, which, it is stated, the magistrates have great difficulty in settling.

§ 60. The exercise, on the parts of the lowest classes, of the feeling, in itself so laudable and apparently susceptible of great moral good, under proper guidance, has, in those districts where the burial societies are conspicuous and numerous, led to dreadful incidental consequences, displaying, amongst other things, the dangers of disturbing natural responsibilities, and allowing interests to be placed in operation against moral duties.

§ 61. The insecurity of the burial societies has, under the anxiety of feeling of the working classes, lest they might fail of their object from the failure of the club, led to multiplied insurances for adults, thence for families, and for children; and thence has arisen high gains on the death of each child,—in other words, a bounty on neglect and infanticide. Those who are aware of the moral condition of a large proportion of the population, will expect that such an interest would, sooner or later, have its operation on some depraved minds to be found in every class.

§ 62. Mr. Robert Hawksworth, the Visitor to the Manchester and Salford District Provident Society, recently stated to me,—"Here, the mode of conducting the funerals—the habits of drinking at the time of assemblage at the house, before the corpse is removed, renewed on the return from the funeral, when they drink to excess, the long retention of the body in the one room, are all exceedingly demoralizing. The occasion of a funeral is commonly looked to, amongst the lowest grade, as the occasion of ' a stir;' the occasion of the drinking is viewed at the least with complacency." A minister in the neighbourhood of Manchester expressed his sorrow on observing a great want of natural feeling, and great apathy at the funerals. The sight of a free flow of tears was a refreshment which he seldom received. He was, moreover, often shocked by a common phrase amongst women of the lowest class—" Aye, aye, that child will not live; it is in the burial club."

The actual *cost* of the funeral of a child varies from 1*l.* to 30*s.* The allowances from the clubs in that town on the occurrence of the death of a child are usually 3*l.*, and extend to 4*l.* and 5*l.* But insurances for such payments on the deaths of children are made in four or five of these burial societies; and an officer mentioned to me an instance where one man had insured such payments in no less than nineteen different burial-clubs in Manchester. Officers of these societies, relieving officers, and others whose administrative duties put them in communication with the lowest classes in those districts, express their moral conviction of the operation of such bounties to produce instances of the visible neglect of children, of which they are witnesses. They often say—" You are not treating that child properly; it will not live; is it in the club?" and the answer corresponds with the impression produced by the sight. Mr. Gardiner, the clerk to the Manchester Union, in the course of his exercise of the important functions of registering the causes of death, deemed the cause assigned by a labouring man for the death of a child unsatisfactory, and on staying to inquire found that popular rumour assigned the death to wilful starvation :—

The child (according to a statement of the case) had been entered in at least ten burial clubs; and its parents had six other children, who only lived from nine to eighteen months respectively. They had received 20*l.* from several burial clubs for one of these children, and they expected to receive at least as much on account of this child. An inquest was held at Mr. Gardiner's instance, when several persons, who had known the deceased, stated that she was a fine fat child shortly after her birth, but that she soon became quite thin, was badly clothed, and seemed as if she did not get a sufficiency of food. She was mostly in the care of a girl six or seven years of age: her father bore the character of a drunken man. He had another child, which was in several burial clubs, and was a year old when it died; the child's mother stated that the child was more than ten months old, but she could not recollect the day of her birth; she thought its complaint was convulsions, in which it died. It had been ill about seven weeks; when it took ill, she had given it some oil of aniseeds and squills, which she had procured from Mr. Smith, a druggist. Since then she had given it nothing in the way of medicine, except some wine and water, which she gave it during the last few days of its life, when it could not suck or take gruel. It was in three burial clubs; her husband told her that they had received upwards of 20*l.* from burial clubs in which the other child had been entered; none of her children who had died were more than eighteen months old.

A surgeon stated, that he made a *post-mortem* examination of the body of deceased; it was then in an advanced state of decomposition, but not so far gone as to interfere with the examination. There was no appearance of external violence on the body, but there was an extreme degree of emaciation. The brain was healthy, and gave no indication of convulsions having been the cause of death; the process of teething had not commenced; had such been the case, it might have led to the supposition that fits might have occurred; the lungs, heart, stomach, and intestines were in a natural and healthy state.

The jury having expressed it as their opinion that the evidence of the parents was made up for the occasion, and entitled to no credit, returned the following verdict:—" Died through want of nourishment; but whether occasioned by a deficiency of food, or by disease of the liver and spine, brought on by improper food and drink, or otherwise, does not appear."

No further steps were taken upon this verdict; and the man enforced payments upon his insurances from ten burial clubs, and obtained from them a total sum of 34*l.* 3*s.* for the burial of this one child. Two similar cases came under the notice of Mr. Coppock, the Clerk and Superintendent-Registrar of the Stockport Union, in both of which he prosecuted the parties for murder. In one case, where three children had been poisoned with arsenic, the father was tried, with the mother, and convicted at Chester, and sentenced to be transported for life, but the mother was acquitted. In the other case, where the judge summed up for a conviction, the accused, the father, was, to the astonishment of every one, acquitted. In this case the body was exhumed after interment, and arsenic was detected in the stomach. In consequence of the suspicion raised upon the death, on which the accusation was made in the first case, the bodies of two other children were taken up and examined, when arsenic was found in the stomach. In all these cases payments on the deaths of the children were insured from the burial clubs: the cost of the coffin and burial dues would not be more than about 1*l.*, and the allowance from the club is 3*l.*

§ 63. It is remarked, on these dreadful cases, by the Superintendent Registrar, that the children who were boys, and therefore likely to be useful to the parents, were not poisoned; the female children were the victims. It was the clear opinion of the medical officers that infanticides have been committed in Stockport to obtain the burial money.* Cases of the culpable neglect of children

* Recently, April the 4th, at the Liverpool assizes, a woman named Eccles was convicted of the murder of one child, and was under the charge of poisoning two

who were insured in several clubs had been observed at Preston. The collector of a burial society, one of the most respectable in Manchester, stated to me strong grounds for believing that it had become a practice to neglect children for the sake of the money allowed. The practice of insuring in a number of these clubs was increasing. He gave the following description of the frauds to which the clubs were exposed :—

A great number of individuals have themselves and family in two or more societies, and by that means realize a great sum of money at the death of any one of them ; and I have no doubt at all in saying that a great many deaths are occasioned through neglect, when there is a great sum to be obtained at their decease. Such cases as these generally happen amongst the lower orders of society.

In reference to cases of undoubted imposition, I will just name a few out of a great many. A person residing in Manchester wished to enter herself and grandchild into our society. We went to the house, and there were from ten to twelve individuals present, the greater part of them children,—two of them somewhere about three months old. I asked who it was that was going to enter? The mistress of the house spoke up, and said it was herself and her grand-child. I asked which was her grandchild ? She took a very fine child in her arms and said that was it, and asked me would it do ?—to which I answered yes. The other was a very thin ghastly-looking child. I asked what was the matter with it ? She said they could not tell ; it had been so from the time it was born. I assure you, sir, it was an awful sight to look at. A thought struck me when I came out, that if that child died they might say it was the child I entered, so I determined to keep my eye on it every time I called, which was once a fortnight. In four months afterwards this thin child died, and according to my anticipations they brought a notice of death for the child I had not entered. I went down to visit, and on looking at it, and examining it, I pronounced it not the child I had entered. She said it was, and a great contest arose for about an hour, during which time I asked her were there not two children about the same age when first I came into her house ? which she denied at first, but afterwards admitted it. I then asked her was not one of them a very fine and the other a very thin child ? to which she answered, yes. I then asked her whether it was the finest or the thin one I entered ? She answered, the finest one. I then asked her was that the fine one ? She said, yes. I then asked her where was the thin child ? She pointed to one that was sleeping in a bed, and said that was it. I looked at it, and said this was the child I entered. I then asked her how it was that this child which was sleeping had become so fat and the other so thin ? to which she said she could not tell. Now I said to her, it is clear enough how you have done this ; you showed me that living child, and gave me the name of the one that is dead, which she denied having done ; and so we were compelled to give her the money because we had no means of finding it out but by some one in the house telling of her. But since, a little light has been thrown on it by her husband uttering a saying when he was drunk one day when I was there. This was the saying :—"A bright set of boys you are, burying the living for the dead !"—meaning that we gave burial money for a living child ; but he was immediately stopped by his wife.

Another case, a woman in Salford, entered herself and two sons, and one of them was far gone in consumption ; this we discovered and on asking, why she did it, she said she thought she could get a few pounds to bury him. Another, a man entered his wife, and she lay dying at the same

---

others, with arsenic. Immediately the murders were committed, it appeared she went to demand a stated allowance of burial money from the employers of the children.

time. When we asked him where his wife was, he pointed to a woman that was sitting by the fireside, and said that was her; but his wife died before she became a member. Another person, in order to obtain the funeral money. kept his child three weeks, until it was in a state of decomposition. The last case, out of many more that might be named, is rather ludicrous.

A man and his wife, residing in Cotton-street, agreed that one of them, namely, the husband, should pretend to be dead, in order that the wife might receive his funeral money; accordingly the wife proceeds in due form to give notice of his death; the visiting officer on behalf of the society, whose duty it was to see the corpse, repairs to the house, enters the chamber, and inquires for the deceased; the should-be disconsolate widow points him to the body of her late husband, whose chin was tied up with a handkerchief in the attitude of death; he surveys the corpse—the eyelids seem to move; he feels the pulse, the certain signs of life are there: the officer pronounceth him not dead; she in return says, *he is dead,* for there has not been a *breath* in *him* since 12 o'clock last night. The neighbours are called in; a discussion ensues between the wife and the officer: some declare they saw the husband at the door that morning giving a light. He (the officer) requires her to bring a doctor; she goes, and says she can't get one to come; the officer goes and brings one, who ordered him to be raised up in the bed, and having obtained some water, the doctor, while the man was sitting up, dashed it in his face.

The man was apprehended and taken before the magistrates for the fraud. Sir Charles Shaw, the Commissioner of Police, directed that he should be produced in court in the same dress in which he had been laid out and was apprehended, which produced a very salutary effect.

§ 64. The evidence in respect to the crimes committed under such circumstances may be carried into wider ramifications. Some of the better constituted societies have perceived the evil of insurances, carried to the extent of entirely removing responsibilities, or creating bounties, to the promotion of the event insured against, and have endeavoured to abate the evil, as far as they could, by the adoption of a condition, that no payment should be made where a party was found to have been a member or to have insured in another club.

§ 65. The collector of the society, whose exemplification of one class of frauds is above cited, stated, that they were about to adopt the common rule of the insurance societies, that all claims should be forfeited for an act of suicide; for they had even instances which showed that men held their own lives on so loose a tenure as to throw them away on apparently slight motives. In one instance a man went to the secretary, and asked whether, if he were to commit suicide, his widow would be entitled to the burial money? The secretary stated that, there being no rule against it, he thought the survivor would be entitled. The man, having fully satisfied himself on this point, went away and took poison. The amount of burial money gained was supposed to be 50*l.* In another case, the letter announcing to the widow the benefit he had secured, grew indistinct from the working of the poison and the sinking of life whilst the man was writing it, until it was nearly illegible. But the occurrence of such facts, showing a recklessness of life, with a degree of strength of domestic affections which induces them to encounter violent deaths for the sake of the survivors, is not confined to one class of society. Soon after the practice of insuring from insurance companies, the payment of large sums on the deaths of parties began to extend as a mode of providing for families, instances occurred where tradesmen and persons of the higher and middle classes, having effected insurances on their own lives, committed suicide with the view apparently of securing to their families the benefit of the sums insured. It is understood that the experience of such cases, and the obvious inducement which persons having in view to commit suicide to effect insurances on their lives, and thus defraud the offices, led to the precaution, now almost universal, of inserting the condition, which, however, is confined to insurance by persons on their own lives; that "if the assured shall die by his own act, whether sane or insane," the policy shall be void. Yet frauds are occasionally committed by persons who must know that they have not long to live.

§ 66. Multiplied payments on one death are contrary to the spirit, at the least, of the law. A payment of a sum certain to parish officers, to be relieved from any future payments in respect to an illegitimate child, has been declared to be illegal. "One of the principles on which that decision is founded is, that the payment of a large sum for the support of a child gives the parish a degree of interest in the child's death, and might have a tendency to induce the officers to relax in their duty towards it."[*]

§ 67. In the higher order of life insurances, the legislature has endeavoured to arrest the dangerous tendency of insuring beyond the interest, by providing, by statute 14 Geo. III., c. 48, that persons insuring the lives of others shall have an interest in such lives; and it is a principle of insurance law that where a risk paid for has not been run, the premiums shall be returned; and it would seem to be a principle of common law that insurances beyond the actual interest are void. In the case of Fauntleroy, the banker, who insured his life in the Amicable Office for 6000*l.*, the claim was resisted on the fact that he had been attainted, convicted, and executed for forgeries committed since the insurance, and the House of Lords held the insurance to be void on the plainest principles of public policy. The Lord Chancellor, in delivering the judgment of the house, said—" Is it possible that such a contract could be sustained? Is it not void upon the plainest principles of public policy? Would not such a contract (if available) take away one of those restraints operating on the minds of men against the commission of crimes,—namely, the interest we have in the welfare and prosperity of our connexions? Now, if a policy of that description, with such a form of condition inserted in it in express terms, cannot, on grounds of public policy, be sustained, how is it to be contended that in a policy expressed in such terms as the present, and after

[*] Clarke *v.* Johnson, 11 Moore, 319.

the events which have happened, that we can sustain such a claim ?"*

§ 68. The Benefit clubs in large towns cannot easily take effectual measures against the multiplication of insurances, 'which indeed their own instability to some extent justifies, and they may find their account, in paying sums beyond the legal authority, as the higher insurance offices avowedly do, in paying on policies to parties who have had no legal interest in the life insured. An officer of one of these large insurance establishments declared, that if they had acted upon the decision of the courts in the case of Godson *v.* Boldero, " they might as well have shut their doors."

§ 69. Although the practice referred to, of multiplied insurances of sums payable on the death of children, appears happily to have broken out into infanticides only in the districts mentioned, yet as the means and the temptation are left equally open in all, the necessity of preventing them, as far as a direct legislative act may, is submitted, by a short provision prohibiting payments beyond the actual cost of interment, and directing the return of the premiums or subscriptions where they have been given to more than one club.

§ 70. The means for the most direct protection of infantile life, and for giving additional security for life in general, will be subsequently submitted for consideration, with the evidence as to the means and the necessity of the appointment of medical officers for the protection of the public health.

§ 71. A collateral means of security, and of the abatement of other evils incidental to the practice of interments, will be found in the practicable administrative measures for reducing the unnecessary expense of interments, and, by consequence, of the temptations to crime constituted by the apparent expediency of the insurance of the payment of large sums to meet that expense.

It will, moreover, on further examination, become apparent, in this as in some other branches of public expenditure, that a course which attains increased efficiency with the popular desiderata in respect to interments is a course of economy.

Total Expenses of Funerals to different Classes of Society.

§ 72. In the following table is given a proximate estimate of the total expenses of funerals of the persons of each class in the metropolis :—

* Bligh's 4th Parl. Reports, N. S. 194.

Class.	Total Number of Funerals of each Class that have taken place in the Metropolis in the Year 1839.	Number of Children under 10 Years of Age.	Present Average Expenses of each Funeral of each Class, inclusive of burial dues.		Total Expenses of the Funerals of all the Persons of each Class, inclusive of Children.	Annual Expense of Funerals in England and Wales: estimating the proportions of Deaths of each Class to be the same as in the Metropolis, and the Average Expenses of each Class to be the same.
			Adults.	Children.		
			£. s.	£. s.	£.	£.
Gentry, &c. . .	2,253	529	100 0	30 0	188,270	1,735,040
Tradesmen, 1st clss.	5,757	2,761	50 0	14 0	250,792	2,370,379
Tradesmen, 2nd cls. and undescribed	7,682	3,703	27 10	7 15	103,728	..
Artisans, &c. .	25,930	13,885	5 0	1 10	81,053	766,074
Paupers . .	3,655	593	13s.		2,761	..
Total Expense for the Metropolis . . .					626,664	
Proximate Estimate of the Expense for the Total Number of Funerals in one Year, England and Wales						4,871,493

The above, which can only be submitted as a proximate estimate, certainly shows an amount of money annually thrown into the grave, at the expense of the living, which exceeded all previous anticipations; and yet, from the information derived from the inspection of collections of undertakers' bills for funerals, I cannot but consider it an under rather than an over estimate, and that the actual expenses of interment in the metropolis would be found, on a closer inquiry, to be nearly a million per annum. Hypothetical estimates of the amount of money which must be expended to maintain so large a body of men as that engaged in the business and service of the undertaker are confirmatory of this view. Even in Scotland the expense of the decent burial of a labouring man is not less than 5l., exclusive of the expense of mourning. I have been shown the payments on account of burials of an affiliated association of a convivial and benevolent character called the "Odd Fellows," which has upwards of 150,000 affiliated members, chiefly of the better class of artisans, in different parts of the country. With them, the payments usually amount to 10l. per funeral. The expenses of burial of some of the smaller descriptions of shopkeepers may not much exceed the expense of the undescribed class, which is taken as an average between the sum set down for labourers and that for tradesmen; but the latter is certainly a low average for the metropolis. All the information tends to show that the expenses of the funerals of persons in the condition of gentry are, on the average (inclusive of burial dues), much higher than the sum stated. From inquiries I have made as to the practice in the offices of the Masters in Chancery, where executors' accounts are examined, I learn that if an undertaker's bill is 60*l.* or 70*l.* (exclusive of burial dues), for a person whose rank in life was that of the clergy, officers of the army or navy, or members of the legal or medical professions, " it would, according to all usage, be allowed as of course, and notwithstanding it should turn out that the estate was insolvent."* The cost of the funerals of persons of rank and title, it will have been seen, varies from 1500*l.* to 1000*l.*, or 800*l.*, or less, as it is a town or country funeral. The expenses of the funerals of gentry of the better condition, it will have been seen, vary from 200*l.* to 400*l.*, and are stated to be seldom so low as 150*l.* § 45.

§ 73. The average cost of funerals of persons of every rank above paupers in the metropolis may, therefore, be taken as 14*l.* 19*s.* 9*d.* per head. In some of the rural districts, and in the smaller provincial towns, where the distinct business of an undertaker has not arisen, coffins are made by carpenters, and services are supplied at a very moderate cost; but the allowances from the benefit and burial clubs throughout the country, of which instances have been given, may be stated as instances of the general expense to the labouring classes. To persons of the middle or higher classes, who give orders to undertakers in the metropolis, for funerals to be performed in the country, the expense is further enhanced by the extra expense of carriage; so that there is ground for believing that the same average prevails throughout Great Britain, and that the total annual expense of funerals cannot be much less than between four and five millions per annum.

§ 74. Out of 5*l.* expended for the common funeral of an adult artisan in the metropolis, about 15*s.* will be the burial dues. Of this 15*s.* about 3*s.* may be stated as the amount the clergyman will receive. The surplice fees vary in different places from 2*s.* for the lowest class, rising with the condition to 5*l.* 5*s.*, or more; but taking the average of all cases which occur in the metropolis, and on the experience of the ministers of several parishes, the burial fees, which form their chief emolument, that which was anciently denominated " Soul Scot," might perhaps be fairly taken as at 7*s.* 2*d.* per case, which is the average of the burial fees in some of the principal parishes in London.†

Different proportions of the Expenses of Burials to the Community in healthy and unhealthy Districts.

§ 75. It is a prevalent popular error, not unsanctioned by doctrines held by several eminent public writers, that " as one disease

* *Vide* Appendix No. 12 for examples of undertakers' ordinary bills for funerals of different classes.
† *Vide* Return in the Appendix.

disappears so another springs up," that the positive "amount of mortality, the common lot," is the same to all classes. But death, besides differing in the period to different individuals, differs widely in the numbers of burials, and in the consequent expenses to different families, classes, and districts. It is the *number* as well as the separate expense of each of the funerals which occur during the year to each *class* of persons, or to different districts, which determines the total expense of burial to the class or district. Tbus, to the poorer classes, living in wretched habitations, as those comprised in Bethnal Green and Whitechapel, there is one burial to every 31 of the inhabitants, whilst in the contiguous district of Hackney there is only one burial to every 56 of the inhabitants yearly. In Liverpool there is one burial per annum to every 30 of the inhabitants, whilst in the county of Hereford there is one burial only to every 55 of the inhabitants. If the existing charge of burial, at the above rates of expense to each class of individuals, were commuted for an annual payment, commencing at birth, as a premium for the payment of 100*l.* 50*l.*, and 5*l.*, payable at the undermentioned periods respectively, it would in the metropolis and the county of Hereford be nearly as follows :—

CLASS.	METROPOLIS.		HEREFORDSHIRE.	
	Average Age at Death.	Annual Payment for Burial to every Individual.	Average Age at Death.	Annual Payment for Burial to every Individual.
	Years.	£. s. d.		£. s. d.
Gentry	44	1 1 10	45	1 1 0
Tradesmen or Farmers . . .	25	1 6 8	47	0 9 9
Labourers	22	0 3 2	39	0 2 9
Average of all Classes . . .	27		39	

Supposing each member of the family to have been assured at birth, a labourer's family in Herefordshire consisting of five persons would have to pay yearly 13*s.* 9*d.*, and there a farmer's family of the same number would have to pay 2*l.* 8*s.* 9*d.* yearly; whilst in London for an artisan's family of five, the yearly payment would be 15*s.* 10*d.* and for a tradesman's family it would be 6*l.* 13*s.* 4*d.* per annum. To insure the payment of the average cost of funerals, 14*l.* 7*s.* 5*d.* at the end of 27 years, on the metropolitan chances of life, the annual payment would be 7*s.*, whilst on the Herefordshire chances of life of 39 years to all born high or low the sum would be only 4*s.* Or to take another form of displaying the comparative burthen; the general average cost of each burial being 14*l.* 7*s.* 5*d.*, and the annual *proportions* of deaths being different from the average duration of life—being 1 of every 40 in the metropolis, a poll-tax to defray the burial expenses must there be 7s. 2¼d.; whilst in Hereford the proportions of deaths being one in every 55, the poll-tax on all of the inhabitants to meet the charge would be 5s. 3d. per head.

§ 76. It appears, therefore, that in considering the means of relief from the evils connected with the number and expenses of burial, it should at the same time be borne in mind that the primary means of abatement and relief of the misery of frequent funerals will be found in the means of the removal of the developed and removable causes of premature mortality. Had the annual mortality amongst the population in the high, open, and naturally-drained district of Hackney been the same proportionate amount of mortality as that in the contiguous, but low, ill-drained, ill-cleansed, and ill-ventilated district of Bethnal Green and Whitechapel, instead of 759 deaths per annum, Hackney would have upwards of 1138 deaths, and an expense of 5448l. more for funerals during the year than it has. So the county of Hereford, if it were afflicted with the same amount of mortality as that which prevails in Liverpool, would have 1488 more deaths annually and an additional expenditure of 21,390l. per annum in burials. How directly, certainly, and powerfully, defective sanitary measures in respect of drainage and cleansing, bear upon health and life, and, by consequence, on the frequency of burials, will be seen in the latter portions of the examination of Mr. Blencarne, surgeon, one of the medical officers of the City of London Union, and of Mr. Abraham, surgeon, one of the Registrars of Deaths in the same Union; which I select as an instance, because the City stands high in wealth, in endowed charities, and in supposed immunity from the removable or preventible causes of disease.*

§ 77. Two individual cases which were narrated by the physician who attended them, will serve to convey a conception of a large proportion of the common cases denoted by the units of the statistical evidence derived from towns, and will illustrate more clearly the economy of the prevention of sickness and death, as a superior economy of the incidents of sickness as well as of funerals.

One case was that of an intelligent industrious man who had been foreman to a tradesman, and having married and established himself as a master tradesman, had a family of children. To diminish the expense of his family he took a house which he let off to lodgers, retaining to himself only the garrets and the underground or kitchen floor. He had five children who became unhealthy and were attacked with cachectic diseases and scald head; and the expense of an apothecary to the family during one year was 59l.: but still more serious disease afterwards appearing, a physician was called in, who perceiving the impure air of the apartments, pointed out the causes of the varied illness which had prevailed, and the remedy—removal from the house.

* *Vide* Appendix.

In another case the foreman of a brewery married a healthy wife, who gave birth to seven children, of whom six died at various ages, while young, from diseases evidently springing from impure air. The source of this impure air was an ill-constructed cesspool in the lower part of the house, the stench of which was pointed out by the physician, who happened to have a perception of such causes, and advised the immediate removal of the family. Since that time they have had two other children, who with the third which escaped, are now living in their better lodging in the enjoyment of good health; the last of the children who died, when " ailing," was sent to the purer atmosphere of a rural district, and returned in robust health, but soon after his exposure to the impure atmosphere was attacked with fever, of which he died within a fortnight.

It was in the power of neither of these persons to obtain an amendment of the general system of drainage, which occasioned the atmospheric impurity under which they suffered; but the actual expenses of structural measures of prevention would not, as an entire outlay, have amounted to half the apothecary's bill for drugs in the first case, or of the expenses of the funerals (superadded to the expenses of drugs) in the second case; but if the expenses of those structural arrangements were defrayed by an annual payment of instalments of principal and interest, spread over a period of 30 years, or a period coincident with the benefit, the expense of the extended or combined measure of prevention would not be more than 1l. 5s. 10d. per tenement, or perhaps a small proportion of that sum, to the indvidual family.*

§ 78. But to return to collective examples. Mr. Blencarne, on a view of the sanitary condition of the population, and the causes of mortality within his district, expresses a confident opinion that in that district the average amount of mortality might be reduced one-third by efficient sanitary measures. The saving by a reduction of 71 funerals yearly, or one-third of the burials in that district, at the average expense of funerals for the metropolis, would amount to nearly 1020l. per annum. If, as appears to be practicable, there were a reduction of one-half of the expenses of the other two-thirds of the average number of funerals, the total saving from this source would be 2040l. per annum to the population inhabiting, according to the last census, 1416 houses. Now the annual share of the expense of the chief structural sanitary arrangements, supposing every house in the district to be deficient, would, on the proximate estimate, amount to a sum of 1829l., or less than the amount saved by the reduction

* *Vide* General Report on the Sanitary Condition of the Population, p. 443 and p. 395, for proximate estimates of the chief structural expenses, *i. e.* main drains, house drains, annual supply of water, water tank, and water closet, and means of cleansing, and also an exemplification of the practical rule for the distribution of the expense, so as to render it coincident to the benefit.

of the funeral expenditure, giving the health and longevity, and all ' the moral and social savings, *plus* the mere pecuniary saving; these remoter savings being in themselves unquestionably far greater than can be represented by the pecuniary items directly economised.

§ 79. Whosoever will carefully examine what has been done in scattered and fortuitous instances amongst persons of the same class, following the same occupation, living in the same neighbourhoods, and deriving the same amount of incomes, and will from such examinations judge of the inferences as to what may be done by the more systematised application of the like means, will not deem the representation extravagant, that the same duration of life may be given to the labouring classes that is enjoyed by professional persons of the first class; or that it is possible to attain for the whole of a town population such average durations of life as are attained by portions of existing towns; or say, such an average as is attained by the population of the old town of Geneva, that is to say of 45 years, or six years higher than appears to be attained by the whole population of the county of Hereford, which, as we have seen, is 39 years.

§ 80. To take another example. If the proportion of deaths to the population in the Whitechapel Union were reduced to the proportion of deaths to the population in Herefordshire, then, instead of 2307 burials, there would only be 1305 burials per annum; and if the cost of the remaining burials were reduced 50 per cent. of the average present cost, then the saving of funeral expenses to the Whitechapel district would be at the rate of more than 23,000*l*., or ، nearly 3*l*. per house on the inhabited houses of the district ; about half that sum being deemed sufficient to defray the expense of the proposed structural improvements. The funeral expenses in the parish of Hackney on the proportion of burials amongst them, are at the rate of 5*s*. 2*d*. per head on the living population. Were the burials in Liverpool reduced to the same proportion, 1 in 56 instead of 1 in 30,* at the rate of expenses for funerals in London, nearly 50,000*l*. per annum would be saved to the population of Liverpool, being more than sufficient to enable them to pay 30 years' annual instalments, the principal and interest, at five per cent., of a sum of 845,065*l*. sterling for structural arrangements.

§ 81. Strong barriers to the improvement of the sanitary condition of the population are created by the common rule and practice of levying the whole expense of permanent works, immediately or within short periods, on persons who conceive they have no immediate interest in them, or whose interest is really transient, and who under such circumstances will see no *per contra* of benefit to themselves to compensate for the expenditure. It may

---

* In all cases the mortuary registries of 1839 are referred to; but the data are varying, and are submitted, as they will be understood, only as proximate estimates. I have every reason to believe them to be on the whole below the truth.

be of use to exemplify the *contra* of advantage to the inhabitants at least, to make it a good economy to them to pay the proportions of rates required for the additional expenditure in efficient means of preventing sickness and mortality.

The following may be given as an instance of the superior economy of prevention, by the appliance of vaccination, afforded by the experience obtained under the partial operation of the Vaccination Act in the metropolis as compared with the experience in Glasgow, to which the same arrangements do not extend. In the metropolis, in the year 1837, the deaths from small-pox were 1520. The deaths from small-pox in the metropolis, and in Glasgow for the years after the Vaccination Act came into operation are thus compared in a report by Dr. R. D. Thompson.

DEATHS FROM SMALL-POX.

	Glasgow.		London.
Population	282,134	Population . .	1,875,493
1838	388	. . . . .	3,090 Epidemic.
1839	406	. . . . .	634*
1840	413	. . . . .	1,233
1841	347	. . . . .	1,053
1842	334	. . . . .	350
Mean	377, or about one inhabitant daily dies of small-pox in Glasgow.		

A confident opinion is expressed that the decrease of small-pox in the metropolis is ascribable to the extension of vaccination. The rate of reduced mortality from that disease has continued during the present year; and the average of the present rate, as compared with the average preceding the extension of vaccination, would give a reduction of 946 deaths and funerals from 1652 annually. But as not one attack in ten of small-pox usually proves fatal, the reduction of the number of deaths may be taken as representing a reduction of some 9,460 cases of sickness. The amount paid from the poor-rates for vaccination in the metropolis was 1701*l*., which at the average fee gives 22,680 of the worst conditioned and most susceptible cases out of about 56,000, in which vaccination was successfully performed. The attention directed to the subject has also promoted the extension of vaccination, by others than the appointed vaccinators. The various expenses of each case of sickness to the sufferers, inclusive of medicines, may perhaps, on a low estimate, be represented at 1*l*. each case; and taking half the average expenses of funerals for the 946 funerals saved, the total expense of funerals and of sickness saved by the expenditure of the sum stated of 1701*l*. in well-directed measures of prevention, would exceed 16,000*l*. in the metropolis alone. Throughout the whole country, the deaths from small-pox in 1840 were 10,434, as compared with 16,268

---

* A severe epidemic, by sweeping off the most susceptible cases, usually diminishes the proportionate mortality from that cause during the following year.

in 1838, on which, if the reduction may be ascribed to the exten-sion of vaccination solely, pounds of immediate expenses must have been saved by the expenditure of half crowns,—in other words, upwards of 90,000*l.* in money has been saved by the expenditure of about 12,000*l.* in vaccination.

The excess of deaths in the metropolis above the healthy standard of Islington or Herefordshire, of 1 in 55, is 11,266 (vide returns, Appendix) ; the expense of burial of this excessive number, at the average cost, is 168,990*l.* per annum, which (without taking into account the expenses of the corresponding excess of sickness) as an instalment, would in 30 years liquidate the principal and interest, at 5 per cent., of a loan of 2,856,168*l.* towards house drainings and the structural improvements and arrangements, by which the excess might be prevented. To the charge of the ex-cessive deaths must be added the charge of the births which take place to make up the ravages of the mortality in the most de-pressed districts. Taking the proportion of the births to the population in the Hackney Union, 1 in 42, as the standard of proportion of births in a healthy district, the excess of births for the whole metropolis during that year was upwards of 8000 : or 52,609 instead of 44,541.*

§ 82. The grounds will hereafter be submitted which appear to sustain the position that all the solemnity of sepulture may be in-creased, and solemnity given where none is now obtained, con-currently with a great reduction of expense to all classes.—Vide post, § 113 to § 120.

In considering the expenses of funerals, the arrangements and consequent expenses of the funerals of the wealthy are of im-portance, less perhaps for themselves than as governing by example the arrangements and expenses of the poorest classes, even to the adoption of such arrangements, and consequently ex-pensive outlay as to have hired bearers and mutes with silk fittings even at the funerals of common labourers. The expenditure by the wealthy, in compliance with supposed demands at which their own taste revolts, for a transient effect which is not gained,† would

---

* *Vide* District Returns, Appendix.

† On a question of fact as to the effect of the common funeral arrangements on the imagination, the testimony of a poet, whose accuracy of description is uni-versally admitted, may be cited. The Rev. Mr. Crabbe thus describes the effect of the funeral array :—

> Lo ! now what dismal sons of darkness come
> To bear this daughter of indulgence home !
> Tragedians all, and well arranged in black !
> Who nature, feeling, force, expression lack ;
> Who cause no tear, but gloomily pass by,
> And shake their sables in the wearied eye,
> That turns disgusted from the pompous scene,
> Proud without grandeur, with profusion mean !
> The tear for kindness past affection owes ;
> For worth deceased the sigh from reason flows ;

suffice to produce permanent effects of beneficence and taste worthy of their position in society. A gentleman who recently, in distaste of the ordinary undertaker's arrangements, reduced them on the occasion of the burial of his daughter, applied the money in erecting to her memory, and partly endowing, a small school for 25 children of a village, in which, as the tablet on the school recorded, the deceased had, when alive, taken a kindly interest. Where no such objects are offered for the surplus expenditure, that which would be unsucessfully thrown away for the transient effect would suffice for a statue or some work of art that would ensure permanent admiration. The aggregate waste on funerals in the metropolis would, in the course of a short time, suffice for the endowment of educational or other institutions, that would go far to retrieve the condition of the poorer classes. The waste of two years in the metropolis would suffice for the erection of a magnificent cathedral, and of a third year for its endowment for ever.

§ 83. In justification of the funeral exactions from the labouring classes, it is sometimes alleged that if they did not expend the money in the funereal decorations, they would expend it in drink. But this would only occur in a minority of cases, and in those only for a time. The reduction would be an immediate and most important relief in an immense number of cases of widowhood, and especially in those cases where there has been no insurance, where the widow incurs debts which often reduce her to destitution and dependence on the poor's rates, or on charity. It forms a large part of the business of some of the small-debt courts in the metropolis to enforce payments of the undertakers' bills, incurred under such circumstances. For all classes, what is deemed by them respectful interment is to be considered a necessity ; and in general the expenditure beyond what is necessary to ensure such interment competes not with extravagancy, but with high moral obligations. By the arrangements which throw the savings of the poor family into the grave, children are left destitute, and creditors are often defrauded, and heavy taxes levied on the sympathies of neighbours and friends.*

E'en well-feigned passions for our sorrows call,
And real tears for mimic miseries fall :
But this poor farce has neither truth nor art,
To please the fancy or to touch the heart.

　　*　　　　*　　　　*

Dark but not awful, dismal but yet mean,
With anxious bustle moves the cumb'rous scene ;—
Presents no objects tender or profound,
But spreads its cold unmeaning gloom around.

　　*　　　　*　　　　*

When woes are feigned, how ill such forms appear ;
And oh ! how needless when the woe 's sincere.

The Parish Register.

* Amongst the higher classes the tendency is to reduce the number of cases in which mourning is worn, and to diminish the time of wearing it. It would be a

Failure of the objects of the common Expenditure on Funerals.

, § 84. Notwithstanding the immense sacrifices made by the labouring classes for the purpose, neither they nor the middle classes obtain solemn and respectful interment, nor does it appear practicable that they should obtain it by any arrangement of the present parochial means of interment in crowded districts.

§ 85. Few persons can have witnessed funeral processions passing in mid-day through the thronged and busy streets of the metropolis, without being struck with the extreme inappropriateness of the times and places chosen for such processions. This want of regulation as to appropriate times is the subject of complaints, which must attach, even to a greater extent, to numerous processions, without regulation, from the centre of the populous town districts to the suburbs.

Mr. Wild, the undertaker, was asked—

What besides the expense, and the objection to the ground, do you find is the objection entertained to the existing mode of burial in the crowded

---

great boon to persons in inferior condition and of limited means, who are governed by the examples of those above them, and who are put to ruinous expense for putting a whole family into mourning, at a time when the expense can be the least spared, if the custom could be further altered to the wearing of a piece of crape only on the hat or on the arm, as in the army and navy; or by limiting the wearing of full mourning to the head of the family, and using only crape bands for the rest. Some conception may be formed of the inconvenience incurred by the extent to which mourning is carried, even amongst the poorest classes, if we suppose that on such occasions it were necessary to clothe the whole of the men of the army and navy in black. The very excess of deaths above a healthy standard in Great Britain necessitates mourning to nearly forty thousand families per annum. The extent to which custom has carried mourning appears to have no Scriptural authority. Bingham, speaking of the primitive Christians, states, " that they did not condemn the notion of going into a mourning habit for the dead, nor yet much approve of it, but left it to all men's liberty as an indifferent thing, rather commending those that either omitted it wholly, or in short time laid it aside again, as acting more according to the bravery and philosophy of a Christian. Thus St. Jerome commends one Julian (Hieron. Ep. 34 ad Julian), a rich man in his time, because having lost his wife and two daughters, that is his whole family, in a few days, one after another, he wore the mourning habit but forty days after their death, and then resumed his usual habit again, and because he accompanied his wife to the grave, not as one that was dead, but as going to her rest. Cyprian, indeed, seems to carry the matter a little farther; he says he was ordered by divine revelation to preach to the people publicly and constantly, that they should not lament their brethren that were delivered from the world by divine vocation, as being assured that they were not lost, but only sent before them : that their death was only a receding from the world, and a speedier call to heaven; that we ought to long after them and not lament them, nor wear any mourning habit, seeing they were gone to put on their white garments in heaven (2 Cypr. de Mortal., p. 164). No occasion should be given to the Gentiles justly to accuse us, and reprehend us for lamenting those as lost and extinct, whom we affirm still to live with God; and that we do not prove that faith which we profess in words, by the outward testimony of our hearts and souls. Cyprian thought no sorrow at all was to be expressed for the death of a Christian, nor consequently any signs of sorrow, such as the mourning habits, because the death of a Christian was only a translation of him to heaven. But others did not carry the thing so high, but thought a moderate sorrow might be allowed to nature, and therefore did not so peremptorily condemn the mourning habit, as being only a decent expression of such a moderate sorrow, though they liked it better if men could have the bravery to refuse it." (Bing., book xxii. chap. 3, sec. 22).

districts of the metropolis?—One very common objection, is the inconvenient time ; the average time is about 3 o'clock, but it varies from 2 to 4 o'clock. This is very inconvenient for persons in business, who wish to attend as mourners. From this cause, interments are frequently delayed; at this time, also, the streets are very much crowded ; sometimes boys crowd round the gates, and shout as ill-educated boys usually do ; sometimes there are mobs ; I have known the service interrupted more than once during the ceremony ; sometimes the adults of the mob will make rude remarks. I have heard them call out to the clergyman, " Read out, old fellow ;" some-times I have known them make rude remarks in the hearing of the mourners ; on the clergyman frequently ; but this has been on the week days, when, of course, the numbers attending are very great. At times, the adults and mob at the gates have an idle and rude curiosity to hear the service. I have known them rush in past the mourners, and go in indis-criminately. It is part of my business to see the mourners and corpse safe in, before I go in ; and I have been sometimes severely hustled, and have had great difficulty in getting in myself.

Are the crowds in the town, or districts, ever characterized by any reverence for the dead?—Not the slightest : quite the contrary, and it makes part of the annoyance of interments in town to have to encounter them.

Are you not aware that on the Continent it is generally the custom for passengers of every condition in the streets, to stop and take off the hat, on the approach, and during the passage of the dead ?—I have met with several instances of persons stopping in our streets in London, and taking off their hats. On looking at them, I had reason to believe they were foreigners.

Have you ever known carriages or common coaches, or carts or waggons, stop in the streets on the approach of a funeral ?—I have seen gentlemen pull their check-strings, or tap at their windows, and stop their coachmen in towns ; but, if the carriage were empty, there was no stoppage. But none of the common conveyances ever stop. I have several times ran the risk of being knocked down by them. I have known cabmen and omnibus men drive through the procession of a walking funeral, and separate the mourners from the corpse. These characters display complete indifference to such scenes.

§ 86. In the rural districts the population appears to be so far bet-ter instructed and more respectful; but, according to the testimony of living persons, the same indifference has not always characterized labouring classes in the town districts, even of the metropolis. It is described as an unavoidable consequence of the increasing numbers of funerals, and familiarity with them arising from the neg-lect of appropriate general arrangements, a neglect from which not only the relations and parties engaged in such services, but strangers have to complain, that their feelings are not duly regarded. In a rural parish, the deceased who is interred is generally known, and the single funeral arrests attention and excites sympathy. In crowded districts neighbourship diminishes ; a vast portion of the population of the metropolis pass their lives without knowing their next-door neighbours, or even persons living in the same building ; the great majority of burials are, to the mass of the population, burials of strangers, for whom no per-sonal sympathies can be awakened ; the inopportune and unex-pected passage of small funeral processions through busy and un-prepared crowds of the young and active, create a familiarity that stifles all respectful or reverential feelings, whilst the numbers of separate funerals make undue demands on the sympathies, and harass the minds of the sickly and the solitary by their continued passage, and the perpetual tollings of the passing bells. Examples in some of the German cities might be cited of refined and successful arrangements by which the feelings of all are consulted, by interments either in the quiet of evening or of early morning, or by the selection of retired routes for the processions. The funeral processions to the cemetery of Frankfort are generally held at early morning for the labouring classes.

§ 87. The celebration of religious ceremonies in a satisfactory manner at some of the populous parishes, appear to be often extremely difficult, if not impracticable. Mr. Wild further answers:—

What are the matters objected to that are of common experience in our burials, when the corpse and attendants have arrived within the churchyard?—In certain seasons of the year, when the mortality is greater than usual, a number of funerals, according to the present regulation of the churchyards, are named for one hour. During last Sunday, for example, there were fifteen funerals all fixed during one hour at one church. Some of these will be funerals in the church; those which have not an in-door service must wait outside. At the church to which I refer, there were six parties of mourners waiting outside. My man informed me, that all these parties of mourners were kept nearly three-quarters of an hour waiting outside, without any cover, and with no boards to stand upon. The weather last Sunday was dreadfully inclement. I have seen ten funerals kept waiting in the church-yard from twenty minutes to three-quarters of an hour. I have known colds caught on the ground by parties kept waiting, and more probably occurred than I could know of. It is the practice on such occasions to say the service over the bodies of children and over the bodies of the adults together, and sometimes the whole are kept waiting until the number is completed. Even under these circumstances, the ceremony is frequently very much hurried.

How many are there in some parochial burial grounds to be buried at one time?—Sometimes fifteen.

With such a number to bury is it physically possible that the separate service should be other than hurried, and in so far as it is hurried unsatisfactory to the mourners?—According to the present system I do not see that it is at all times practicable to be other than hurried and unsatisfactory.

Would not an in-door service be acceptable to the labouring classes?— I conceive highly so. In some parishes, as at Camberwell, the custom is to give an in-door service to all, whether rich or poor. This is considered highly acceptable. Where the labouring classes are excluded they not only feel the inconvenience of having to wait, but they feel very much the exclusion on account of their poverty. They frequently complain to me, and question me as to whether it is right, and ask me the reason.

What other inconveniences are experienced in the service in churchyards?—It is a frequent thing that a grave-digger, who smells strongly of liquor, will ask of the widow or mourners for something to drink, and, if not given, he will follow them to the gates and outside the gates, murmuring and uttering reproaches.

Is that ordinarily the last thing met with before leaving the churchyards?—Yes, that is the last thing.

That closes the scene?—Yes, that closes the scene.

Mr. Dix was asked—

In the crowded districts is the funeral ceremony often impeded?—Besides the state of the parochial burial grounds, the mode of performing the ceremony is very objectionable, in consequence of the crowd and noise and bustle in the neighbourhood. I have had burials to perform in St. Clements Danes' burial ground, when the noise of the passing and the repassing of the vehicles has been such that we have not heard a third of the service, except in broken sentences.

§ 88. On this very important subject it is observed, by the Reverend William Stone, the rector of Spitalfields :—

It must, I think, be admitted, that, in a crowded population, the parochial system, as it generally stands at present, is utterly inadequate to meet the demand for interment—the demand, I mean, which would exist, if that system were universally acquiesced in, and all our parishioners were brought for interment to our parochial burial grounds. To say nothing of the inability of many parishes to provide adequate grounds, there could not be an adequate supply of clergymen or of churches. Indeed, it has always seemed to me, that, in practice, this *has been* admitted ; for, in London, that considerable and important part of the burial service which is performed within the church, unless specially desired and paid for, has, from time almost immemorial, been left out ; and I think that the highest ecclesiastical authorities could hardly have introduced or sanctioned such an anti-rubrical omission, had it not served some more popular or more necessary purpose than that of merely raising the fees of the church. From this consideration, added to the frequent inconvenience of my burial services, I have been led to regard the fees for the in-church service, like the payments for the erection of monuments and tablets in our churches, as a kind of necessary preventive duty. And certain it is, that unless our burial services were limited by some such restrictive system, they would be not only overwhelmingly laborious, but absolutely impracticable and incompatible with our other professional engagements. How, for instance, could the densely-built parish of Christ-church, Spitalfields, yielding a clerical income less than 380*l.* a-year, possessing one burial-ground, and one church attached to that burial-ground, accommodate, in any enlarged sense of the word, an *interrable* population of 23,642, with the addition of the many proprietors of our vaults and graves, who must always be resident at a distance ? Even now, with our present very scanty demand for interment, I sometimes find, as I have intimated, extreme inconvenience from this part of my duties. For obvious reasons the working classes make choice of Sunday for their burials ; the very day, above all others, when the clergy and the church are almost wholly pre-engaged for other purposes. No wonder, then, that one purpose should often clash with another—that burials *in* church should clash with burials *out* of it—that clergymen should be hurried, discomposed, and exhausted—and mourners kept waiting in a cold, damp burial-ground, so as to verify the old objection urged by the Puritans against our service there, that " in burying the dead we kill the living." On other days, too, the clergy have other engagements, so as to render it necessary to appoint burials for a particular hour—an appointment, however, often more necessary to the clergy than agreeable to the undertakers and their employers. And yet, with every precaution, the clergyman is most seriously incommoded ; for, however he may try to accommodate, by allowing parties to fix their own hour of burial, his time and patience are fearfully encroached upon. Burials are very seldom punctual. They arrive from 20 minutes up to an hour and a half after the hour fixed. Mourners linger at home over their cups. The undertaker pleads that he " couldn't get them to move.' Sometimes he has another " job " in hand elsewhere—nay, an undertaker has had two " jobs " in my own burial-ground—he has fixed them for the same hour ; yet, after having, with my assistance, completed one of them, he has coolly left me to wait till he could fetch the other ; so that, what with wasted time, exhausted patience, and trials of temper owing to incivility and other annoyances from such persons as a clergyman is thus brought into contact with, he has, to say the least, as much inconvenience as the public have to complain of.

Among the inconveniences which the necessities of our parochial system impose upon the working-classes, may be mentioned the practice just now alluded to, viz., the omission of the *in*-church service in all cases where it is not specially paid for. Looking at my parishioners in a religious light, and at a moment when all ranks and conditions are literally levelled in the dust, I feel this to be an invidious distinction between rich and poor; and I think it but natural that the poor should prefer burial in places where such a distinction is less strongly marked.

In another part of his highly important communication, he observes—

In the course of my remarks I have adverted to our inadequate parochial provision for the burial of the dead in populous places, and to the consequent inconvenience which has placed the churchyard in unfavourable contrast with the dissenting ground. There is another inconvenience, however, which attaches to both, and which is inseparable from the burial of the dead in a crowded population: I mean the impossibility of maintaining a due solemnity on such an occasion.

If the working-classes of a populous city are less awfully affected by the sight of death, from an unavoidable familiarity with it in their own homes, it is to be feared that they and others meet with much to prevent or impair a wholesome sensibility upon it in public; for there the touching associations of a burial, and the sublime spirituality of our burial office are broken in upon by the exhibition of the most vulgar and even ludicrous scenes of daily life.

The eastern end of my parish ground, for instance, abuts upon Brick-lane, one of our most crowded and noisy thoroughfares, and at one corner stands a public-house, which, of course, is not without its attraction to all orders of street minstrels. In performing the burial service, I have left the church, while the organ has been playing a beautiful and impressive requiem movement, and proceeded to the grave, where it was purely accidental if I did not hear the very inappropriate tune mentioned by my medical friend.

Indeed, as my church extends along one side of another crowded street, I have had most inappropriate musical accompaniments, even during that part of the burial service which is performed *within* the church. My burial ground is partially exposed to the street at the west end also; and there, as at the east, it is liable to be invaded by sounds and sights of the most incongruous description. Boys clamber up the outside of the wall, hang upon the railing, and, as if tempted by the effect of contrast, take a wanton delight in the noisy utterance of the most familiar, disrespectful, and offensive expressions;—of course, all attempts to put down this nuisance from within the burial ground serve only to aggravate it, and nothing *could* put it down but a police force ordered to the outside every time that a burial takes place. To this wilful disturbance is added the usual uproar of a crowded thoroughfare,—whistling, calling, shouting, street-cries, and the creaking and rattling of every kind of vehicle—the whole forming such a scene of noisy confusion as sometimes to make me inaudible. On all these occasions, indeed, I labour under the indescribable uneasiness of feeling myself out of place. Amidst such a reckless din of secular traffic, I feel as if I were prostituting the spirituality of prayer, and profaning even the symbolical sanctity of my surplice. And yet, the exposure of my burial-ground is but partial, and is little or nothing compared with that of many others. The ground is hardly less desecrated by the scenes within it; on Sundays, especially, it is the resort of the idle, who pass by the church and its services to lounge and gaze in the churchyard. It is made a play-ground by children of both sexes, who skip and scamper about it, and, if checked by our officers, will often retort with impertinence, abuse, obscenity, or profaneness. I generally have to force my way to a grave through a crowd of gossips, and as often to pause in the service, to intimate that the murmurs of some or the loud talk of others will not allow me to proceed.   I hardly ever witness in any of these crowds any indication of a religious sentiment.   I may sometimes chance to observe a serious shake of the head among them; but, with these rare exceptions, I see them impressed with no better feeling than the desire to while away their time in gratifying a vulgar curiosity.   On the burial of any notorious character,—of a suicide, of a man who has perished by manslaughter, of a woman who has died in child-birth, or even of a child who has been killed by being run over in the street, this vulgar excitement rises to an insufferable height.   If, in such a case, the corpse is brought into my church, this sacred and beautiful structure is desecrated and disfigured by the hurried intrusion of a squalid and irreverent mob, and clergyman, corpse, and mourners are jostled and mixed up with the confused mass, by the uncontrollable pressure from without.   I will not, indeed, venture to say that, on these occasions, the mourners always feel and dislike this uproar, for I believe that among the working classes they often congratulate themselves upon it.   There is an éclat about it which ministers to the love of petty distinction before alluded to; but, whether through the operation of this feeling or the many other abominable mischiefs attending the burial of the dead in populous places, there is much to counteract or impair the solemn and impressive effect of religious obsequies.

§ 89. The feeling of a large proportion of the population appears to be dissatisfaction with the intra-mural parochial interments, less on sanitary grounds than from an aversion to the profanation arising from interment amidst the scenes of the crowd and bustle of every-day life.   This feeling is manifested in the increasing numbers who abandon the interments, even in parishes where the places of burial are neatly kept, where, if there be nothing to satisfy, there is nothing to offend the eye, where the service is solemnly and attentively performed, and where the amount of the burial fees cannot be supposed to influence the choice.   The increasing feeling of aversion is indeed manifested by acts less liable to error than any verbal testimony, by the increasing abandonment of parochial family-vaults by the gentry and middle classes of the population, by payments from the labouring classes, even of increased burial dues for interments in places apart from the profanation of every-day life.   The feeling manifested may be stated to be a national one, and to call for measures of a corresponding extent and character.

Means of diminishing the evil of the retention of the Remains of the Dead amidst the Living.

The most predominant of the physical, if not of the moral evils which follow the train of death, to the labouring classes, being the long retention of the corpse in their one room, the means of altering this practice claims priority in the consideration of remedies.

§ 90. The delay of interment, it has been shown, is greatly increased by the expense of the funerals; but in a considerable proportion of cases, where the expense is provided for, the delay still occurs, chiefly from feelings which require to be consulted,—the fear of interment before life is extinct.

§ 91. It has been proposed by an arbitrary enactment, without qualification or provision of securities, to forbid all delay of interments beyond a certain number of hours. Such a provision would, in the shape proposed, and without other securities, run counter to the feelings of the population, and standing as a self-executing law it would have but little operation.

The proposed compulsory clause stood thus in the bill of the session of 1842 without any qualification :—

"And be it enacted, That from and after the First day of October, One thousand eight hundred and forty   , if any dead body shall continue unburied between the First day of May and the Thirty-first day of October, both days inclusive, more than   hours, or between the First day of November and the Thirtieth day of April, both days inclusive, more than   hours, the executors or administrators to the estate and effects of such deceased person, or the friends or relatives of the same, or any one of such friends or relatives present at the burial, or the occupier of the house from which such dead body shall be removed to be buried, shall forfeit the sum of Twenty shillings for every Twenty-four hours after the expiration of such respective periods."

From the closeness of the rooms in which the poorer classes die, and from large fires being on such occasions lighted in them, decomposition often proceeds with as much rapidity in winter as in summer. The mental sufferings from the prolonged retention of the body amidst the living, §§ 26, 3, 39, and the moral objections to it also, § 42, would be as intense in the winter as in the summer, or more so.

§ 92. In several of the continental states, about half a century ago, similar enactments were passed ; but it was found necessary to accompany them with various securities ; and where these securities, such as the medical inspection and certificate before interment, have been loose, events have occurred which have convinced the public of the necessity of strengthening them. In a recent report on the subject at Paris, by M. Orfila, he adduces an instance.

"In October, 1837, M. Deschamps, an inhabitant of la Guillotière, at Lyons, died at the end of a short indispositon. His obsequies were ordered for the next day. On the next day the priests and the vergers, the corpse-bearers and conductors of funerals, attended. At the moment when they were about to nail down the lid of the coffin, the corpse rose in its shroud, sat upright, and asked for something to eat. The persons present were about to run away in terror, as from a phantom, but they were re-assured by M. Deschamps himself, who happily recovered from a lethargic sleep, which had been mistaken for death. Due cares were bestowed upon him, and he lived. After his recovery he stated that in his state of lethargy he had heard all that had passed around him, without being able to make any movement, or to give any expression to his sensations. * * * It is fortunate for M. Deschamps that the funeral, which was to have taken place in the evening, was deferred until the morning, when the lethargic access terminated, otherwise he would have been interred alive. · * * ··

In the last number of the Annalés d'Hygiene, the following recent instances are cited, as proving the necessity of a regular verification throughout the kingdom of the fact of death ;—

A midwife of the commune of Paulhan (Herault) was believed to be dead and was put in a coffin. At the expiration of twenty-four hours she was carried to the church and from thence to the cemetery. But during its progress the bearers felt some movement in the coffin, and were surprised and frightened. They stopped and opened the coffin, when they found the unfortunate woman alive! she had merely fallen into a lethargy, She was carried back to her home, but in consequence of the shock she received she only survived a few days the horrible accident.

It is stated from Bergerac (Dordogne), of the date of the 27th of December, 1842, that—

An individual of the Commune d'Eymet, who suffered from the continued want of sleep, having consulted a medical practitioner, took on his prescription a potion which certainly caused sleep; but the patient slept always, and the prolongation of the repose created great anxiety, and occasioned his being bled. The blood flowed feebly, drop by drop. Then he was declared to be dead. At the expiration of a few days, however, the potion given to the patient was remembered, and an uneasy sensation that it might have been the cause of an apparent death, caused the exhumation of the body. When the coffin was opened the horrible fact was apparent to all present that the unfortunate man had really been buried alive: he had turned round in the coffin! His distorted limbs showed that he had long struggled against death.

In the "Journal des Débats," bearing date February 21, 1843, a letter is given from Caen of the 17th February, informing us "that Madame * * * dwelling in the Rue Saint-Jean, appeared, after a long sickness, to expire on Tuesday evening. The sad functions of preparing her for the tomb were performed during the night. On the Thursday morning the coffin was brought, and as the two men were about to lay her in it, she moved in their hands, and woke up from the profound lethargy in which she was plunged. Madame * * * is in a state of health which leaves little hope. We shudder to contemplate the horrible end which awaited her if the trance had continued some hours longer."

§ 93. I am informed of one case, which occurred in a private family in this country, of a disentombment, made under very similar circumstances to those of the case related from Bergerac, which revealed a similarly horrible event, the body being found turned in the coffin. The belief of the occurrence of such cases in this country is sometimes founded on statements of the bodies being found out of their proper position in the coffins; but nothing is more probable than the discomposure of the body from its recumbent position, by jolting at the time of its removal down steep and narrow staircases. Sir Benjamin Brodie observes:—" Mistakes such as these here alluded to must be very rare, and can be the result only of the grossest neglect. The movements of respiration are always perceptible to the eye, and cannot be overlooked by any one who does not choose to overlook them, and there is no doubt that the heart never continues to act more than four or five minutes after respiration has entirely ceased. But it is not always easy to say what is the *exact moment* at which death hath taken place, as in some instances the inspirations for some time previously are repeated at very long intervals. Thus I have watched a dying person, and supposed that he was dead, when, after a minute's interval, there has been a fresh inspiration; then one or two more presently afterwards; then another long interval, and so on. I have no doubt that persons in this condition are often sensible, and even hear and understand all that is said.

" It may be doubtful whether sensibility is always immediately extinguished when the heart has ceased to act. In persons who have died of the Asiatic cholera convulsive movements of the body have been observed even several hours after apparent death. If the nervous system has remained in such a state as this implies, who can say that it did not retain its sensibility? There is no account of persons in whom such convulsions (after apparent death) have taken place having recovered; but this occurrence, even without chance of recovery, forms a strong argument against the immediate burial of persons who have died of the cholera."*

---

* Dr. Bently states, that " allowing for much of fiction, with which such a subject must ever be mixed, there is still sufficient evidence to warrant a diligent examination of the means of discriminating between real and apparent death." (*Ency. Prac. Medicine*, vol. iii. 316.) " As respiration is a function most essential to health, and at the same time the most apparent, the cessation of it may be considered as an indication of death. But as in certain diseases and states of exhaustion it becomes very slow and feeble, and so to the casual observer to appear quite extinct, various methods have been adopted for ascertaining its existence. Thus, placing down or other light substances near the mouth or nose; laying a vessel of water on the chest, as an index of motion in that cavity; holding a mirror before the mouth, in order to condense the watery vapour of the breath; have all been proposed and employed, but they are all liable to fallacy. Down, or whatever substance is employed, may be moved by some agitation of the surrounding air; and the surface of the mirror may be apparently covered by the condensed vapour of the breath, when it is only the fluid of some exhalation from the surface of the body. We therefore agree fully with the judicious observations of Dr. Paris on this subject :—' We feel no hesitation in asserting, that it is physiologically impossible for a human being to remain more than a few minutes in such a state of asphyxia as not to betray some sign by which a medical observer can at once recognize the existence of vitality; for if the respiration be only suspended for a short interval we may conclude that life has fled for ever. Of all the acts of animal life, this is by far the most essential and indisputable. Breath and life are very properly considered in the scriptures as convertible terms, and the same synonym, as far as we know, prevails in every language. However slow and feeble respiration may become by disease, yet it must always be perceptible, provided the naked breast and belly be exposed; for when the intercostal muscles act, the ribs are elevated, and the sternum is pushed forwards; when the diaphragm acts the abdomen swells. Now this can never escape the attentive eye; and by looking at the chest and belly we shall form a safer conclusion than by the popular methods which have been usually adopted.' "

The looking-glass and the feather have been the standing test for time immemorial. When Lear enters with Cordelia dead in his arms, he says:—

" I know when one is dead, and when one lives;
    She 's dead as earth.—Lend me a looking-glass;
    If that her breath will mist or stain the stone,
    Why, then she lives.
Kent.—Is this the promis'd end ?

§ 94. The extreme ignorance and terror of the lowest class of the population on the occurrence of a death which they may never have witnessed before, must be expected to stand in the place of gross neglect.   Of the lower class of officers in public establishments, when unsuperintended by well qualified and responsible persons, the occurrence of gross neglect must be anticipated. Cases have recently occurred, and have at other times, though rarely, occurred, where the sick are laid out for dead, who have afterwards recovered.   "To the skilful medical practitioner," says Dr. Paris, (Paris and Fonblanque's Medical Jurisprudence, vol. ii., p. 44,) "we apprehend such signs must ever be unequivocal, but we are not prepared to say that common observers may not be deceived by them."   And he adduces instances where they have been.   He cites the testimony of Howard, who, in his work on prisons, says, "I have known instances where persons supposed to be dead of the gaol fever, and brought out for burial, on being washed with cold water have shown signs of life, and have soon afterwards recovered."

Dr. Paris also states that—

At the period when the small-pox raged with such epidemic fury, and physicians so greatly aggravated its violence by their stimulating plan of cure, there can be no doubt but that many persons were condemned as dead who afterwards recovered ; amongst the numerous cases that might be cited in support of this opinion, the following may be considered as well authenticated :—the daughter of Henry Lawrens, the first president of the American Congress, when an infant was laid out as dead, in the small-pox ; upon which the window of the apartment, that had been carefully closed during the progress of the disease, was thrown open to ventilate the chamber, when the fresh air revived the supposed corpse, and restored her to her family ; this circumstance occasioned in the father so powerful a dread of living interment, that he directed by will that his body should be burnt, and enjoined on his children the performance of this wish as a sacred duty.   We can also imagine, that women after the exhaustion consequent on severe and protracted labours may lie for some time in a state so like that of death, as to deceive the by-standers ; a very extraordinary case of this kind is related in the Journal de Savans, Janvier 1749.

Dr. Gordon Smith, in his work on Forensic Medicine, has observed, that in cases of precipitancy or confusion, as in times of public sickness, the living have not unfrequently been mingled with the dead, and that in warm climates, where speedy interment is more necessary than in temperate and cold countries, persons have been entombed alive.   We feel no hesitation in believing that such an event *may be possible ;* but the very case with which the author illustrates his position is sufficient to convince us that its occurrence would be highly culpable, and could only arise from the most unpardonable inattention ; "I was," says Dr. Smith, " an eye wit-

---

Edgar.—Or image of that horror?
Lear.—This feather stirs ; she lives ! if it be so
  It is a chance which does redeem all sorrows
  That ever I have felt."
  Shakespeare, King Lear, Act V. Sc. 3

ness of an instance in a celebrated city on the continent, where a poor woman, yet alive, was solemnly ushered to the margin of the grave in broad day, and whose interment would have deliberately taken place, but for the interposition of the bystanders." If the casual observer was thus able to detect the signs of animation, the case is hardly one that should have been adduced to show the difficulty of deciding between real and apparent death.

Although the chances may be as millions to one against such a horrible occurrence, yet the existence of the painful feeling of the possibility of such an event, even if the apprehended possibility were utterly unreal, is as valid ground for the adoption of measures to prevent and alleviate the painful feeling, as if the danger were real and frequent. A large proportion of the population, especially in Scotland, are deeply impressed with the horror of being buried alive. Amongst the working-classes the feeling is sometimes manifested in a dying request that they may not be " hurried at once to the grave."

One consequence of abandoning the rite of burial, as a trade and source of emolument to persons without instruction or qualification, who employ for important ministrations agents of the lowest class, § 51, is, that only the superficial, ceremonial, and profitable portions of the service are usually attended to, and that important private and public securities are lost. One of the proper ministrations after death, a purification or ablution of the body, is generally omitted. On inquiring, as to the effects produced amongst the lower class of Irish by the retention of the body amidst the survivors under circumstances of imminent danger, a comparative immunity has been ascribed to the practice which they maintain of washing the corpse immediately after death. Amongst the lower class of the English and Scotch population of the towns, this important sanitary rite is extensively neglected, and the corpse is generally kept (except the face) with the *sordes* of disease upon it. The occurrence of such cases as have already been mentioned, § 31 and § 40, of the propagation by contact of diseases of a malignant character, may probably be sometimes ascribed to this neglect. The ablution, whether with tepid or cold water, as a general practice, is a protection against cases of protracted syncope or suspended animation. Besides these cases, there are others of a judicial nature which cannot be termed extraordinary amidst a population where deaths from accidents or one description of violence or other, a large proportion of them involving criminality, amount in England and Wales alone to between 11,000 and 12,000 per annum. Cases have occurred of violent deaths discovered on exhumation, and on judicial examination where marks of violence have been covered by the shroud, and where the coffin has been closed on *primâ facie* evidence of murder.

Between the every-day dangers arising from the undue retention of the dead amidst the living, and all real dangers and painful apprehensions, a course of proceeding has been taken at Franckfort, and several cities in Germany, which has hitherto been perfectly successful as a sanitary measure, and highly satisfactory to the population.

§ 95. A case is stated to have occurred at Franckfort, where, on taking to the grave a child which had died immediately after its mother, who had been just interred, on opening her coffin the eye of the supposed corpse moved, and she was taken out and recovered. She stated that she retained sensation, but had utterly lost all power of volition, even when the coffin was closed, and she heard the earth fall upon it.

§ 96. This case, and some others which have undoubtedly occurred in Germany, led to the establishment of houses at Franckfort and Munich for the reception and care of the dead until their interment; and similar establishments have now been attached to a large proportion of the German cities, under regulations substantially the same. The State regulations of interments at Munich (translations of which, and of those at Franckfort, together with plans showing the construction of the houses of reception, I have given in the Appendix) have this recital:—

" Whereas it is of importance to all men to be perfectly assured that the beings who were dear to them in life are not torn from them so long as any, the remotest, hope exists of preserving them,—so death itself becomes less dreadful in its shape when one is convinced of its actual occurrence, and that a danger no longer exists of premature interment.

" To afford this satisfaction to mankind, and to preclude the possibility of any one being treated as dead who is not actually so ; to prevent the spread of infectious disorders as much as possible; to suppress the quackeries so highly injurious to the health of the people ; to discover murders committed by secret violence; and to deliver the perpetrators over to the hands of justice ;—is the imperative duty of every wise government; and in order to accomplish these objects, every one of which is of the greatest importance, recourse must be had to the safety, that is to say the medical police, as the most efficient means, by a strict medical examination into the deaths occurring, and by a conformable inspection of the body."

The regulations provide that, on the occurrence of the death, immediate notice shall be given to the authorities, who shall cause the body to be removed to the house of reception provided (which at Munich is a chapel where prayers are said) for its respectful care. At the edifice of the institution at Franckfort, an appropriate apparatus is provided for the requisite ablutions with warm or tepid water: the body is received, if it be of a female, by properly

appointed nurses, who perform, under superior medical superintendence, the requisite duties. The spirit of the regulations of
these institutions (vide Appendix) may be commended to attention; for if it be a high public duty, which is not questioned, to
treat the remains of the dead with respect and reverence, it follows
that public means should be taken in every stage of proceeding,
to protect individuals against the violation of that duty; where
private individuals are, as they almost always are and must be,
especially in populous districts, compelled to call in the aid of
strangers for the performance of such ministrations as those of
purifying and enshrouding the corpse, such securities as are exemplified in these regulations should be taken that those duties are
confided to hands invested with responsibilities, and having a
character of respectability, if not of sanctity. At Munich, they
are intrusted to a religious order of Nuns. At Franckfort a
private room is appropriated for the reception of each corpse,
where regular warmth and due ventilation and light, night and
day, are maintained. Here it may be visited by the relations or
friends properly entitled. On a finger of each corpse is placed a
ring, attached to which is the end of a string of a bell,* which on
the slightest motion will give an alarm to one of the watchmen
in nightly and daily attendance, by whom the resident physician
will be called. Each body is daily inspected by the responsible
physician, by whom a certificate of unequivocal symptoms of death
must be given before any interment is allowed to take place.
The legislative provisions of the institution of the house of reception at Franckfort are thus stated :—

The following are the regulations regarding the use of the house for the
reception and care of the dead, which are here made known for every one's
observance.
    (1.) The object of this institution is—
        a. To give perfect security against the danger of premature inter-
        ment.
        b. To offer a respectable place for the reception of the dead, in order
        to remove the corpse from the confined dwellings of the survivors.
    (2.) The use of the reception-house is quite voluntary, yet, in case the
physician may consider it necessary for the safety of the survivors that the
dead be removed, a notification to this effect must be forwarded to the
Younger Burgermeister to obtain the necessary order.
    (3.) Even in case the house of reception is not used the dead cannot
be interred, until after the lapse of three nights, without the proper certificate of the physician that the signs of decomposition have commenced.
In order to prevent the indecency which has formerly occurred, of preparing too early the certificate of the death, the physician shall in future
sign a preliminary announcement of the occurrence of death, for the sake
of the previous arrangements necessary for an interment, but the certificate
of death is only to be prepared when the corpse shows unequivocal signs of
decomposition having commenced. For the dead which it is wished to
place in the house of reception, the physician prepares a certificate of re-

---

* Vide Appendix.—Regulations and Plans of the Building, forming part of the
Institution.

moval. This certificate of removal can only be given after the lapse of the different periods, of six hours; in sudden death, of twelve hours; and in other cases, twenty-four hours.

§ 97. A German merchant, now resident in London, who took great interest in the institution, informs me that he visited it in company with his friend, one of the inspecting physicians of this house of reception. His attention was there attracted by the corpse of a beautiful child:—that child turned out not to be dead, and he himself saw it alive and recovered. No such event is known to have occurred at Munich.

This gentleman, and Mr. Koch, our consul at Franckfort, who obtained for this Report the plans of the house of reception and the regulations for interment in that city, both attest from extensive knowledge of its population, that the effect of this institution, of which all classes avail themselves, is, on the part of the poorest and most susceptible classes, to allay all feelings of reluctance to part with the remains, and to create, on the contrary, a general desire for their removal from the private house early after death, that they may be placed under the care of skilful and responsible officers. The aggravation and extension of disease to the living is thus prevented; the protraction of the pain of the weaker and more susceptible of the survivors, arising from the undue retention of the remains, and the demoralizing effect of familiarity with them on the parts of the younger, and those of the least susceptible of the survivors, are equally avoided.

The following is an extract from an official report made for this inquiry through the English Ambassador, on the operation of similar regulations at Munich :—

" The arrangements made for the speedy removal of the body after death are considered highly beneficial in a sanative point of view, as tending to check the spread of contagious and unclean disorders, more particularly in the crowded parts of the town.

" At the same time the great care and attention paid to the bodies in the place where they are deposited, the precautions taken in cases of re-animation, and the ascertaining beyond a doubt the actual occurrence of death, are sufficiently satisfactory to the surviving relations.

" The examinations also which take place immediately after death have been found equally useful in detecting the employment of violent or improper means in causing death, as well as in discovering the existence of any contagious disease against which it is of importance to guard.

" There is only one burial ground for the whole city of Munich, on a scale sufficiently large for the population, and open to Protestants as well as Catholics, without distinction."

§ 98. The practical means for the accomplishment of such an alteration of custom in the mode of keeping the remains of the deceased, preparatory to interment, in the towns of England, may be further considered in connexion with the remedial measures, for the reduction of the great and unnecessary expense of funerals.

Mr. Hewitt states the practical, need of some such accommodation of survivors for the temporary reception of the dead in the crowded districts, independently of the high considerations on which the intermediate houses of reception at Franckfort and Munich and other parts of Germany were established.

The house in which my foreman lives is seldom unoccupied by a corpse. During the last week there were three at one time. The poor people speak of the inconvenience of having the corpse in their house, where they have only one room for their family. It is customary for me to say, "Very well, then, you may be accommodated; the body may be brought to our house, and kept until the time of the funeral, when you and your friends may come to the house and put on your fittings and follow the body to the ground." This is done: men and women come to the house, put on hoods, scarves, coats, and hatbands, and follow the body to the ground. The body is sometimes removed under these circumstances from the room of the private house where the death has taken place, but it is most frequently done when the death of a poor person has occurred in an hospital, a workhouse, or a prison, and it is wished to bury them respectably, but where it would be inconvenient to remove them to the only room which the family have to live in. I believe that all the undertakers receive deceased persons in their houses and keep them for burial.

Judging from the particular instances coming within your own experience, do you believe that if arrangements of a superior order were made for the reception of bodies and keeping them under medical care previous to interment, the accommodation would be deemed a boon?—Yes; it would be a boon to a great many classes, especially the poorest. It would be a great accommodation also to many persons of the middle classes— shopkeepers, who only keep the under part of their houses and let off the upper parts. On the occurrence of a death these classes are as much inconvenienced by the presence of a corpse as are persons of the labouring classes. And yet there are few who like to have a burial take place in less time than a week. To such persons as these it would certainly be a very great accommodation to have an intermediate house of reception for the due care of the body until the proper time of interment.

. Mr. Thomas Tagg, jun., an undertaker of extensive business in the city of London, states, that "besides the poorest classes who die at hospitals and are buried. by their friends, and are sometimes taken to the undertaker's premises, when more convenient to the relatives of the deceased than to be removed to their own houses, that respectable persons also from the country, who die at an hotel or inn, or in apartments, are occasionally removed to the undertaker's until the coffins are made, and they can be conveyed to the residence of their family, or their vaults in the country."

§ 99. Mr. Wild gives other examples of the practice; and states that instances sometimes occur of persons of respectable condition in life who cannot bear the painful impressions produced by the long continued presence of the corpse in the house, and who quit it, and return to attend the funeral.

§ 100. Mr. P. H. Holland, surgeon and registrar of Chorlton-upon-Medlock, in Manchester, states an instance where a mother who had lost two of her children from small-pox (as she conceived, from the retention in the house of the corpse of a child belonging to another woman which had also died of the small-pox) stated that it would be a great boon to the poorer classes to provide proper places to receive bodies until the convenient time of interment.   The extent of benefit which such a provision would confer, and which is attested by other witnesses of extensive experience, will indeed be sufficiently manifest on consideration of the circumstances under which they are placed.

§ 101. It is only submitted that suitable accommodation should be provided for the removal and care of bodies, and given, as it would be, as a boon.   Confident statements are frequently made that the removal of the deceased from private houses to any public place of reception would be resisted; but it appears on an examination of the cases in which resistance was made, that in most of them the arrangements were really offensive, coarse-minded, and vulgar, and such as to prove that the feelings of the relations and survivors were little cared for by those who ought to have understood and consulted them.   In some cases of the lowest paupers the retention of the body has been proved to have arisen from a desire to raise money, on the pretext of applying it to defray the expenses of the funeral long after it had been provided for; but the objection of the respectable portions of the labouring classes are objections not to the removal itself, but to the mode and sort of place in which it is commonly performed on the occurrence of a death from contagious disease, in a bare parish shell, by pauper bearers, to the " bone-house" or other customary receptacle for suicides, deserted or relationless, or, as they are sometimes termed, " God-forsaken people."   On the occurrence of the cholera little difficulty was interposed by any class to the immediate removal of the dead. The success of such a measure would depend entirely on the mode in which it is conducted.

§ 102. In reference to all such alterations, it may here be premised that very serious practical errors are frequently created by taking particular manifestations of feeling or prejudice, and assuming those prejudices to be impregnable, and assuming, moreover, that any or every prejudice pervades the entire population.

Not only does the extent of the prejudices which are supposed to stand in the way of regulations of the practice of interments, but the difficulties of overcoming them, appear, from an examination of the evidence, to be commonly much exaggerated; but it appears that the nature of the objections themselves is much mistaken: it appears, for example, that the prejudice against dissection often arises less from a desire to preserve the remains in their living form than to preserve them from profanation and disrespect.   In no part of the country has a more intense feeling been manifested to preserve the remains of the dead from dissection than in Scotland, where the expense of safes made of iron bars, strongly riveted down, and of a watchman to watch it, forms a prominent item of the funeral charges.   Yet when the studies of the schools of anatomy were allowed to depend chiefly on the supplies of subjects stolen from the graves, it is stated by practitioners who, whilst students, were themselves driven to that mode of procuring subjects, that their labours were frequently frustrated by the precautions the survivors had taken to render the use of the remains for dissection impossible, by putting quick lime into the coffin to destroy them.   The same precaution has been known to have been sometimes taken for the same purpose in London; and yet by proper care and attention to the feelings of the survivors, the practice of post-mortem examinations has been extended, and the consent to the use of the remains even for dissection in the schools has been frequently obtained from the survivors.   A witness of peculiar and extensive opportunities of experience in several thousand cases was asked on this point—

Have you had any reason to believe, that by careful and kind treatment of the labouring classes, their prejudices may be extensively overcome ?—Yes, certainly.   There was no prejudice stronger or more general than that to post-mortem examinations, or to any dissection; yet by care, and by the inducement of the allowance of a better funeral, that prejudice has been extensively overcome.   The teachers of the medical schools, after dissection of a body, and its use for the advancement of medical knowledge, have made a liberal allowance for the interment of the remains; such sums as three or four pounds have been allowed for that service. When the relations of the poorest classes have expressed the common aversion to a pauper funeral, and their pain at having to submit to it on account of their necessity, I have told them if they would allow the remains to be taken to a medical school, and be examined, the teachers would allow them such a respectable funeral as they wish; I have sometimes added, " It is for the advancement of science; persons of the highest rank and condition in society have directed their remains to be examined, and I do not see what sound objection there can be to any of the poorest classes doing so." Whenever I have made the offer under such circumstances it has generally been accepted.

· Of course after the examination at the schools, the remains were properly and respectfully interred ?—Yes they were, wherever the parties requested, whether in or out of the parish—They frequently chose places of interment out of the parish, and in some instances places two or three miles distant, and almost always out of the town.

Why was the burial mostly chosen out of the parish ?—Generally from a dislike to the places and mode in which paupers were buried; to their being put into a hole, where, perhaps, fifty others were, instead of having a separate grave.   They frequently made it a main condition, that the remains should be buried out of the parish.

The means to ensure voluntary compliance with all salutary regulations for the better ordering of interments, are those which ensure real respect to the remains of the interred; and thus to the feelings of the survivors.   The widows' and the mothers' feelings of reluctance to part with the corpse would, from such measures, receive appropriate alleviation.

Proposed Remedies by means of separate Parochial Establish-
ments in Suburban Districts.

§ 103. A set of remedies, as proposed in the Committee of the House of Commons, and agreed to, has been before the public, and the chief part of them embodied in a bill proposed to the House at the close of the Session of Parliament of 1842. All the evidence of disinterested persons which I have met with, all paid and experienced officers connected with parishes, whose interests would perhaps be the least disturbed by parochial establishments, concur in the conclusion that the measures proposed for creating such establishments would not diminish, but would rather diffuse, and might even aggravate the evils intended to be remedied.

By the first clause it was proposed to enact—

That the rector, vicar, or incumbent, and the church-wardens of every parish, township, or place in every such city, town, borough, or place respectively, shall form a parochial committee of health for every such parish, township, or place.

§ 104. The first observation which occurs on this proposal is, that it involves the formation of " a committee of health," for the execution of a sanitary measure, requiring the application of a very high degree of the science applicable to the protection of the public health, and omits all provision of services of the nature of those which would be required from a well-qualified medical officer. A provision on a parochial scale would indeed preclude the regular application of such service, except at a disproportionate expense. As a remedy against undue charges on the smaller parishes, a power of forming unions for the purpose is provided by the clause.

Or it shall be lawful for the rectors, vicars, or incumbents and church-wardens of any two or more parishes, townships, or places therein, to form such parishes, townships, or places into a Union for the purposes of this Act ; and in such cases the rectors, vicars, or incumbents, and church-wardens of each parish, township, or place so united, shall form a parochial committee of health for such Union ; and all the powers hereinafter given to any such committee may be executed by the majority of the members of any such committee at any meeting.

It is agreed by the most experienced public officers, that even a compulsory power to form unions of two parishes, but leaving the union beyond that number optional, would be equivalent to a provision, that two and *no* more shall unite; but that a merely permissive power to unite would be nugatory, except perhaps in the case of the smallest parishes : in other words, since there are in the district to which the enactment would apply, in the metropolis, upwards of 170 parishes, it would imply the establishment of upwards of 100 places of burial in such places as the following clauses would enable the parishes to provide.

And be it enacted, that every such committee may provide a convenient site of land for the burial of the dead of the district for which such committee shall be formed, which land shall not be in or within the distance of two miles from the precincts or boundaries of the city of London or West-minster, or the borough of Southwark, or in or within one mile of any other city, town, borough, or place ; and no land which shall be purchased for such purpose shall be within 300 yards of any house of the annual value of 50*l.*, or having a plantation or ornamental garden or pleasure-ground occupied therewith (except with the consent in writing of the owner, lessee, and oc-cupier of such house).

An undertaker who has an extensive business, states that he has for some time been desirous of purchasing a piece of ground for interments in the suburbs of the metropolis, as a private speculation of his own, and that he had been three years in looking out for a plot that was suitable and purchasable, but has hitherto been unable to procure one. Other witnesses, on similar grounds, doubt the practicability of parishes procuring land, unless at enormous prices.

Supposing it were possible to procure separate plots for all the parishes which will require them in the suburbs, there are pre-liminary objections to the plan which relate to the suburbs them-selves.

§ 105. The suburbs, it may be submitted, not only require careful protection on their own account, but on account of the population of the crowded districts of the metropolis, which are relieved by the growth of the suburbs. The progress of the new in-crements to towns is, therefore, as a sanitary measure, entitled to favourable protection. But the appropriation of vacant places, without reference to any general plan, must create very frequent impediments to the regular or systematic growth of the suburbs, and can scarcely fail ultimately to deteriorate them. And by the proposed measure the place of interments being removed, not only without any securities for the adoption of new measures of precaution, such as will be shown to be requisite in the formation, and also in the management, of places of burial for a large popu-lation, and the proposed machinery being such as to render it very nearly certain that no improved arrangements can be executed in such burial-grounds, the measure would simply effect the trans-ference of common grave-yards from the old to the midst of new suburbs; and this transference must be accompanied by the creation of a new and apparently economical, but really extrava-gantly expensive and permanently inferior, agency, for the manage-ment of the new ground.

§ 106. These results admit of proof derived from the actual trial of a system of parochial interments apparently differing in no essential point, and especially in the nature of the agency and the scale of establishments, from the plan proposed.

In the parishes of St. Giles-in-the-Fields, St. George, Hanover-square, St. James, Westminster, and St. Martin's-in-the-Fields, over-crowding of the burial grounds within the parish, between forty and fifty years ago, led the parish officers to obtain local acts for the establishment of burial grounds in the suburbs. The spaces then obtained were apart from any buildings. They are

H

all now closely surrounded by them. The burial grounds of the parish of St. Giles-in-the-Fields having been the subject of an investigation before the Committee of the House of Commons, I have not made any inquiries with relation to them. In the suburban burial ground which belongs to the parish of St. George, Hanover-square, which consists of two acres of land, the interments have been for many years at the rate of about 1000 corpses per annum. It is now in the centre of a dense town population. It has become the subject of complaints similar to those made in respect to burial grounds in the ancient parts of the metropolis; and it appears that there are equally good grounds for the discontinuance of the practice of interment there, and for the selection of a burial place at a greater distance, notwithstanding that the payments from individuals produce to the collective funds of that parish a surplus beyond the expenditure of the management of the ground.

§ 107. The arrangements for burial in the parishes of St. Martin-in-the-Fields, which has a population of 25,000, and of St. James, Westminster, which has a population of 37,000, where the suburban burial grounds have not been crowded to the same extent, may be adduced as a high class of examples of a change of practice to extra-mural or suburban burials, and of management by a parochial machinery. In the parish of St. James, Westminster—

The gross expenditure of the chapel and ground between the years 1789 and 1835 (46 years) amounted to £73,879 1s. 11d., and it is estimated that the cost of maintaining the chapel and ground during that period over and above the receipts was not less than £50,000, the whole of which was drawn from the churchwardens under authority of the Act of Parliament.

But the chapel attached to the burial ground of this parish has been converted into a chapel of ease, for the accommodation of the inhabitants of the parish where it is situate. The vestry clerk of the parish states—

The pew rents, which formerly averaged only £150, now amount to upwards of £500 per annum, while the burial fees have decreased, and are still decreasing in amount.

The interments of the middle class and more wealthy among the inhabitants of the parish of St. James, which do not take place either in the vaults or grounds of or belonging to the parish, are presumed to be made in the neighbouring cemeteries, while the labouring class resort chiefly, as I am informed, to the burial ground in Spa Fields, where the fees are less by 2s. 9d. than at the Hampstead Road ground, the undertaker's charges being the same for each.

Is the church to be considered part of the burial ground ?—Yes; it is. The Act apparently contemplated only a place for the performance of a service over the dead, not for services to regular congregations. The minister has a house on the ground, and derives a portion of his emoluments from pew rents, derived from persons who attend the chapel from the immediate neighbourhood—parishioners of St. Pancras parish; very few, if any, of the parishioners of St. James, have pews there. The minister, Dr. Stebbing, has a moiety of the pew rents, which now amount to nearly £500 per annum. His proportion of the burial fees may be about £70 per annum.

Since the commencement, has the income defrayed the expenses of the burial ground ?—Since Dr. Stebbing has been the minister it has only just paid the expenses ; but I am apprehensive that it will not continue to do so. By the Act for the regulation of the chapel, any deficiency in the expenditure is directed to be made good out of the moneys in the churchwardens' hands. Since the establishment of the chapel it has been a drag on the funds : a very severe one.

When the chapel was established were there any houses round it ?—Not any.

What is its condition in that respect now ?—It is now in the midst of houses which are increasing in numbers.

When asked, what was the condition of the burial ground, notwithstanding the expenditure made upon it, he states that—

The ground, consisting of four acres, is in a very watery condition, but is considered capable of being effectually drained, the expense being the only obstacle.

Is it considered that the ground will hold more than it does ?—Many more ; and a much larger amount of burials for a number of years.

What are the objections to the ground ?—One objection among the higher classes, and a very serious one, is that it is very wet. After a grave has been dug, the water in it has risen, and the coffin is lowered into the water.

Has there been any expenditure upon it for rendering it attractive by planting or ornamenting it ?—In former years it was planted with trees or shrubs ; but as compared with the cemeteries it cannot pretend to any attractions.

Is there anything in the circumstances of the establishment of the burial ground and chapel for St. James which do not render it a fair example of any similar measure for an equivalent population in these times ?—There appear to be no circumstances to prevent it being considered a fair example.

§ 108. The following is the account of the St. Martin's suburban burial ground, given by Mr. Le Breton, the clerk to the guardians of the parish :—

What is the provision made for the burial of the poorer classes in the parish of St. Martin-in-the-Fields ?—The burial ground in Drury-lane in 1804 was considered to be full, when four acres of ground, situate at Camden-town, were purchased and used as a cemetery. The plot was then in what was considered the country : the distance of the spot is rather more than two miles from the workhouse. Since its institution it has been completely surrounded by houses, and they are now building close against the wall of the burial ground. Originally it was designed as a better sort of burial ground, but since loss has been incurred by it and it has not been found to be attractive ; two hundred pounds have recently been expended upon it in planting it. Formerly it was so wet that when persons went to funerals there they often found that the coffin was let down several feet in water or mire. This created an unpleasant sensation, and the ground was drained at a great expense into the Fleet-ditch. The objection as to the wetness of the ground does not now exist.

What have been the expenses, and the numbers of interments and charges of the burial ground ?—(The following statement was given in answer to this question.)

The original cost of forming ground, &c., was about . £2,000
The price is a perpetual rent-charge of, for the 4 acres,
per annum . . . . £100 = £3,000

Establishment Charges :—

Chaplain's salary per annum	£60
Sexton's „ „	£50
Keeping up ground by gardener	£20
Paving rate per annum	£30
Compensation to St. Pancras	£5

The chaplain and sexton have houses to dwell in, which are kept in repair, insured, and the taxes paid by the parish at a considerable expense £30

A private Act of Parliament was obtained, but at what cost does not appear.

The burial ground was formed in 1804, and the charges of it to this date have exceeded £10,000 beyond the fees received.

From 29*th March,* 1806, *to* 1*st December,* 1842.

Total number of burials at Camden-town since the formation of the ground	10,982
Of these were non-parishioners	1,987
„　　　paupers	4,624
„　　　buried in the cheapest ground where monuments are not allowed	1,062
All burials for St. Martin in the Fields, 1841	522
Registered deaths, 1841	589

Beyond the expense of the establishment, have any inconveniences been the subject of complaint by the parishioners ?—Yes; that the hours appointed by the chaplain are not those most suited for interments; that they are often driven off until late in the evening, and in consequence of the time being limited the service is performed in a hurried manner. In respect to position, the cemetery appears to be convenient, and no one within the district complains of any offence arising from it. My own view is that there ought to be a central or some other supervision over cemeteries : if there be not there will only be abuses and grounds of dissatisfaction.

Do you conceive that the experience of the parish of St. Martin, of a separate parochial cemetery, is applicable as an index to the general charge upon the rate-payers in the other parishes of the metropolis, resulting from the simple prohibition of interments in the town, and the permission to any two or more parishes to provide cemeteries for; in other words, to the transference of burial grounds from the centre of the town to the midst of the suburbs ?—Yes, I do consider it applicable : moreover, that at the present time, it would be still more difficult to obtain sites within a reasonable distance than it was in 1804 : the expenses of separate parochial grounds must therefore be much more considerable.

§ 109. The Rev. Wm. Stone, the rector of Spitalfields, whose position, as the minister of a large and populous parish, possessing one of the best managed places of burial in the metropolis, gives him peculiar opportunities of judging of the most advantageous administrative arrangements, and entitles his observations to peculiar weight, concludes his testimony in the following terms :—

1. As the clergyman of a poor and populous parish, I should regret the necessity of imposing any additional rate upon my parishioners, especially any one which was likely to be regarded as a church rate ; and I feel certain, that a rate assessed for the burial of the dead, and collected under the tauthority of the rector and churchwardens, would be so regarded. Under our present system, the burial of the dead is a source of profit ; it yields an annual surplus towards defraying the other expenses of the church ; and it

thus conspires with other circumstances to make the church-rate fall light upon my parishioners. But in a population like mine any additional impost would be felt; and confounded, as in such a population it certainly would be, with church-rate, it might operate mischievously or even fatally against the church establishment of my parish. The same objection would apply in principle to all poor and populous parishes. As a clergyman, too, I might add more personal considerations; for, though the incumbent, as the only permanent member of the committee of health, might have some local prominence and weight, more, perhaps, than might everywhere be satisfactory to dissenters; yet, in imposing pecuniary charges on his parishioners, and levying penalties for the non-payment of those charges, he would have duties unpopular enough to outweigh the advantage of any distinction conferred on him.

2. If it is said, that a rate of 1*d.* in the pound would be too light to be felt; it may be said also that it would be too much so to answer its purpose. It is commonly calculated, that, in my parish, a rate of 6*d.* in the pound realizes barely 500*l.*, yet the population to be provided with interment is above 20,000. And as all the parishes about us are in much the same circumstances this objection would apply equally to a union of parishes.

3. There is much that is objectionable in the proposed local committees of health.

A local board would be less likely to possess the confidence of the people. Indeed, it would be exposed to the influence of personal interest and local partialities; and still more so, if the majority of its members were in office for a year or two only. A board of this kind may be said to exist already in my own parish, where a local Act of Parliament places the burial ground in the hands of the parish officers. And it is but a few years since my attention was forcibly called to the insecurity of this local arrangement by one of my parishioners. This parishioner, who was intimately and practically acquainted with the working of our parochial system, represented to me the necessity of adopting increased precautions for the protection of our burial ground, " for," said he, " a partial or interested parish officer might do almost anything he pleased with it;" and he proceeded to name an individual, who had even intimated his intention to do so as soon as he should come into office. There can be no doubt, indeed, that any individual might do so. It is impossible to say, to what extent a tradesman so disposed might oblige his friends and customers, and benefit himself; for as senior officer of the year he would have the sole disposal of the burial ground, and receive all payments for burials, private graves, vaults, and the erection of monumental tablets, without any demand upon those receipts, but a limited sum payable to the rector, and without any inspective control over them but that of a board of auditors chosen from his brother vestrymen. From my own observation, I do not think that parish auditors are generally very accurate in their investigations. But on a subject like the one in question, they hardly could be so. Even supposing what is seldom, if ever, the case, that they had a practical knowledge of the subject, and conducted their investigations with the authorized table of fees before them, they might in many instances be eluded. During the first four years of my incumbency, the parish officers reported their receipts for burials at the average amount of 215*l.* a-year, which sum, after the deduction of 125*l.* secured to the rector, left an annual surplus of 90*l.* At that time it was generally held to be a point of official honour, that the amount of this surplus should be kept secret out of doors. It was kept secret even from the rector; and it may serve at once to show the impolicy of secrecy, and the extent to which local authorities are distrusted, that my predecessor always had his misgivings on the subject. Though remarkable for the mildness and amiability of his disposition, he could never surmise any more innocent misapplication of this surplus, than that it was alienated from the church for the relief of the poor rate.

A constant change in the majority of a local board would be most unfavourable to uniformity of system, efficiency, and economy. Upon this ground I believe the church to be a great loser by the office of churchwarden. An individual charged with raising and expending the ecclesiastical finances of a parish for a year only is little likely to perform those duties as well as if he had a more permanent authority. To say nothing of his having more temptation to indolence, and to an ostentatious or interested profusion, he labours under the unavoidable disadvantage of inexperience. By the time that he becomes efficient in his office, he is called upon to retire from it.

A local board would want many other advantages of a more publicly constituted authority. Supplied with members by the casualties of parochial office, it could not always command a high order of intelligence. It would necessarily be limited in its opportunities of observation; and, as it could not make its purchases and regulate its current expenditure to the same advantage as if it acted on a more extensive scale, it would, of course, prove less economical to the public.

In fact, from all my local observation, I am led to hope that, in removing the interment of the dead from populous towns, the Legislature will adopt not a parochial but a comprehensive national plan for the purpose.

Mr. Drew, the vestry clerk and superintendent registrar of Bermondsey, makes similar objections to the proposed machinery; that "the persons nominated to carry out such a measure in parishes would not be satisfactory to the inhabitants, even if they were disposed to act."

Mr. Corder, the clerk to the Strand Union, was asked upon this subject—

What do you believe to be the prevailing opinion in your Union on the subject of town interments?—I believe there is a strong and growing opinion against the practice of interring in London and its immediate environs. I believe that public feeling generally is opposed to that custom, as being prejudicial to health, and often more distressing to the feelings of the survivors than interments would be in a more distant and less familiar and frequented spot.

Do you think the parishioners of London parishes would approve of separate and distinct parochial cemeteries?—No, I think they would prefer having one or more cemeteries on a very extensive scale to having parochial cemeteries which, in the neighbourhood of the metropolis, would, I think, be found almost impracticable.

Do you think that parishes generally would object to the expense of providing cemeteries?—I think that if separate parochial cemeteries were established, the expense incurred would be so serious as to induce parishes almost to submit to the evils resulting from town interments rather than incur so heavy an expenditure. One of the advantages of having one or more cemeteries on a large scale would be that the expense would be thereby proportionably and very considerably diminished.

George Downing, a mechanic, and secretary to a burial society, it will be found, represents sentiments extensively prevalent amongst persons of his own class in the metropolis.

Do you conceive that any arrangements for the improvement of interments would be carried on more acceptably to the labouring classes if they were conducted by officers connected with the parish, or by a larger and superior agency?—The working people would sell their beds from under them sooner than have any parish funerals: it is heart-rending to them, and they would prefer any other officers to the parish officers.

Do you find that they are prepared to have interments in the towns prohibited?—Yes, it has been very much debated upon since the scenes in the churchyards are made known, and they wish the bill to be carried. I am confident that every man in our club would petition to have the bill carried, so that such scenes may be put a stop to. I find the opinion of the working men on the subject is quite universal about it. They expect that Government will provide the grounds and some means of conveyance.

Mr. Dix was asked—

Is it the expectation of the labouring and poorer classes that large public cemeteries will be provided?—Yes, that I think is the general opinion.

Do you conceive that large cemeteries, on a national scale, will be more acceptable to the labouring classes than parochial burial grounds, whether in the present grounds or in burial grounds in the suburbs of the metropolis? —I think the national cemeteries will be much more popular.

If the burials of the working population could be performed in the more ornamented and attractive cemeteries, such as those at Highgate and Kensal Green, at the same expense as in any of the grounds within the town, would there be any who would not be buried there?—I think very few.

Unequivocal proof is given of the dispositions of the labouring classes in this respect by the fact that the number of interments of persons of those classes in cemeteries is increasing, even under increased charges. For example, on examining the mortuary registries of the Westminster cemetery, to see what were the class of persons interred, it appeared that the majority of the persons interred in that, which is the cemetery most heavily charged with burial fees, was of the labouring classes from St. George's, Hanover-square. The fees for interment in the suburban burial ground in the Bayswater-road, belonging to their own parish, were 15*s.*; and interments in the trading burial grounds might have been obtained at lower rates: but the fees paid for interment at the more distant cemetery are 30*s.* for each burial. The registries contained similar evidence in an increasing number of interments of the labouring classes from immediately adjacent suburban parishes, such as Chelsea, Brompton, and Kensington, of a disposition to make sacrifices, to obtain interments in places that are more free from offensive associations to them than those which attach to the parochial burial grounds.

Mr. Wild was asked—

So far as your experience goes, does the practice of interment in cemeteries result from motives of economy or from choice of situation?—From choice of situation, or from dislike of the parochial burial-grounds; in nine cases out of ten from preference of the situation and mode of interment in cemeteries; the choice would indeed be general, if it were not for the increased charges made by undertakers. The undertakers have generally increased the funeral charges at the cemeteries above one-third. The number of men taken out, whose whole day is occupied, make up the increased charge.

You state, that but for the increased charge, the custom of interment in cemeteries would be general; has the strength of the attachments to the parochial churchyards diminished?—Yes, under the recent inquiries and ex-

posures of the state of the churchyards they have almost vanished.   But at
no time was the attachment to the parochial churchyards in town so strong
as in the country.   In the country, even the poorer classes will pay the
sexton a fee of from 1*s*. 6*d*. to 2*s*. 6*d*, for "keeping up the grave."   This
cannot.be the case in the towns for want of space; parties who appoint their
places of burial, generally select a place on account of its quiet.

Do you believe that the wish to be buried where kindred are buried, is,
or would continue to be stronger, than a desire to be buried in well-provided
cemeteries?—No; this is shewn by the increasing frequency with which
parties who have family vaults, desire to be buried in the cemeteries.   Very
recently I performed the funeral of a lady belonging to a family who had a
vault in a church at Westminster—her husband had been buried in it.   By
her will she desired to be buried at Kensal Green, and she had requested
that if the churchyard at Westminster was closed, her husband's remains
might be brought and placed next to hers in the cemetery.   There were
other members of the family besides her husband buried in the family vault.
Such instances are now becoming very frequent.

Inasmuch as interments in cemeteries have generally increased the
charges of interment, is it not to be apprehended that unless some regulations on a larger scale than of small localities be adopted, the inconvenience
arising in towns will increase the charges of these calamities to the poorest
of the middle classes and to the working classes, not to speak of the charges
on the poor's rates, for the interments of paupers will also be increased by
districts?—Yes; it has occurred to me that it will be so.

He expresses his conviction, however, that so strong is the
feeling at present against parochial interments, that if there should
be no legislative provision or interference for the public protection,
the parochial burial places being left open to the competition of
private and trading burial grounds, in a very short time not one-
third of the present number of burials would take place in the
parochial grounds.

§ 110.   The expense to the rate-payers of parishes for the transference of the interments to the suburbs would be necessarily very
high ; the expense of numerous separate parochial establishments,
if only on the scale of the establishments for the performance of
the funeral ceremony, and for such imperfect care of the ground as
that given in those described would be, at the least, between 25 and
30,000*l*. per annum.   The proposed regulation of the distance of
cemeteries from human habitations—that they shall in every case
be two miles, not from houses, but from the metes and bounds of
London and Westminster, and " of any other city, town, or
borough," as defined by the Municipal Act, and " which shall
contain more than 500 houses, the occupiers of which shall be
rated to the relief of the poor more than 10*l*. or upwards," appear to be made without any local examination, or reference to
proper observations or experience.—Vide post, §§ 162, 163, and
164.   The metes and bounds of several towns and places include
common lands and sites, sufficiently distant from any collections
of houses, to be the most eligible sites, and suitable soils for
cemeteries, which according to the best ascertained rule, should be
at distances proportioned to the numbers of inhabitants and probable burials, varying according to these numbers, from 150 to

500 paces. All unnecessary increase of distance must be attended with proportionately increased charges of interment to the poorer classes : arrangements for preventing an increase of the expense of conveyance of the remains to distant places of interment, though practicable under general regulations for large national cemeteries, would be impracticable on the plan of numerous places of interment with small separate establishments. Mr. Jeffryes, an undertaker, who chiefly inters the poorest classes in the Whitechapel district, where the *parochial* interments are generally diminishing, was more particularly questioned on this topic.

What has been your experience in respect to the interment of people of the working classes at cemeteries, and at a distance from their residence, as compared with burials near their residence ? At what cemeteries have you interred persons ?—At Mr. Barber Beaumont's cemetery ; which is about a mile and a half from Whitechapel ; and also at the cemetery which is at the Cambridge Heath, Cambridge Road. I have attended, but not on my own account, funerals at all the other cemeteries—Highgate, Kensal Green, and others.

Supposing that interments within towns be prohibited for all classes, and that funerals for the future must be performed beyond the gas lamps or the pavements ; judging from the cases you have already had, what must be the effect on the funerals of the labouring classes ;—supposing that no other arrangements are made than that of allowing parishes, or any two of them, to provide cemeteries at a distance from town ?—It will certainly increase the expenses to the labouring classes, and increase the expenses to the parishes generally. I perform funerals for the working classes at one-third less than most others ; yet I find that the extra expense of a funeral only a mile or a mile and a quarter distance, is about one pound per funeral extra ; this consists chiefly of the extra expense of conveyance.

Have you seen carriage conveyances or hearses for the conveyance of bodies to the cemeteries without the use of bearers ?—Yes, I have : but to get a coffin out of the house, which sometimes has to be got down stairs, and is very heavy, four men at the least will be required, and then four men will be required to take it from the hearse at the cemetery, so that men's labour cannot be much less, even if they provide bearers at the cemeteries, which is talked of : there will still be the extra expense of the carriage, whatever that is.

§ 111. From the practical evidence already cited, §§ 87, 88, it will be perceived, that notwithstanding this increase of expense, the chaplain or curate, if unaided, cannot be expected to perform the service in a manner that will be more satisfactory to the survivors than in those parochial grounds which are now the subject of complaint. The numerous successive services that may be expected to arrive on the Sunday must often unavoidably have the appearance of being hurried over, and without assistance and appropriate superintendence will sometimes really be so, whilst the funeral of the person of better condition which takes place separately, and at an appointed time, has its separate attention under circumstances, giving rise to the appearance and creating the feeling of an undue " acceptation of persons," which it is said ought not to be, and which the examination of practical examples will show, need not be. Inasmuch as, in the present mode, the clergyman's attention must be absorbed with his own clerical duties, the grave-yard and the material offices connected with it must be left to be managed, as it is now, by a sexton and common grave-digger. No multiplication of the numbers of such poor men in numerous extra-mural and parochial establishments will give them education, or elevate their minds to act without super-intendence, up to the solemnity and delicacy of the duties to be performed in any proposed alteration of custom. In such hands the institution and service for the reception and care of the dead, (which, with all its appliances, is one of the most elevated that can adorn the civic economy of a large and civilized community,) would be impracticable, or would become a common "dead-house," or a revolting charnel. It may be confidently affirmed, that to accomplish what is needed to satisfy the feelings of the population, on the points on which they are so painfully sus-ceptible, and to gain the public confidence requisite to carry out all the sanitary appliances and improvements that are requisite in connexion with the practice of interment, would task the zeal and ability, and unremitting attention of any, the best staff of educated medical men that could be procured for such a service. The improvements which appear to be practicable, may be per-ceived on a consideration of the information hereafter submitted, as to what is already gained under arrangements of a compre-hensive character.

§ 112. The chief conclusions in respect to the proposed suburban parochial interments deducible from the present experience appear then to be,

1. That the change of the practice of interments on the plan of suburban parochial or establishments of separate unions of parishes, while it gave immediate relief to the centre of the town, would create impediments to the regular growth of the suburbs, and, ultimately, as the interments increase, diminish the salubrity of the suburbs. §§ 107, 108.

2. That it would not *ultimately* diminish any injurious effects arising from the practice of interments amidst the abodes of the living; and that its chief effect would be to transfer such evils from the districts where they now prevail to the midst of the population of other districts. §§ 105, 110.

3. That these results would only be obtained at a considerable expense to the rate-payers of the parishes from whence the practice of interments is transferred. §§ 107, 108.

4. That if burial in parochial grounds were transferred to such a distance as not to interfere with the growth of the suburbs, the increased distance of interments would occasion a propor-tionate increase of the expense of interments to the labouring classes of the community. § 110.

5. That inasmuch as the difficulty of obtaining the means of defraying the expense of such classes of interments is frequently a

powerful means of increasing the evil of the long delay of the interments, the measures proposed would tend to increase the most extensive and direct source of injury to the health and morals of the survivors of the labouring classes—the long retention of the corpse in their crowded and ill-ventilated places of abode. §§ 43, 44.

6. That interment by a parochial agency would aggravate or leave untouched the other objections to the present practice of interments in the metropolis. §§ 98, 99, 111.

Practicability of ensuring for the Public superior Interments at reduced Expenses.

The subject which may next be presented for consideration is how far the pecuniary burthens may be reduced consistently with the sentiments expressed by Jeremy Taylor, who deems it " a great act of piety, and honourable, to inter our friends and relatives according to the proportions of their condition, and so to give testimony of our hope of their resurrection. So far is piety ; beyond, it may be the ostentation and bragging of grief to serve worse ends. In this, as in everything else, as our piety must not pass into superstition or vain expense, so neither must the excess be turned into parsimony, and chastised by negligence and impiety to the memory of their dead.".

§ 113. It appears, from detailed inquiries, made of tradesmen of experience and respectability, who have answered explicitly the questions put to them, that the expense of the materials at present supplied for funerals admit of a reduction under general arrangements of, at the least, 50 per cent. The practical experience of these witnesses would justify a dependence on their testimony as to the possible reduction of expenses, especially in case the public feeling should be gained to change from the practice of having processions through the town to the practice of processions nearer to the cemeteries, by which the expenses of conveyance included in Mr. Wild's estimate would be diminished. It is stated by the latter that the disposition evinced by the higher classes, is to reduce expensive trappings. He states :—

Is it not an occurrence of increasing frequency amongst the respectable classes to express in their wills a wish to be buried plainly, and at moderate expense ?—Yes, it is ; and they sometimes fix sums. They fix such a sum as £150, where it has been usual to expend such sums as £400 or £500. Parties of respectability now begin to object to wearing cloaks and long hatbands. They are also beginning to object to the use of feathers, and to the general display. The system of performing funerals by written contract is also becoming very prevalent. It is so frequent with me that I must have some printed forms.

Mr. J. Browning of Manchester, member of the large society alluded to, as comprehending 150,000 members, states that they have evinced similar tendencies.

I have belonged to the Odd Fellows' Society and to the Foresters' Society, and have served office in both in this town, Manchester. I have belonged to them about 13 years.

Do you find any alteration in the dispositions of the members of those societies in respect to the ceremonies observed and the array at funerals? —Yes, a very great alteration.

In what respect ?—In Manchester and Liverpool it used to be the practice, when a member of either society died, that the members and the officers attended decorated with their regalia; and followed the corpse in procession. They used to assemble in bodies, as many as two or three hundred, and there was a great deal of drinking. Now these sort of processions are put a stop to by members, and there is no regalia or processions used. Only a few members attend the deceased member, and they attend only with black scarfs, white gloves, and a black silk hatband, which is considered respectful. But in some of the country places they still follow the practice, and they will have the processions.

But the general tendency is to render the ceremony more simple ?—Yes, and there is much less drinking in the towns.

§ 114. These manifestations are ascribable to a consciousness of the incompatibility of funereal displays through the crowded streets of populous districts, and are consistent with the desire to obtain proper respect for the deceased, shown in the objections to brief, meagre, and hurried services, and in the selection of secluded and decorated places of burial; it is shown, indeed, by the removal of the meretricious trappings, which have lost their effect, and the preference of a more quiet simplicity which, under such circumstances, forms a better means of ensuring that respect.

§ 115. Assuming the practicability of the accomplishment in this country of administrative arrangements such as have been accomplished, and are in habitual execution, abroad, to the great satisfaction of every class of society, a primary regulation, which would be practicable, would be to obtain for the public the opportunity of obtaining, at various scales, supplies of goods and services for funerals. To Mr. Wild the following questions were put :—

Do you believe it to be practicable, by proper regulations, greatly to reduce the existing charges of interments ?—Yes, a very great reduction indeed may be made—at least 50 per cent.

May it be confidently stated that under such reductions, whatever of respectability in exterior is now attached to the trapping, or to the mode of the ceremony, might be preserved ?—Oh, yes; I should say it might, and that they could scarcely fail to be increased.

Might not the expenses of the funerals of *the labouring classes* be greatly reduced without any reduction of the solemnity, or display of proper and satisfactory respect?—Very considerable reductions may be made, and attention to propriety very greatly increased. One large item of expense is the expense of bearers: they cost, for a walking funeral of an adult, 12s. Nine shillings of this expense would be dispensed with if the burial were at a cemetery. This would go towards the expense of conveyance, and contribute to the compensation: besides, it would avoid for the mourners the inconvenience and annoyance of walking through the crowded streets, often in wet weather. One circumstance attending burial in cemeteries would be, a diminution of the number of mourners: this would occasion a diminution of the expense of funeral fittings.

What is the lowest price for which a coffin is made ?—The lowest priced coffin at this time, is the adult pauper's coffin, with a shroud, but with no cloth or nails, or name-plate or handles, and costs 3s. 6d.; the contract is usually for deal, inch thick, but they never are; if they were, they could not be supplied under 4s.; they often break when taken to the grave.

What would be the price of a coffin deemed respectable by the labouring classes, with name-plate and appropriate fittings complete, if manufactured for an extensive supply?—The average price of such coffins is now about 35s.; but the same quality of coffin might be supplied on a large scale for about 17s.

What would be the price of coffins for persons of the middle class, if supplied on a similar scale?—The prices vary with them from 3l. to 10l.; they have frequently double coffins; the same coffins might be supplied from 30s. to 5l., or 50 per cent. less.

§ 116. Mr. Hewitt, whose testimony has already been referred to, states, that under general arrangements, it would be practicable to alleviate the evil of the expense to an extent which would appear incredible. He says—

I have so far carefully considered the subject, that I should be ready to take a contract for the performance of burials at the following rates:—For a labouring man, 1l. 10s. without burial fees; for a labourer's child, 15s., for a tradesman, 2l. 2s.; for a tradesman's child, 1l. 1s.; for a gentleman, 6l. 7s. 6d.; for a gentleman's child, 3l. 10s. These expenses are for "walking funerals;" the expenses of hearses and carriages would depend on the distance, and would make from one to two guineas each carriage extra.

All these, with the same descriptions of coffins, and with the same respectability of attendance?—Yes, on the scale of about half the existing burials in the metropolis; if it were for the whole, it might be done much better, and in some instances perhaps at a greater rate of reduction.

§ 117. Mr. Wild gives, on similar grounds, the following estimate of the practicable rates of expenses of interment with all decent appliances:—

	Tradespeople.				Mechanics.			
	Adults.		Children.		Adults.		Children.	
	From.	To.	From.	To.	From.	To.	From.	To.
	£. s.	£. s.	£. s.	£. s.	£. s.	£. s.	£. s.	£. s.
Coffin	1 5	4 4	0 15	1 10	0 17	1 5	0 10	0 15
Fittings, &c. . .	0 15	2 0	0 10	1 0	0 10	0 15	0 5	0 10
Sundries . . .	..	..	..	..	..	..	..	..
Conveyance . .	1 1	4 4	1 1	2 2	0 17	1 1	0 10	1 1
Totals . . .	3 1	10 8	2 6	4 12	2 4	3 1	1 5	2 6

§ 118. Next to the arrangements practicable for the regulation of the supplies of goods, the most important practicable arrangements for reduction of expense are those which may regulate the services necessary for interments. The item set forth in the above estimate of the charge for conveyance is on the supposition of separate conveyance in the present mode to the distant cemetery. With reference to the charge for the poorer classes, Mr. Wild was asked—

Might not several sets of mourners be carried in one conveyance?—

Yes; that has often occurred to me, and it would tend to reduce the expense materially. When two or three children have died in one street, and they have had to be buried in the same cemetery, I have asked the parents whether, as they had to go to the same place, they objected to go in the same conveyance, and they have frequently stated that they had no objections. These were of the more respectable classes of mechanics.

In the fittings up of the coffins, is it considered that these would be as good as those now used?—Quite as good.

§ 119. One large item in the expense of funerals in the metropolis and populous districts is the expense of bearers, § 115, who are provided for each separate funeral. This expense is about 12*s.* for a set of bearers for the funeral of an adult of the working classes. Formerly common bearers were provided by the several parishes in the metropolis. Any arrangements of a national character would include the provision of a better regulated class of bearers at a greatly reduced expense. In the course of the examination of Mr. Dix, the following information was elicited:—

It has been suggested that, if the hearse were always used, the expense of bearers would be dispensed with in walking funerals. What do you conceive would be the case?—I conceive that that would not be the case, inasmuch as it would require bearers to remove the body from the house to the hearse, and from the hearse to the grave. But this difficulty might, I would suggest, be, to a great extent, obviated by the establishment of public bearers, who should have the exclusive right of removing all corpses, and whose rate of payment should be fixed.

What is the present rate of payment of bearers to the grave for the labouring classes?—It is 2*s.* 6*d.* each.

If public bearers were appointed, what might be the expense?—Much less than one-half.

Do you think that this principle of management would be satisfactory to the working classes?—It is in fact an old method. Formerly there were bearers in all parishes, appointed by the churchwardens. In the parish of St. Margaret's, Westminster, and in most of the city parishes, the practice continues to this day.¹ In the form of bills of the various parish dues the charge for bearers remains to the present day.

Were these parish bearers less expensive than others?—No; they were not.

Why were they discontinued?—In consequence of these bearers often becoming undertakers themselves, which created a jealousy amongst the trade, who refused to employ them, and the parishes had no power to compel their employment. Also in consequence of the men being elected by the churchwardens; they were seldom elected until they became of an age that rendered them incapable of performing the duties properly. They were not properly dressed, and were under no control. In recommending public bearers, I presume they would be under a different control than a parochial one or than the churchwardens. I would add, however, that as one set of bearers cannot carry a corpse more than a mile, I would only propose them in aid of the hearses.

§ 120. Mr. Wild, who had previously volunteered the suggestion as to the means of reducing the expenses of conveyance, by arrangements on an extensive scale, observes, further, in reference to the bearers—

" My first view as to the possible economy of funerals, was derived from seeing that parish bearers were often made use of. The present charge for bearers for mechanics is 12s. for the adults, or 3s. per bearer. I was asking one of the parish bearers what he was allowed, as the charge was included in the burial dues, which were 1l. 5s. 6d.. He told me they were paid 6d. per bearer, or 2s. the set. He told me that they had borne six to the grave that morning, and he had earned 3s. himself. This at the usual charge would have been 3l. 12s.; but properly provided bearers at the cemetery might reduce the charges still further, perhaps to 3d. each case."

§ 121. Before submitting for consideration any detailed arrangements for securing, in a manner satisfactory to the people, better funerals at less oppressive charges, it is necessary to premise, that there appear to be no grounds to expect the extensive spontaneous adoption of improved regulations by the labouring classes without aid *ab extra.* The labour of communicating information to them, to be attended to at the time it is wanted, would be immense. Their sources of information on the occurrence of such events are either poor neighbours, as ignorant as themselves, or persons who are interested in misleading them and profiting by their ignorance, to continue expensive and mischievous practices. As against such an evil as the undue retention of the bodies amidst the living the usual mode of effecting a change would be simply by a prohibitory ordinance, § 91, of which information would be conveyed practically by the enforcement of penalties for disobedience of the law, which it is assumed they know. The appointment of a responsible agency, which would be respected, to convey the information of what may be deemed requisite for the protection of the living and exercise influence to initiate a change of practice, appears to all the practical witnesses examined, § 102, to be a preferable course, as being the most suitable to the temper of the people, and as being the least expensive, as well as the most efficient. The very desolate and unprotected condition of the survivors of the poorest classes, on the occurrence of a death in large towns, appears to render some intervention for their guidance and protection at that moment peculiarly requisite, as a simple act of beneficence. Mr. Wild was asked—

Amongst the poorer classes, is not the widow often made ill during the protracted delay of the burial?—Yes, very often. They have come to me in tears, and begged for accommodation, which I have given them. On observing to them, you seem very ill; a common reply is, " Yes, I feel very ill. I am very much harassed, and I have no one to assist me." I infer from such expressions that the mental anxiety occasioned by the expense, and want of means to obtain the money, is the frequent cause of their illness. My opinion is, that unless the undertaker gave two-thirds of them time or accommodation for payment, they would not be able to bury the dead at all.

You state that they have no persons to assist them; do they frequently, or ever, on such occasions, see any persons of education, or of influence, from whom they might receive aid or advice?—I never hear of such persons unless they happen to be connected with some local association, when the survivors are visited and get advice, and sometimes relief.

If any gentleman were to visit them as a public officer, as the officer of a board of health, would his recommendations have influence with them?—

Very great: the doctor now has the greatest influence with them, but he does not attend them after the death.

John Downing, a mechanic, the secretary of a Burial Society, whose duty it was to visit the remains of the deceased members, was asked—

After the death of the party have you ever, in visiting the deceased, met any professional person or any gentleman attending to give advice or consolation to the widow?—No. Never to my knowledge.

Then on what advice will the widow act on the occurrence of a death?— On the advice of the poor people in the neighbourhood, or of any friends or relatives that may chance to call upon them; but I never knew either medical man or minister attend professionally to give advice or consolation.

Is any notice of the death sent to the minister?—The working-classes never think of that; the first thing and the only thing thought of by them is to scrape together the money for the funeral.

Do you think that a medical officer, an officer of public health, attending gratuitously to inspect the body and register the cause of death, and to give advice as to the proper means of conducting the funeral, and the steps to be taken for the health of the living would be respectfully received and have influence?—I am very confident that he would have a very hearty welcome. I think a deal of benefit would be derived from it to the feelings as well as the health of the parties.

§ 122. The curate of a populous district mentioned to me, as illustrative of the practice in the crowded neighbourhoods in the metropolis, that he had for a time lived in a house let off in lodgings to respectable persons in the middle ranks of life, and though his profession was known in the house, yet three deaths had taken place in it of which he had no notice whatever, and only knew of them at the time of the funeral. All the witnesses who have had experience amongst the labouring classes, concur in the expression of confidence that the visits and intervention of a public officer would at such a time be well received by the poorest classes.

Mr. Hewitt was asked—

Do you conceive that respectable officers visiting the house of all classes of the deceased immediately after the death, as medical officers and officers of public health, to inquire as to the causes of death and register them, would long fail to acquire powerful influence in the suggestion of voluntary and beneficial sanitary arrangements?—I think that an officer appointed from the first class of physicians would be better received than a local medical man—as an officer of the public health, whose opinions would be more prized, and consequently would be sure to be received by all most respectfully. Such an officer is calculated to do more good than can easily be conceived, and would be able to execute such duties over an extensive district.

Would they have that sort of faith in a physician that they would not have in any local medical officer?—They would receive well any gentleman, and would act upon his advice.

On the occurrence of a death, is there any one person of education, or of superior condition in life, who comes near the working classes?—Not one that I am aware; no one attends for such a purpose; if any such person comes it must be accidental.

It may perhaps be presumed that it is rare that any death occurs without some medical man or medical officer having attended the case?—Very few, and in those cases inquests are usually held.

In the majority of cases, therefore, the labouring classes, on the occurrence of a death, are left either to the advice of any interested person who may come amongst them, or to the influence of their equally uninformed neighbours?—Yes, certainly, that is the case.

§ 123. The principle of the measure proposed, *i. e.* a certificate of the fact, and the cause of death, given on view of the body, and the non-interment without such certificate, has been in operation perhaps during two centuries. In the year 1595, orders were issued by the Privy Council to the justices, enjoining them, that wherever the plague appeared, they would see that the ministers of the church, or three or four substantial householders, appointed persons to view the bodies of all who died, before they were suffered to be buried. They were to certify to the minister or the churchwarden, of what disease it was probable each individual had died. The minister or the churchwarden was to make a weekly return of the numbers in his parish that were infected, or had died, and the diseases of which it was probable they had died. These returns were to be made to the neighbouring justices, and by them to the clerk of the peace, who was to enter them in a book to be kept for the purpose. The justices, who assembled every three weeks, were to forward the results to the Lords of the Privy Council. It is supposed that this scheme of registration gave rise to the bills of mortality, which have been preserved without interruption from the year 1603 until the present period. It is conjectured also, that the appointment of " searchers " originated at the same time. The alarm of the plague having subsided, the office of searcher was, until the recent appointments of registrars under the new Registration Act, given by the parish officers to two old women in each parish, frequently pew-openers, who, having viewed the body, demanded a fee of two shillings, in addition to which they expected to be supplied with some liquor, and gave a certificate of the fact and cause of death as they were informed of it, and this certificate was received by the minister as a warrant for the interment.

§ 124. The Rev. Mr. Stone observes on this topic—

It would be well if the burial of the dead could be expedited by some agency created for the purpose ; something, for instance, like the obsolete office of searcher. I never heard but one person make an objection even to those inferior functionaries, and that one was an educated person, who would probably have withdrawn the objection, had the agency been one of a more refined, intelligent, and conciliatory character. It might be a more delicate matter to secure the removal of the corpse to be deposited elsewhere for any considerable time before the burial ; though, judging from one practice, which has fallen under my observation, I feel justified in supposing, that even this would not be met with universal repugnance. A similar thing is now often done spontaneously from a pecuniary motive, and for the purpose of evading burial dues. In my parish ground, and, I believe, in others, the fees for the burial of a non-parishioner, or person dying out of the parish, are double those payable for a parishioner. But, if the undertaker employed is a parishioner, this extra payment is easily evaded, by his accommodating the corpse on his own premises. It is brought there some time before the burial, and frequently from a considerable distance; it then becomes a resident parishioner, and forthwith claims the privilege of a parishioner. It claims to be admitted into our burial ground at single fees; and, of course, the claim so made cannot easily be disallowed. Indeed, by a little management, this smuggling of dead bodies may be effected so that my clerk and sexton, the only officers in my preventive service, may themselves know nothing about it. It is probable, however, that such sanitary arrangements as those adverted to would be best facilitated, and it is certain that much mischief would be entirely prevented, by a reduction in the amount of burial expenses. Indeed these expenses ought, if possible, to be reduced for the sake of all classes, whether they arise from too high a rate of burial fees, from the prejudices of the people, or from the advantage that may be taken of those prejudices or other circumstances by a class so directly and deeply interested as the undertakers.

§ 125. Several physicians of eminence in the metropolis, who are conversant with the state and feelings of families of the middle and higher classes on the occurrence of a death, have expressed their confidence, that the most respectable families, who are stunned by the blow, and are ignorant of the detail of the steps to be taken when a death has occurred, would gladly pay for the attendance of any respectable and responsible person, on whose information they might, under such circumstances, rely. As already stated, the physician takes no cognizance of the arrangements for interments, and knowing the feelings that commonly arise when the undertaker's bill is presented, carefully avoids giving advice, or doing anything that may implicate him with the arrangements for the interment.

§ 126. In opening the consideration of remedial measures, it appears incumbent to represent that there are many who, viewing what has been accomplished abroad, and the inconvenience experienced in the metropolis in respect to the oldest private trading burial grounds, object on principle to the abandonment of acknowledged public functions and services, and to leaving the necessities of the public as sources of profit to private, and (practically for every-day purposes) irresponsible associations. They submit, that if the steps in this direction cannot be retraced, the public have claims that at all events they shall be stayed. Such opinions may, perhaps, be the best represented in the following portion of the communication from the Rev. Wm. Stone.

It may be thought that, in alluding to these private burial grounds, I have expressed myself strongly, and indeed I am not anxious to disavow having done so. The subject seems to me to justify such a tone of expression. In all ages and nations, the burial of the dead has been invested with peculiar sanctity. As the office that closes the visible scene of human existence, it concentrates in itself the most touching exercise of our affections towards objects endeared to us in this life, and the most intense and stirring anxieties that we can feel respecting an invisible state. And, appealing thus to common sympathies of our nature, it has been universally marked by observances intended to give it importance or impressiveness. The faith and usage of Christians have given remarkable prominence to this duty. The ecclesiastical institutes of our own country indicate a jealous solicitude for the safe and religious custody of the receptacles of the dead; and there are few of us, perhaps, to whom those receptacles are not hallowed by thoughts and recollections of the deepest personal interest. It is reasonable, then, that the reverential impressions thus accumulated within us should shrink from the contact of more selfish and vulgar associations. And one may be excused for thinking and speaking strongly in reprobation of a system which degrades the burial of the dead into a trade. Throughout the whole scheme and working of this system, there is an exclusive spirit of money-getting, which is revoltingly heartless; and in some of its details there is an indecency which I have felt myself compelled to allude to in the tone of strong condemnation.

It is surely desirable that a state of things so vulgar and demoralizing, should be put an end to, but at present there seems no prospect of it. Of course, during the continuance of a competition such as I have described, our parishioners will never return to our parish burial grounds, and I have already remarked, that if they did, they might not get interment there, inasmuch as it would, perhaps, be found impossible to make our parochial system meet the wants of any crowded population. There is little better chance of the present offensive system of burial being superseded by the joint stock cemeteries; for to the mass of our population these cemeteries hold out hardly any advantages which are not possessed by the private burial grounds, while they have to compete with those grounds under disadvantages greater, in some instances, than those which our churchyards have to contend with.

Indeed, even if it were practicable, I should be sorry to see our people handed over for burial to a joint stock company. I am very far from saying this out of any sympathy with the popular, and often indiscriminate and unreasonable jealousy felt towards all joint stock companies. Nay, I see obvious reasons why the cemeteries of such companies should be a great improvement upon the present system of private speculation in burial grounds. And it may be thought that, as a clergyman and an interested party, I may naturally prefer these cemeteries, because their proprietors, unlike the private speculators, are required to indemnify the clergy for loss of fees by some amount of pecuniary compensation. But I do sympathize with the common repugnance to consign to joint stock companies the solemnities of Christian burial; and I believe that this repugnance is not more common than it is strong. "And so," said a highly intelligent gentleman, pointing to a cemetery of this class, "the time is come when Christian burial is made an article of traffic." And since the legislature has been reported to be contemplating the removal of burials from populous places, it has been commonly suspected of having been led to entertain the measure through the influence of joint stock cemetery proprietors. In fact the repugnance in question is no more than what I have already adverted to. It is the state of feeling which shrinks from associating the touching and impressive solemnities of burial with the profits of trade. So far as the trading principle is involved, the joint stock company is no better than the private speculator. However disinterested may have been the motives which have induced some to become shareholders in these companies, and I have been assured upon authority which I respect, that many have done so without any expectation or hope of profit upon their shares, yet the primary and effective character of these associations is undeniably that of trading associations, and they cannot be rescued from that character by even numerous individual exceptions. Their managers, like the proprietors of the private grounds, are assiduous in soliciting attention to their lists of prices; and affiches, painted in large letters, and placed at various outlets of the metropolis, with genuine mercantile officiousness, direct the public, as in a case close by my own parish, "To the E. L. Cemetery, only one mile and a-half." Surely we may say, that this system also involves much that is inconsistent with reverential impressions of the sanctity of burial, much that must either offend or deteriorate the better feeling of our population. Then again, as regards burial services, and other details in the working of the system, with what security can we consign these to the tender mercies of a trading company? Why should not the money-getting principle eventually come to operate upon these points also, and, as in the private burial grounds, tempt shareholders to sanction indecent and mischievous condescensions to the interests, habits, tastes, and caprices of the people? What security, at least, is there equal to that which is afforded by a clergy and parochial establishments, responsible to the civil and ecclesiastical authorities of the country, or which would be afforded by what, for reasons before mentioned, I should think still preferable, a national plan of burial, placed under a departmental control of Government?

The remedial measures hereafter submitted for consideration have been deduced directly from the actual necessities experienced within the field of inquiry, and such only are submitted as clearly suggested themselves without reference to any external experience. The following preliminary view of the experience of other nations is presented for consideration on account of the confirmatory evidence which it contains, as well as the instances to be avoided.

Examples of successful Legislation for the Improvement of the Practice of Interment.

§ 127. It appears that the evil of the expensive interments consequent on the monopoly which the nature of the event, and the feelings of survivors, gives to the person nearest at hand for the performance of the undertaker's service, is checked by special arrangements in America. In Boston, and most of the large towns in America, there is a Board of Health which nominates a superintendent of burial grounds, who is invariably a person of special qualifications, and generally a medical man. All undertakers are licensed by the Board of Health, by whom the licence may at any time be revoked. The sexton of the church which the deceased attended is usually the undertaker. The bills of the undertaker are made out on a blank form, furnished by the public superintendent of interment, to whom all bills are submitted, and by whom they are audited and allowed, before they are presented for payment to the relations or friends of the deceased. Previous to interment, the undertaker must obtain from the physician who last attended the deceased, a certificate specifying the profession, age, time of illness, and cause of death of the deceased. This certificate is presented to the superintendent of funerals. An abstract of these certificates, signed by the superintendent of funerals, is printed every week in the public journals of the city. The cost of a funeral for a person in the position of life of the highest class of tradesmen in Boston, is about fifty dollars, or 10*l.* English, exclusive of the cost of the tomb. The price of a good mahogany coffin would be fifteen dollars, or 3*l.* 5*s.* The price of a most elegant mahogany coffin would be perhaps double that price. The price of a pine coffin, such as are used for the persons of the labouring classes, would be about four dollars. There is a peculiarity in the coffins made in the United States,—that a portion of the lid, about a foot from the upper end, opens upon a hinge. This, when opened, exposes to view the face of the deceased, which is covered with glass. The survivors are thus enabled at the last moment to take a view of the deceased, without the danger of infection. In Germany, the coffins are nailed down, every blow of the hammer frequently drawing a scream from the female survivors.

§ 128. In the chief German states it is adopted as a principle, that provision shall be made, and it is made successfully, for meeting the necessities of the population in respect to the undertakers' supplies of service and materials; and that on the occurrence of a death, those necessities shall not be given up as the subject of common trading profits to whatsoever irresponsible person may obtain the monopoly of them. At Franckfort provision is made for these services and supplies of material at the lowest cost to the public as part of a series of arrangements comprehending the verification of the fact of death on view of the body, the edifice for the reception and care of the dead previous to interment, and the public cemeteries, all under the superintendence of superior and responsible medical officers. The expenses of the supplies of materials are reduced so low under these arrangements, that they no longer enter into serious consideration as a burthen to be met on such occasions.

§ 129. At Berlin, a contract is made by the Government with one person to secure funeral materials and services for the public at certain fixed scales of prices. The materials and services are stated to be of a perfectly satisfactory character; and yet the undertaker's charge for a funeral such as would here cost for an artisan 4*l.* and upwards, is not more than 15*s.* English money; the charge for a middle class funeral is about 2*l.*, and for a funeral of the opulent class of citizens is about 10*l.* And yet I am assured that the contractors' profits on the extensive supplies required are deemed too high, and that the Government will, on the renewal of the contract, find it necessary to protect the poorer classes by a contract at a lower rate.

§ 130. At Paris, interments are made the subject of a *fisc;* but a contract is made with one head to secure services and supplies to the private individual at reduced rates, and so far the system works advantageously to the public.

§ 131. The whole of the interments are there performed, and the various burial and religious dues collected and paid under one contract, by joint contractors for the public service at regulated prices, called *the Service des Pompes Funèbres.* This establishment annually buries gratis, upwards of 7000 destitute persons, or nearly one-third of all who die in the city. The funerals and religious services are divided into nine classes, comprehending various settled particulars of service, for which a price is fixed.

The appointed service for any of these classes may be had on the terms specified in a tariff. This is found to be a great benefit to testators and survivors, as it enables them to settle the ceremonial with certainty, and without the possibility of any extortion. The first class of funerals are of great pomp: they include bearers, crosses, plumes, eighteen mourning coaches and attendants, grand mass at church, 120 lbs. of wax tapers, an anniversary service, and material of mourning cloth; and also the attendance of Monsieur le Curé, two vicars, twenty-one priests, six singers and ten chorister boys, and two instrumental performers, at a cost of 145*l.*, for a funeral superior in magnificence perhaps to any private funeral in England. The charge for the service and materials of the ninth class, in which there is the attendance of a vicar and a priest, and of a bass singer or chorister for the mass, is about 15*s.* of English money. In the service ordinaire there is less religious service, and that is performed gratuitously. The only charge made is the price of the coffin, which is five or seven francs, according to the size: the coffin is covered by a pall, and carried on a plain hearse, drawn by two black horses. This funeral is conducted by a superintendant and four assistants, exclusive of the driver. The following is the scale of charges, and the numbers interred under each, during two years:—

	1st Class.	2nd Class.	3rd Class.	4th Class.	5th Class.	6th Class.	7th Class.	8th Class.	9th Class.	Total of the Nine Classes.	Service Ordinaire.	General Total.
Religious Funeral Service	£. 24	£. 19	£. 11	£. 8	£. s. 5 10	£. 2	£. 1	£. s. 0 16	s. 11	..	..	..
Anniversary Religious Service . . .	26	20	12	9	6 0	3	..	..	..	..	..	..
Undertaker's Material and Service . . .	95	83	49	23	14 10	5	3	1 11	4	..	..	..
Total Expenses .	145	122	72	40	26 0	10	4	2 7	15	..	..	..
Number of Burials { 1839 .	23	52	138	256	828	1,457	2,523	141	530	5,958	14,087	20,045
{ 1841 .	30	47	188	201	816	1,655	2,377	78	715	6,107	14,185	20,292

§ 132. On the number of burials in Paris for 1841, the gross income would be about 80,000*l.* per annum. Out of this sum the contractor pays the fixed salaries of the staff of officers, which consists of a chief inspector of funeral ceremonies, of 27 other directors besides, 78 bearers, one inspector of cemeteries and four keepers; officers chiefly appointed by the municipality. The total amount of the salaries which he pays is 5862*l.*, English money. He keeps an establishment of 30 hearses and 76 carriages, with suites of minor attendants properly clothed, and inters the 7000 of the pauper class gratuitously. The last contractor paid annually to the municipality 17,000*l.*, which sum was chiefly devoted to ecclesiastical objects. The large profits which he realized led to considerable competition, and a new contract was recently sealed for nine years, securing for public purposes an annual income of 28,000*l.*

Besides this amount, there is a revenue of about 20,000*l.* per annum derived by the municipality from the sale of tombs, and from the tax on interments, which is twenty francs for the inter ment of every adult, and ten francs upon children under seven years of age. One-fifth of this revenue, or about 4000*l.*, is devoted to the hospitals.

§ 133. The remains of those who die in the public hospitals in Paris, and are not claimed by their friends, are, after dissection, merely enclosed in a coarse cloth and deposited in the ground, without any funereal rites. This number amounts, as stated, to no less than 7000 annually. The total average deaths in Paris is from 28,000 to 30,000 annually. This, in a population of 900,000, gives about one burial to every thirty of the population annually, which is nearly as large a proportion of annual deaths and burials as that in Manchester. The deaths and burials in the British metropolis (though varying in different parts, from 1 in 28, as in White-chapel, to 1 in 56, as in Hackney, chiefly according to the condition of the locality) average for the entire population of 1,800,000 inhabitants, one death or burial in every forty-two of the inhabitants, or one-fourth less of burials than at Paris in proportion to the population. In Paris the average number of inhabitants to every house is 36. If the mortality were there in the proportion of London there would be 7,000 fewer burials yearly. An assertion may be ventured, that more than this excess of mortality is ascribable to the still lower sanitary condition of the labouring population in Paris, which has its concomitant in a still lower moral condition than yet prevails amongst the population of our large towns.*

* In a paper read on the 2nd January last before the Academy of Sciences at Paris, by M. le Baron Charles Dupin, on the increase of savings' banks and their influence on the Parisian population, some most startling facts are mentioned in the conclusion, showing the deplorable moral condition of a large portion of that population. "Le nombre proportionnel des indigents, au lieu d'augmenter, diminue, ainsi que celui des bâtards, mais avec lenteur déplorable ; au commencement de l'époque dont nous résumons les progrès, le peuple de Paris abandonnait chaque année 205 enfants sur 1,000 nouveau nés ; il n'en abandonne plus que 120 : c'est beaucoup moins, et pourtant c'est *cent vingt* fois trop. Encore aujourd'hui, le *tiers* du peuple vit dans le concubinage ou dans le libertinage ; un *tiers* de ses enfants sont bâtards ; un *tiers* de ses morts expirent à l'hôpital ou sur le grabat du pauvre ; et ni père, ni mère, ni fils, ni filles, n'ont le cœur, pour dernier tribut humain, de donner un cercueil, un linceul, au cadavre de leurs proches :—du côté des mœurs, voilà Paris, et Paris amélioré !"— It may on this point of comparison be a relief to state, the numbers who die in the workhouses in the British metropolis, do not exceed 4000 for nearly double the population, and that of these, on the average of the last ten years, not more than 293 have been so given up or abandoned as to be applicable to the public service in the schools of anatomy. The total number who are abandoned in all the hospitals of London, for that service, has not, on the average, exceeded 168 out of upwards of 2000 deaths per annum. The total number of subjects requisite for teaching in the

§ 134. In Paris the law requires that the dead shall be interred within twenty-four hours after the decease, but this law may be evaded by neglect to give notice of the death. The general prac-

schools of anatomy would be about 600. Notwithstanding that the prejudice against dissection has much abated, the full number deemed requisite has never been obtained of late years from all sources. In some instances, persons of education set an example by giving up their own bodies for dissection; in some other instances, the use of the remains is obtained by persuasions, and the promises of more respectful interment afterwards, than could otherwise be obtained. There are actually very few real "abandonments" by relations, the greater proportion of cases being of persons who have outlived near relations, of whom none, after due enquiry, which is always made, can be found. In respect to illegitimate births, it appears from the last parliamentary return of the number of illegitimate children born in the several counties of England (that of Mr. Rickman,) for 1833, that the proportion of illegitimate to legitimate births, was in Middlesex, 1 in 38; and in Surrey 1 in 40. This was most probably an understatement, but, whatever may be the real proportions they are below any comparison with the proportions in Paris. The highest proportion of illegitimate to legitimate births given in the returns, were those of the county of Pembroke, 1 in 8; and Radnor, where it is 1 in 7. It may be important to state for the sake of the example, and in illustration of the principle, as to the comparative economy of sanitary arrangements that this excess of 7,000 miserable deaths and burials per annum in Paris, at the least, might be saved by structural sanitary arrangements, which would prevent the accumulation of human beings in winding streets, (some of which are not more than eight or nine feet wide,) under circumstances which render decency, morality, health, or contentment impossible. The whole excess of deaths, as well as the demoralization that arises from overcrowding, might in all probability be saved even by the last vote of expenditure, five millions sterling, (which, at English prices, of 100*l.* for a tenement for a family, would have provided improved tenements, at improved rents, for fifty thousand labourers' families) for maintaining the war on the Arabs, or by the interest of the money expended in building the immense wall and fortifications round the dangerous population (kept "desperate," as Jeremy Taylor expresses it, "by a too quick sense of a constant infelicity,") which those works encircle in Paris. In a copy of a report of the medical commissioners, appointed to examine the cholera, with which I have been favoured by one distinguished member, M. Villerme, and in which I have found powerful corroborative evidence on the influence of structural arrangements on the health and moral, not to speak of the political, condition of the population; they observe, "Le fléau qui a pesé si cruellement sur la capitale s'est fait sentir d'une manière particulièrement désastreuse dans les quartiers étroits, sales et embarrassés de l'ancien Paris; n'y aurait-il pas lieu de signaler ici quelques améliorations utiles à introduire dans ces localités? Les raisons d'état ont souvent; dominé les intérêts matériels des villes; autrefois les voies étroites et tortueuses appliquées même aux rues pouvait faire partie des moyens de défense à l'usage de l'état; aujourd'hui des rues larges et droites deviennent dans l'intérieur des villes un premier élément de sécurité publique autant que d'hygiène; il y a donc double avantage à favoriser dans ces conditions, soit des percements nouveaux, soit l'élargissement des voies actuelles." They give forcible descriptions of population analogous to that found— happily in less proportions,—in the worst part of our cities, and they also attest, from the examination of the inferior population of that capital: "C'est une vérité de tous les temps, de tous les lieux, une vérité, qu'il faut redire sans cesse parceque sans cesse on l'oublie; il existe entre tice, however, appears to be, that interments take place within two days.

· § 135. In America, the later regulations manifest the tendency of the general experience to connect the regulations of interment with the general regulations for the protection of the public health,

l'homme et tout ce qui l'entoure, de secrets liens, de mystérieux rapports dont l'influence sur lui est continuelle et profonde. Favorable, cette influence ajoute à ses forces physiques et morales, elle les develope, les conserve ; nuisible, alors elle les altère, les anéantit, les tue. Mais son action n'est jamais plus redoutable que lorsqu'elle trouve à s'exercer sur une population entassée, quelle qu'elle soit d'ailleurs, et voilà pourquoi l'on observe dans certains arrondissements une mortalité plus grande ; voilà pourquoi le germe des maladies s'y developpe plus constamment, pourquoi la vie s'y éteint plus rapidement, enfin pourquoi l'on y compte habituellement un décès sur trente-deux habitants, quand il n'y en a qu'un sur quarante dans les autres." They also indicate as part of the effects of the noxious physical causes the moral depravity and the predominance of bad passions which impede amendment. "Ces obstacles sont réels, ils ne sauraient être méconnus, mais qui peut douter de les voir s'affaiblir, si d'une part la classe aisée de la population, comprenant mieux les intentions de l'autorité et ses intérêts véritables, se prête plus aisément à l'action des règlements sur la propreté et la salubrité publique, et si d'une autre part l'instruction, pénétrant dans cette portion de la population qui doit une partie de ses vices et de sa misère à l'ignorance, fait naître chez elle, avec des mœurs plus pures, des habitudes plus réuglières et plus en harmonie avec l'hygiène publique?" But these representations of the Medical Commissioners of Paris have not been heard by the classes appealed to, and relief is sought by the mode of " giving vent" to the dangerous passions in preference to the superior treatment recommended, of the removal of the physical circumstances by which those passions must continue to be generated. Thus it may be mentioned in illustration of the important principle of the superior economy and efficiency of structural means of prevention, that the expenditure of money on Algiers appears to have been upwards of four millions sterling per annum, during the twelve years of its occupation. The capital sunk on the permanent structural arrangements for supplying London with water being about three millions and a half, it may be safely alleged that one year's expenditure on Algiers would have sufficed for the structural arrangements for a supply of water for the cleansing of every room, and house, and street in Paris ; or on the scale of the expense of the works completed for supplying Toulouse with water, one year's expenditure on Algiers would have sufficed to supply one hundred and fifty towns of the same size as Toulouse with the like means of healthful, and thence of moral improvement ; or such a sum would have sufficed to have effected for ever the "percements et enlargissements des voies actuelles," and thence to have advanced the health and achieved the comparative security of four or five such cities as Lyons. One year's cost of any one regiment maintained in the war on the Arabs would suffice to build and endow a school, or to have constructed between one and two miles of permanent railway. The total amount of capital so applied exceeds nearly by one-fourth the amount expended on the existing railroads in Great Britain. It may be confidently averred that the cost of the forts detaches, or *encientes-continues*, said to be on a reduced scale upwards of ten millions sterling, would, if properly directed, with the accessaries of moral appliances in addition to such physical means as those indicated by the officers of public health, suffice within the period of the living generation, to renovate the physical and moral condition of the great mass of the population in the interior of that capital.

and to do this by single, specially qualified, paid, and responsible officers, rather than by Boards, or by any unskilled and honorary agency. The revised statutes of Massachusetts introduce the alternative of the appointment of a single officer. Every town is empowered to appoint a Board of Health, " or a health officer:" and the Board so appointed may appoint "a physician to the Board." The Board acting by such officer may destroy, remove, or prevent, as the case may require, all nuisances, sources of filth, and causes of sickness. "Whenever any such nuisance or source of filth, or cause of sickness shall be found on private property, the Board of Health, or health officer, shall order the owner or occupant thereof at his own expense to remove the same within twenty-four hours, and if the owner or occupant shall neglect so to do, he shall forfeit a sum not exceeding one hundred dollars," c. 21, s. 10. In cases of the refusal of entry into private property, on complaint to a magistrate, the magistrate may thereupon issue his warrant, "directed to the sheriff, or either of his deputies, or to any constable of such town, commanding them to take sufficient aid, and being accompanied by two or more members of the said Board of Health, between the hours of sunset and sunrise, to repair to the place where such nuisance, source of filth, or cause of sickness complained of may be, and to destroy, remove, or prevent, the same, under the direction of such members of the Board of Health." The cleansing of the streets and houses is in most cases included in the functions of the Board of Health, or of the health officer, who regulates the removal of all refuse. Sec. 14, c. 21.

Every householder, when any of his family are taken ill, is required, on a penalty of one hundred dollars,—and every physician in the like penalty, on ascertaining that any person whom he visits is infected with the small-pox, or other disease dangerous to the public health,—to give immediate notice to the officers of public health, and they may, "unless the condition of such person is such as not to admit of his removal without danger of life," remove him at once to the public hospital, whatever may be his station in life. Sec. 43 and 44, c. 21.

I have been favoured by Dr. Griscom, the inspector of interments at New York, with the copy of a report on the sanitary condition of the population of that city ; which points out the great extent of deaths that are preventible by the adoption of means similar to those recommended in the General Report for the improvement of the sanitary condition of the population in Great Britain. This report, revealing extensive causes of death in New York, of which a large proportion of the population must have been unaware, may be adduced in proof of the immense services derivable from such an office, when zealously executed, in guarding against evils more destructive than wars.[*]

* Vide Appendix—Explanations of the District Mortuary Returns.

§ 136. In Munich, and in other towns in Germany, the visits and verification of the fact of death as the warrant for interment, is felt to be an important public security, and is highly popular ; but one cause of its popularity is the jurisprudential functions of the officer of health, as means of preventing premature interments, and the escape of crime ; for comparatively little attention appears yet to have been given to the practical means afforded by the office of tracing out and removing the causes of disease. The difficulty appears to be in respect to the jurisprudential functions of the officers of health to satisfy the public anxiety for the exercise of solemn care in *every* case of a multitude, where only one case in that multitude will, on the doctrine of chances, be a case calling for intervention ; and where it is not provided, as it may and ought to be, that the discovery of that one shall be a matter of deep personal interest, instead of a mere source of trouble to the officer himself, his examinations may be expected to degenerate into a routine in which the intended security will fail in the less obvious cases.

In later times very comprehensive regulations as to the sites and management of cemeteries, and the service of officers of health, who have charge of the cemeteries, have been adopted throughout the Austrian dominions, and it is stated that they work very satisfactorily. On the occasion of every death by accident or violence, or of suspicion, a close inquiry as to the causes is made by the town physician. In Vienna a strict inquiry is made into every such death by the following officers, who all attend for that purpose ;—namely, the town physician, the surgeon in chief, the professor of pathological anatomy, a lawyer, and in some cases, when analyses are required, a chemist. The results of their examinations are set forth in a "protocol," a carefully prepared document, *" bien motivé,"* which sometimes takes two or three days in drawing up. The effect of this inquiry is the prevention, to a great extent, of crimes of violence, and the production of public confidence. It is stated to be highly popular.

§ 137. In Paris some cases have of late occurred, which have created much public uneasiness by the evidence they afforded of the defective organization of the service of the officers of health, and occasioned it recently to undergo an examination with the view to the adoption of better securities. It appears that, from a very early period, to satisfy the public solicitude, the law required the fact of the reality of a death to be verified by the personal visit and inspection of the Maire of the district of the city where the death had taken place. Subsequently, the Maires were allowed to delegate this duty to officers of their own nomination, persons qualified for the duties by a medical education, and who were called *Officiers de Santé.* But the appointments thus made by the Maires did not give public satisfaction ; and in the year 1806 it was required that the persons appointed as " officiers de santé" by the Maires, should be chosen by them from amongst the doctors in medicine and surgery who were attached to the public hospitals. They appear, however, to have been mostly chosen without reference to public qualifications, from their own medical friends in private practice. This arrangement of appointing persons in private practice appears to have prevailed in other countries, and to have frustrated much of the benefits otherwise derivable from the institution. Thirty-five of these private practitioners are now appointed to perform the duty. Reports have gained ground that from negligent discharge of the duty, persons had even been buried alive, and that the verification had been given in cases of murder. On a recent commission of inquiry, the celebrated surgeon, M. Orfila, thus speaks of the necessity of the verification of the fact of the decease.

" It is possible to be interred alive! Interments may take place after murder, committed with the knife or by means of poison, without a suspicion being created that the death has been occasioned by violence. Ignorance or malevolence may attribute to crime deaths that have occurred from natural causes !"

After referring to ancient cases in which evidence was recorded of parties having been buried alive, he adduces the following recent instances of parties having been interred without due verification of the cause of death by the *Officier de Santé :—*

" We all know the case of the death of the grocer in the Rue de la Paix, who died of poison by arsenic. The interment took place after the verification of the death. In about a month afterwards I was called upon to examine the body as to the poison. Although the putrefaction of the corpse of the person who was of a very full habit had been much advanced, I was enabled to discover the presence of the arsenic by which the crime had been perpetrated.

" The widow Danzelle, of the Rue Beauregard, was found dead in her bed on the 1st of January, 1826. The certificate of the decease was given in due form to the relations to authorise the interment. In that certificate, given to M. le Commissaire de Police, the medical practitioner declared, ' the death has taken place, and it appears that it has been occasioned by a commotion of the brain with hæmorrhage.' ' The deceased' added he, ' lived alone ; she was found dead in her chamber, where she appeared to have fallen down.' The municipal authorities caused the interment to be adjourned, and required a new examination of the body in the presence of the Commissioner of Police, assisted by two doctors in medicine. The result of the examination was, ' that Madame the widow Danzelle had fallen under the blows of an assassin ; the corpse bore five recent wounds in the neck, made with a cutting instrument, and the carotid artery had been divided.'

" In the month of July, a child of Dame Revel, Rue de Siene Saint Germain, died very suddenly. The authorities being informed that the child had been the subject of much ill-treatment on the part of the parents, ordered an inquiry and *une expertise medico-legale.* The examination of the body showed that the rumours as to the barbarous conduct of Dame Revel, the mother, were but too well-founded. Dr. Olivier testified to the fact, that the body bore twenty-seven recent contusions on the body and members, and a fracture of nearly five inches in extent, which almost entirely broke through one of the bones of the cranium.

" The death of this poor child, which was three years and three months old, awakened suspicions which had arisen on the death of its eldest brother, of eight years of age, which had been interred on the 28th of February preceding. The body was disinterred, and Dr. Olivier, to whom this second examination was confided, notwithstanding the length of time that had occurred since the death, found traces of numerous contusions on the body and members, and a wound above the right ear, with a fracture and disjunction of the bones of the cranium."

And notwithstanding in this, as in the other case, the interment was effected without observations.*

After giving instances where the innocent were justified or suspicions were allayed by post mortem examinations, which proved that deaths suspected to have been from murder had occurred from natural causes, M. Orfila concludes by stating :—

"I do not believe that it often happens that persons are interred alive in Paris, though I must admit that such events may take place; but I am convinced that the earth has covered and continues to cover crimes without any suspicion being raised in respect to them."

§ 138. Another report imputes the neglects of the "officiers de santé," to the forgetfulness of duties, the force of habit or routine, the results of age and infirmities; and the chief remedy recommended, and now apparently in course of adoption in Paris, is the erection on the unsubstantial foundation of service by a number of private practitioners, of two additional stages as securities, namely, of three paid medical officers, who are to devote their time to the superintendence of the performance of the public duties by the private practitioners, and, secondly, a certain number of high honorary officers, who are to superintend both classes of paid officers. This is an example of one of those superficial alterations, in which, from want of firmness on the part of the legislature to compensate fairly and amply the interests which it is obviously necessary to disturb, and from not duly regarding and estimating the immense amount of pain and public evil which requires measures of alleviation of corresponding extent and efficiency; consequently from allowing that amount of pain and mortality to weigh as dust against local patronage and latent sinister interests,—that evil is only masked, and more widely and deeply spread by the intended remedy. Of a certainty the attention of every private practitioner, as he gains practice, whilst acting as a public officer, must every hour of the day be *from* his public duties, and *with* the means of adding to his emoluments. That the least possible time may be taken from them, the public duties are slurred over, conclusions are snapped from the readiest superficial incidents ; extensive and removable, but latent causes of evil, the development of which would require sustained and laborious examination, are perpetuated, by being stamped authoritatively as "accidental" or arbitrarily classed under some general term assigning the evils as the results of some inscrutable cause. The three superior paid inspectors will not long be able to stimulate the thirty-five private prac-

* Vide other instances cited in the Annales d' Hygienne.—Number 59, p. 153 to 159.

titioners to a close attention to their public duties against their paramount and ever-pressing interests, or will soon tire of doing so. The service will become one of mere routine and of short and easy acquiescence in all except the most extraordinary cases which present an appearance of danger to the officer himself if he overlook them; Under such arrangements, the functions of the office degenerates into a highly prejudicial form, protracting the evil; by creating an impression from the fact of the existence of the office, that all has been done in the way of prevention or remedy that can be done by such an officer. The admixture of private practice with important public duties in such cases, is attended with further evil in depriving the public of much volunteer service from the whole class of private practitioners, for many who would give information to advance science, or to aid the public service, can scarcely be expected to give cordial aid that may add to the credit and promote the interests of a rival. To the people themselves such services, from a locally connected private practitioner, are generally less acceptable than those of an independent and responsible public officer. The official service must, in time, fail to inspire confidence, for it must fail to elicit evidence to justify public confidence. The additional expense of the three additional officers will only have created an additional interest, in slurring over cases that may have been overlooked by the other class of officers, involving blame for remissness to the superior officers. When exposures do take place, these two classes of officers will only add to the means of perplexing public attention, and of dividing and weakening responsibility. If less than half the number of officers, devoting their whole time to the service, would be sufficient (as will be shown they would), for the efficient discharge of these highly important duties in London, less than one-third of the number would suffice in Paris.

§ 139. Except in the regulation of the expenses of the funerals, there appears to be nothing in the practice of interments in Paris, that deserves to be considered with a view to imitation. Indeed, the whole arrangements there are now under revision, and exertions are being made for their improvement. The little account that appears to have been at any time made of the feelings of the labouring classes, and the burial after dissection, of the poor dying in hospitals, without funereal rites, the almost total omission of any marks of sympathy or respect towards their remains,—cannot but have a most demoralizing effect on the survivors. The mode in which the evil of the retention of the corpse amidst the living is provided for by the law, which requires that interments shall take place within twenty-four hours after notice; must frequently oppress the feelings of the dying and of survivors; and harass them with alarms which the medical inspection provided, as we have seen, § 137, is not of a character to allay. The intermediate stage of removal provided at Franckfort and other German towns; the retention of the corpse in a separate room warmed and ventilated, and watched at all hours, and lighted during the night; the regular medical attendance and inspection, and other cares bestowed until there are unequivocal signs of dissolution, and the minds of all classes are satisfied, appears to be a superior arrangement, salutary in its effect and principle.* Beyond these benevolent arrangements may be commended the acts of real good will and charity by which the feelings of the labouring classes are consulted and satisfied by community of sepulture, and the benevolent care and spirit of good will in which it appears to be maintained.

Experience in respect to the sites of Places of Burial, and sanitary precautions necessary in respect to them.

There appear to be very important questions connected with the consideration of the site of the place of burial to populous districts.

§ 140. The question of the distance of places of burial (irrespective of convenience of conveyance) appears to be dependent on the numbers buried,—on the composition and preparation of the ground,—on the elevation or depression of the place of burial,—and its exposure to the atmosphere and the direction of the prevalent winds for the avoidance of habitations.

§ 141. The extent of burial ground requisite for any district will be determined by the rate of decomposition.

§ 142. At Franckfort and Munich, and in the other new cemeteries on the continent, where qualified persons have paid attention to the subject, the general rule is not to allow more than one body in a grave. The grounds for this rule are,—that, when only one body is deposited in a grave, the decomposition proceeds regularly,—the emanations are more diluted and less noxious than when the mass of remains is greater; and also that the inconvenience of opening the graves, of allowing escapes of miasma, and the indecency of disturbing the remains for new interments, is thereby avoided; and in the case of exhumations, the confusion and danger of mistaking the particular body is prevented.

§ 143. The progress of the decay of the body is various, according to the nature of the soil and the surrounding agencies. Clayey soils are antiseptic; they retain the gases, as explained by Mr. Leigh; they exclude the external atmosphere, and are also liable to the inconvenience of becoming deeply fissured in hot weather and then allowing the escape of the emanations which have been retained in a highly concentrated state. Loamy, ferruginous, and aluminous soils, moor earth, and bog, are unfavourable to decomposition; sandy, marly, and calcareous soils are favourable to it. Water, at a low temperature, has the tendency, as already explained, to promote only a languid decomposition, which sometimes produces adiposcire

* Vide Regulations at Franckfort and Munich, Appendix.

in bodies : a high and dry temperature tends to produce the consistency and permanency of mummies. A temperature of from 65 degrees Fahrenheit and upwards, and a moist atmosphere, is the most favourable to decomposition. The remains of the young decompose more rapidly than those of the old, females than males, the fat than the lean. The remains of children decompose very rapidly. On opening the graves of children at a period of six or seven years, the bodies have been found decomposed, not even the bones remaining, whilst the bodies of the adults were but little affected. The process of decomposition is also affected by the disease by which the death was occasioned. The process is delayed by the make of some sorts of coffins. The extreme variations of the process under such circumstances as those above recited is from a few months to 30 years or half a century. Bones often last for centuries.

§ 144. The regulation of the depth of the graves has been found to be a subject requiring great attention, to avoid occasioning too rapid an evolution of miasma from the remains, and at the same time to avoid its retention and corruption, to avoid the pollution of distant springs, and also to avoid rendering increased space for burial requisite by the delay of decomposition usually produced by deep burial, for the ground usually becomes hard in proportion to the depth, and delays the decomposition. Attention to these circumstances by qualified persons in Germany has led to different regulations of the depth of graves at different ages. At Stuttgart the different depths are as follows: for bodies of persons—

	ft.	in.
Under 8 years	3	9
„ 8 to 10	4	7
„ 10 to 14	5	7
Adults	6	7

At the Glasshutte, in the Erzgebirge, the depths are as follows :

	ft.	in.
Under 8 years	3	8
„ 8 to 14	4	7
Adults	5	0

At Franckfort the average depth prescribed for graves is 5 ft. 7 in.; at Munich 6 ft. 7 in.; in France 4 ft. 10 in. to 6 ft.; in Austria 6 ft. 2 in., if lime be used.

§ 145. Space between graves is also a matter requiring attention to avoid the uncovering of the coffin in one grave in opening another, and to avoid the accidents arising from the falling in of the sides of the graves : this space must vary according to the consistency of the ground and the depth of the graves. At Munich and Stuttgart the space prescribed, is in round numbers, rather more than 32 square feet to each adult. To avoid treading on the graves, and to allow the access of friends, spaces must be allowed also for walks.

These circumstances considered, the space requisite for the interments in a town may be determined by the multiplication of the average square superficies of a grave, by the average yearly mortality, and the period of years which the grave is to remain closed. " As an example," says Dr. Reicke, " of the mode of calculating the necessary space for the burial ground of a populous district, I will take a town of 35,000 inhabitants. Accordingly of this number it may be reckoned there will yearly die 1000. Of the number 500 will be adults, 50 children, from 7 to 14, and 450 children from 0 to 7 years. For the adults, allowing more than the most economical space, I calculate graves of 48 square feet Wirtemburg (*i. e.* 54·72 square feet English); for the children between 7 and 14 years, 24 square feet (27·36 English feet); and for those under 7, 20 square feet (22·80 English). For the adults I take a period of 10 years, for the youth 8 years, for the infants 7 years, as the time during which periods the grave must not be opened. According to this calculation the space required for the interment of the several classes would be—

	English Square Feet.		Numbers Dead.		Years.		English Square Feet.
1. Adults.—	54·72	×	500	×	10	=	273,600
2. Youth.—	27·36	×	50	×	8	=	10,944
3. Infants.—	22·80	×	450	×	7	=	71,820

$$\text{Total} \quad . \quad . \quad . \quad . \quad 356,364$$

" According to the usual calculation the requisite space would be :—

$$39\cdot90 \times 1,000 \times 10 = 399,000.$$

So that, by the above calculation and classification, there is a saving of 42,636 square feet.

" I must, however, beg to be understood that this calculation is only meant to serve as an example, and that the factors on which it is grounded must undergo the necessary variations, according as the soil is more or less favourable to decomposition, and therefore requiring a longer or shorter period of rest ; and according to the greater or less consistency of the soil, and therefore requiring the space between the graves to be greater or less; and, lastly, according as the average mortality varies, and especially the rate of mortality of the three classes of ages."

These factors would give different results for different populations, according to their different proportions of death. As an example of a town population, in Whitechapel the proportion of deaths for every 35,000 of the population will be 1125 deaths yearly. As an example of a rural population, for every 35,000 of the population in Hereford, there will only be 562 deaths annually, and the space required for interments for the two popu-

K

lations will be as follows, at the actual rate of deaths per 35,000 amongst the population in the Whitechapel Union in 1839 :

	English Square Feet.		Number of Deaths.		Age of Grave.		Total Area in Square Feet.	Average Square Feet.
1. Adults.—	54·72	×	568	×	10	=	310,810	
2. Youths.—	27·36	×	31	×	8	=	6,785	
3. Children.—	22·80	×	524	×	7	=	83,639	
			1,123				401,234	39·07

Rate of deaths per 35,000 in the Herefordshire Unions in 1839 :

	English Square Feet.		Number of Deaths.		Age of Grave.		Total Area in Square Feet.	Average Square Feet.
1. Adults.—	54·72	×	382	×	10	=	209,030	
2. Youths.—	27·36	×	16	×	8	=	3,502	:
3. Children.—	22·80	×	164	×	7	=	26,174	:
			562				238,706	44·62

This gives for a rural population .   976 graves per acre.
For a town population . . . 1,117   ,,

But in consequence of the smaller proportion of children dying in the rural district, a larger space is requisite than would appear from a comparative number of the interments if the graves were of the same size. The average size of the different graves may be taken as an epitome of the strength of the same numbers of the two populations : that of the town grave being in round numbers 39 feet, while the rural grave is 44 feet.

Nevertheless, the extent of land requisite for cemetery, on a decennial period of renewal, for a population of 20,000 in a rural district would be only $4\frac{4}{10}$ acres, whilst for 20,000 of such a town population as that of Whitechapel, it would be $7\frac{4}{10}$ acres.

§ 146. In 1838 the deaths in the metropolis were nearly 52,000 ; and for round numbers the average may be taken as 50,000 annually. Such an amount of mortality would require on the scale proposed by Dr. Riecke, for the several classes of graves, about 48 acres, or a space of nearly the size of St. James's Park within the rails, annually. On the same scale, supposing the interments generally renewable in decennial periods, the space required for national cemeteries in the metropolis would be 444 acres, or a space co-extensive with Hyde Park, which has 350 acres, and the Green Park and St. James's Park put together ; or rather more than one-fourth more than the Regent's Park, which has 350 acres ; or one-fourth less space than the Hyde Park and Kensington Gardens taken together. But besides the spaces for the cemeteries, spaces would be requisite as belts of land surrounding them, and to be kept clear of houses.

§ 147. The proper distance of places of interment from houses, is calculable according to the number of interments. On this subject there have been some, though not complete observations.

There is a church-yard at Stuttgart, in which 500 bodies are interred yearly, at depths varying with the age, according to the scale of regulations stated, with no more than one corpse in each grave, yet a north-west wind renders the emanations from the ground perceptible in houses distant from 250 to 300 paces. The stench of the carrion pits at Montfaucon is almost insupportable to a person not used to it, at a distance of 6500 feet, and with certain winds at double that distance, and under some circumstances even to the distance of five miles. Besides the surface emanations, the pollution of the subsoil drainage and springs have to be regarded. Captain Vetch states, that on some plains in Mexico, where animals have been slaughtered and buried in pits in permeable ground, the effects on vegetation were to be seen along the edges of a brook for a distance of three-quarters of a mile. In some parts they actually slaughtered and buried animals for the purpose of influencing the surrounding vegetation. By the best regulations in Germany, as already stated, wells are forbidden to be sunk near grave-yards, except at certain distances, such as 300 feet. *Ante,* §§ 13, 14.

§ 148. On such data as have been obtained, the distance of a cemetery ought to vary according to its size, or the number of the population for whom burial is required. The cemetery for a small population of from 500 to 1000 inhabitants, should, Dr. Reicke considers, be not less than 150 paces; for 1000 to 5000 inhabitants, not less than 300 paces; for above 5000, not less than 500 paces. In Prussia, the distance from houses at which cemeteries may be built, is fixed at not less than 500 paces; at Stralsund, in Prussia, at 1000 paces.

§ 149. It is recommended that in general public cemeteries should be placed at the east or the north, or the north-east of a town : the south and south-west winds, being usually moist, hold the putrefactive gases in solution more readily than the north, or northeast winds, which are dry. The higher the elevation of a cemetery, the nearer may it be permitted to a city, as putrefactive gases are lighter than the atmosphere and ascend. For the same reason, cemeteries lower than the houses should be at a greater distance. A site, with a slope to the south, is deemed the best, as it will be drier and warmer, and facilitate decomposition.

§ 150. Competent witnesses declare, that by a careful preparation of the ground, and without any appliances that would be otherwise than acceptable to the most fastidious minds, the escape of miasma may be so regulated as to avoid all injury to the health, and springs may be protected from pollution by drainage; and that by these means the necessity of far distant sites, and the inconvenience and expense of conveyance of the remains, and obstructions to the access of friends to the place of burial, may be avoided.

§ 151. Amongst these means, one for preventing the escape of emanations at the surface by absorbing and purifying them, is entirely in accordance with the popular feeling. The great body of English poetry, which it has been remarked is more rich on the subject of sepulture than the poetry of any other nation, abounds with reference to the practice of ornamenting graves with flowers, shrubs, and trees. A rich vegetation exercises a powerful purifying influence, and where the emanations are moderate, as from single graves, would go far to prevent the escape of any deleterious miasma. It is conceived that the escapes of large quantities of deleterious gasses by the fissuring of the ground would often be in a very great degree prevented by turfing over the surface, or by soiling, that is, by laying vegetable mould of five or six inches in thickness and sowing it carefully with grasses whose roots spread and mesh together. At the Abney Park Cemetery, where the most successful attention is paid to the vege- tation, this is done; but in some districts of towns it marks the impurity of the common atmosphere that even grass will not thrive; and that flowers and shrubs which live on the river side, or in spaces open to the breeze, become weakly and die rapidly in the enclosed spaces in the crowded districts. Several species of ever- greens, and the plants which have gummy or resinous leaves, that are apt to retain soot or dust, die quickly. The influence, there- fore, of a full variety of flowers and a rich vegetation, so necessary for the actual purification of the atmosphere, as well as to remove associations of impurity, and refresh the eye and soothe the mind, can only be obtained at a distance from most towns. It occasion- ally happens that individuals incur expense to decorate graves in the town churchyards with flowers, and more would do so, even in the churchyards near thoroughfares, but that they perish.

§ 152. Mr. Loudon recommends for planting in cemeteries, trees chiefly of the fastigiate growing kinds, which neither cover a large space with their branches nor give too much shade when the sun shines, and which admit light and air to neutralize any mephitic effluvia. Of these are, the Oriental Arbor Vitæ, the Evergreen Cypress, the Swedish and Irish Juniper, &c. For the same reason, trees of the narrow conical forms, such as the Red Cedar, and various pines and firs are desirable. In advantageously situated cemeteries, some of the larger trees, such as the Cedar of Lebanon, the Oriental Plane, the Purple Beech, the dark Yew, and the flowering Ash, sycamores, Mountain Ash, hollies, thorns, and some species of oaks, such as the Evergreen Oak, the Italian Oak, with flowering trees and shrubs, would find places in due proportion.

§ 153. There is one point of view in which the site of cemeteries does not appear to have been considered on the continent, and per- haps in no place could it be of so much importance as in London, namely, the convenience of access for processions, including in the consideration the protection of the inhabitants of particular quarters from an excess of funereal processions, and the mourners from the conflicting impressions consequent on a passage through thoroughfares crowded by a population unavoidably inattentive. It might be found on a survey that the banks of the river present several eligible sites for national cemeteries, and one pre-eminent recommendation of such sites would be the superior and eco_nomical means of conveyance they would afford by appropriate funereal barges, for uninterrupted and noiseless passage over what has been denominated " The Great Silent Highway."

Extent of Burial Grounds existing in the Metropolis.

§ 154. The rule, as deduced (§ 142.) from the German practice, would give an average of 110 burials per acre per annum in a town district.

§ 155. In 1834, some returns of the extent of burial grounds and the number of burials during the three years preceding, in the places of burial within the diocese of the Bishop of London and the bills of mortality, were laid before the House of Commons. From those it appeared that the ground occupied as burial ground within the diocese amounted to 103 acres, and that the average number of burials was 22,548, or 219 per acre, being from 108 to 117 more per acre than the preceding rule would give. In some grounds the number of interments were as high as 891 per acre. But that return did not include the burials in the whole of the metropolis. From the results of a systematic inquiry which has been recently made throughout the whole district of the metropolis (as defined in the report of the Registrar-General) into the extent of the burial-grounds and the average weekly number of burials at each place, it appears that the total area now occupied as burial ground, including the new cemeteries, and the annual rate of burial in each class, is, as nearly as can be ascertained, as follows :—

Burial Grounds in the Metropolis.	Area in Acres.	Annual Number of Burials, exclusive of Vault Burials.	Average Annual Number of Burials per Acre.	Highest Number of Burials per Acre in any Ground.	Lowest Number of Burials per Acre in any Ground.
Parochial Grounds	$176\frac{3}{10}$	33,747	191	3,073	11
Protestant Dissenters' Grounds	$8\frac{7}{10}$	1,715	197	1,210	6
Roman Catholics	$0\frac{3}{10}$	270	1,043	1,613	814
Jews	$9\frac{3}{10}$	304	33	52	13
Swedish Chapel	$0\frac{1}{10}$	10	108	..	..
Undescribed	$10\frac{5}{10}$	3,197	294	1,109	5
Private Grounds	$12\frac{6}{10}$	5,112	405	2,323	50
Total of Intra-mural Grounds	$218\frac{1}{10}$	44,355	203	1,080	46
Total of New Cemeteries	$260\frac{5}{10}$	3,336	13	155	4
Vault Burials	..	789	..	..	..

The total numbers of burials, as ascertained by verbal inquiry at each graveyard, approximate so nearly to the total numbers of deaths as to afford a presumption in favour of the general accuracy of these returns.*

§ 156. The most crowded burial grounds, on the average, are, it appears, the grounds which belong to private individuals, usually undertakers. In these places an uneducated man generally acts as minister, puts on a surplice, and reads the church service, or any other service that may be called for. These grounds are morally offensive, and appear to be physically dangerous in proportion to the numbers interred in them. In one of them the numbers interred appears to be at the rate of more than 2,300 per acre per annum. Names are given to these places by the owners, importing connexion with congregations, but without any apparent authority for doing so. They are repudiated by the most respectable Dissenters. On this point it appears to be just to submit an extract from a communication (on his individual responsibility) from the Rev. John Blackburn, Pentonville, one of the secretaries of the Union of Congregational Dissenters :—

I have no facts to communicate relating to the *physical* effects produced by the present crowded state of the old grave-yards, but I am sure the moral sensibilities of many delicate minds must sicken to witness the heaped soil, saturated and blackened with human remains and fragments of the dead, exposed to the rude insults of ignorant and brutal spectators. Immediately connected with this, allow me to mention that some spots that have been chosen both by episcopalians and dissenters, are wet and clayey, so that the splash of water is heard from the graves, as the coffins descend, producing a shudder in every mourner. I may with confidence disclaim the imputation that the grave-yards of dissenters were primarily and chiefly established with a view to emolument. Many grave yards that are private property, purchased by undertakers for their own emolument, are regarded as dissenting burial grounds, and we are implicated in the censures that are pronounced upon the unseemly and disgusting transactions that have been detected in them.—These are not dissenting but general cemeteries : dissenters use them for the reasons already stated [which are omitted, being the objections urged by dissenters against the indiscriminate use of the burial service.] The pastor of the bereaved family accompanies them to the grave, or meets them there, adapts his ministrations to their known circumstances, and without fee or reward— except in rare cases—discharges them as part of his pastoral work. By far the greatest portion of the persons buried in these grounds are not dissenters at all; and to meet the feelings of their connections the proprietors of these grounds obtain the services of men, who, without scruple, ape the clergyman, assume the surplice, and read the service of the church; a fact which is sufficient to show that they are not dissenters themselves, nor seeking to conciliate dissenting objections. The congregational or independent denomination, to which I belong, have about 120 chapels in and around London, and I believe there is not more than a sixth part of them that have grave yards attached, and all those are not in the hands of trustees appointed by the people. But, as far as I know and believe, there are but very few of these open to the sweeping censures that have been pronounced upon them.

* Vide Appendix for the list of burial places returned, and a view of the spaces requisite on the preceding scale, § 145, and the relative space occupied as burial ground by the chief religious denominations.

At a recent meeting of the congregational ministers of the metropolis they resolved, " That this board will always hail with satisfaction the adoption of any efficient means to correct abuses connected with burial grounds, as well general as parochial, where such abuses are proved to exist;" and I trust that the character of dissenters in general for good citizenship, is sufficient to assure you that they will never permit their private interests to oppose any great measures for our social improvement that are really national in their spirit and design.

As the sufficiency of the burial grounds existing within the metropolis does not properly come into question under the general conclusion that there ought to be none there, the only observation I at present submit upon the space of ground now occupied is that it would serve hereafter advantageously to be kept open as public ground.

§ 157. The well considered regulations then, give about 1452 common graves per acre for a town population. § 145. In the arrangements made for cemeteries belonging to a joint stock company, it is calculated that every acre of ground filled with vaults and private graves, will receive no less than 11,000 bodies. On the average size of coffins of 6 feet 3 by 1 foot 9, the common estimate is that the floor of an acre will receive 3,887 coffins laid side by side.

§ 158. Another calculation for the produce of a company's cemetery, is that each grave will be 6 feet by 2 feet, or 12 square feet, or 3630 graves to the acre (which contains 43,560 square feet), and that every grave shall contain 10 coffins in each grave. Twenty-five shillings is charged for each coffin interred: hence each acre is calculated to produce, when filled (without reference to the public health), a gross sum of 45,375*l.* In one instance, where the burials in a company's cemetery were five deep, the sales of graves actually made were at a rate of 17,000*l.* per acre, gross produce.

§ 159. The retention of bodies in leaden coffins in vaults is objected to, as increasing the noxiousness of the gases, which sooner or later escape, and when in vaults beneath churches, create a miasma which is apt to escape through the floor, whenever the church is warmed.* In Austria, and in other states,

---

* It is due to the medical profession to state, that they have always discountenanced as injurious the practice of entombment in vaults under churches. A Parisian physician had the following epitaph to his memory :—

> " Simon Pierre, vir pius et probus
> Hic sub dio sepeliri voluit
> Ne mortuus cuiquam noceret
> Qui vivus omnibus profuerat."

At Louvain, there is the tomb of a celebrated anatomist, with the following :—

> " Philippus Verhagen,
> Med. Dr. et prof.
> Partem sui materialem
> Hic in cœmeterio condi voluit,
> Ne templum dehonestaret
> Aut nocivis halitibus inficeret."

interment in lead is prohibited. In the majority of cases in England, burial in lead, as well as in other expensive coffins, appears to be generally promoted by the undertakers, to whom they are the most profitable. The Emperor Joseph, of Austria, on the knowledge of the more deleterious character of concentrated emanations from the dead, forbade the use even of coffins, and directed that all people should be buried in sacks; but this excited discontent amongst his subjects, who agreed in the sanitary principle of the measure, but complained that, putting them in sacks, was treating them as the Turks would do, and the regulation was altered for burial in coffins made of pine, which decays rapidly.

§ 160. It is to be observed as an improved direction of the public mind in the British metropolis, that on the part of persons who have the means of defraying the expenses of vaults, an increasing preference of inhumation is manifested, and that it is found by cemetery companies that catacombs prepared for sale are not so much in demand as was anticipated from the proportion in which they were in demand in the parochial burial grounds. The state of some of the places of common burial has evidently been such as to lead to the practice of entombment in preference to inhumation. The associations commonly expressed with inhumation (*redditur enim terræ corpus, et ita locatum ac situm, quasi operimento matris obducitur,* Cic. de legibus) were with a purer earth. In the most carefully regulated cemeteries in Germany the sale of any portions in perpetuity is entirely prohibited. The recent investigation of the disorders which have arisen in the management of the Parisian cemeteries, has led to a conclusion for the adoption of the same regulation, it having been found that, in time, families become extinct, or fall into decay; that a proportion of the tombs and vaults are neglected and fall into ruins, and detract from the general good keeping of the rest. Under such circumstances the private tombs too frequently raise associations of a character the very opposite of those intended by the purchasers. Their numbers at the same time increase and continually encroach on the spaces for general burial, and would ultimately occupy the whole of the cemeteries; and in the progress of population would absorb and hold large tracts of most important land near towns, in what would literally be one of the worst species of mortmain.* It has, therefore, been found necessary to restrict the sale of perpetuities in vaults or graves, and to give only what may be called leases for years, renewable on conditions, for the public protection.

---

* Perpetuities in burial grounds may be said to have been declared illegal by Lord Stowell's decision in the case of Gilbert v. the Churchwardens of St. Andrew's, Holborn, on the use of iron coffins. His lordship, in his judgment in that case, remarked, that "All contrivances that, whether intentionally or not, prolong the time of dissolution beyond the period at which the common local understanding and usage have fixed it, is an act of injustice, unless compensated in some other way."— Haggard's Rep. v. 2, p. 353. *Vide* statement of the principle of this decision, in the extracts from the judgment given in the Appendix, No. 12.

§ 161. In the common grave-yards in the metropolis, the bones are scattered about, or wheeled away to a bone-house, where they are thrown into a heap. The feeling of the labouring classes at the sight of the removal of the bones, from an overcrowded churchyard was expressed in a recent complaint, that those in charge of the place "would not give the poor bones time to decay." In Paris it is the custom to arrange skulls and bones, in various forms, in catacombs: but they are offensive objects; and the feelings of the poor man must be but ill consulted in presenting to him, in these decayed and debased remains, the prospect of the use of his own skull and bones to form part of a great and revolting monument. A more beneficial arrangement is that in the better regulated German cemeteries, where it is the invariable rule to remove from the sight and to re-inter carefully, all bones, the, object being to preserve the associations of a gradual, inoffensive, and salutary restoration of the material elements.

§ 162. By the Code Napoleon any one was permitted to be interred in his own garden, or wheresoever he pleased. By the better considered jurisprudence in Germany this liberty is withheld: because if the practice were to become general, such decomposing remains would be spread about without order, to the injury of the public health : it would facilitate the burial of persons murdered; many by precipitate and ill-regulated burial would be buried alive; many would be buried in this mode to evade proper inquiries. An examination of the circumstances of private and speculative burial grounds in this country developes many facts, in corroboration of the soundness of the German jurisprudence on this subject.

§ 163. The information with relation to material arrangements of the public cemeteries in Germany is submitted, as showing how much there is in their details of important questions of scientific appliances for consideration, which, in the new cemeteries as well as in the old burial grounds in this country, have generally been overlooked: appliances which, even if they were practicable on a parochial scale of management, would surely be little understood by the ordinary class of parochial officers. Though the practice in Germany appears to be on most points in advance, the inquiry has elicited various suggestions of probable important improvements upon it, which it is thought unnecessary to discuss, as being more fitted for investigation when new cemeteries have been determined upon than at present. It may for the present suffice to state, that a confident expectation is entertained by the best informed witnesses, that were the attention of the most competent persons who have hitherto been scared away, secured to the subject, still further useful improvements would be in a very short time effected.

§ 164. The following portion of evidence from Dr. Lyon Playfair, which adverts to the management of the evil in the common grave-yards, may however be adduced as an example of the character of some of the improvements already suggested.

You have examined into the state of certain church-yards with reference to their sanitary effects; have you not?—I have examined various church-yards and burying-grounds for the purpose of ascertaining whether the layer of earth above the bodies is sufficient to absorb the putrid gases evolved. The carbonic acid gas would not in any case be absorbed, but it is not to this that the evil effects are to be attributed. The slightest inspection, however, shows that the putrid gases are not thoroughly absorbed by soil lying over the bodies. I know several church-yards from which most fœtid smells are evolved, and gases with similar odour are emitted from the sides of sewers passing in the vicinity of church-yards, although they may be above 30 feet from them. If these gases are thus evolved laterally they must be equally emitted in an upward direction. The worst burying-grounds which have come under my notice are those belonging to private persons, generally undertakers, who make their livelihood by interring at a cheap rate. I visited one of these only a few days since. It was about 150 feet long and about 30 broad, and had been used for 80 years as a burying ground, and was still a favourite place of interment among the poor. Of course many bodies are placed in one grave, and when the ground becomes too much raised by bodies, it is levelled, and the boxes, &c., exhumed during the levelling, are thrown into a large cellar fitted to receive them. This whole ground was a mass of corruption, as may well be supposed, and it is situated in a densely populated neighbourhood. I mention this case as one among many other similar cases of private burying-grounds, in order to suggest that attention should be paid in any alteration respecting the laws regulating interments, to prevent burying-grounds being kept as objects of pecuniary speculation, at least within towns; for this practice gives much inducement to violate every feeling of decency and regard for public health in the desire for gain.

Can you suggest any method for preventing the escape of miasmata from graves, or from places for the interment of the dead?—I cannot suggest any methods as the results of experiment; but, at the same time, I think it possible that the evil might be much abated by the use of certain materials. For example, in a theoretical point of view, chloride of lime would be quite effectual, but it might not be applicable in practice, both from its expense, and from its great tendency to be decomposed. A cheap method of absorbing putrid effluvia, is by a mixture of charcoal from burnt tar, burnt clay, and gypsum. When such a mixture is mixed with putrid matter, all smell is immediately removed, and the matter is rendered inoffensive to health. When this mixture is strewed over decomposing animal and vegetable matter, it ceases to emit disagreeable odours. In like manner, if a layer of such a cheap mixture as this were thrown around and over a coffin, it would absorb probably the greatest part, if not all, of the putrid miasmata arising from the decomposition of the body. It possesses also this advantage, that it would not impair by keeping, even though the coffin did not burst for some years. I beg, however, again to state, that I throw this out as a mere suggestion, as I have never tried it in the case of graves, although I think it would be well worthy of a trial. Vegetation also ought to be encouraged over the graves. The legitimate food of plants is derived from decaying animal matter; for indeed all the food existing in the air, from which they derive their nutriment, is furnished to the atmosphere by the decay of organic matter. Plants assist in absorbing the emanations which escape from graves.

§ 165. It has been mentioned as an objection entertained in Germany to the use of clayey soils, on the ground that they retain the gases, and prevent that regular access of air which is necessary (as explained in a portion of evidence already adduced) to allow decay to proceed without putrefaction, which is the most dangerous condition. Good sand and good gravel are of value in the metropolis. It is stated by a gentleman connected with one of the cemeteries, and it is here mentioned to show the prevalent want of knowledge, that it is the common practice when sand and gravel are dug out to form a grave, not to return it, but to fill in with the cheap and coarse, but retentive, London clay. Now the grave-diggers frequently suffer severely in re-opening the graves which are thus filled in by the retentive clay, and require to be stimulated to their work by ardent spirits; and their ghastly appearance, as Mr. Loudon observes, attests the sufferings which they undergo. In another new cemetery, where the grass was very poor, the turf-mounds covering some of the graves was trodden down; on inquiring the reason, it was stated that sheep had been let in to eat the grass, to save the expense of cutting it. Some of the trees and shrubs first planted had not thriven well, and the officers stated that they had not yet been able to persuade the directors to go to the expense of renewing them. In most other cemeteries the plantations were in very good order, and several presented points of improvement in the architectural arrangements. But, as observed by Mr. Loudon, "nearly all the new London cemeteries, and most of the provincial cemeteries, adopt the practice of interring a number of bodies in the same grave, without leaving a sufficient depth over each coffin, to absorb the greater part of the gases of decomposition." It may indeed be confidently affirmed that there is scarcely one of the new cemeteries in which one or other of the well established principles of management, in the choice of the site, or the preparation of the soil, or in the drainage, or in the mode of burial, or in the numbers interred in one grave, or in respect to the precautions to prevent the undue corruption of the remains and escapes of dangerous morbific matter, or in the service and officers, or in jurisprudential securities, is not overlooked. (§ 20.)

§ 166. In the cemetery at Liverpool, where Mr. Huskisson is interred, it is the practice to pile the coffins of the poorest class in deep graves or pits, one coffin over the other, with only a thin covering of earth over each coffin until the pit is filled, when it holds upwards of thirty, as the sexton expressed it, about "thirty-four big and little." The observation of several of the joint stock cemeteries, and their estimates of future amounts of interments, not of one body in one grave, but of bodies piled one over the other by five and even ten deep, without any new precautions in respect to the emanations, the general experience of the difficulty of effecting any change through commercial associations that does not promise an immediate return for the expense incurred, prove that, although they may be kept in a better condition to the eye, there is no security that they will not be as injurious as any common burial grounds, and stand as much in need of some regulations for the protection of the inhabitants of the dwellings which in time may be driven closer around them.

§ 167. Besides the improvements in formation of the cemeteries and management of the interments, the regulations of the Franckfort and Munich cemeteries present instances which it may here be proper to submit for consideration, of the advantages derivable in aid of the religious service from a better organized staff of officers in maintaining superior order in the grounds on all occasions of solemnity.

§ 168. It will have been perceived how little support the clergymen have in any appointed staff of officers to maintain order in the burial-grounds of the more populous parishes. §§ 87, 88, and 111. On occasions of several interments taking place in burial-grounds in the metropolis at the same time, the master undertakers will. volunteer their services to get the crowd of by-standers into some order, and show how much might be done by other and better superintendence to add to the impressiveness of the last scene. The inferior attendants, the grave-diggers, at the interments which I have witnessed at the new cemeteries, attended, as they usually do at the parochial grounds, in a disorderly condition—unshaven, dirty in person, in dirty shirts and in the old and the common filthy dress. During the burial service the undertakers' men only concerned themselves in removing the feathers from the hearse and preparing for an immediate return; all the attendants began talking on other matters, and went their different ways immediately the coffin was lowered; the mourners were left with the utmost unconcern, except by the grave-diggers, who followed them in the attitude of the usual solicitations of money for drink.

§ 169. A conception of the alterations required and practicable in public establishments for conducting such a ceremony with due regard to the feelings of the survivors and the public, may be formed by inspecting the regulations of the cemetery at Franckfort, from which it will be perceived that the superintendence of the cemetery, and of the sextons in their various employments, is given to a cemetery inspector, whose duties are described in the second section of the regulations, and who must be a person of medical education, an officer of public health, examined by the Sanitary Board, and found by them to be qualified. It is specified as an important duty that he shall be present at the interment, " in order that by his presence nothing may be done by his subordinates, or by any other person, which should be contrary to the dignity of the interment or to the regulations."

The regulations also provide as follows :—

(3.) For the performance of all the necessary arrangements preceding the interment, commissaries of interments are appointed to take the place of the so called undertakers. These commissaries have to arrange every thing connected with the funeral, and are responsible for the proper fulfilment of all the regulations given in their instructions.

(4.) In order to prevent the great expense which was formerly occasioned by the attendance with the dead to the grave, bearers shall be appointed who shall attend to the cemetery all funerals, without distinction of rank or condition.

To these bearers shall be given assistants, who shall be equally under the control of the interment commissaries.

The commissary must see that the bearers are always cleanly and respectably dressed in black when they appear at a funeral, and must be particularly careful that they conduct themselves seriously, quietly, and respectably.

He must also see that the carriage of the dead is not driven quickly either in the town or beyond it, but that it is conducted respectably at a proper quiet pace.

When the dead is covered, and not until then, the commissary and the bearers shall leave the cemetery in perfect silence.

For any impropriety which may, through the conduct of the bearers, arise during the interment, the commissary is responsible.

(35.) The sextons must always be respectably dressed in black during the interment, and those who go to the house of mourning must always appear in neat and clean attire, and must be studious at all times, whether engaged within or without the churchyard, to preserve a modest and proper behaviour. Drunkenness, neglect of duty, or abuse of their services, will be punished by the Church Yard Commission, and on repetition of the offence, the offender will be dismissed.

A Christian attention and civility to all is required from the highest public officer, without any fees or expense, and mendicancy on the part of the inferior attendants, and the rapacity of the uneducated and of the ill-educated, which always rushes in most strongly on the helpless, are equally prohibited. Of the inspector himself, it is by these regulations provided :—

(17.) It is the duty of the inspector to treat all who have to apply to him with politeness and respect, and to give the required information unweariedly and with ready good will.

Under no pretext is he allowed either to demand or receive any payment, as he has a sufficient salary.

And in respect to the other officers :—

(40.) Besides, or in addition to the authorised payment printed in the tax roll, and determined by the Cemetery Commission as the sufficient remuneration of the Inspector, Commissioners of Interments, the bearers and sextons, no one is on the occasion of a death, either to give money, or to furnish food and drink.

The practice of furnishing crape, gloves, lemons, &c., by the friends of the dead, is also given up, and the persons engaged in conducting the interment, must take all the requisites with them, without asking or receiving any compensation, under pain of instant dismissal.

§ 170. It is now a prevalent complaint, which, so far as the present inquiry has proceeded, appears to be a just one, that in the management of the common grave-yards in this country, human remains are literally treated as earth, by the sextons and grave-diggers, and ignorant men to whom that management falls. The popular sentiments are offended by such open practices as that of using an iron borer, to bore down and ascertain whether the ground is occupied by a coffin, and whether it and the contents are sufficiently decayed for removal. Were proper registries kept of all interments and their sites, these, and a knowledge of natural operations, would render such offensive processes unnecessary. There appear to be few parochial grounds in which the remains of any individual of the poorer classes could be found with certainty, for exhumation, or for judicial or other purposes.

§-171. In the German regulations cited as examples, the public feeling is carefully consulted, and the general principle is acted upon, that the remains, so long as they last, are sacred, and must even be dealt with as sentient. Year after year the regulations for the care of the dead in the house of reception preparatory to interment are scrupulously maintained, on the presumption that a revival may take place, and the action upon the presumption is not relaxed, although perhaps there is no actual probability of such an event taking place. . Persons are kept in attendance at the cemetery on this presumption, and with respect to them it is expressly provided :—

(7.) If roughness be shown by a nurse to the dead, he must be punished with instant dismissal, and a notification of the same must be given by the Cemetery Commission, to the police, in order that proper inquiry and punishment be given.

Moral influence of seclusion from thronged places, and of decorative Improvements in National Cemeteries, and arrangements requisite for the satisfactory performance of Funeral Rites.

§ 172. The images presented to the mind by the *visible* arrangements for sepulture, are inseparably associated with the ideas of death itself to the greater proportion of the population. Neglected or mismanaged burial grounds superadd to the indefinite terrors of dissolution, the revolting image of festering heaps, disturbed and scattered bones, the prospect of a charnel house and its associations of desecration and insult. With burial grounds that are undrained, for example, the associations expressed by the labouring classes on the occasion of burial there, are similar to those which would arise on plunging a sentient body into a " watery grave." Where there is nothing visible to raise such painful associations, a feeling of dislike is manifested to the " common" burial grounds in crowded districts, or to their " dreariness " in the districts which are the least frequented.

The Rev. H. H. Milman, the rector of St. Margaret's, Westminster, probably adverts to these associations when questioned before the Committee of the House of Commons with reference to the expediency of discontinuing burial in his own parish.

2744. In reference to the churchyard of St. Margaret's, is that full or not ?—It is very full.

2745. Can you with convenience inter there?—My own opinion is, that interment ought to be discontinued there for several reasons ; not because I have ever heard of any noxious effect upon the health of the neighbourhood, *but on account of its public situation; it is a thoroughfare,* and, in point of fact, it has been a cemetery so long, and it is so crowded, that interment cannot take place without interfering with previous interments.

Mr. Wordsworth, in a paper first published by Mr. Coleridge, has thus expressed the same sentiments, and the feelings, which it is submitted, are entitled to regard, in legislating upon this subject :—

" In ancient times, as is well known, it was the custom to bury the dead beyond the walls of towns and cities, and among the Greeks and Romans they were frequently interred by the way sides.

" I could here pause with pleasure, and invite the reader to indulge with me in contemplation of the advantages which must have attended such a practice. We might ruminate on the beauty which the monuments thus placed must have borrowed from the surrounding images of nature, from the trees, the wild flowers, from a stream running within sight or hearing, from the beaten road, stretching its weary length hard by. Many tender similitudes must these objects have presented to the mind of the traveller, leaning upon one of the tombs, or reposing in the coolness of its shades, whether he had halted from weariness, or in compliance with the invitation, ' Pause traveller,' so often found upon the monuments. And to its epitaph must have been supplied strong appeals to visible appearances or immediate impressions, lively and affecting analogies of life as a journey—death as a sleep overcoming the tired wayfarer—of misfortune as a storm that falls suddenly upon him—of beauty as a flower that passeth away, or of innocent pleasure as one that may be gathered—of virtue that standeth firm as a rock against the beating waves;—of hope undermined insensibly like the poplar by the side of the river that has fed it, or blasted in a moment like a pine tree by the stroke of lightning on the mountain top—of admonitions and heart-stirring remembrances, like a refreshing breeze that comes without warning, or the taste of the waters of an unexpected fountain. These and similar suggestions must have given formerly, to the language of the senseless stone, a voice enforced and endeared by the benignity of that nature with which it was in unison.

" We in modern times have lost much of these advantages; and they are but in a small degree counter-balanced to the inhabitants of large towns and cities, by the custom of depositing the dead within or contiguous to their places of worship, however splendid or imposing may be the appearance of those edifices, or however interesting or salutary may be the associations connected with them. Even were it not true, that tombs lose their monitory virtue when thus obtruded upon the notice of men occupied with the cares of the world, and too often sullied and defiled by those cares; yet still, when death is in our thoughts, nothing can make amends for the want of the soothing influences of nature, and for the absence of those types of renovation and decay which the fields and woods offer to the notice of the serious and contemplative mind. To feel the force of this sentiment, let a man only compare, in imagination, the unsightly manner in which our monuments are crowded together in the busy, noisy, unclean, and almost grassless churchyard of a large town, with the still seclusion of a Turkish cemetery in some remote place, and yet further sanctified by the grove of cypress in which it is embosomed."

§ 173. Careful visible arrangements, of an agreeable nature, raise corresponding mental images and associations which diminish the terrors incident to the aspect of death. Individuals who have purchased portions of decorated cemeteries for their own interment in the metropolis, make a practice of visiting them for the sake, doubtless, of those solemn but tranquil thoughts which the place inspires as personally connected with themselves. The establishment of a cemetery at Highgate was strongly opposed by the inhabitants, but when its decorations with flowers and shrubs and trees, and its quiet and seclusion were seen, applications were made for the purchase of keys, which conferred the privilege of walking in the cemetery at whatever time the purchaser pleased. If the chief private cemeteries in the suburbs of the metropolis were thrown open on a Sunday, they would on fine days be often thronged by a respectful population. Such private cemeteries as have been formed, though pronounced to be only improvements on the places of burial in this country, and far below what it would yet be practicable to accomplish, have indisputably been viewed with public satisfaction, and have created desires of further advances by the erection of national cemeteries. Abroad the national cemeteries have obtained the deepest hold on the affections of the population. I have been informed by an accomplished traveller, who has carefully observed their effects, that cemeteries have been established near to all the large towns in the United States. To some of these cemeteries an horticultural garden is attached; the garden walks being connected with the places of interment, which, though decorated, are kept apart. These cemeteries are places of public resort, and are there observed, as in other countries, to have a powerful effect in soothing the feelings of those who have departed friends, and in refining the feelings of all. At Constantinople, the place of promenade for Europeans is the cemetery at Pera, which is planted with cypress, and has a delightful position on the side of a hill overlooking the Golden Horn. The greatest public cemetery attached to that capital is at Scutari, which forms a beautiful grove, and disputes in attraction, as a place for readers, with the fountains and cloisters of the Mosques.

§ 174. In Russia, almost every town of importance has its burial place at a distance from the town, laid out by the architect of the government. It is always well planted with trees, and is frequently ornamented with good pieces of sculpture. Nearly every German town has its cemetery at a distance from the town, planted with trees and ornamented with public and private monuments. Most of the cemeteries have some choice works of art or public monument, which alone would render them an object of attraction. For instance, at Saxe Weimar, the cemetery contains the tombs of Goethe and Schiller placed in the mausoleum of the ducal family. In Turkey, Russia, and Germany the poorer classes have the advantages of interment in the national cemeteries. In Russia it is the practice to hold festivals twice a-year over the graves of their friends. In several parts of Germany similar customs prevail. At Munich, the festival on All Saints' Day (November the 1st) is described as one of the most extraordinary spectacles that is to be seen in Europe.* The tombs are decorated in a most remarkable manner with flowers, natural and artificial, branches of trees, canopies, pictures, sculptures, and every conceivable object that can be applied to ornament or decorate. The labour bestowed on some tombs requires so much time, that it is commenced two or three days beforehand, and protected while going on by a temporary roof. During the whole of the night preceding the 1st of November, the relations of the dead are occupied in completing the decoration of the tombs, and during the whole of All Saints' Day and the day following, being All Souls' Day, the cemetery is visited by the entire population of Munich, including the king and queen, who go there on foot, and many strangers from distant parts. Mr. Loudon states that, when he was there, it was estimated that 50,000 persons had walked round the cemetery in one day, the whole, with very few exceptions, dressed in black. On November the 3rd, about mid-day, the more valuable decorations are removed, and the remainder left to decay from the effects of time and weather.

§ 175. A review of the circumstances influencing the public feeling, and of the tendencies marked by the recent changes of practice in this country, and of the effects of the public institutions for interment amongst other civilised nations, enforce the conclusion that those arrangements to which the attention of the population is so earnestly directed, should be made with the greatest care, and that places of public burial demand the highest order of art in laying out the sites, and decorating them with trees and

---

* The neglect of the cemeteries at Paris, and especially of those portions dedicated to the interment of the poorer classes, has been the subject of public complaint, and means are now being taken to redress them. A friend, who aided me with some inquiries in respect to them, states,—

The English tourist in visiting Père la Chaise is attracted by splendid monuments in the midst of cypress trees, and little gardens filled with flowers planted round a majority of the tombs; but the graves of the humbler classes lie beyond these, and to them the stranger is seldom conducted. The contrast is painful. When I last visited Père la Chaise, on a fine day in November, and after a week of unusually fine weather for the season, I found the paths quite impracticable in the poorer quarter of the cemetery, and as I watched a man, in the usual blouse dress worn by the working class, picking his way through the mud to lead his little boy to pray over the grave of his mother, I could but deplore the economy of an administration which had neglected to provide, at least, a dry gravel path for the humble and pious mourner.

architectural structures of a solemn and elevating character.
National arrangements with such objects, would be followed up
and supported by the munificence of private individuals, and by
various communities.   It is observable in the metropolis, and in
the larger towns that the direction of private feeling in the choice
of sepulture is less affected by locality or neighbourhood, than
by classes of profession or occupation, or social communion when
living, and that such feeling would tend to association in the grave
and monumental decoration.   A proposal has been in circulation
for the purchase of a portion of one of the new cemeteries, for the
erection of a mausoleum for persons of the naval and military
professions—members of the United Service clubs.   At the public
cemetery of Mayence are interred 150 veteran soldiers, officers
and privates, natives of the town, who were buried in one spot,
denoted by a monument on which each man's name and course of
service is inscribed in gold letters, and the monument is sur-
mounted by a statue of the general under whom they served.
At Berlin there is a cemetery connected with the *Invaleiden haus*
founded by Frederick the Great, in which many of the generals
are buried with the private soldiers.   The ground is well laid
out, and ornamented with monuments, the latest of which are
executed by Tieck, and other celebrated sculptors.   This
cemetery forms the favourite walk of the old soldiers.   The
great moral force, and the consolation to the dying and the incen-
tive to public spirit whilst living, derivable from the natural regulations of a public cemetery, is almost entirely lost in this country,
except in the few cases where public monuments are provided in
the cathedrals.   In the metropolis it would be very difficult to find
the graves of persons of minor fame who have advanced or adorned
any branch of civil or military service, or have distinguished
themselves in any art or science.   Yet there are few occupations which could not furnish examples for pleasurable contemplation to the living who are engaged in them, and claim
honour from the public.   The humblest class of artisans would
feel consolation and honour in interment in the same cemetery
with Brindley, with Crompton, or with Murdoch, the artisan who
assisted and carried out the conceptions of Watt; or with
Emerson, or with Simpson, the hand-loom weaver, who became
professor of mathematics at Woolwich; or with Ferguson, the
shepherd's son; or with Dollond, the improver of telescopes,
whose earliest years were spent at a loom in Spitalfields; or with
others who " have risen from the wheelbarrow" and done honour
to the country, and individually gained public attention from
the ranks of privates ; such for example as John Sykes, Nelson's
cockswain, an old and faithful follower, who twice saved the life of
his admiral by parrying the blows that were aimed at him, and at
last actually interposed his own person to meet the blow of an
enemy's sabre which he could not by any other means avert,

and who survived the dangerous wound he received in this act of heroic attachment. The greater part of the means of honour and moral influence on the living generation derivable from the example of the meritorious dead of every class, is at present in the larger towns cast away in obscure grave-yards and offensive charnels. The artisans who are now associated in communities which have from their beneficent objects a claim to public regard, might if they chose it have their spaces set apart for the members of their own occupation, and whilst they derive interest from association with each other, they would also derive consolation from accommodation within the same precincts as the more public and illustrious dead.

§ 176. It is due to the memory of Sir Christopher Wren, to state that extra-mural or suburban cemeteries formed part of his plan for the rebuilding of London after the great fire. " I would wish," says he, "that all burials in churches might be disallowed, which is not only unwholesome, but the pavements can never be kept even, nor pews upright : and if the church-yard be close about the church, this is also inconvenient, because the ground being continually raised by the graves, occasions in time a descent by steps into the church, which renders it damp, and the walls green, as appears evidently in all old churches. It will be inquired where, then, shall be the burials?—I answer, in cemeteries seated in the outskirts of the town; and since it has become the fashion of the age to solemnize funerals by a train of coaches (even where the deceased are of moderate condition), though the cemeteries should be half a mile or more distant from the church, the charge need be little or no more than usual ; the service may ·be first performed in the church : but for the poor and such as must be interred at the parish charge, a public hearse of two wheels and one horse may be kept at small expense, the usual bearers to lead the horse, and take out the corpse at the grave. A piece of ground of two acres, in the fields, will be purchased for much less than two roods amongst the buildings. This being enclosed with a strong brick wall, and having a walk round, and two cross walks, decently planted with yew trees, the four quarters may serve four parishes, where the dead need not be disturbed at the pleasure of the sexton, or piled four or five upon one another, or bones thrown out to gain room. In these places beautiful monuments may be erected; but yet the dimensions should be regulated by an architect, and not left to the fancy of every mason; for thus the rich with large marble tombs would shoulder out the poor : when a pyramid, a good bust, or statue on a proper pedestal will take up little room in the quarters, and be properer than figures lying on marble beds : the walls will contain escutcheons and memorials for the dead, and the real good air and walks for the living. It may be considered, further, that if the cemeteries be thus thrown into the fields, they will bound the excessive growth of the city with a graceful border which is now encircled with scavenger's dung-stalls."*

§ 177. I might submit the concurrent opinions of several distinguished clergymen, communicated in reference to the general view of the importance of a large change in the practice of town interments, and the formation of suburban cemeteries, as being indeed conformable to the practice of the Jews and early Christians, and recognised in the words "There was a dead man carried *out*." It was the ancient practice, as is perhaps indicated in the term exsequies, to bury outside of the town.† To this practice it is clear that the earliest Christians conformed. It was their custom to assign to the martyrs the most conspicuous places, over which altars or monuments were erected, where the believers used to assemble for nightly worship, so that it may rather be said of them that their burial places were their churches, than that their churches were their burial places.‡ When the temples of the heathen gods were converted into Christian churches, the *bones* or relics of these illustrious persons, together with the altars, were removed and placed within the churches. The early practice of burial in the cemeteries near the earthly remains of those holy persons, being deemed a great privilege when those remains were removed, naturally led to the idea of its continuation, by the interment of *bodies* in or about the first accustomed objects of worship. Nevertheless, interment in the interior of the church was held to be an unusual piece of good fortune, and when the Emperor Constantine, who had constituted Christianity the religion of the state, had granted to him a grave within the porticos of the church, it was esteemed the most unheard-of distinction. The ancient Greeks and Romans thought that a corpse contaminated a sacred place, and this idea as to the corpse was retained by the early Christians. When some persons in Constantinople began to make an invasion upon the laws, under pretence that there was no express prohibition of burying in churches, Theodosius, by a new law, equally forbade them burying in cities and burying in churches; and this whether it was only the ashes or relics of any bodies kept above ground in urns or whole bodies laid in coffins; for the same reasons that the old laws had assigned, viz., that they

---

* Vide Appendix for an exemplification of the excess of deaths and funerals, and other losses incurred by setting aside Sir Christopher Wren's plan for the rebuilding of the city of London.

† One of the twelve tables was in these words, "*Hominem mortuum in urbe ne sepelito neve urito.*" Cicero, in one of his epistles, Epist. ad Div. iv. 12, in which he describes the assassination of his friend M. Marcellus, at Athens, mentions that he had been unable to obtain permission of the Athenians that the body should be buried in the city; they said that such permission was inadmissible on religious grounds, and that it never had been granted to any one.

‡ Bingham's Christian Antiquities, b. xxiii. ch. 1, s. 2.

might be examples and memorials of mortality and the condition of human nature to all passengers, and also that they might not defile the habitations of the living but leave it pure and clean to them. St. Chrysostom, in one of his homilies upon the martyrs, says, " As before when the festival of the Maccabees was celebrated all the country came thronging into the city; so now when the festival of the martyrs who lie buried in the country is celebrated, it was fit the whole country should remove thither." In like manner, speaking of the festival of Drossis the martyr, he says, " Though they had spiritual entertainment in the city, yet their going out to the saints in the country afforded them both great profit and pleasure." The Council of Tribur, in the time of Charlemagne, to prevent the abuse of burying within churches, decreed that *no layman* should thenceforth be buried within a church; and that if in any church graves were so numerous that they could not be concealed by a pavement the place was to be converted into a cemetery, and the altar to be removed elsewhere and erected in a place where sacrifice could be religiously offered to God.

Amongst the distinct clerical orders of the Primitive Church, Bingham (book iii. chap. 7) reckons the *Psalmistæ*, the *Copiatæ*, and the *Parabolani*. The Psalmistæ, or the canonical singers, were appointed to retrieve and improve the psalmody of the church. The business of the Copiatæ was to take care of funerals and provide for the decent interment of the dead. St. Jerome styles them *Fossarii*, from digging of graves; and in Justinian's Novels they are called *Lecticarii*, from carrying the corpse or bier at funerals. And St. Jerome, speaking of one that was to be interred, " The *Clerici*," says he, " whose office it was, wound up the body, digged the earth," and so, according to custom, " made ready the grave." Constantine incorporated a body of men to the number of 1100 in Constantinople, under the name of *Copiatæ*, for the service in question, and so they continued to the time of Honorius and Theodosius, junior, who reduced them to 950; but Anastatius augmented them again to the first number, which Justinian confirmed by two novels, published for that purpose. Their office was to take the whole care of funerals upon themselves, and to see that all persons had a decent and honourable interment. Especially they were obliged to perform this last office to the poorer people without exacting anything of their relations upon that account. The *Parabolani* were incorporated at Alexandria to the number of 500 or 600, who were deputed to attend upon the sick, and take care of their bodies in time of weakness.* [Cod. Theod., leg. 43:—Parabolani, qui ad curanda debilium corpora deputantur, quingentos esse ante præcipimus; sed quia hos minus sufficere in præsenti cognovimus, pro quingentis sex centos constitui præcipimus," &c.] They were called *Parabolani* from their undertaking (Παραβολον ἔργον) a most

---

* *Vide* Leviticus, chap. xiv, verse 33 to 48, for early sanitary measures of purification.

dangerous office in attending the sick. The foundation of a great city like Constantinople must have brought the magnitude of the service of the burial of the whole population distinctly under view, and have necessitated comprehensive and systematic arrangements of a corresponding extent, by the superintendence of superior officers through the gradations of duty of a disciplined force, which, even with the Eastern redundance of service, could scarcely have failed to be efficient and economical as compared with numerous separated and isolated efforts. A great prototype was thus gained, and the well-considered gradations of duty and service of the great city was carried out as far as practicable in the small parish. In some churches, where there was no such standing office as the Copiatæ or the Parabolani, the Penitents were obliged to take upon themselves the office and care of burying the dead; " and this by way of discipline and exercise of humility and charity which were so becoming their station." *Bingham,* book xviii. cap. 2. The state of administrative information in these our times may surely be deplored, when any views can be entertained of making the small parish and the rude and barbarous service (multiplied, at an enormous expense) of the really unsuperintended common gravedigger and sexton, the prototypes for this most important and difficult branch of public administration of the greatest metropolis in the modern world.

On a full consideration I think it will be apparent that the exclusion of the burial of corpses in churches or in churchyards, and the adoption of burials in cemeteries, and the conspicuous interment there of all individuals whose lives and services have graced communities, will, in so far as it is carried out, be in principle a return to the primitive practice, restoring to the many the privilege, of which they are necessarily deprived by burials in churches, of association in sepulture with the illustrious dead, and giving to these a wider sphere of attention and honour, and beneficent influence.

On the immediate question of the arrangements for sepulture I beg leave to submit for consideration the following extracts from a communication from the Rev. H. Milman, which is more peculiarly due to him, as his examination before the Committee of the House of Commons does not appear to have elicited his full and matured opinions on the important subject :—

I cannot but consider the sanitary part of the question, as the most dubious, and as resting on less satisfactory evidence than other considerations involved in the inquiry. The decency, the solemnity, the Christian impressiveness of burial, in my opinion, are of far greater and more undeniable importance.

It must unquestionably be a government measure in its management as well as its organization. If you have understood my evidence as recommending parochial, rather than a general administration, such was not my intention. I thought that I had left that point quite open. When I stated (2729) the alternative of cemeteries provided by the national funds, and by parochial taxation, I represented the unpopularity of the latter mode of taxation : and (in 2782) I suggested certain advantages to be derived from the more general and public administration. The Committee, however, who seemed to incline strongly towards the parochial system, went off in that direction, and the questions turned rather on the practicability of that system, and the manner in which it might be organized.

Further reflection leads me to the strong conviction that the parochial system, even if there were no difficulties in forming the union of the smaller parishes for this object, could only furnish so loose and uncertain a superintendence over an affair of such magnitude, and requiring such constant vigilance, as to be altogether inadequate to the purpose. It is not easy, with their present burthens and responsibilities, to fill the parochial offices with men competent to the duty, and with sufficient leisure to devote to it. They are usually filled by men in business of some kind, with considerable sacrifice of their time, and of that attention which is required by their personal concerns. These duties, however are confined, onerous as they sometimes are, to their own immediate neighbourhood. But if we add to their responsibilities, the care of a remote and large churchyard, with all its complicated management, we impose upon them duties so arduous and so incompatible with their own interests and avocations, that the conscientious would shrink from undertaking them, and they would fall into the hands of a lower class of busy persons, anxious for notoriety, or with some remote view of advantage to themselves. It will be absolutely necessary to relieve the parish officers from a burthen which they cannot undertake without a sacrifice, which is more than can be expected from men engaged in business or in some of the active professions. Besides all this, the administration would be constantly passing from one to another; the objection to the whole parochial system, that a man no sooner learns the duty of his office, than he is released from it, would apply in a tenfold degree to an affair of such magnitude. The only way to secure the proper organization and conduct of a remote cemetery, would be by officers, judiciously selected, and adequately paid, who should devote their whole time to the business. Many of these objections, as the want of sufficient time without neglecting more serious duties, would apply to the clergyman of a large town parish, and if the cemetery be made an object of parochial taxation, the less he is involved in it the better.

On the wise and maturely considered organization, and on the provisions for the careful, constant, and vigilant superintendence of the whole system, will depend entirely its fulfilment of its great object, the re-investment of the funeral services, and of the sacred abode of the dead, in their due solemnity and religious influence. Nothing can be more beautiful, more soothing under the immediate influence of sorrow, or at all times more suggestive of tranquil, yet deep religious emotion, than the village churchyard, where the clergyman, the squire, or the peasant, pass weekly or more often by the quiet and hallowed graves of their kindred and friends, to the house of prayer, and where hereafter they expect themselves to be laid at rest under a stone perhaps, on which is expressed the simple hope of resurrection to eternal life, and where all is so peaceful, that the tomb may almost seem as if it might last undisturbed to that time. I am inclined to think that some of the unbounded popularity of Gray's Elegy, independent of its exquisite poetic execution, may arise from these associations. Of these tranquillizing and elevating influences, so constantly refreshed and renewed, the inhabitants of large cities are of necessity deprived. The churchyard, often very small, always full, and crowded with remains of former interments, either carelessly scattered about, or but ill concealed, is in some cases a thoroughfare, where the religious service is disturbed by the noises, if not of passing and thoughtless strangers, with those of the din and traffic of the neighbouring street; and the new made grave, or the stone, which has just been fixed down, is trampled over by the passing crowd, or made the play-place of idle children. Where, as in some of the larger parishes in the west of London, the burial place is not contiguous to the church, it is more decent, but then it is secluded within high walls, or perhaps by houses, and is only open for the funeral ceremony, at other times inaccessible to the mourning relatives.

But will it not be possible, as we cannot give to the population of the metropolis, and other crowded towns, the quiet, the sanctity, the proximity to the church of the village place of sepulture, to substitute something at least decent, and with more appearance of repose and permanence; if not solemn, serious, and religiously impressive? The poor are peculiarly sensible of these impressions, and to them impression and custom form a great part, the most profound and universal influence of religion; and to them they cannot be given but by some arrangement under the sanction, and with the assistance, of the Government. Private speculation may give something of this kind to the rich, but private speculation looks for a return of profit for its invested capital. To my mind there is something peculiarly repugnant in Joint-Stock Burial and Cemetery Companies. But, setting that aside, they are and can be of no use to the *people* of the metropolis and the large towns. There always has been, and probably always will be, some distinction in the burial rites (I beg to say that to the credit of my curates, they refuse to make any difference between rich and poor in the services of the church) and in the humbler or more costly grave of rich and poor—

> Here lie I beside the door,
> Here he I because I am poor;
> Further in the more they pay,
> Here lie I as well as they.

But it may be a question whether the very numbers of funerals, which must take place for a large town, with the extent of the burial places, may not be made a source of solemnity and impressiveness, which may in some degree compensate for the individual and immediate interest excited by a funeral in a small parish. That which at present, when left to a single harassed and exhausted clergyman, and one sexton, and a few wretched assistants, can hardly avoid the appearance of hurry and confusion, might be so regulated as to impose, from the very gathering of such masses of mortality, bequeathed together to their common earth, not (let me be understood) in one vault or pit, but each apart in his decent grave. The vast extent of cemetery which would be required for London (suppose six or eight for the whole metropolis and its suburbs), if properly kept, and with such architectural decorations, and the grand and solemn shade of trees appropriate to the character of the ground, could scarcely fail to impress the reflective mind, and even to awe the more thoughtless. Our national character, and our more sober religion, will preserve us, probably, from the affectations and fantastic fineries of the Père la Chaise ground at Paris. From some of the German cemeteries we may learn much as to regulation, and the proper character to be maintained in a cemetery of the dead.

National sepulture is a part, and a most important part of national religion; of all the beautiful services of our Church, none is more beautiful (I might wish, perhaps, two expressions altered) than our service for burial. I could have wished that the Church had taken the initiative in this great question. I trust that she will act, if the State can be prevailed upon to move, in perfect harmony with the general feeling on the subject. It is fortunate, that in the Bishop of London we have not merely a person of liberal mind, and practical views, but one who brings the experience of the parish priest of a large London living to his Episcopal authority and influence.

One further practical suggestion occurs to me as likely most materially to diminish the expenditure of funerals of all classes, and therefore to render any great scheme more feasible. A funeral procession through the streets of a great and busy town can scarcely be made impressive. Not even the hearse, in its gorgeous gloom, with all the pomp of heraldry, and followed by the carriages of half the nobility of the land, will arrest for an instant the noise and confusion of our streets, or awaken any deeper impression with the mass than idle curiosity. While the poor man, borne on the shoulders of men as poor as himself, is jostled off the pavement; the mourners, at some crossing, are either in danger of being run over or separated from the body; in the throng of passers no sign of reverence, no stirring of conscious mortality in the heart. Besides this, if, as must be the case, the cemeteries are at some distance, often a considerable distance, from the homes of the deceased, to those who are real mourners nothing can be more painful or distressing than this long, wearisome, never-ending—perhaps often interrupted—march; while those who attend out of compliment to the deceased while away the time in idle gossip in the mourning coach, to which perhaps they endeavour to give—but, if their feelings are not really moved, endeavour in vain to give—a serious turn. Abandon, then, this painful and ineffective part of the ceremony; let the dead be conveyed with decency, but with more expedition, under trustworthy care, to the cemetery; there form the procession, there assemble the friends and relatives; concentrate the whole effect on the actual service, and do not allow the mind to be disturbed and distracted by the previous mechanical arrangements, and the extreme wearisome length of that which, if not irreverent and distressing, cannot, from the circumstances, be otherwise than painfully tedious.

It may be worth observing that, in London, even the passing bell seems almost lost in the din and confusion. This is the case even in the old churches, which retain their deep, full, and sonorous bells. The quick shrill gingle, or the feeble tone of those which are placed in the chapels of the more recent burial-grounds, instead of deepening to my ear, are utterly discordant with the solemnity of the service. In the country nothing can be finer than the telling from some old grey church tower—

> Over some wide watered shore,
> Swinging slow with solemn roar

What would be the effect of a bell as large as St. Paul's, heard at stated times, or in the event of the funeral of some really distinguished persons, from the distant cemetery?

§ 178. The formation of national cemeteries would give the means of more special and appropriate service for the interment of the dead than it is now possible to provide by small parochial establishments. In the more populous parishes, the service is unavoidably hurried. In all, the feelings of survivors require the most full, respectful, and impressive service. In many of the rural districts, the friends and fellow-workmen of the deceased accompany the remains to the grave, and one object of subscriptions to burial and general benefit clubs is to secure the advantages of arrangements for the attendance of fellow-workmen, who are members of the same club. When a waterman dies, to whom his brethren would pay respect, the body is conveyed by them in an eight-oared cutter, to the churchyard by the water-side. On their return, the seat which the deceased would have occupied is left vacant, and his oar, tied with a piece of crape, is placed across the boat. One of the most popular and impressive of funeral ceremonies is that on the interment of a private soldier. When a private of the metropolitan police dies, a number of members of the force, and a superior officer, attend his funeral in their uniforms. It is not unfrequent when a member has been invalided and left the force, that he will make it a dying request that his funeral may be attended by the officer and men with whom he served. This request is generally complied with. Old soldiers who have been invalided frequently make it a dying request to the commanders of the regiments in which they have served that they may be buried as if they had died in the service ; and unless there be an exception to the respectability of their conduct, the honour and consolation is bestowed.

§ 179. In Scotland, it is a subject of intense desire on the part of the labouring classes to gain the attendance of some person of higher condition at their funerals. When an aged and exemplary member of a congregation dies, it is not unfrequent that the minister's eldest son will pay respect, by acting as one of the bearers of the corpse. In many of the rural districts in England, the persons composing the procession will sing hymns. In the churches, anthems are still sung, and funeral discourses given in the manner described by the Rev. Dr. Russell, the rector of Bishopsgate.

When I was a boy (says the reverend gentleman), nothing was more common, in the parish of which my father was rector, than for the body to be brought into church before the commencement of the evening service on Sundays. The psalms and lessons appointed for the burial service were read instead of the psalms and the second lesson of the evening. At the time of singing, a portion of those psalms which have reference to the shortness of life was sung ; and sometimes an ambitious choir would attempt a hymn—'Vital spark of heavenly flame,' or the like. Since I have been in orders, I have myself occasionally, in the country, buried persons with a similar service. Sometimes funeral sermons were preached.

§ 180. The natives of the provinces, when they attend the remains of their friends to the grave in London, frequently express a wish to have anthems or such solemnities as those to which they have been accustomed.*

§ 181. The formation of national cemeteries would enable the ecclesiastical authorities to provide means for complying with the desire thus expressed. Under general arrangements, with reduced expenses, it will be seen that ample pecuniary provision for it may be made to give to the funerals of the many the most im-

---

* It is perhaps an important fact, that the great majority of burials in some burial-grounds are stated by the undertakers who perform them to be burials of persons who are not subscribing members of the congregations who are reputed to be the owners of the grounds, and whilst only one out of three of the parishioners of many parishes choose burial in the ground belonging to their parish church, the solemnization of the marriage ceremony being generally satisfactory to the population, and all of them having the option to have the marriage solemnized with or without the religious ceremony, only one out of twenty-four in the metropolis prefer solemnization elsewhere than at the established church. From the Registrar General's Report it appears that, in 1839, out of 18,648 marriages celebrated in the metropolis, only 772 were not solemnized in the established church ; and out of 124,329 marriages performed that year in the whole of England and Wales, only 7,311 were performed out of the established church.

pressive solemnity.   On this subject, the Rev. Mr. Stone, rector of Spitalfields, observes—

Should the legislature determine upon removing the burial of the dead from populous places, it would get rid of these mischiefs; and should it adopt a national system of burial instead of the highly objectionable parochial system sketched out in Mr. Mackinnon's Bill, it might do much more—it might greatly add to the solemnity of our burial obsequies, and so make them at once more impressive and more attractive.   This might be done by concentration; instead of the parochial clergyman, hurried to the performance of this affecting service, when his time, attention, and sympathies are engaged by other duties, summoned desultorily to it, and often compelled to repeat it over and over again at the same grave, just as the interest or the convenience of undertakers, the caprice, the bigotry, or the carousals of mourners may choose to prescribe, let ministers appointed to officiate in national cemeteries perform the service over great numbers at once, and at two or three stated hours in every day.   But the performance of the burial service over great numbers at the same time would add incalculably to its solemnity.   In the present state of things, simultaneous interments are supposed, as they certainly are primarily intended, merely to save the time and labour of the clergy; and they may sometimes be hurried through in a manner so careless, slovenly, and unfeeling, as not even the necessities of the clergy can excuse.   But it is quite a confusion of ideas to suppose that the practice itself is slovenly and unfeeling.   On the contrary, I find it more impressive in its effect upon myself; and I think it must prove so to others.   Two or three coffins, placed with their sable draperies in the body of the church, are in themselves an awful spectacle; and the attendant mourners, occupying the surrounding pews clothed in the same livery of death, form a congregation at once appropriate, and large enough to give effect to a religious service.   By their numbers, too, they operate against the intrusion of idle gossips and inquisitive gazers, and, associated as they are with each other in a bereavement of the same kind, they are thus brought into a contact calculated to kindle emotions of social sympathy and religious sensibility.   Assembled in the burial ground round the same grave, or disposed in groups by the side of graves within a reasonable distance of each other, they form a picture of the same affecting and impressive character.   If the sympathy of a public assembly is perceptible or intense in proportion to the numbers that compose it, this aggregation of burials need only be limited by the effective power of the human voice.

Judging from an experiment of my own, I think that these salutary effects would be heightened to a thrilling degree by music.   And from the practice of the highest civil and ecclesiastical authorities, I presume that the introduction of music into the burial office is not inconsistent with the rubric.   At a burial already alluded to, I acceded to a special request by allowing the introduction of some organ-music; and, having no rubrical directions on the point, I selected two parts of the service as those in which music seemed to me to be most admissible, and most likely to prove impressive.   After the officiating minister has preceded the corpse from the entrance of the church and read the introductory sentences, there is an interval, during which he ascends the desk, the mourners take their places in the pews assigned to them, and the corpse is deposited in the body of the church; and there is a still longer interval, during which the melancholy procession leaves the church for the burial ground.   I found that both these intervals, which are unavoidably disturbed by somewhat bustling and noisy arrangements, were most usefully and effectively filled up by the introduction of music.   The subjoined scheme of the music performed at royal burials will prove that I was not mistaken in supposing music consistent with the rubric, nor much so in selecting those parts of the service, at which I prescribed its introduction. It will also serve to show to what an extent music might be made to give effect and attractiveness to a national burial of the dead.

Parts of the Service.		Musical Composer.
" I am the resurrection," &c.	Sung .	Croft. .
" I know that my Redeemer liveth," &c. . .	Ditto .	Ditto.
" We brought nothing into this world," &c. .	Ditto .	Ditto.
The Psalms are chanted	Chant in G minor Purcell.

After the lesson, and before the removal of the corpse from its station in the choir, an anthem is introduced *ad libitum.*

" Man that is born of a woman," &c. . . .	Sung .	Croft.
" In the midst of life," &c.	Ditto .	Ditto.
" Yet, O Lord God, most holy," &c. . . .	Ditto .	Ditto.
" Thou knowest, Lord, the secrets," &c. . .	Ditto .	Purcell.
" I heard a voice from heaven," &c. . . .	Ditto .	Ditto.

Immediately before the Collect, " O merciful God," or sometimes, though very seldom, before " the grace of our Lord Jesus Christ," an anthem is introduced *ad libitum.*

At the close of the service, while the mourners are moving off, the Dead March in Saul is played on the organ.

The anthems usually selected are two of the following :—

" When the ear heard," &c.	Handel.
" I have set God always before me," &c. . .	Blake.
" The souls of the righteous," &c.	Dupuis.
" Hear my prayer," &c.	Kent.

On the burial of esteemed members of the cathedral choirs, the other choristers have sung the highest and most solemn of the church music.

§ 182. Where the circumstances described, in respect to the Protestant population, have prevented compliance with the popular desire for hymns or anthems to be sung or sermons to be spoken at the burial at the parochial churches in London, interment has been purchased for the express purpose of obtaining them at the trading burial grounds. And yet it may be submitted that the desire is consistent with the earliest recognized practice for all classes,* and that a system of national cemeteries would in pro-

---

* Bingham observes that St. Chrysostom speaks against those who use excessive mourning at funerals, showing them the incongruity of that with this psalmody of the church, and exposing them at the same time to the ridicule of the Gentiles. For what said they are these men that talk so finely and philosophically about the resurrection? Yes, indeed! But their actions do not agree with their doctrine. For whilst they profess in words the belief of a resurrection, in their deeds they act more like men that despair of it. If they were really persuaded that their dead were gone to a better life, they would not so lament. " Therefore," says Chrysostom, " let us be ashamed to carry out our dead after this manner. For our psalmody, and prayers, and solemn meeting of fathers, and such a multitude of brethren, is not that thou shouldst weep and lament, and be angry at God, but give him thanks for taking a deceased brother to himself." St. Jerome also frequently speaks of this psalmody as one of the chief parts of their funeral pomp. He says at the funeral of the Lady Paula at Beth-lehem, which was attended with great concourse of bishops and clergy and people of Palestine, there was no howling or lamenting as used to be among the men of this world, but singing of psalms in Greek, Latin, and Syriac (because there were people of different languages present) at the

portion to the numbers interred in them, furnish valuable cases as examples for its beneficial exercise, and must, to a great extent, prevent the misapplication of the service to such cases as have apparently caused it to fall in public esteem.

" The honour," says Hooker, " generally due unto all men maketh a decent interring of them to be convenient, even for very humanity's sake. And therefore so much as is mentioned in the burial of the widow's son, the carrying him forth upon a bier and accompanying him to the earth, hath been used even amongst infidels, all men accounting it a very extreme destitution not to have at least this honour due to them." * * * * " Let any man of reasonable judgment examine whether it be more convenient for a company of men, as it were, in a dumb show to bring a corpse to a place of burial, there to leave it, covered with earth, and so end, or else to have the exsequies devoutly performed with solemn recitals of such lectures, psalms, and prayers, as are purposely framed for the stirring up of men's minds into a careful consideration of their estate both here and hereafter.

" In regard to the quality of men, it hath been judged fit to commend them unto the world at their death amongst the heathen in funeral orations; amongst the Jews in sacred poems; and why not in funeral sermons amongst Christians? Us it sufficeth that the known benefit hereof doth countervail millions of such inconveniences as are therein surmised, although they were not surmised only, but found therein." * * * " The care no doubt of the living, both to live and die well, must needs be somewhat increased when they know that their departure shall not be folded up in silence, but the ears of many be made acquainted with it. The sound of these things do not so pass the ears of them that are most loose and dissolute in life, but it causeth them one time or other to wish, ' Oh that I might die the death of the righteous, and that my end might be like his.' Thus much peculiar good there doth grow at those times by speech concerning the dead; besides the benefit of public instruction common unto funeral with other sermons."—*Hooker, Ecclesiastical Polity,* b. v. ch. lxxv.

" When thou hast wept awhile," says Jeremy Taylor, in his Holy Dying, " compose the body to burial; which, that it be done gravely, decently, and charitably, we have the example of all nations to engage us, and of all ages of the world to warrant; so that it is against common honesty and public fame and reputation not to do this office."—" The church, in her funerals of the dead, used to

procession of her body to the grave." " And being so general and decent a practice, it was a grievance to any one to be denied the privilege of it. Victor Uticensis, upon this account, complains of the inhuman cruelty of one of the kings of the Vandals. Who can bear, says he, to think of it without tears, when he calls to mind how he commanded the bodies of our dead to be carried in silence without the solemnity of the usual hymns to the grave." (Vol. vii. 335.)

sing psalms and to give thanks for the redemption and delivery of the soul from the evil and dangers of mortality."—"Solemn and appointed mournings are good expressions of our dearness to the departed soul, and of his worth and our value of him, and it hath its praise in nature, and in manners, and in public customs; but the praise of it is not in the gospel, that is, it hath no direct and proper uses in religion; for if the dead did die in the Lord, then there is joy to him, and it is an ill expression of our affection and our charity to weep uncomfortably at a change that hath carried my friend to the state of a huge felicity."—"Something is to be given to custom, something to fame, to nature and to civilities, and to the honour of deceased friends; for that man is esteemed to die miserable for whom no friend or relation sheds a tear, or pays a solemn sigh. I desire to die a dry death, but am not very desirous to have a dry funeral; some flowers sprinkled on my grave would do well and comely; and a soft shower, to turn those flowers into a springing memory or a fair rehearsal, that I may not go forth of my doors, as my servants carry the entrails of beasts."   *   *   *   *

" Concerning doing honour to the dead the consideration is not long. Anciently the friends of the dead used to make their funeral oration, and what they spake of greater commendation was pardoned on the accounts of friendship; but when Christianity seized on the possession of the world, this charge was devolved on priests and bishops, and they first kept the custom of the world and adorned it with the piety of truth and of religion; but they also ordered it that it should not be cheap; for they made funeral sermons only at the death of princes, or of such holy persons ' who shall judge the angels.' The custom descended, and in the channels mingled with the veins of earth, through which it passed; and now-a-days, men that die are commended at a price, and the measure of their legacy is the degree of their virtue. But these things ought not so to be; the reward of the greatest virtue ought not to be prostitute to the doles of common persons, but preserved like laurels and coronets to remark and encourage the noblest things. Persons of an ordinary life should neither be praised publicly, nor reproached in private; for it is an offence and charge of humanity to speak no evil of the dead, which I suppose, is meant concerning things not public and evident; but then neither should our charity to them teach us to tell a lie, or to make a great flame from a heap of rushes and mushrooms, and make orations crammed with the narrative of little observances, and acts of civil, necessary, and eternal religion. But that which is most considerable is, that we should do something for the dead, something that is real and of proper advantage. That we perform their will, the laws oblige us, and will see to it; but that we do all those parts of personal duty which our dead left unperformed, and to which the laws do not oblige us, is an act of great charity and perfect kindness."—" Besides this, let us right their causes and assert their honour:" * * " and certainly it is the noblest thing in the world to do an act of kindness to him whom we shall never see, but yet hath deserved it of us, and to whom we would do it if he were present; and unless we do so, our charity is mercenary, and our friendships are direct mer. chandise, and our gifts are brocage : but what we do to the dead, or to the living for their sakes, is gratitude, and virtue for virtue's sake, and the noblest portion of humanity."

Necessity and nature of the superior agency requisite for private and public protection in respect to interments.

§ 183. Having given a view of the evils arising from the existing practice in respect to interments in towns, and an outline of what appears to be justly desired as necessary objects to supply the wants of the population, I now beg leave to submit for consideration the information collected as to the practical means of obtaining them.

§ 184. The most pressing of the evils being physical or sanitary evils, the first means of amendment required is the appointment and arrangement of the qualifications, powers, and duties and responsibilities of an officer of health, to whom the requisite changes of practice may be most safely confided.

The functions of such an officer, as marked out by the evidence of existing necessities, may be divided into the ordinary and the extraordinary. The immediate necessities are those which arise from the want of a trustworthy person who may be looked up to for counsel and direction to survivors in the event of a death, §§ 121, 122, 123, 124, and guide a change of the practice of interment. It is only by an arrangement that will carry a man of education, a responsible officer, to the house of even the poorest person in the community, just at the time when a competent and trustworthy person is most needed to give advice, that the effect of ignorant or interested suggestions may be prevented, and the beneficent intentions of the legislature, or the salutary nature of any public arrangement for the general advantage can be made known with certainty.

185. The ordinary service of such an officer would consist of the verification of the fact and cause of death, and its due civic registration. From the exercise of these duties would follow the extraordinary duties of directing measures of immediate precaution and prevention, which it is to be feared whatsoever general sanitary measures might be adopted would, at the outset, and for too long a period, constitute ordinary and every-day duties. Out of the ordinary duties of the officer of health, would arise extraordinary jurisprudential duties of protecting the interests of the community in cases of deaths which have occurred under circumstances of suspicion or of manifest criminality.

§ 186. Assuming the necessity of the establishment of adequate national cemeteries at proper sites, it is proposed that a body of officers properly qualified by service, as in the example § 185, should have charge of the material arrangements, and take the place of the churchwardens and overseers in respect to all places of burial, and be responsible for the control of the servants of the establishment, and shall, moreover, be enabled to regulate and contract for supplies, at reduced prices, of materials and service of the nature of those now supplied by the undertaker. §§ 150, 153, 154, 155.

§ 187. In order that the officer of public health may be brought to the spot, it is proposed that the last medical attendant on the deceased should, on a small payment, be required to give immediate notice of the death, in a form to be specified, or in case there happened to be no medical attendant, it should then be incumbent on the occupier of the house, or the person having charge of the body, to give the required notice.

Before particularising the course of practice of such an officer, it appears requisite to state other grounds on which intervention appears requisite for the verification of the fact of death, and the mode of death, by the inspection of the body previously to interment.

§ 188. It is admitted that some additional arrangements are yet wanting for the complete attainment of the proper civic and technical purposes of registration:—as depositaries of pre-appointed evidence of the fact of death, to determine questions of private rights:—as depositaries of evidence for purposes of medical science and public health, to show the extent and prevalence of common causes of disease incident to different occupations and different localities—and of the data for tables of insurance, as well as for the recovery of sums assured, where the proof of age is not admitted in the policy. Any one who is unknown to the local registrar may go and register as a fact his own death, of which a certified copy of the registry will, according to the 38th clause of the Act, be evidence in a court of law. Cases of the registration of false statements have already been detected ; some have been made with the view to successions and to the obtainment of property. False registrations have been made amongst the labouring classes as to the place of death, to gain interments in distant parishes at cheaper rates. Fictitious deaths have been registered to defraud burial societies, and the registrar's certificate of such deaths have got in use by vagrants as a means of obtaining alms. In Manchester a woman having obtained and used one certificate of a fictitious death, soon after obtained another similar certificate, and in order to deter parties from visiting the house, she got the cause of death registered as " malignant fever."

§ 189. On the continent, wherever the mortuary registers are well kept, and arrangements are made for the protection of the public health, the fact and time of death, and the identity of the deceased, is verified on the spot, by inspection of the body by a competent responsible officer of public health. Vide instance and effects at Geneva, stated in the General Sanitary Report, p. 174.

§ 190. It is proposed that the verification of the fact of death, and ascertaining its cause, by inquiry on the spot, should be confided to the officer proposed to be appointed as an officer of public health. The present local registrars might act as auxiliaries; the proposed appointment would be an additional security for the acccuracy of the mortuary registration, and would improve that branch of the local machinery for registration.

Postponing the consideration of other collateral grounds for the appointment of a district officer of health, and to illustrate more clearly the course of alteration of the practice of interments, we will suppose the physician or officer of health brought by the proper notice to the habitation where the body lies in the presence of the survivors.

§ 191. In visiting the habitations of the labouring classes, he would be more careful to denote his office, profession, and condition, by his dress, and in his address, even than with other classes. On his arrival at the place of abode of a person of the working class, he would, after announcing his office and duty, inspect the body, and then require the name, age, occupation, and circumstances of the death of the deceased, enter them, and take the attestations of witnesses present. If the death occurred from any ordinary cause, he would, nevertheless, speak of the expediency of the early removal of the body to the chapel or house of reception, where it would be placed under proper care until the appointed time of the attendance of the relations and friends at the interment. The exercise of a summary power of removal in the case of rapid decomposition of the corpse, or in case of deaths from epidemic disease, for the protection of the living, is frequently suggested and claimed by neighbours. On inquiry in Manchester as to the periods during which the bodies of persons dying in the poorest districts were retained in the rooms where they died, the superintendent-registrar, Mr. Gardiner, observed, "they are not retained so long in these districts, because the houses to which the rooms belong are generally inhabited by several families, and those other families feel the inconvenience of the retention of the body amongst them, and they press for an early interment." With females or survivors who cannot endure to part with the remains, the exercise of a friendly will would sometimes be necessary, and if properly exercised would generally be effectual. The name of an officer of public health would carry with it very general voluntary obedience to whatever he recommended, and in a majority of cases the prostrate survivors would be glad that he should order everything, and would feel it a relief if he were to do so. He would be prepared with a tariff of the prices of burial, and

with instructions as to the regulations adopted for the public convenience, and for the more respectful performance of the ceremony
of interment, and should be empowered and required, on the
assent or application of the parties, to carry them out completely,
as he might do with very little inconvenience or expenditure of
time. He might be empowered to take such a course as this.
Speaking to the widow or survivor of the lowest class, he might
say—

" The inspectors of public health have been empowered to regulate the practice and the charges for interment, and to contract for
and on behalf of the public to ensure the means of burial in a proper
and respectful manner for the highest, as well as for the most humble
classes. Formerly, the charge for the funeral of a person of the
condition in life of your husband was four or five pounds, but by
the new regulations, an equally respectable interment is secured
to you for little more than half the amount. You are, nevertheless,
at liberty to obtain the means of burial from any private undertaker. You may also, if you prefer it, have burial in any private
cemetery, or elsewhere."

§ 192. It is anticipated that, except on private canvass, and that
only for a time, interment under the auspices of a public officer
would be preferred in the great majority of cases, if the business
were conducted with moderate care, in a manner really satisfactory, and if the minor but really important conveniences of
all classes were duly consulted. For example, one frequent cause
of the delay of interments amongst the poorer classes in crowded
districts, is the delay of notification of deaths to distant relatives
and friends, whose attendance may be required. More than one-
half of the poor cannot write, and many of all classes who can
write are unable to collect their thoughts even for a simple announcement of the event. The poorer classes generally get some
one to write for them ; and the regular payment for each letter is
fourpence and a glass of liquor, or sixpence, exclusive of paper
and postage. In the charges for funerals of the labouring classes
in Scotland, five shillings is set down as the item of expense of
letters of notification of the death of an artisan, and fifteen shillings for the notifications of the deaths of persons of the middle
ranks of life. Under practicable regulations, such notifications
might be prepared in a manner suitable to persons of every condition, at the rate of threepence per letter, or at one-half the ordinary rate of payment, paper, and envelope, and postage stamp
included. The service might be rendered at an expense of a few
minutes' time to the officer in taking down a list of the names
and addresses of the persons to be sent to. This list he would
on his return to his office, hand to a clerk, by whom they would
be immediately prepared and despatched in proper and well
considered form. The Inspector might, therefore, add—

" If you will give me the names and addresses of those relatives and friends who may be desired to attend the funeral, I will cause notice of the time and places of attendance to be sent to them. Amongst the highest classes it is now the practice to diminish the number of followers to the grave, and to commit that duty only to a few ; and it is desirable, for the sake of preventing unnecessary expense, that too many should not be invited. All the friends of the deceased who attend at the national cemetery will have an opportunity of joining in with the procession. Besides, the requests to attend, I can also, if you wish it, and will give me the names and addresses, cause notifications of the fact of the death to be sent to any persons in any part of the country."

In the cases of illness amongst the survivors, or of a death from epidemic disease, indicating an infected atmosphere, he might add—

"For the protection of your own health, and the health of your children and of your neighbours, it is requisite that the body be immediately removed to a place where it will be kept under the care of a physician, and inspected until the appointed time of interment, when it will be received by the friends and relations who attend."

§ 193. It is considered that, in general, this course would be complied with, but it is considered by physicians, that if it were found necessary in the first instance, in the case of the poorest and most ignorant and highly-excitable people, to concede the point, the officer might give directions to have the body enclosed with cloth of a material to resist the immediate escape of effluvia, and to be closed down, which might be done at a few shillings extra expense. Mr. R. Baker, the surgeon, who has paid great attention to the means for the improvement of the sanitary condition of the population at Leeds, observes—

I believe that where persons die of epidemic diseases, there is not much regard paid to the necessity of early interment. There is what is called the making up of the body, which is often done very early after death, and even in some cases of supposed contagion, before it is absolutely necessary. But an application is used in coffins of those whose friends can afford it which deserves naming, because it is at once safe and economical, and renders any sanatory precautions unnecessary, where there is a desire from any requisite family arrangements to keep the body; it is to place the body in a deal shell, and then to place this shell within the coffin, between which and the shell are affixed at the sides and bottom. a few pieces of circular wood about the thickness of two crown pieces, here and there, to keep the shell and coffin apart, forming a considerable interstice, which is filled in with boiling pitch. The lid of the shell is then laid on, having a glass over the face, and over this is poured more pitch till the shell is incased in a pitch coffin between the wooden ones. The cost of this process, which is next to that of embalming, is about 9s. 6d., and is easily paid out of the seven or ten pounds which the club supplies. I would only add that this experiment deserves well of every one's consideration, being far superior to lead, and equally useful, in all ordinary interments, and admirable for the purpose of avoiding contagion, while it admits the opportunity of keeping the body for any arrangement that is required to be made. If this plan could be enforced upon all

M 2

occasions where death had occurred from contagious disease, I look upon it, that a great benefit would be conferred upon the community.

§ 194. In the cases where decomposition, as sometimes occurs, commences even before death and proceeds with extreme rapidity after it, even an immediate removal is not effected without producing depressing effects on the bearers; and when there is an in-door church service, in some districts in the metropolis, it is not unfrequently necessary to have the body left at the church door, on account of the extremely offensive smell which escapes from the coffin. These coffins are generally constructed without knowledge, or care, or adaptation to the circumstances of the remains, or to any sanitary service. Mr. W. Dyce Guthrie, surgeon, who has paid much attention to some of the structural means for the protection of the public health, specifies various modes in which the evils arising before interment, as well as after, may be prevented, at a cost so inconsiderable as not to be sensibly felt, even by the poorest classes, and yet be as efficient as the most expensive arrangements now in use. For example : " Coffins may," he says, " be rendered perfectly impervious to the escape of all morbific matter, at an expense not exceeding 1s. 6d. or 2s. each, by coating the interior over with a cement composed of lime, sand, and oil, which soon sets and becomes almost as hard and resisting as stone. Pitch, applied hot, would answer the same purpose as the compound I have mentioned, but it would be more expensive." In the cases of such rapid decomposition as bursts leaden coffins, or renders " tapping " necessary, he recommends the application, at a few shillings expense, of safety-tubes to the foot of the coffin, so as to secure and carry away into a chimney flue, or a current created by a chauffer, the mephitic matter. These are adduced as instances of the detailed appliances of which the officer of health would judge in each case on the spot and suggest to the survivors, and if necessary write directions, or a prescription, for their appliance.

§ 195. A cause of the delay of interments might, it is stated, be diminished by arrangements, under which coffins of every size being kept prepared, one might be brought to the house, with the name of the deceased, and his obituary duly inscribed on a plate, in about one-third the time that is now usually employed for the purpose. By this service, the rapid progress of decomposition, and the escape of noxious effluvia would be arrested.

§ 196. Before leaving the abode of the deceased, the officer of health would, in the case of death from diseases likely to have been originated or precipitated by local causes, inspect the premises, inquire closely as to the antecedent circumstances of the decease; and note directions to be given in respect to the premises to officers having charge of drainage or sewerage, or public works, for cleansing and lime-washing the premises, at the charge of the owner, before renewed occupation.

In respect to the poorest classes, those who stand the most in need of protection : the measure of prohibiting burial, except on a verification of the fact and cause of death, by a certificate granted on the sight and identification of the body at the place where the death occurred, has its chief importance as being the means of carrying a person of education into places rarely, if ever entered, by them, except by accident. The functions of the officer of health when there are marked out by instances of acts done by force of humanity and charity, which as yet have no authority in law, or in administrative provision. For example, in the following instance, of a house owned by a landlord of the lowest class.

Shepherd's-court consists of about six houses. It was notorious that fever had prevailed to a great extent in this court ; in the house in question, several cases of fever had occurred in succession. The house is small, contains four rooms,—two on the ground-floor and two above; each of these rooms was let out to a separate family. On the present occasion, in one of the rooms on the ground-floor there were four persons ill of fever; in the other room, on the same floor, there were, at the same time, three persons ill of fever ; and in one of the upper rooms there were also at the same time three persons ill of fever; in the fourth room no one was ill at that time. It appeared that different families had in succession occupied these rooms, and become affected with fever ; on the occasion in question, all the sick were removed as soon as possible by the interference of the parish officers. An order was made by the board of guardians to take the case before the magistrates at Worship-street. The magistrates at first refused to interfere, but the medical officer stated that several cases of fever had occurred in succession in this particular house ; that one set of people had gone in, become ill with fever, and were removed ; that another set of people had gone in, and been in like manner attacked with fever ; that this had occurred several times, and that it was positively known that this house had been affected with fever for upwards of six weeks before the present application was made. On hearing this, the magistrate sent for the owner of the house, and remonstrated with him for allowing different sets of people to occupy the rooms without previously cleansing and whitewashing them ; telling him that he was committing a serious offence in allowing the nuisance to continue. The magistrate further gave the house in charge to the medical officer, authorizing him to see all the rooms properly fumigated, and otherwise thoroughly cleansed; and said that, if any persons entered the house before the medical officer said that the place was fit to be inhabited, they would send an officer to turn them out, or place an officer at the door to prevent their entrance. The landlord became frightened, and allowed the house to be whitewashed, fumigated, and thoroughly cleansed. Since this was done the rooms have been occupied by a fresh set of people ; but no case of fever has occurred.*

This occurred seven years since, and on a very recent inquiry made at this same house, it was stated that comparative cleanliness having been maintained, no fever had since broken out, no more such deaths have been occasioned, no more burthens had been cast upon the poor's rates from this house. The law already authorizes the house to be condemned, and its use arrested, when it is in a condition to endanger life by falling ; if it be deemed that the principle should be applied to all manifest causes of disease or death, or danger to life, then, instead of the remote

* Dr. Southwood Smith's Report, Poor Law Commissioners' Fifth Annual Report, Appendix, p. 160.

and practically useless remedy by the inspection of an unskilled and unqualified ward inquest (Vide General Sanitary Report, p. 300), the skilled and responsible medical officer, with such summary powers and duties of immediate interference, as were successfully exercised in the case above cited, should be appointed.

§ 197. It is proper to observe, that it occurs not unfrequently that such scenes arise from negligences and dilapidations of a succession of bad tenants, of which the chief landlord is himself unaware : but whether aware of it or not, the prompt intervention of an officer of health in such cases would not be without its compensation to the owner. A bricklayer, who himself owned some small houses occupied by artisans, which he had himself built, was asked in the course of another inquiry :—

In what periods do you collect the rents?—Some monthly; about one-third monthly; the rest we collect quarterly.

What may be your losses on the collections?—They will average, perhaps, about one-fifth; we lose rather the most on the quarterly tenements.

What are the chief causes of your losses from this class of tenants?—Loss of work first; then sickness and death; then frauds.

Are the frauds considerable?—Not so much as the inabilities to pay. I find the working classes, if they have means, as willing to pay and as honourable as any other class. Within the last 18 months there have been a great many people out of work; at other times there is as much loss to the landlord from sickness as from any other cause. Three out of five of the losses of rent that I now have, are losses from the sickness of the tenants, who are working men.

When children are sick, there is of course no immediate interruption to the payment of rent?—Very seldom.

What sort of sicknesses are they from which the interruption to work and to the payment of rent occurs?—Fevers, nervous disorders, and sickness that debilitates them.

Then anything which promotes the health of the tenants will tend to prevent losses of rent to the owners of the lower class of houses?—Yes, I have decidedly found that rent is the best got from healthy houses.

In some of the cellar dwellings in Manchester the losses of rent, chiefly from sickness, amounted to 20 per cent.

§ 198. In all cases of deaths from epidemic diseases, one of the first duties of the officer of health would be to inquire whether there were any other persons in the house attacked with disease, and examine them. In all such cases as those cited, §§ 26, 27, 28, 29, 30, 31, he should have adequate power, which, that it may be efficient must be summary, to take measures to protect the parties affected and others, by ordering their immediate removal to fever wards. It is only in a deplorable state of ignorance of the nature of the evils which depress such districts that there could be any hesitation in granting such powers from the fear of abuse; the most serious legislative difficulty would be to ensure their constant and efficient application. Mr. S. Holmes, the builder of the Stockport viaduct, and formerly an active member of the Liverpool town council, gives the following illustration of the extreme miseries witnessed in that town, and it is certainly not an exaggerated description of the scenes to which the officer of health must at the commencement of his duties be frequently carried on the occurrence of deaths.

The melancholy facts elicited by the corporation clearly show that Liver-pool contains a multitude of inhabited cellars, close and damp, with no drain nor any convenience, and these pest-houses are constantly filled with fever. Some time ago I visited a poor woman in distress, the wife of a labouring man. She had been confined only a few days, and herself and infant were lying on straw in a vault through the outer cellar, with a clay floor, impervious to water. There was no light nor ventilation in it, and the air was dreadful. I had to walk on bricks across the floor to reach her bed-side, as the floor itself was flooded with stagnant water. This is by no means an extraordinary case, for I have witnessed scenes equally wretched; and it is only necessary to go into Crosby-street, Fremasons'-row, and many cross streets out of Vauxhall-road, to find hordes of poor creatures living in cellars, which are almost as bad and offensive as char-nel-houses. In Freemasons'-row, about two years ago, a court of houses, the floors of which were below the public street, and the area of the whole court, was a floating mass of putrified animal and vegetable matter, so dreadfully offensive that I was obliged to make a precipitate retreat. Yet the whole of the houses were inhabited!

§ 199. In cases of epidemics the saving of life by the prompt intervention of an officer of health, on the occurrence of the first death, and the immediate removal of the survivors affected, would be very considerable. In cases of fever, on the removal of patients to the fever hospital, they are often received in a state of violent delirium, or in a state of coma succeeding to violent delirium. After they have been washed in a bath, and placed in a clean bed, in the spacious and well-ventilated ward of the hospital, in a few hours, often before the visit of the physician, the violent delirium has subsided, or the state of coma having passed away conscious-ness has returned. Although in a great majority of cases the patients are only sent to the hospital in the last stage of disease, this mere change in the locality and external circumstances of the sufferers diminishes the proportion of deaths from one in five to one in seven. Supposing the cases occurred in equal numbers daily, the functions of registration in the metropolis would carry the officers of health to upwards of 20 cases per diem of deaths from epidemic disease, for the most part in the most wretched districts.

§ 200. The principle of this part of the proposed arrangement is in necessitating visits of inspection, and thence necessitating the initiation of measures of relief where there has hitherto been, and whence it may safely be said there will be, no complaint or initiation of measures of relief by the sufferers themselves. It is observed by Dr. Southwood Smith, in confirmation of the obser-vations made on the demoralizing effects of the physical evils which depress the bodily condition of large classes that, as they have not the bodily vigour, so they have not the intelligence of a healthy class. One of the most melancholy proofs of this, he observes, is, that they make no effort to get into happier circumstances; their dulness and apathy indicate an equal degree of mental as of physical paralysis. And this has struck other observers who have had opportunities of becoming acquainted with the real state of these people. " The following statement impressed my mind the more, because it recalled to my recollection vividly similar cases witnessed by myself. ' In the year 1836,' says one of the medical officers of the West Derby Union, ' I attended a family of thirteen, twelve of whom had typhus fever,— without a bed in the cellar, without straw or timber shavings— frequent substitutes. They lay on the floor, and so crowded that I could scarcely pass between them. In another house I attended fourteen patients: there were only two beds in the house. All the patients lay on the boards, and during their illness never had their clothes off. I met with many cases in similar conditions; yet amidst the greatest destitution and want of domestic comfort, *I have never heard, during the course of twelve years' practice, a complaint of inconvenient accommodation.*' Now this want of complaint, under such circumstances, appears to me to constitute a very melancholy part of this condition. It shows that physical wretchedness has done its worst on the human sufferer, for it has destroyed his mind. The wretchedness being greater than humanity can bear, annihilates the mental faculties—the faculties distinctive of the human being. There is a kind of satisfaction in the thought, for it sets a limit to the capacity of suffering which would otherwise be without bound."

§ 201. In respect to any such services proposed, involving inquiry on the spot, an objection is apt to be suggested, that the exercise of such functions would be unpopular and objected to. By the sufferers it certainly would not, § 122. With portions of the population, in such a deplorable state of ignorance as that manifested, even in this country, at the time of the invasion of the cholera, when they imbibed the notion that the wells had been poisoned by the medical men, the creation of any monstrous impressions by others must be admitted to be possible; but the existence of that notion would have been no justification for closing the hospitals, for staying the work of beneficence, and suspending the performance of medical duties. Such an objection, however, implies a very large misconception as to the *general* state of intelligence of the working classes. There is, on this point, as regards the metropolis, the direct and decisive evidence of experience. In consequence of the difficulty of dealing satisfactorily with common hearsay evidence, some of the local registrars have, with praiseworthy care, proceeded to verify the facts of the death by inquiries made at the house where it took place, which inquiries are strictly supererogatory. The following evidence, though in part substantially a repetition of scenes already described, is here adduced less for the descriptions of places visited than as showing the manner in which these officers were received.

Mr. James Murray, the registrar of births, deaths, and marriages for the Hackney Road district of Bethnal Green, having
stated that sometimes he made inquiries on the spot for the registration of deaths, speaking of the poorer population of that district, states that they have usually only a single room, and that
" they never speak of occupying the same house, but the ' same
room.' "

In what proportion of cases do the bodies of those persons remain in the
room in which the persons live and sleep ?—It would depend upon the part
of the district, for part of the higher district is highly respectable.   In that
district nine-tenths of them have only a single room, and no opportunity of
placing the body elsewhere.

In nine-tenths of the cases the body remains in the same room ?—It must
be so, they have no other room.

In a coffin ?—Yes; I have seen it so repeatedly.

Is the retention of the body injurious ?—I think so.

When you go to register the deaths is it deemed an intrusion, or are you
received with civility ?—I am always received with civility in all cases.

It is not considered an intrusion?—Not at all.   I myself have rather cul-
tivated the good feeling and opinion of the working classes ; they know me
exceedingly well, and I have never met with any instance of incivility among
them.

Mr. John Johnson, the registrar of one part of the Shoreditch
district, was asked—

Of the labouring classes, what proportion of the families have more than
two rooms ?—I cannot say the number; but there is a vast number who
occupy one room, and some occupy two rooms ; some occupy a kitchen and
one room, or a little parlour and kitchen, and some two rooms up-stairs,
some one room ; perhaps if they have two rooms up-stairs they have a family
in each.

Do you find, on visiting those places, upon the occurrence of a death, that
the dead body is retained in the living and sleeping room ?—Frequently we
find it so.

And the family are eating and pursuing the ordinary offices of life in the
room where the body lies ?—Yes.

Have you found the body retained for a long time?—No, they do not
usually keep it longer than five or six days ; but I have known instances
where the body has been kept two and three weeks.

But in that time does it not acquire a putrid smell ?—Yes, and in rooms
where I have gone to register births I have found the effluvia so bad that I
have been obliged to go out of the house without effecting the register.

It had an effect upon your health for the time being ?—Yes.

When you go to register deaths at the houses of the labouring classes,
are you on the whole well received ?—Generally very well; they consider
we pay them a compliment by calling upon them.

They do not deem your registration or inquiry an intrusion ?—Not at all.

Mr. W. H. Wheatley, the registrar for the Old Church district of Lambeth, was asked—

You think it necessary, in order to ascertain the causes of death with correctness, to go to the spot and ascertain the fact on the spot ?—Yes: I get
much more correct information in that way than from parties calling upon
me.

If you were to remain at your desk, without local inquiry, do you conceive your registration would be at all correct, or would it not be widely different from the fact ?—I do not think it would be correct. I think in every case of death the registrar ought to go to the house, not only for the purpose of registering the death, but that there ought to be some means of ascertaining from what cause the party died ; that the body ought to be seen by the registrar, or some authorized person, or that it should be compulsory to produce a medical certificate, certifying the precise cause of death. The searchers, who were two women, appointed in open vestry, under an old Act of Parliament, to call and investigate every case of death that occurred, and to examine the body and see that the party had come fairly by his or her death, have been done away with since the passing of the Registration Act, and there is now no means of ascertaining how the party has met with his death.

Can you state to the Commissioners instances of error which you have obviated or prevented by going and inquiring upon the spot, that would have occurred by your not going ?—I cannot mention individual cases ; but it has come under my knowledge that parties have called upon me to register a death, and when I have asked the cause they have said, " I do not exactly know what it was, I believe it was a fever, or something of that kind." I have said, " I must trouble you to get me a medical certificate, or I will call at the house." I have gone to the house, and found it widely different in many cases from the statement they gave to me, from error on their parts.

Are you satisfied from the experience of your office, though it has been short, that there can be no correct registration without examination on the spot, and a sight of the body ?—I think so ; it would entail upon the registrars a very arduous and a very unpleasant office, but that the registration would be more perfect, and it would be a check upon crime, I have very little doubt.

Do you find any obstruction given on the part of the poorer classes to your going to the spot and making inquiries ?—Not the slightest. My opinion is that the poorer classes pay more attention to the registration than the middling classes.

Have you met with any manifestation of prejudice or bad feeling from the poorer classes ?—No, not the slightest, but really a wish that the registration should be effective.

They do not view the registrar as an intrusive officer ?—Not in the least.

In the worst conditioned places the only persons who are seen as public officers are policemen and the rate-collectors or the tax-gatherers. When commissioners of inquiry have been seen taking notes in them, the popular impression was that they were tax-gatherers, an impression which it required some trouble to remove. In a little time the officer of health would be most popular and would exercise extensive and beneficial influence. The practical evidence of the registrars was of an uniform tenor, establishing, as far as actual experience may establish, not only the acceptability of the more elevated and extensive service proposed, but that it must develope most important civil as well as medical facts, the correct knowledge of which is necessary for the relief of the most afflicted portions of the population.

Jurisprudential value of the appointment of Officers of Health.

§ 202. In the lamentable state of the population, which in England and Wales produces annually upwards of 700 committals to prison for crimes of passion, and of these 450 for murder, manslaughter, and attempts upon life, it may scarcely be deemed necessary to adduce many particular examples of the importance of the extraordinary jurisprudential services and securities for life to the community obtainable by the exercise in all cases of the ordinary functions of the verification, as far as may be, of the fact as well as the cause of death. On examining the grounds of the fears of life and suspicions of the poorer classes, inhabiting the worst conditioned districts, it is evident that obstructions to crime, or safeguards, which are carefully preserved in the well regulated communities (marked by security of life and the rarity of crimes of violence) are here absent, and that wide openings are left for the escape of the darkest crimes. Had there been an officer of public health, and a verification of the cause of death by him on inspection, as at Geneva, Munich, or other towns on the continent, and inquiry for registration of the causes of death, it is probable that, with the certainty of such inspection, the murders of the children at Stockport or at Little Bolton would not have been attempted; or, if perpetrated, they might have been detected in the first case. The whole class of murders verified on examination after disinterment may be cited as coming within the same category. The crime of burking, which appears to have originated in Scotland, and was extended to England, could scarcely have been attempted systematically, except under the temptation of the absence of such a security; and with such service as that proposed, it is highly improbable that it could have been carried on to the extent there is reason to believe it was.

On this point Mr. Corder, the superintendent registrar of the Strand Union, gives important testimony.

From your knowledge of the actual state of much of the population in the worst part of the metropolis. derived from your experience in the several local offices you have held, and especially your experience as a superintendent registrar, do you believe that the inspection of the body to verify the fact of death, and, as far as inspection and inquiry on the spot may do so, to determine the cause of death, would be important securities not merely for the truth of the registration, but valuable securities for life itself?—Most certainly I do. Had there been such an inspection and verification prior to the year 1831, the horrible system of destroying human beings for the purpose of selling their bodies could not have been carried on to the extent to which I know it existed at that period. Being then the vestry clerk of St. Paul, Covent Garden, the officers of which were bound over to prosecute Bishop, Williams, and May, for the murder of the Italian boy, the duty of conducting the prosecution entirely devolved upon me. In the course of my inquiries, I elicited beyond all doubt that the practice of burking, as it was then called, had prevailed to a considerable extent in the metropolis.

Would inspection, do you conceive, and proper inquiry as to the cause of death, have prevented such murders?—Most effectually so, I conceive. I may mention that they took out the teeth of the younger subjects, and sold them to the dentists. The Italian boy, it would have been seen. had no teeth; the teeth had been punched out in such a manner as to have been remarkable.

Though the motives to such dreadful practices are removed under the securities for the public safety imposed in connexion with the Anatomy Act, yet in cases of other attempts against life, do you consider that the requiring a certificate of the fact of death, verified on inspection before burial, would interpose useful practical obstacles for the prevention of murder, and the protection of life?—Most assuredly,

Mr. Partridge, the surgeon of King's College, at whose instance the murderers were taken into custody, in the cases referred to, expresses a similar opinion as to the importance of the proposed verification of the fact and cause of death by a proper officer.

§ 203. It may here be stated that only a small proportion of the local registrars are either medical officers or members of the medical profession; but the short experience of those registrars who have those qualifications has elicited abundant indications of the extent to which proper securities are wanting for the protection of life in this country. Nearly all who have for any length of time exercised their functions have had occasion to arrest cases of *prima facie* suspicion on the way to interment that had escaped the only existing security and initiative to investigation, the suspicion of neighbours and popular rumour. Mr. Abraham, surgeon and registrar of deaths in the City of London Union, was asked on this subject—

You are Registrar of Deaths in the City of London Union. Since you have been Registrar, have you had occasion to send notice to the coroner of cases where the causes of death stated appeared suspicious?—Yes, in about half-a-dozen cases. One was of an old gentleman occupying apartments in Bell Alley. His servant went out to market, and on her return, in less than an hour, found him dead on the bed, with his legs lying over the side of it. He had been ailing some time, and was seized occasionally with difficulty of breathing, but able to get up, and when she left him she did not perceive anything unusual in his appearance. I went to the house myself, and made inquiries into the cause of death; and although I did not discover anything to lead to the suspicion of his having died from poison or other unfair means, I considered it involved in obscurity, and referred the case to the coroner for investigation. Another case was of a traveller who was found dead in his bed at an inn. The body was removed to a distance of forty miles before a certificate to authorize the burial was applied for. His usual medical attendant certified to his having been for several years the subject of aortic aneurism, which was the probable cause of his sudden death, although the evidence was imperfect and unsatisfactory, and could not be otherwise without an examination of the body, and I therefore refused to register it without notice from the coroner.

A third case occurred a few days ago. A medical certificate was presented to me of the death of a man from disease of the heart and aneurism of the aorta. He was driven in a cab to the door of a medical practitioner in this neighbourhood, and was found dead. He might have died from poison, and, without the questions put on the occasion of registering the cause of death, the case might have passed without notice. There was not in this case, as in others, any evidence to show that death was occasioned by unfair means, but the causes were obscure and unsatisfactory, and I felt it to be my duty to have them investigated by the coroner.

But for anything known, you may have passed cases of murder?— Certainly; and there is at present no security against such cases. The personal inspection of the deceased would undoubtedly act as a great security.

Mr. P. H. Holland, surgeon, registrar for Chorlton-on-Medlock :—

My district is of the better description, inhabited either by the higher classes or by respectable working men, in which cases of deaths from crime are not very likely to occur; yet suspicious cases have from time to time happened (say six or eight annually in my district), to which I have thought it necessary to call the attention of the coroner. In one case, for example, a father, a labouring man, came to me to report the death of his infant child, stating the cause to be sickness and purging; there was then no cholera prevalent, and the rapidity of the disease was unusually great. My suspicion was excited as to the cause of the death, of which the father could give no clear account, and I sent word to the coroner that I thought the case was one which required inquiry. An inquest was held, and it turned out that the child had taken arsenic. The jury were of opinion that the death was entirely accidental,—that there had been no criminal intention. Had not the cause of the accident been developed by the inquiry, others of the family might have suffered in the same way. The other cases, which had escaped inquiry, have been chiefly those of accident, in which the death occurred at long periods subsequently, such as five or six weeks. I have found that it is a common practice to represent children as "stillborn," who were born alive, it not being necessary to register still-born children. By passing them off as still-born, burial is obtained for a smaller fee. But by this means cases of infanticide might be concealed. The fact of a married woman having been pregnant, and no proof existing as to the issue may hereafter be of legal importance. I have heard of many suspected cases of the wilful neglect of children, on whose deaths sums were obtainable from different burial societies. I cannot doubt that by inquiring much infantile death, which occurs from ignorance and incorrect treatment, would be prevented.

Inspection on the spot would, I consider, operate much more powerfully in prevention than in detection of crime. It would also occasion the stoppage of many existing but unsuspected causes of death. I have had reason to believe in the existence of a large amount of the preventible causes of death, with respect to which I have had no means of inquiry.

I was, during four years, apothecary to the Chorlton-on-Medlock Dispensary, during which time cases of sickness occurring in houses unfit for healthful habitation were constantly coming under my observation; many particular localities, affording far more than their due proportion of disease, owing to imperfect drainage and ventilation. Any one who had gone to inspect the body on the occurrence of death in those places, with powers to enforce sanitary measures, such as the removal of the survivors, the drainage and cleansing and ventilation of the premises, would, undoubtedly, have had the means of preventing much mortality.

§ 204. Mr. Leigh, the surgeon, whose testimony has already been cited, acts as one of the registrars of Manchester, and adverts to one source of mortality amongst infants which appears to be widely extended in the town districts. It is a practice with mothers who go to work to leave their children in the care of the cheapest nurses, who commonly neglect the infants, and have recourse to Dalby's Carminative in large quantities to quiet them. It is his opinion that a large number of them fall a sacrifice to this and other improper modes of treatment. For example, says Mr. Leigh,

There is one evil of the extent of whose existence I had no conception, till I had for some time held the office of registrar. In decrying this, I would beg distinctly to disavow any private professional feeling. I allude to the great number of cases in which either no medical treatment at all, or what is nearly as bad, improper medical treatment, had been resorted to. I think, in nearly one-fourth of the deaths of infants reported to me, on inquiry I find that the little patients had been attended by incompetent and unqualified practitioners, chiefly retail druggists. Cases of croup and inflammation of the lungs which are eminently benefited by medical treatment, and in which prompt and decisive measures often preserve life, are treated by them, and I have reason to know by inquiry into the details of the cases that bleedings, calomel, and the remedies absolutely requisite in such cases are never, or very rarely, employed, whereas, under proper medical treatment, most of such cases would recover. Under these circumstances, these men themselves become fertile sources of mortality to the young.

In a subsequent communication, he states—

I find that in the month of January just passed I registered the deaths of 33 children under 4 years of age, of these 9 were attended by druggists ; I believe all by one who has received no medical education : this is at the rate of 108 per annum. Three of the children had no assistance at all, making 12 out of 33 that might possibly have been saved. This number 33, however, is below the average of the year, for in the three months preceding there died in the district, of children under 4 years, 133, or 44 per month; and during the quarter ending 30th September, 1842, 169, or 56 per month; and the general number of those having no attendance, or being attended by druggists, is fully one-third, so that 100 per annum is much below the truth. I some time ago requested Mr. Bennet, the registrar for the Ancoats district, to make similar notes on the cases reported to him, and on inquiry from him I have reason to believe that the evil exists to as great an extent in his district as in mine.

I find that in most of the cases no efficient medical treatment was adopted. Cases of pneumonia are seldom or never bled, or proper remedies applied : the disease is probably not recognized, and if it were, the treatment and extent to which it should be pursued is not known to the parties prescribing.

A similar practice appears to be prevalent also in the mining districts of Staffordshire and Shropshire. (Vide Reports of the Sub-Commissioners for inquiring into employment in Mines, vol. I., pp. 22, 23; articles 182-6 : and pp. 38, 39; pp. 305 to 315, and the recent report respecting the employment of children at Nottingham.) In the course of some recent inquiries by Dr. Lyon Playfair he found the increasing sale of opium in the manufacturing towns was ascribable to the increasing use of it in the form of carminative, or as it was named " quietness " for children, and that the consumption of opium by adults had diminished. On inquiring from the druggists who sold the opium what was the cause of the diminished consumption by the adults, the uniform answer was, the " distress of the times," which compelled them to dispense with luxuries. He however ascertained clearly that from this terrible practice great numbers of children perish, sometimes suddenly from an overdose, but more commonly slowly, painfully, and insidiously. He was struck, however, with the fact of the increased proportions and rapidity of the births in the places where this infantile mortality was prevalent. It was remarked by the people themselves. So that there was no diminution of the numbers of children, but a woeful diminution of their strength and a proportionate increase of their burthensomeness. Those who escaped with life, became pale and sickly children, and it was very long before they overcame the effects arising from the pernicious practice; if indeed they ever did do so.*

The most serious consequences, arise from the omission of proper administrative securities for the safety of life in Scotland. On these Dr. Scott Alison states:—

In Scotland there is full opportunity for the perpetration of murder and burial without investigation by any responsible officer. There is no coroner and no inquest. I have known cases of the occurrence of deaths from culpable negligence, to say the least of it, which required public proceedings to be taken, but where interment took place without the slightest notice. I had myself a young man of about 20 years of age under treatment who, in my opinion, died from culpable maltreatment whilst in prison. He had in a drunken frolic committed an assault, and was imprisoned in a damp cold cell without a fire. He certainly died of disease which was very likely to be produced by the cold which he then endured, and to which he ascribed it. Before his imprisonment he was a remarkably strong, fine healthy man. No inquiry was made or thought of in the case. I have known several cases, and they were not uncommon. I remember two, within two or three days, of children having been overlaid and killed by their parents when in a state of drunkenness. They were buried without any notice being taken of the circumstance by any party, though if punishment were not inflicted upon them public notice would have been of importance for the sake of the morals of the population.

I have known deaths of grown up people from burning when in a state of intoxication, and deaths from intoxication take place without inquiry; also deaths from accidents, such as falling into coal pits, deaths from machinery, as to which in many cases no public inquiry whatsoever was ever made. I have known cases of children burned to death who were left without any care. It was a common case in Tranent for persons to drink for a wager who would drink most. I know of the case of three tradesmen who drank for a wager; two of them died within a few days, and the widow of one of them committed suicide shortly afterwards; and I was informed that they were all buried without any notice being taken of the fact. There is certainly a facility for the perpetration of murder in Scotland from the absence of securities, and for protection of life against culpable negligence. The visits of an officer of public health would be of very great utility.

Mr. William Chambers observes:—

It seems to me not a little surprising that in Scotland, which is signalized for its general intelligence, love of order, and I may add really beneficent

---

* Whosoever may feel inclined not to attach much weight to infantile mortality on any such theory as that the "pressure of population" is thereby diminished, may be requested to consider the evidence of the fallacy, and proof that in the very districts where such mortality is the greatest, so is the amount of births. Vide General Sanitary Report, Note, p. 175; Tables, p. 182 and 183, et seq; and the subsequent corroborative evidence adduced in connexion with the district returns of the proportions of deaths and funerals given in the Appendix to this Report—Appendix.

laws, the country should be so far behind in everything connected with vital statistics. I have already noticed that it possesses no coroner's inquest. This is a positive disgrace. Deaths are continually occurring from violence, but of which not the slightest notice is taken by procurators fiscal, magistrates, or police; indeed, these functionaries seldom interfere except when a positive complaint is lodged. Some time ago, the medical gentleman who attends my family, mentioned to me incidentally that that morning he had been called to look at, and if possible recover, a lady who had been found hanging in her bed-room. His efforts were ineffectual; the lady was stone dead; and it was announced by her relatives that she had died suddenly. In the usual course of things, she was buried. Now, in this case, not the slightest inquiry was made by any public officer, and whether it was a death from suicide or from murder nobody can tell. The procurator fiscal, whose duty it is to take cognizance of such deaths, is, of course, not to blame, for he has not the faculty of omniscience.

The preventive and detective functions of the officer of health would be the more efficient from the exercise of any such functions being incidental to ordinary functions of acknowledged every day importance, which must lead his visits and inspection to be regarded as *prima facie* services of beneficence and kindness to all who surround the deceased. The comparative inefficiency of officers whose functions are principally judiciary is well exemplified in some remarks made by Mr. Hill Burton, Advocate, in a communication on the subject of interments in Scotland.

A prominent defect (as he observes) in the means of inquiry into the causes of death in Scotland consists in the circumstance that before any investigation can be entered on there must be ostensible reasons for presuming the existence of violence and crime. On the occasion of a death having occurred in circumstances out of the ordinary course, the only person authorized to make any inquiry as to its cause is the officer whose proper and ostensible duty it is to prosecute to conviction. It hence arises that the simple institution of an inquiry is almost equivalent to a charge of crime, and that the proper officer, knowing the serious position in which he places those concerned, by taking any steps, is very reluctant to move, until the public voice has pretty unequivocally shown him that the matter comes within his province as a public prosecutor. There is no family in Scotland that would not at present feel a demand by a Procurator Fiscal, or by any individual to inspect a body within their house, as very nearly equivalent to a charge of murder; and I should think it is of very rare occurrence, that any such inspection takes place, in a private house, unless when a prosecution has been decided on.

The absence of any machinery, through which an inquiry can be calmly and impartially made into the cause of death, without in itself implying suspicion of crime, is frequently illustrated in the creation of excitement and alarm in the public mind, which the authorities cannot find a suitable means of allaying. I remember some years ago being present at a trial for murder, which, as it involved no point in law, has unfortunately not been reported. It was a trial undertaken by the Crown for the mere purpose of justifying an innocent man. Two butchers were returning tipsy from a fair; some words arose between them, and soon after, one of them was found stabbed to the heart by one of the set of knives which both carried. On investigation, it appeared that the deceased had fallen on his side, from the effects of drunkenness, and that one of the knives which hung at his side, dropping perpendicularly with its heavy handle to the ground, pierced through his ribs to his heart as he fell. It was impossible, however, to satisfy the public that such was the case. The feeling of the neighbourhood ran high, and the Crown was induced, out of humanity, or from a desire to preserve the public peace, to concede the formality of a trial. I know it to be of the most frequent occurrence, especially in the north of Scotland, that suspicions which must be destructive to the peace of mind of those who are the objects of them, take wing through society, and can never be set effectually at rest.

§ 205. Mr. W. Dyce Guthrie, after reciting several cases of strong suspicion which came under his observation whilst acting as a medical practitioner in Scotland concludes by observing—

· Whether on an inquest before a coroner the real truth would have been elicited I cannot determine, but I think there can be but one opinion as to the propriety of having all obstacles removed which may presently stand in the way of arriving at the truth of all circumstances connected with sudden and suspicious deaths. Were it necessary, I could cite many instances of sudden deaths attended by circumstances of such a nature as not only rendered an investigation highly proper in a legal point of view, but necessary in charity to those individuals whose characters were tarnished by the cruelly unjust insinuations of some black-hearted enemies. The business not having been thoroughly probed at the time of its occurrence leaves great latitude for the villanous conjectures of parties whose interest it may be to damage others in the estimation of the public.

§ 206. Besides supplying the defect of administrative arrangements in respect to the cases of suspicion which at present escape inquiry, the proposed appointment of officers of health presents as a further incidental advantage the means of abating an evil which has been the subject of much complaint, namely, the grievous pain inflicted on the relations and survivors, and the expense to the public by the holding of inquests, which the subsequent evidence and the terms of the verdicts have shown to have been unnecessary. In the metropolis, and in many extensive districts inquests are chiefly moved on the representations of common parish beadles, or by common parish constables, to whom the inquest is usually a source of emolument. This will be admitted to be one of the least secure and satisfactory agencies in towns that could well be employed for so important a purpose. I have been informed of instances where they have been paid to avoid the annoyance of inquests in cases where from sudden but natural deaths, as from apoplexy, inquests might have been held, and that there is reason to believe that such payments have not been unfrequent. Such agency cannot be said to be a secure one either as to integrity or discretion.

§ 207. I am informed by Mr. Payne, the coroner for the city of London, that he has in some cases felt it to be his duty to send a confidential person to make inquiries for him, before he would act on the ordinary sources of information in holding inquests. I have also been informed that other coroners adopt the same laudable practice, and frequently incur the trouble and expense of previous inquiries by more trustworthy persons, in cases where the alleged cause of death is not manifest. The appointment of medical officers of health might be made without the exercise of any new or anomalous powers to relieve the coroners from such necessity, and at the same time give the public cause to be better satisfied that no really suspicious cases were shrouded and concealed, and that none escaped from inadvertence.* I believe that on the uses to be derived from the appointment of the officers in question most coroners would concur in the opinions expressed in the following answer received from Mr. Payne.

In reply to your inquiry (respecting the Medical Registrars of Deaths giving notice to the Coroner of such deaths as may appear to them to inquire to be investigated by him), I beg to say that I have long felt there has been something wanting in the machinery by which inquiries into deaths are, or ought to be regulated.

In cases of death from external violence, where the injury is apparent, the constable of the district is fully aware of the necessity of applying to the coroner; but in cases of sudden or other deaths where there is no cause apparent to a common observer, there is a necessity for some qualified person forming a judgment as to the expediency of a judicial inquiry into the cause of death, and I know of none so well qualified to form such a judgment as a member of the medical profession. The office of *searcher*, when properly carried out, was useful as far as it could be in the hands of old women, but that could only apply to cases in which external violence was apparent to the view on searching the body. I believe, however, that the office has now ceased to exist, and the present mode of registering deaths does not supply any means of detecting unnatural or violent deaths.' I am therefore quite of opinion that a Medical Registrar (chosen for his ability and *discretion*) who would not unnecessarily annoy the feelings of private families, and yet make himself acquainted with the death by personal knowledge, would be a valuable addition to the present mode of ascertaining and registering deaths.

Advantages to Science from the Improvement of the Mortuary Registration.

§ 208. Extending the view from the private and public immediate and extraordinary necessities which may be met by a staff of well qualified public officers, exercising the duties and powers proposed, to the ordinary but higher public wants, it will be found they may in that position obtain in years, or even in months, indications of the certain means of prevention of disease, for which the medical experience of ages has supplied no means of cure, and only doubtful means of alleviation.

§ 209. There is not one medical man who has acted as a registrar of deaths who has been consulted on this subject, who does not state as a result of his short experience under the registration of the fact of deaths, and even of the distant and imperfect statements of the causes of death, that it has given them such a knowledge as no private practice could give of the effect of habits of life and of locality in producing disease.

§ 210. As a practical instance of the immediate advantages of

* Vide on the subject of defective registration of the causes of deaths : a letter to the Registrar-general from Mr. Baker, coroner to Middlesex, printed in the Minutes of Evidence on the practice of coroners, given before a Select Committee of the House of Commons, p. 128 of paper 549, Sess. 1840.

placing the business of registration under the guidance of medical knowledge, may be cited the following from the statement of Mr. Jones, a medical officer, who acts as registrar of the Strand Union. Speaking of the working of the registration, he says—

I find that neither my experience as a medical officer, for many years in the parish, nor my experience as a private practitioner, give me the same extended view of the causes of death as the mortuary registration. It brings to my knowledge cases which I could not know as a private practitioner: for example, as to the occurrence of small-pox or epidemics. In such instances, it is of use to me, as it sometimes enables me to go to places where I believe children have not been vaccinated, and suggest to the family the necessity of vaccination as a measure of prevention. When I have received information of one or two cases of small-pox, I have looked to the register of births, and sent to other people to warn them of the necessity of vaccination.

§ 211. On the advantages which inquiries for the registration of death would give, the concurrent opinions of several eminent medical men may be expressed in the terms used by Dr. Calvert Holland, of Sheffield, who observes that, " From an inquiry on the spot concerning the train of symptoms preceding death, the general examination of the body, or from conversation with the medical attendant, the cause of death, with few exceptions, would probably be assigned with as much accuracy as by any plan that can possibly be devised. We should hail such an appointment as one of great value. Even in those instances in which it is difficult, from the obscurity or undefined character of the symptoms, to say precisely what is the cause of death, the inquiry would tend to dissipate the doubts or obscurity in which it might be involved. The duties of the officer, if he possessed first-rate professional abilities, would give to him a power of analyzing symptoms, of tracing cause and effect, which few practitioners possess or can acquire in a long life of professional exertions. Were the causes of death analyzed and recorded by one having no other duties, and fitted by his accomplishments to undertake the task, the medical and statistical inquirer would possess a body of information on the influence of general local circumstances as well as on particular agents in connexion with manufactures, the just value of which it is not possible to appreciate."

§ 212. For the promotion of the new science of prevention, and the knowledge of causes necessary to it, a primary requisite is to bring large classes of cases as may be duly observed, under the eye of one observer. It would be a practicable arrangement, on the receipt of the notices of deaths, to direct the visits of one officer chiefly to cases of the same class, for the purpose of collecting information as to the common causes or antecedents. The amount of remuneration included in the estimate hereafter given might be made the means of obtaining additional time and services for carrying the inspections of the officers of health still further into the circumstances of the living; as in cases of consumption or fever, where numbers came from the same place of work or occupation, to visit and ascertain whether there was any overcrowding or any latent cause of disease.

§ 213. In an important paper which Dr. Calvert Holland has written " On the Diseases of the Lungs from mechanical causes," he gives an account of the physical and moral condition of the cutlers' dry grinders of Sheffield, whose case may be cited not only as further exemplifying the large evils, § 200, which, in the absence of protective public arrangements, will pass without complaint from the *immediate* sufferers, but as showing the advantages derivable from any arrangements which bring large classes of cases within one intelligent view, *i. e.* before an officer of health, in presenting clearly common causes of evil, and in suggesting means of prevention, which in single cases or smaller groups of cases might not have challenged attention or justified any confident conclusions as to the remedies available.

It is known that the steel and stone dust arising in the processes of grinding cutlery, is peculiarly injurious to the class of workpeople engaged in it, and that those who continue at the work are generally cut off before they are thirty-five or forty-five years of age. Formerly the same workmen completed several processes in the making of knives, of which processes grinding was only one.   At that time the " grinders' disease was very little known, and the men lived to about the average age, and were considered the most respectable class of the Sheffield workmen.   As the manufacture advanced the labour became subdivided, and one class of workmen were wholly occupied with the destructive process of grinding. Whether their numbers were kept down by the excessive mortality, or a monopoly were maintained by the destructive effects of the process, wages were so high as to allow them to play during a part of the week.   Then arose that avidity for immediate and reckless enjoyment, common to all uneducated minds under the perception of a transient existence.   When trade was good they would only work a part of the week; they spent the remainder in the riot and the dissipation characteristic of soldiers after a siege.   Many of them each kept a hound, and had it trained by a master of the hunt, and their several hounds formed a pack with which they hunted lawlessly, and poached over any grounds within their reach.   The grinders pack is still kept up amongst them.   They became reckless in their marriages.   " The more destructive the branch of work," says Dr. Holland, " the more ignorant, reckless, and dissipated are the workmen, and the effects may be traced in the tendency to marry, and generally at exceedingly early ages."   He further observes of one class of them, that amongst them " nature appears not only precocious but extremely fruitful."   Their short and improvident career is attended by a proportionately large amount of premature and wretched widowhood and destitute orphanage.

This one class of cases was brought fortuitously under the observation of Dr. Holland, and he has done what a competent officer of health could scarcely have omitted to attempt to do,—to devise means of prevention and reclaim their execution.

One benevolent inventor proposed the adoption of a magnetic guard, or mouth-piece, the efficiency of which consisted in the attraction of the metallic particles evolved in the process of grinding. But the dust to which the grinder was exposed consisted of the gritty particles of the stone as well as of the metallic particles of the instruments ground, and if the invention had been adopted, it would still have left the men exposed to the gritty particles. It was not, however, adopted, nor does it appear that any efficient preventive would be voluntarily adopted by these reckless men. Dr. Holland invented another mode, which acts independently of the men, and which is very simple, and, it is confidently stated, that after a trial of some years, it has proved equal to the complete correction of the evil. It consists of an arrangement by which a current of air, directed over the work, carries from the workman clear out of the apartment all the gritty as well as all the metallic particles. The expense of the apparatus would scarcely exceed the proportion of a sovereign to each grinder. But it is not adopted; and Dr. Holland is in the position of an officer of health, on behalf of mothers and children, to reclaim authoritative intervention and the interests of society to arrest the suicidal and demoralizing waste of life. Having consulted his experience on the advantages of such an office as that in question to the working classes, he speaks in strong and confident terms of the benefits to be derived from it:—

Perhaps in no manufacturing community is human life, in large classes of men, so shortened or accompanied with such an amount of suffering or wretchedness as in this town, in connection with certain staple manufactures. Were the legislature to interfere and enforce the correction of the evils, by a system of ventilation, which is neither difficult nor expensive to put in operation, the duties of this officer, if directed to the superintendence of this system, would save numerous lives and prevent an incalculable amount of misery. At present, in consequence of these evils, a majority of the artisans is killed off from twenty-five to thirty-five years of age, and numbers annually leaving widows and children in great destitution, and, in most cases, dependent on the parish. The evils are not inseparably connected with the occupation; they admit of redress. An officer of health, by maintaining the system of ventilation in efficient operation, would save numerous lives, would create a better tone of mind among the artisans—for wretchedness is closely allied with ignorance and immorality—would diminish the high rate of mortality amongst the young under five years of age—left by the premature death of the parent unprovided for, and lastly, would greatly relieve the parish funds. The officer, having the power to remove at once any case of fever from a densely populated locality, as well as to enforce measures of prevention, such as the removal of accumulated filth, stagnant pools of water, or the correction of any other local circumstances, would perform duties which would redound considerably to the advantage of the community.

§ 214. In confirmation of the views of the benefits derivable to medical science from such arrangements as those proposed, § 211, various instances might be adduced besides the last cited, § 213, and that already given in the General Report, p. 355, of the discoveries made, on an examination of 1000 cases, by M. Louis, on the nature of consumption, now generally recognized as presenting facts at variance with all ancient and previous modern opinions: but in respect of the views there stated, as to the great public importance of well-ascertained medical statistics, I submit the high confirmation derivable from the following statement contained in the recently published outlines of pathology and practice of medicine, by Dr. W. Pulteney Alison, fellow and late president of the College of Physicians at Edinburgh, and professor of the practice of medicine in the University of Edinburgh:—

"The living body," he observes, "assumes, in many cases, different kinds of diseased action, varying remarkably in different periods of life, without any apparent or known cause; but in the greater number of cases it is generally believed that certain circumstances in the situation or condition of patients, before diseases appear, can be assigned with confidence as their causes. The efficacy of these, however, is seldom established in any other way than simply by the observation that persons known to be exposed to their influence become afflicted with certain diseases in a proportion very much greater than those who are not known to be so exposed.

"This kind of evidence is in many *individual* cases very liable to fallacy, in consequence of the great variety of the circumstances capable of affecting health, in which individuals are placed, and of the difficulty of varying these so as to obtain such observations, in the way of induction or exclusion, as shall be decisive as to the efficacy of each. Hence the importance of the observations intended to illustrate this matter being as extensively multiplied as possible; and hence also the peculiar value, with a view to the investigation of the causes of diseases, of observations made on large and organized bodies of men, as in the experience of military and naval practitioners. All the circumstances of the whole number of men whose diseases are there observed, are in many respects exactly alike; they are accurately known to the observer, and are indeed often to a certain degree at his disposal; they are often suddenly changed, and when changed as to one portion of the individuals under observation, they are often unchanged as to another; and therefore the conditions necessary to obtaining an *experimentum crucis* as to the efficacy of an alleged cause of disease are more frequently in the power of such an observer than of one who is conversant only with civil life.

"But when the necessary precautions as to the multiplication of facts, and the exclusion of circumstances foreign to the result in question, are observed, the efficacy of the remote causes of disease may often be determined *statistically*, and with absolute certainty; and the knowledge thus acquired as leading directly to the *prevention* of disease, is often of the greatest importance, especially with a view to regulations of medical police. And if the human race be destined, in future ages, to possess greater wisdom and happiness in this state of existence than at present, the value of this knowledge may be expected to increase in the progress of time; because there are many diseases which the experience of ages has brought only partially within the power of medicine, but the causes of which are known, and under certain circumstances may be avoided; and the conditions necessary for avoiding them are in a great measure in the power of *communities*, though at present beyond the power of many of the individuals composing these.

"There are, indeed, various cases, of frequent occurrence, in which the study of the remote causes of disease is as practically important as anything that can be learnt as to their history, or the effects of remedies upon them. This is particularly true of epidemic diseases, and of diseases to which a tendency is given by irremediable constitutional infirmities."

Having had the honour to be associated with the late Dr. Cowan of Glasgow, Dr. Alison, and some other gentlemen, in a committee to consider of the means of obtaining a system of mortuary registration for Scotland, and having conversed with many qualified persons who have also paid much attention to the subject, I may state confidently that the exposition above given of the advantages derivable to the public service from the improvement of vital statistics would meet with extensive concurrence, independently of the very high sanction conferred by any expression of an opinion on such a subject from Dr. Alison. The towns where the greatest mortality prevails present precisely the opportunities so highly appreciated, of observations on large and organized bodies of men, § 213, often as similar in the chief circumstances which govern their condition, as the classes presented to the observation of medical officers in the army or in the navy.

Lord Bacon observes, in his suggestions for an inquiry into the causes of death—" And this inquiry, we hope, might redound to a general good, if physicians would but exert themselves and raise their minds above the sordid considerations of cure ; not deriving their honour from the necessities of mankind, but becoming ministers to the Divine power and goodness both in prolonging and restoring the life of man; especially as this may be effected by safe, commodious, and not illiberal means, though hitherto unattempted. And certainly it would be an earnest of Divine favour if, whilst we are journeying to the land of promise, our garments, those frail bodies of ours, were not greatly to wear out in the wilderness of this world." It would accord with his great views that adequate public provision and arrangement should be made to enable physicians to render the services desired. From the earliest time to the present, when the subject of sanitary evil and desecration of grave-yards was brought before the public by the long-continued exertions of Mr. Walker, members of the medical profession have made the most strenuous exertions and sacrifices for the attainment of such objects.

It is submitted that, in whatsoever place a proper system of the verification and registration of the fact and cause of death has not been introduced, as in Ireland and Scotland, and in all populous and increasing districts, that the appointment of an officer of health, having charge and regulations of all interments, would be the most economical as well as the most efficient mode of introducing it: in every place it must be a measure of paramount importance.

§ 215. As an instance of the incompatibility of such duties as those of the proposed officer of public health, with service in connexion with any existing local administrative body, it may be mentioned that every local Board in such a town as Sheffield would comprehend some of the chief householders, who would most probably be the chief manufacturers and employers of the class of workmen, and that even the official connexion would to such minds as the workmen expose him to suspicion, and diminish his influence, for the effectuation of any voluntary changes of practice. On other grounds, such as the absence of qualification in such Boards to give superior directions; and such grounds as those specified in p. 322 and p. 349 and 350 of the General Report, it is submitted that the functions of the officer of health would be the best exercised, independently of any other local administrative body. He would, in an independent capacity, be the most powerful auxiliary of any well-intended and zealous administration of local works, and as his functions must bring him at once to the chief spots where the consequences of neglects and omissions would be often manifest in fatal events, he would, as an independent and yet responsible officer, exercise an extensive influence and an efficient check on behalf of the public at large.

§ 216. Every efficient measure of improvement of the sanitary condition of the population, must be in its mere pecuniary results a measure of a large economy (§ 80). Physicians and medical officers are of opinion that all the ordinary and extraordinary duties specified, and even more, may be done by an officer of health with the same average expenditure of time (taking one case with another), that occurs to a physician in visiting a patient, examining the case, writing out a prescription and giving instructions to attendants. I shall be able to show that it may be accomplished at a charge no greater than that now paid by the labouring classes to one of their body as a steward or officer of their burial clubs who is required to inspect and identify the body of a deceased member.

Proximate Estimate of the comparative Expense of Interments under arrangements for National Cemeteries.

Having shown the chief desiderata in respect to the improvement of the practice of interment, and the means of protecting the public health, I proceed to submit the substance of the information collected as to the means of obtaining them.

§ 217. In submitting for consideration a proximate estimate of the extent to which it is practicable to carry that reduction of the expense of interments, which is so important to the middle and lower classes, the expense of interments of gentry and persons of the middle class of life is taken at double the amount at which persons of great experience in providing for the interment of large numbers have estimated they may be executed for without any reduction of the essentials to a decent solemnity.

§ 218. The estimate takes the existing scale of burial fees of the parish of St. James, Westminster, as fees to be continued, which would, if received in a fee fund, not only provide compensation for vested interests, but go far to provide the expense of new services.

§ 219. To the estimate of the expenses of interment is superadded a fee to defray the expenses of medical officers of a board of public health. The reduction of that great source of waste and expense, the payment of two or three stages of profits, for materials, &c. of funerals (by placing them under general arrangements), would admit of this charge, which is really a means to a still greater economy, the economy of health and life, and consequently of the number of funerals themselves. Objection to these charges would scarcely have place where the pecuniary economy is immediate. The medical service proposed may be procured to the working classes (supposing it were necessary to charge the expense on the funeral) at all distances, for the same sum as that which they now pay to the unlearned inspectors, officers of their clubs, for inspection within short distances, namely, 2*s*. 6*d*. It is declared by competent witnesses, that a respectable officer of public health, a physician, performing such services as those described, would be welcomed in most families on such a charge as 10*s*. 6*d*. for the middle classes, and 1*l*. 1*s*. for the higher classes, charged as a part of the reduced funeral expenses.

Estimated Scale of Charges for Interments in the Metropolis, inclusive of Compensations; the payment for the purchase of new Cemeteries; and new Establishment Charges.

		Existing Burial Dues.	Proposed Charge for Officer of Health and Registration of Death.	Scale of Expense for Undertaker's Materials and Services.	Charge for New Cemeteries and Establishments.	Total estimated Scale of Expense of Burials.	Annual Number of Cases of each Class.	Total estimated Expense of Interments to each Class per annum.
		£. s. d.	£. s. d.	£. s. d.	£. s. d.	£. s. d.		£
Gentry	Adults	10 10 0	1 0 0	21 0 0	6 0 0	38 10 0	1,724	66,374
	Children	5 5 0	1 0 0	3 10 0	4 5 0	14 0 0	529	7,406
1st Class	Adults	2 10 0	0 10 0	10 10 0	3 0 0	16 10 0	3,979	65,655
Tradesmen 2nd Class	Children	1 5 0	0 10 0	2 10 0	2 0 0	6 5 0	3,703	23,144
Tradesmen (Undescribed)	Adults	1 12 9	0 6 3	6 0 0	1 10 0	9 9 0	2,996	28,312
	Children	0 16 9	0 6 3	1 12 6	0 10 0	3 5 6	2,761	9,042
Artisans	Adults	0 15 6	0 2 6	1 10 0	0 2 0	2 10 0	12,045	30,113
	Children	0 8 9	0 2 6	0 15 0	0 1 9	1 8 0	13,885	19,439
Paupers	Adults	..	..	..	..	0 13 0	3,655	2,376
	Children							
Totals								251,861

Or an annual saving on the estimated total expense of the interments and parochial charges for the whole metropolis	374,743

§ 220. In this estimate the expense of the funerals of the classes "undescribed" in the mortuary registries may be taken as representing the second or third class of tradesmen. In the estimate of the expense of funerals of persons of the first class, no account is taken for a long cavalcade of mourning coaches; but those who are conversant with the details agree that several may be supplied, with a full retinue of hired mourners, and the expense be yet kept below one-half the present amount of charges. A confident opinion is expressed that interments might be performed, under general arrangements, with all the advantages specified, and full compensation be given, at a rate of between 5l. and 6l. each funeral, instead of about 15l., the present average.

§ 221. On the eight chief cemeteries opened in the metropolis by private companies, and comprising about 260 acres, or considerably more than the space occupied by all the parochial and private burial grounds whatever, a capital of about 400,000l. has been invested. The expenses of litigation and of procuring Acts of Parliament, and purchasing grounds, must have been excessively heavy; and it appears probable that, for an amount not much greater or not exceeding it by more than one-fifth, superior national cemeteries, with houses of reception and appropriate chapels, may be formed on the present scale of expenditure of these companies, and in a style commensurate with what is due to the metropolis of the empire. If the charge of the purchase of the land and the structural arrangements be spread over 30 years, and the payment of the money charged, with interest, on the burials of persons of the higher and middle classes, the amount might be included in the total charges for funerals above estimated for the several classes, which charges, though so much below the amount at present usually paid, are yet higher than asserted to be necessary by respectable trades- men, ready to verify their assertions by sureties to supply the materials and service of an equal or of a better description for the public than that which they now obtain. If the charges of the new cemeteries and establishments at such rates as those sug- gested were taken as substitutes for the existing rates of charge for graves, the new rates would be for the middle and higher classes greatly below the charges usually found in undertakers' bills and executors' accounts. If those new expenses were levied in the shape of a poll tax, or as burial dues, a sum of about 5*d.* per head per annum (exclusive of the expense of collection) would suffice in the metropolis to repay the principal and interest of purchase-money in 30 years, and also to defray the annual establishment charges.

§ 222. The establishment charges of the existing eight principal cemeteries, amount, it is stated, to about 7500*l.* per annum. I believe, that by appropriate arrangements of a public establishment a far more efficient service might be obtained for national cemeteries for the same money. Assuming that the greatest solemnity and the highest cathedral service is due to funerals, four full choirs of 20 choristers and four organists to lead them might be obtained for less than 10,000*l.* per annum for four national cemeteries to meet the wishes of those who desire a service of the highest solemnity. The lowest aggregate charge for the separate establishments of paro- chial and suburban burial grounds, if only on the scale of that of St. Martin's-in-the-Fields, must be at the least 25,000*l.*; and would probably extend to 30,000*l.* or 40,000*l.* per annum. Such an amount in connexion with national cemeteries would suffice to maintain, in addition to the superior religious establishments above described, a superior description of intermediate houses of recep- tion for the dead, with houses and offices for the residence of the officers of public health in care of them : it would beyond that suffice to provide the means for accommodation, on a large scale, for the reception and treatment of all persons labouring under infectious diseases. It might also suffice for the establishment of public baths, in which the metropolis is also deficient.

§ 223. The number of the officers of health requisite for the due execution of the service could only be determined by experience ; but, judging from analogous experience, a much smaller staff than on the first view might be expected would suffice for the per- formance of all the duties specified, if their whole time were devoted to them. Medical officers of dispensaries, within their districts, visit, examine, and treat twenty or thirty cases per diem ; physicians in full practice, and driving to distant parts of the town, on the average (which includes cases of short visits of a few minutes and cases where a long attendance would be required), visit about three cases in the hour. This appears to be the best analogous experience.   On this experience, and considering that it would be good economy to provide each officer with a one-horse vehicle, he may be expected to visit fifteen cases a-day, one day with the other, out of the daily number of deaths.   The two public medical departments, the navy and the army, have rendered the highest, if not the only, public service in the prevention of disease—the navy medical department especially;   which service it has been enabled to achieve from having the subjects of its care under the most complete control. . The scale of remuneration to these officers, who, whatever diploma they may possess, are required to undergo, and do undergo, a special re-examination, is taken for estimating the expense.   There are various grounds that, at all events at the outset, and for their superior responsibility, this class of officers should be selected.   The proposed staff would be as follows :—

	Per Annum.		
	£.	s.	d.
An inspector of public health, of the rank of an inspector-general of hospitals in the army, or of fleets in the navy, at full pay of 1*l*. 16*s*. per diem, at the rate given after ten years' service	657	0	0
A deputy inspector-general, at the rate of the army full pay of 1*l*. 4*s*. per diem . . .	438	0	0
Eight inspectors of public health, of the rank of staff surgeon, at the rate of the army full pay of 19*s*. per diem	2,774	0	0
Two supernumeraries, of the pay of regimental surgeons, at the rate of the army pay of 15*s*. per diem	547	10	0
Ten single horse vehicles, and ten drivers, at 1*l*. 1*s*. per week, total 3*l*. 3*s*. per week each .	1,638	0	0
Total	6,054	10	0

Ten officers, visiting fifteen cases per diem, would suffice to take order such as described, for the burial of 45,000 persons. They will also be enabled in upwards of 8000 cases to direct measures for the protection of the survivors and their neighbours from the spread of contagious disease.   Supposing that each class of deaths occurred daily, with the same regularity that they occur yearly, the distribution of the duties of verification and examination may be seen from the following table, made from the Registrar-General's returns.

	Metropolis Pop. 1,870,727			Liverpool Pop. 223,045	Manchester Pop. 192,408	Leeds Pop. 168,627
—	Daily Number of Deaths of Children under 15.	Daily Number of Deaths of Adults.	Total Number Daily.	Weekly Number of Deaths in Liverpool.	Weekly Number of Deaths in Manchester.	Weekly Number of Deaths in Leeds.
Epidemic, Endemic, and Contagious Diseases .	18	$4\frac{2}{10}$	$22\frac{2}{10}$	$52\frac{6}{10}$	$34\frac{8}{10}$	$20\frac{3}{10}$
Sporadic Diseases:—						
Nervous Disease . .	$14\frac{6}{10}$	$6\frac{6}{10}$	$21\frac{2}{10}$	$28\frac{7}{10}$	18	$15\frac{6}{10}$
Diseases of the Respiratory Organs . .	$13\frac{2}{10}$	$25\frac{6}{10}$	$38\frac{6}{10}$	$46\frac{8}{10}$	$34\frac{6}{10}$	24
Diseases of the Organs of Circulation . .	$\frac{1}{10}$	$2\frac{1}{10}$	$2\frac{7}{10}$	$1\frac{8}{10}$	$1\frac{1}{10}$	$\frac{8}{10}$
Diseases of the Digestive Organs . . .	$5\frac{5}{10}$	$3\frac{8}{10}$	$9\frac{3}{10}$	$10\frac{6}{10}$	$9\frac{5}{10}$	$6\frac{1}{10}$
Other Sporadic Diseases	$5\frac{4}{10}$	$12\frac{7}{10}$	$18\frac{1}{10}$	$13\frac{5}{10}$	16	$10\frac{2}{10}$
Old Age	..	$9\frac{1}{10}$	$9\frac{1}{10}$	$5\frac{1}{10}$	$5\frac{7}{10}$	$5\frac{6}{10}$
Violent Deaths . . .	1	$2\frac{1}{10}$	$3\frac{1}{10}$	$3\frac{8}{10}$	$4\frac{8}{10}$	$2\frac{7}{10}$
Causes not specified . .	$\frac{2}{10}$	$\frac{3}{10}$	$\frac{5}{10}$	..	..	1
Total . .	$58\frac{1}{10}$	$67\frac{5}{10}$	..	$162\frac{8}{10}$	$124\frac{8}{10}$	$86\frac{3}{10}$
Total Deaths Daily .	..	..	$125\frac{4}{10}$	$23\frac{2}{10}$	$17\frac{8}{10}$	$12\frac{2}{10}$

NOTE.—The data upon which this Table is calculated are taken from the Registrar-General's Fourth Annual Report—the Metropolis, p. 330 ; Liverpool, p. 281 ; Manchester, p. 281 ; Leeds, p. 283. The Metropolis is calculated on the average of the years 1840 and 1841, the other places on the year 1840.

§ 224. The total number of funerals and deaths requiring verification daily would be—for Birmingham about 12, for Nottingham 5, for Leicester 3, for Derby 3. From the data above given it will be seen at how small an expenditure of time a well directed force for the prevention as well as the alleviation of misery—vast interests of the population, that are now neglected—may be placed, under responsible superintendence, and on the most sordid views of economy of money, immense savings, under proper regulations, be made. In Liverpool alone, in the business of cure or alleviation there are now engaged 50 physicians, and 250 surgeons, apothecaries, and druggists, and not one responsible public officer to investigate the causes of disease with a view to prevention. Nor has the city of London, with a population of 125,000, one such officer, though it has an expenditure of 72,000*l.* per annum in hospitals and endowed medical charities alone, for the alleviation of disease.

§ 225. There is much experience to establish the conclusion that very special qualifications are requisite for the performance of the duties of an officer of the public health. The only safe proof of the possession of such qualifications is the fact of a person having investigated successfully some scientific question on the prevention of disease to a practical end, by which the main qualification, the habit of practical investigation, and zeal and ability for the service of prevention may be placed beyond doubt. It would be no imputation on the merits of a general medical practitioner that he was found unsuited to the performance of the duties devolving on an officer of public health. The working of the Parisian administrative arrangements shows the injury done to the public service by the difficulty of retrieving any mistaken appointment, and suggests the desirableness of an arrangement to facilitate changes of the officers of health even where there is the security of a previous special examination as to the qualifications for the office. Cases would occur where officers would themselves choose to withdraw from such a service, for which they felt unsuited, if they might retire without imputation and without any severe sacrifice. If, therefore, officers of health were chosen from amongst those who had long served with honour in the army or navy medical department, the advantage would be gained of a facility of retirement being given to the officer of health (an office, indeed, which would often be trying to the constitution), and without loss of rank or of the means of livelihood.

§ 226. The arrangements for the performance of the funereal rites in public cemeteries would, of course, fall to the proper ecclesiastical authority. The architectural arrangements, and the decoration of the cemeteries, may claim the highest aid that art can give to the production of solemn religious impressions. Public monuments and works of art have of late been extensively thrown open to the population, and there is evidence that this course of proceeding has been productive of beneficial effects on those of the lower classes who have had opportunities of viewing such monuments during their holidays. But the place of burial is the object to which the views of almost every individual of that class, as well as of others, is ever most intently directed. All the structural and decorative arrangements of the national cemetery should, therefore, be made by the highest talent that can be procured, with the purpose of interesting the feelings, under the conviction that in rendering attractive that place we are preparing *the* picture which is most frequently present to the minds of the poorest, in the hours of mental and bodily infirmity, and the last picture on earth presented to his contemplation before dissolution.

§ 227. It will have been seen that if the tendency of the public mind be followed out by the economical regulation of funeral expenses, and if the public be protected from the extortions of undertakers, considerable reductions of expense may be effected, and munificent provision may yet be made for permanent decorations.

These reductions would, also, under practicable regulations of the mode and practice of interment, admit of full and liberal compensation to all legal and proper interests affected by the proposed change of the practice, and to whom Parliament might determine that compensation should be awarded.

§ 228. . In the case of the ministers of the Established Church in large towns, the surplice fees, including the burial dues, are to be considered as the main parts of their incomes. They have no tithes, and no other means of livelihood. But the burial dues are so variously regulated—in some places by custom, in other places by local Acts—that it is scarcely practicable to lay down any one scale in respect to them that would not operate unequally and unjustly. Complaints from cemetery companies are made in respect to the existing scales of, compensation, which did not appear to be within my province to investigate. It appeared to me that the only satisfactory mode of determining the amount of compensation would be an adjudication and examination of the case of. each parish. This would be a service, which the Commissioners for the Commutation of Tithes would be competent to render.

§ 229. The claims of families who have purchased the privilege of interment in private vaults are not, that I find, maintained to any extent by the possessors, but are rather suggested as obstacles by others. That which at the time of purchase was deemed a privilege is now proved to be an injury to the community at large, not to speak of the very families by whom the right of interment in the church which they attend is exercised. When the fact is known of the deleterious character of the miasma which arises wherever bodies waste away, it were inconsistent with all religious feeling to maintain, as a privilege, the right of endangering the health of their families, friends, or neighbours. The same observation is applicable to grave-yards attached to chapels belonging to Dissenting congregations. Burial there is an injury to the congregations themselves, and the removal of interments a benefit to them; and although any one may choose to put up with the injury, or refuse to admit the evidence of it, they can scarcely claim to continue the injury at the expense of others, or against the conviction of the majority of the community and the opinions and customs of all civilized nations by whom the practice of interments in towns is prohibited. The overwhelming evidence that what is deemed a privilege is really an injury, precludes all claim to compensation as for a loss. No claim is set forth by any congregation for compensation as for the loss of a gainful trade of burial. Setting aside, then, the question of right, it may be submitted in respect to the owners of private vaults in parochial burial grounds, whether claimants, within a given time, may not be allowed an equal space in the national cemeteries, and be allowed to transfer the remains of their ancestors thither, and erect suitable monuments to them. It may also be submitted that the sites occupied as burial grounds may be re-purchased from the congregations on liberal terms of compensation, to be kept as open spaces for the public use, and that those congregations may have equivalent spaces allotted to them at a distance from town in the new cemeteries. The authorities carrying out the change, should be enabled, on the like terms, to re-purchase from private companies such cemeteries as may be deemed eligible for the public, and engage their officers in the public service, or otherwise compensate them. The success of national cemeteries, would doubtlessly occasion loss to those who have subscribed capital in what was at the time a public improvement, and it is further submitted for consideration, whether the power of re-purchase for the public, from the proceeds of a reduced burial expenditure, might not be extended to the re-purchase of such sites even where they would not be found eligible for national cemeteries.

§ 230. If it be decided that the protection so much needed by all classes, especially by the poorest, in respect to the expense of interments shall be given, by empowering officers of health to carry out regulations the same in principle as those which have given relief and satisfaction in well regulated communities, it may then be submitted for consideration, whether the cases of the tradesmen who have devoted themselves entirely to the business of supplying funereal materials and service, and who will be wholly superseded, could not be brought within any legitimate principles and precedents of compensation, for the loss of their existing multiform monopoly by the whole or any portion of the supply having been transferred to officers responsible to the public. By means of such transference, the public gain will, in proportion to its completeness be immense. Without it there is no apparent means of change or compensation that will not increase the existing expenses, and also increase the train of existing evils consequent on those expenses. Whatever may be the sacrifice or inconvenience experienced by this class of tradesmen from such a transference, it were a lamentable misdirection of sympathy to sustain their pecuniary interests at the expense of the perpetuation of the enormous pecuniary sacrifices of the poorest and most helpless classes. But it may be submitted that the large work of charity and justice to the public from the change proposed, need not be accomplished by the sacrifice of the real principals in the business of undertaking. If the alterations proposed were not made, it is nevertheless probable that this business will be considerably changed. The practicability and advantage of the consolidation of the business of the supply of funereal materials and services under one general management with the cemetery, and the acceptability of the institution of a place for the reception and care of the dead previous to interment, are attested by the fact of which I am informed, that in consequence of the proposed measures having been necessarily developed by the course of the present inquiry from a multitude of witnesses, joint stock companies are now preparing to adopt, as a source of emolument, similar arrangements. To those persons who are not really principals in the business, as they professed, but agents, whose only service consisted in conveying orders to real principals, and who extorted large profits from those who employed them; to those carrying on the business of undertaker only as an addition to their chief trade, and to whom the orders for a funeral was " an occasional job"—to a large proportion of these classes, the change would cause no ulti-mate loss, and to many it must be an eventual gain. The business as at present conducted is in principle similar to a lottery in the excessive emoluments of death, amounting to upwards of half a million of money in the metropolis alone, and which is chiefly wrested from the poorer and depressed classes. Such an amount is annually distributed in prizes, which fall with the deaths, in sums varying from a few pounds to several hundreds, amongst a crowd of expectants, which even, under the existing manage-ment, is five times more numerous than is necessary (and under the proposed arrangements ten times the number requisite), leaving the greater number poorly paid for all their waiting, not-withstanding the large sums exacted from the suffering survivors. It may confidently be pronounced, that to the majority of the class of inferior labourers, the change of system must be an eventual and very early benefit.

§ 231. As various religious communities would participate in the provision of public cemeteries, it appears preferable, for the avoid-ance of jealousy and any pretext for dissatisfaction, and that such different parties may be freely communicated with, that land should be purchased, and the structural arrangements made, on due con-sultation by the Commissioners of Woods and Forests.

§ 232. The sites for national cemeteries would be determinable on consideration of circumstances affecting public health, and by convenience of access, which the responsible officers of public health should be required to investigate on a view or survey of the circum-stances of the metropolis in these respects as a whole. They would also set forth the arrangements necessary for the preparation of the ground for interment, for drainage, and the protection of the springs; and the prevention of the escape of miasma; from which regulations no class of interments and no places should be exempted.

§ 233. If the whole of the arrangements for sepulture were begun *de novo*, the most eligible principle for defraying all the public charges, and perhaps most of those charges which are now private charges, would be, as respects persons of the lower and middle ranks, by annual payments approximating to an insurance. With the wealthy classes payment at the time of interment par-takes of the nature of a legacy duty, and is then made most con-veniently. With the lower and a large part of the middle classes of society, the death of an adult member of the family is frequently the loss of the most productive member of the family, which occurs at a time when the family has, in almost every case, incurred severe expenses for medical treatment during illness. The charges for interment and for the mourning which custom requires, then press most grievously. A large proportion of the middle and lower classes endeavour to alleviate this pressure by spreading it over long periods by means of insurance, and amongst others by such expensive and uncertain modes as those displayed in the regulations of burial clubs. The commutation of the charge of insurance into an annual charge would be a public insurance, possessing the advantages of superior security, and the means of superior efficiency as well as of economy. The chief obstacle that stands in the way of such an arrangement is the want of a machinery for the annual collection of such a tax. It has been proposed to throw upon the poor's rates some of the additional charges supposed to be necessary, and, in the event of the change being made by means of numerous extra-mural parochial establishments, that certainly would be necessary. But the imposition of such a charge in such a mode as to follow the incidents of the poor's-rates would be unequal and unjust. Large districts of cottage tenements, which are now, chiefly to the benefit of the landlords of those tenements and at the expense of the other rate-payers, exempted from poor's-rates, would escape contribution, and it is precisely in such districts that the deaths are most frequent and the burial charges would be the most burthensome. Lodgers would extensively escape the charges; strangers and foreigners, and the fluctuating population in large districts, would escape them. If there were a machinery for collection, it is submitted that the most equitable mode of levying such charges would be, like those of a burial club, *i. e.* of the nature of a poll-tax, or burial dues payable, per head, on the number of persons inhabiting each house. These might be fixed for the whole community at a minimum rate, leaving it to the friends of the deceased to pay for any higher class of funeral which they think proper.

§ 234. It is, however, to be borne in mind that in burial clubs, and in savings' banks, large sums are now actually set apart by the labouring classes for the payment of funeral charges. Provision is, no doubt, also made by will, by other classes for defraying such charges. In the plan proposed, even including the expense of the new agency of officers of health the consideration of new sources of additional payments is rendered unnecessary. On the whole, therefore (although if bodies are immediately removed from the premises in cases where the removal is requisite for the protection of the lives of the survivors, attempts will be made to shift the expense to the public), it may be recommended that all new charges and compensations should, for the present, at least, still be defrayed from burial dues levied upon each interment. And in so far as any new expenses are for objects obviously beneficial (not to speak of those immediate charges being for the most efficient means of reducing the aggregate expenses), it will meet with ready acquiescence. I have consulted intelligent persons of the labouring classes, and discussed with them step by step the proposed changes. They have unanimously declared that these changes would all be a great gain to them, especially the proposed reduction of the expenses of interments. They have moreover urged that if they were enabled to have the funerals performed in a satisfactory manner, at a reduced expense, the applications for parochial aid would be proportionately diminished, the poorest relations would then subscribe to avert the disgrace of a parochial interment; a large proportion of the applications for such aid being now made by others than regular paupers, and in consequence of the hopelessness of their being enabled to defray the heavy expenses which are at present necessary.

§ 235. The conclusions before stated are deduced principally from the facts obtained by inquiries in the metropolis and the chief towns in the manufacturing districts. The information obtained by correspondence from Edinburgh, Glasgow, Bristol, Birmingham, Coventry, and several towns in Ireland, tends to the conclusion that the leading principles set forth in this report are applicable to all crowded town districts, with but few modifications. In all the practice of interments in towns, the crowded state of the places of burial, the apparent want of seclusion and sanctity pollute the mental associations, and offend the sentiments of the population, irrespective of any considerations of the public health; in almost all, this state of feeling is manifested by the increasing resort of persons of the higher and middle classes to such cemeteries as have been formed out of the towns by private individuals who have associated, and taken advantage of the feelings to procure subscriptions for the formation of more acceptable places of sepulture. In Manchester and Edinburgh, and a few other towns, the business of the undertaker does not appear to be on the same footing as in the metropolis; the expenses of the funerals to the labouring classes appear nevertheless to be no less oppressive, and the whole arrangements to stand in pressing need of regulation. In nearly all the towns where the grave-yards are crowded by the burials of an increasing population, evidence was tendered of outrages perpetrated upon the feelings of the population by the gravediggers in the disposal of undecomposed remains to make space for new interments. And it follows, from the circumstances that these men will not allow their own means of livelihood to be curtailed, and will, if they be permitted, or be unwatched, make way by any means for new interments. The desecrations are suspected, and from time to time are discovered. It requires a high order of education and mental qualification to maintain habitually respect for the inanimate remains of the dead and regard to the feelings of the living connected with them. In the uneducated, any common feelings of respect soon give way to every-day conveniences, and are at once obliterated by any strong necessities. The common tendencies in this respect are attested by the examples cited, of careful arrangements made to guard against them. (§ 169.) In all the populous provincial towns the need of the superior superintendence of the material arrangements for interment, and the exercise of such functions as those described as falling to a superior officer of public health, appear to be even more urgent than in the metropolis.   It is, however, an error to suppose that the evils of the existing practice of interment are confined to the *larger* towns.   The burial-ground at Southampton, for example, is represented to me to be full; it is moreover not more than one-half of the extent requisite for the population of that town, which is about 28,000, and rapidly increasing.   The authorities there are desirous of obtaining grounds and establishing a public cemetery in or near the town, and would, if practicable, do so without the expense of a private Act of Parliament.   The grave-yard of the cathedral of Ely, for the burials arising from a population of about 7,000 is reported to be inconveniently full, and the very reverend the dean is stated to be extremely desirous of closing it and procuring a burial-ground at a distance.   I have been informed by several ecclesiastical authorities, that the clergy are often much distressed by the inadequacy of the old grave-yards to meet the necessities of burial for an increasing population.   The data already given as to the space required for interments will serve to show the adequacy or inadequacy of the existing burial-grounds for any population.   It may be submitted that provision might be made for the relief of any district on the inspection and under the authority of properly appointed officers of health, for the provision of new and separate places of burial, on applications showing the inadequacy or unsuitableness of the existing grave-yards.

It were a reproach to the country, and its institutions and its government, and to its administrative capacity, to suppose that what is satisfactorily done in the German states may not, now that attention is directed to the subject, be generally done at least as well and satisfactorily in this country ; or that the higher classes would not in whatever depends on their voluntary aid, exhibit as good and practical an example of community of feeling in taking a lead in the adoption of all arrangements tending to the common benefit, as that displayed in the states which have achieved the most satisfactory improvement of the practice of interment, by well-appointed officers of public health.

§ 236.   I have thought it unnecessary to occupy attention with many details which would appear to follow the adoption of the general principles deducible from the information collected.   I have given that information so fully in the text, that I have avoided extending the bulk of the Report by repeating it with prefatory or connecting matter in the Appendix.

I would now beg leave to recapitulate the chief conclusions which the information obtained under this inquiry appears to establish.   They are—

I. *As to the Evils which require Remedies.*

§ 237. That the emanations from human remains are of a nature to produce fatal disease, and to depress the general health of whosoever is exposed to them; and that interments in the vaults of churches, or in grave-yards surrounded by inhabited houses, contribute to the mass of atmospheric and other impurities by which the general health and average duration of life of the inhabitants is diminished. (§ 1 to 23.)

§ 238. That the places of burial in towns or crowded districts are usually destitute of proper seclusion or means for impressive religious service, and are exposed to desecrations revolting to the popular feelings; and that feelings of aversion are manifest in the increasing removals or abandonment of family vaults and places of burial, and the preference, often at increased expense, of interments in suburban cemeteries, which are better fitted to raise mental associations of greater quiet, respect, and security as places of repose. (§ 109.)

§ 239. That the greatest injury done by emanations from decomposing remains of the dead to the health of the living of the labouring classes, in many populous districts, arises from the long retention of the body before interment in the single rooms in which families of those classes live and have their meals, and sleep, and where the deaths, in the greater number of instances, take place; and that closely successive deaths of members of the same family, from the same disease, are very frequent amongst the labouring classes; and that, where the disease has not been occasioned by the emanations from the first dead body, as sometimes appears to have been the case, or where the disease has either arisen from a common cause, or may have been communicated before death from the living person, the diseases are apparently rendered much more fatal by this practice of the retention of the dead body in the one living room previous to interment. (§ 24 to 39.)

§ 240. That this practice of the prolonged retention of the dead in such crowded rooms, besides being physically injurious, is morally degrading and brutalizing. (§ 40 to 42.)

§ 241. That this practice is frequently the most powerfully influenced by the difficulty of raising the expenses of funerals, which in this country press grievously on the labouring and middle classes of the community, and are extravagant and wasteful to all classes, and occasion severe suffering and moral evil. (§ 43 to 71.)

§ 242. That, on the best proximate estimates which have been made, the total amount of the whole of the yearly expenses of funerals in the metropolis cannot be less than between six and seven hundred thousand pounds, and for the whole of Great Britain between four and five millions sterling per annum. (§ 72 to 74.)

§ 243. That it appears, upon examination in the metropolis, that notwithstanding the great expense of funerals, the existing

arrangements for conducting them are on an unsatisfactory footing, and that great difficulties stand in the way of any efficient
amendment, whilst the practice of interment in the crowded districts is retained.   (§ 84 to 89.)

§ 244. That on the occurrence of a death amongst the poorest
classes or amongst strangers, the survivors are commonly destitute
of means of precaution against oppressive charges and of trustworthy advice or counsel, as to the modes of burial such as are
afforded by the civic arrangements of other civilized countries.
(§§ 121, 122, and vide Appendix, No. 1.)

§ 245. That on the occurrence of deaths from preventible
causes of disease, there are no appointed means for the detection
and removal of those causes, and that strangers and new-comers,
having no warning, are successively exposed, and frequently fall
victims to them.   (§ 196.)

§ 246. That common causes of diseases which ravage the community, of the extent of operation of which causes it has a deep
interest in knowing, pass unexamined and undetected ; moreover,
that in many districts there are wide opportunities for the escape
of crimes, by which life is also rendered insecure, chiefly by the
omission of efficient arrangements for the due verification of the
fact and causes of death.   (§§ 205 to 215.)

§ 247. That the numbers of funerals, and intensity of the misery
attendant upon them, vary amongst the different classes of society
in proportion to the internal and external circumstances of their
habitations : that the deaths and funerals vary in the metropolis
from 1 in every 30 of the population annually (and even more
in ill-conditioned districts), to 1 in 56 in better-conditioned districts ; from 1 death and funeral in every 28 inhabitants in an ill-
conditioned provincial town district, to 1 in 64 in a better-
conditioned rural district : such differences of the condition of the
population being accompanied by still closer coincidences in the
variation of the span of life, the average age of all who die in
some ill-conditioned districts of the metropolis being 26 years
only, whilst in better-conditioned districts it is 36 years : the variations of the age of deaths being in some provincial towns, such as
Leicester, from 15 years in the ill-conditioned to 24 years in the
better-conditioned districts : and as between town and rural districts
17 or 18 years for the whole population of Liverpool, and 39 years
for the whole population of Hereford ; and that the total excess
of deaths and funerals in England and Wales alone, above the
commonly attained standards of health, being at the least between
thirty and forty thousand annually. (§ 75 to § 80, and district
returns : Appendix.)

II. *As to the Remedies available for the Prevention or Mitiga-
tion of these Evils.*

§ 248. That the most effectual and principal means for the

abatement of the evils of interments are those sanitary measures which diminish the proportionate numbers of deaths and funerals, and increase the duration of life. § 75 to § 82, and General Report, p. 370. But—

§ 249. That on the several special grounds, moral, religious, and physical, and in conformity to the best usages and authorities of primitive Christianity, § 177, and the general practice of the most civilized modern nations, the practice of interments in towns in burial places amidst the habitations of the living, and the practice of interment in churches, ought for the future, and without any exception of places, or acceptation of persons, to be entirely prohibited. (§ 1 to § 23.)

§ 250. That the necessities of no class of the population in respect to burial ought to be abandoned as sources of private emolument to commercial associations, but that national cemeteries of a suitable description ought to be provided and maintained (as to the material arrangements), under the direction of officers duly qualified for the care of the public health. (§ 126.)

§ 251. That for the avoidance of the pain, and moral and physical evil arising from the prolonged retention of the body in the rooms occupied by the living, and at the same time to carry out such arrangements as may remove the painful apprehensions of premature interments, institutions of houses for the immediate reception, and respectful and appropriate care of the dead, under superior and responsible officers, should be provided in every town for the use of all classes of the community. (§ 90 to § 101.)

§ 252. That for the abatement of oppressive charges for funereal materials, decorations, and services, provision should be made (in conformity to successful examples abroad) by the officers having charge of the national cemeteries, for the supply of the requisite materials and services, securing to all classes, but especially to the poor, the means of respectable interment, at reduced and moderate prices, suitable to the station of the deceased, and the condition of the survivors. (§ 186, § 115 to § 120.)

§ 253. That for these purposes, and for carrying out the physical arrangements necessary for the protection of the public health in respect to the practice of interment, officers of health qualified by medical education and special knowledge should be appointed. (§ 223.)

§ 254. That in order to abate the apprehensions of premature interment, § 92 to § 96, to bring responsible aid and counsel, and protection within the reach of the most destitute survivors, §§ 121 and 122 and § 198, to protect the people against continued exposure to ascertained and preventible causes of disease and death, the principle of the early appointment of searchers be revived, and no interment be allowed to take place without the verification of the fact and cause of death by the officer of health. (§ 123, 124, 125, 126, to § 216.)

§ 255. That in all clear and well ascertained cases of deaths from immediately removable causes of disease and death, the officers of health be invested with summary powers, and be responsible for exercising them, for the removal of those causes, and for the protection of strangers from continued exposure and suffering from them.

§ 256. That the expenses of national cemeteries should be raised by loans bearing interest.

§ 257. That the repayment of the principal and interest should be spread over a period of [thirty years?]—and be charged as part of the reduced expenses for future interments.

§ 258. That all burial fees and existing dues be collected on interment, and form a fund from whence be paid the compensations which Parliament may award to such existing interests as it may be necessary to disturb, including the payment of the establishment charges, and the principal and interest of the money expended for the erection of new cemeteries; and that any surplus which may thereafter accrue may be applied to the means of improving the health of the living.

§ 259. That, on consulting the experience of those cities abroad where the greatest attention has been given to the arrangements for the protection of health connected with interments, it appears that by the appointment of medical officers, unencumbered by private practice, as officers of health, and qualified by the possession of appropriate science for the verification of the fact and causes of death, and by committing to them the regulation of the service of interments in national cemeteries, the several defects above specified may be remedied, and that new and comparatively salubrious places of burial may be procured, together with appropriate religious establishments, wherein the funeral service may be better solemnized, and that the expense of funerals may be reduced, in the metropolis, at the least, to one-half of the existing amount, and full compensation be given to all who may have legitimate claims for compensation for losses on the alterations of the existing practice. (§ 219 to § 225.)

§ 260. That the agency of properly qualified officers of health necessary for abating the evils of the practice of interments would also serve powerfully to promote the application of those sanitary measures which in some districts would, there is reason to believe, save more than their own pecuniary expense, merely in the diminished numbers combined with reduced expenses of funerals, consequent on the practical operation of comprehensive measures of sanitary improvement. (§ 201.)

§ 261. The advantages which the measures proposed offer to the classes who now stand most in need of a beneficent intervention, may be thus recapitulated. To take the poorest class : the labouring man would (in common with the middle and higher classes) gain, on the occasion of his demise, protection for his widow and surviving children, that is to say ;

> Protection from the physical evil occasioned by the necessity of the prolonged retention of his remains in the living and sleeping room :

> Protection against extortionate charges for interment, and against the impositions of unnecessary, expensive, and unseemly funereal customs, maintained against the wishes of private individuals and families :

> Protection and redress to his survivors or the living against any unfair or illegal practices, should any such have led to the death :

> Protection against any discoverable causes of ill health, should any have attached to his abode or to his place of work :

> Protection from the painful idea (by arrangements preventive of the possibility) of a premature interment :

> Protection of the remains from profanation, either before or after interment :

> Protection such as may be afforded by the information and advice of a responsible officer, of knowledge, and station, in the various unforeseen contingencies that occur to perplex and mislead the prostrate and desolate survivors on such occasions. (§ 191 to § 207.)

Added to these will be the relief from the prospect of interment in a common grave-yard or charnel, by the substitution of a public national cemetery, on which the mind may dwell with complacency, as a place in which sepulture may be made an honour and a privilege.

§ 262. The advantages derivable to the public at large have already been specified, in the removal of causes of pain to the feelings of the living connected with the common burial places ; they would also gain in the several measures for protection against the causes of disease specified as within the province of an officer of the public health to remove; and they would also gain in the steps towards the creation of a science of the prevention of disease, and in a better registration of the fact and the causes of death.

To use the words of a great Christian writer,—that all this, which constitutes the last office of the living, " to compose the body to burial," should be done, and that it should be done well and " gravely, decently, and charitably, we have the example of all civilized nations to engage us, and of all ages of the world to warrant :—so that it is against common honesty, and public fame and reputation not to do this office."

I would, in conclusion, beg leave to repeat and represent urgently that Her Majesty's Government, should only set hands to this great work, when invested with full powers to effect it completely : for at present there appears to be no alternative between doing it well or ill; between simply shifting the evil from the centre of the populous districts to the suburbs, and deteriorating them ; fixing the sites of interments at inconvenient distances, forming numerous, separate, and weak, and yet enormously expensive, establishments ; aggravating the expense, and physical and moral evils of the delay of interment; diminishing the solemnities of sepulture ; scattering away the elements of moral and religious improvement, and increasing the duration and sum of the existing evils :—there appears to be no distinct or practicable alternative between these results and effecting such a change as, if zealously carried out, will soothe and elevate the feelings of the great bulk of the population, abate the apprehensions of the dying, influence the voluntary adoption of beneficial changes in the practice of obsequies, occasion an earlier removal of the dead from amidst the living to await interment and ensure the impressiveness of the funeral service, give additional securities against attempts on life, and trustworthy evidence of the fact of death, with the means of advancing the protection of the living against the attacks of disease ; and at a reduced expense provide in well arranged national cemeteries places for public monuments, becoming the position of the empire amongst civilized nations.

I have the honour to be, Sir,

Your obedient servant,

EDWIN CHADWICK.

APPENDIX.

APPENDIX.

No. 1.

REGULATIONS FOR PUBLIC INTERMENT AT FRANCKFORT, PASSED 1829.

The transference of the cemetery to the outside of the town required the herewith enacted abolition of the ancient mode and custom of interring the dead, and the substitution of another and more suitable arrangement. For this purpose the following regulations for Sachsenhausen [the suburbs of Franckfort], as well as Franckfort, are published for general observance :—

SECTION I.

(1.) The mixed Church and School Commission has the chief superintendence of all church, cemetery, and interment affairs.

The regulation of all matters relating to interments is conferred upon the legally-appointed Church and Cemetery Commission.

All officers employed in connection with interments are placed under the control of the said Commission, and it will be its duty to report yearly to the mixed Church and School Commission on the expenses and receipts, and the general progress of the institution.

(2.) The superintendence of the cemetery, of the sextons in their various employments, and of the house of reception, is given to an inspector, whose duties are hereafter described in the 2nd section.

(3.) For the performance of all the necessary arrangements preceding the interment, commissaries of interments are appointed to take the place of the so-called undertakers. These commissaries have to arrange everything connected with the funeral, and are responsible for the proper fulfilment of all the regulations given in their instructions.

(4.) In order to prevent the great expense which was formerly occasioned by the attendance with the dead to the grave, bearers shall be appointed who shall attend to the cemetery all funerals, without distinction of rank or condition.

To these bearers shall be given assistants, who shall be equally under the control of the interment commissaries.

(5.) A sufficient number of sextons and assistants shall be appointed to form the graves and assist at the interment.

(6.) There are four classes of funerals and interments. Every house of mourning may choose the class of funeral on paying the sum fixed for that class to the Church and Cemetery Commission.

All Christian interments, without distinction, can be conducted only according to these interment regulations. It remains open to the friends of the dead to attend the burial either in carriage or on foot; but this must be without expense to the house of mourning. The funerals of the town guards and of the soldiers of the line remain the same, but are only to cost a fixed sum.

If it be the wish of a family, the clergyman may attend the funeral, and he may perform a service either at the side of the grave, or, in case of bad weather, in the house of reception.

All interments whatsoever, except in extraordinary cases, where the police determines the time, must take place early—in summer before nine, in winter before eleven o'clock, in the morning.

The blowing of trumpets from the steeples, the attendance of women with napkins, the bearings of crosses, the attendance of the old-fashioned mourning coach, and also the use of the so-called "chariot of Heaven," and the following of young handicrafts-men, which generally were an immense expense, are all given up.   New carriages of a simpler and more respectable form, and such as are better suited to the object and to the greater distance of the cemetery from the town, shall be built.

The bodies of adults who are taken direct from the house of mourning to the grave, must be borne in the funeral carriage to the gate of the cemetery, where the bearers will convey the coffin to the grave.

The dead who have been placed in the house of reception must be borne in the same manner to the grave.

In exceptional cases, the dead may be borne to the grave by other persons; but this is only allowed when there is any particular cause of sympathy with the dead, or with the surviving family, and it must be free of all expense.

(7.) A complete and exact plan of the new cemetery shall be prepared, and all the graves shall be marked upon it.

Every place of interment must be numbered, which number must be engraved upon the plan as soon as it is taken.

The actuary of the Cemetery Commission shall keep a book, in which is entered, along with the number of the grave, the rank, age, name, and surname of the deceased.

(8.) Those who possess family vaults, family graves, or monuments, receive from the Cemetery Commission a document attesting their right, and they must also follow the regulations which are contained in it.

(9.) No grave can be opened till after the lapse of 20 years.

Hence, if a family grave-plot is full, and the oldest grave has not been closed 20 years on the occurrence of another death in the family, if it cannot be placed in the grave-plot of any other relative, it must be interred in the general interment ground, in the regular order and course.

(10.) The printed table of the cost of interment determines what sum is to be paid for funerals to the Church and Cemetery Commission.

SECTION II.—*The duties of the Cemetery Inspector.*

(11.) He is chosen by the Church and Cemetery Commission, and the appointment is confirmed by the mixed Church and School Commission.

In case the latter commission should find reason to delay the ratification, the grounds of the delay are to be reported to the senate, which will then order what is requisite.

The oath of the Cemetery Inspector must be taken before the younger *Herr Burgermeister,* but his dismissal must be conducted in the same manner as his appointment.

He must be examined by the Sanitary Board, and must be found by them to be qualified.   He must also be a burgher.

The Cemetery Inspector retains his situation during good behaviour, exact obedience to the interment regulations, and all other matters contained in his instructions.

(12.) The sextons and their assistants are under the control of the Cemetery Inspector.

He has to enforce the regulation that all those employed in the solemnities of funerals, or in the house of mourning, shall appear in good black clothes, and that no disorder, negligence, or defect, is permitted in the cemetery.

He has further to see that on the part of the sextons, or the gardeners, the neatness of the paths of the cemetery is restored after interments, as also that of the plantations and flower borders, as quickly as possible, and also that the mounds on the graves in the common ground are covered with green turf and kept in a pretty form.

. (13.) The interments are to be notified by writing to the inspector of the cemetery by the Interment Commissary. This notification must be signed by the Church and Cemetery Commission, otherwise the inspector may not venture to order the sextons to form a grave.

One of the principal duties of the inspector is to keep a register of all the interments from these notifications, which register he must weekly lay before the Church and Cemetery Commission.

(14.) The coffins must, without any distinction, be lowered into the graves, and the inspector has to see that the necessary ropes are always in proper condition.

No less important is it for the inspector to be present at an interment, in order that by his presence nothing may be done by his subordinates, or by any other person, which should be contrary to the dignity of the interment or to the regulations.

(15.) The inspector must also inspect the family vaults, graves, and monuments, and keep a book, in which he enters statements of any repairs which may be necessary, and a notification of this is immediately to be sent to the Church and Cemetery Commission, without whose permission no alteration can be made in the graves.

(16.) The inspector has also the superintendence of the house of reception.

(17.) It is the duty of the inspector to treat all who have to apply to him with politeness and respect, and to give the required information unweariedly and with ready good will.

Under no pretext is he allowed either to demand or receive any payment, as he has a sufficient salary.

Section III.—*On the Interment Commissaries.*

(18.) On the motion of the Church and Cemetery Commission, the Consistory names four Interment Commissaries for the Lutheran community.

For the reformed church in Franckfort two Interment Commissaries are chosen by the reformed consistory from those proposed by the Church and Cemetery Commission. Amongst those persons proposed by this commission, there must be included not only the present clergymen of the two reformed communities, but the clergyman at all times must be proposed.

The Catholic has also an Interment Commissary, chosen by the Church and School Commission from those proposed by the Church and Cemetery Commission.

The list proposed for every such appointment must include, at least, three burghers, fit to fill the situation.

The appointment is given during good behaviour, and the commissary must take an oath that he will truly and exactly follow the regulations, and that he feels it his duty to perform all these and any other particular instructions which he may receive.

(19.) To each of the three Interment Commissaries of the Lutheran community four districts are given, in which they must superintend all that has to be done from the death to the interment in their community.

The two Reformed commissaries, as well as the Catholic, have to take care of everything connected with interment in their communities.

(20.) In order that illness or any other unavoidable obstacle may not easily interfere with the function of these commissaries, two Lutheran, one Reformed, and one Catholic commissaries, shall be appointed as substitutes, and shall have the same duties and obligations as their superiors.

(21.) These commissaries must notify to each other at what hour they have an interment in charge, in order that many interments at the same time may be avoided.

(22.) The commissary is to be informed immediately as soon as a death has occurred. Thereon the commissary acquaints the family of the deceased with all that is to be done or observed with regard to the interment.

The commissary must then send to the proper officer a notification of the death, and receive the interment certificate, signed by the Church and Cemetery Commission. If the hour and day of the interment is fixed by the family of the deceased, the interment commissary informs the bearers of it the day before, so that if many funerals occurred on one day, it may be so arranged that no delays or annoyances should take place.

Timely warning is to be given to the friends of those who are placed in the house of reception, of the hour and day of interment, in order that they may, if desirous of doing so, attend the funeral.

(23.) The bearers alone, without any exception, must place the coffin in the ground.

The commissary must see that the bearers are always cleanly and respectably dressed in black when they appear at a funeral, and must be particularly careful that they conduct themselves seriously, quietly, and respectably.

He must also see that the carriage of the dead is not driven quickly either in the town or beyond it, but that it is conducted respectably at a quiet pace.

When the dead is covered, and not until then, the commissary and the bearers shall leave the cemetery in perfect silence.

For any impropriety which may, through the conduct of the bearers, arise during the interment, the commissary is responsible.

(24.) The commissary must keep a register of the deaths which occur in his district. He must close it every month with his signature, and present it in the first three days of the following month to the Church and Cemetery Commission.

(25.) If desired by the family of the deceased to communicate the event to the friends, the commissary shall do so, and for this he is to be paid according to the tax. But it is by no means necessary that he should be employed, as any other person may be employed to announce the death.

(26.) The substitute must receive half of the sum fixed by the tax-roll as belonging to the commissary, whose place he fills.

If the substitute is employed to announce the death, he receives the whole of the remuneration for that service.

Of the Bearers or Attendants of the Funerals.

(27.) The coffin bearers are chosen by the Church and School Commission, according to the sect for which they are to be employed.

The appointment of attendants on funerals and their assistants depends on good conduct.

They are bound by oath, truly and exactly, to do all that is prescribed by the interment regulations, as also all that may further be committed to them by the Church and Cemetery Commission.

(28.) For the interment of the Reformed and Lutheran sects in Franckfort, there shall be appointed thirty-six attendants of funerals and twelve assistants.

The community in Sachsenhausen has also twelve attendants and six assistants.

These attendants and their assistants are chosen from both these evangelical sects, without regard, however, to the particular number which there may be belonging to the one or the other sect.

. They are summoned by writing to the performance of their duties at the four different classes of funeral by the Interment Commissioner belonging to that community, and are subject to the strictest inspection by that commissioner.

The Catholic community has also twelve attendants and six assistants.

The whole of the attendants and assistants must be citizens or burghers of Franckfort, or from the neighbourhood, and of unquestionable reputation.

(29.) On the occasion of every death, whenever they are required, these bearers must appear in a neat and clean dress, and conduct themselves respectfully and quietly.

The dress consists of a frock coat, vest, trousers, a round hat, stockings, and shoes or boots, all of black.

In winter is added a black cloak.

The whole of the dress must be of a particular form and make.

(30.) The bearers shall neither eat nor drink in the house of mourning : they shall neither ask nor receive, under the strongest penalty, any sum for that purpose. since they and their assistants have a fixed and sufficient salary, according to the interment regulations ; any breach of this regulation will be punished by dismissal.

The assistant will pay half the rate to the bearer. That assistant who has signalized himself by the exact fulfilment of his duties, shall be the first to be promoted as bearer in case of a vacancy.

Neglect of duty on the first occasion shall be punished by the Church and Cemetery Commission with suspension from the office for a certain length of time, and on a repetition of the neglect, with dismissal.

It is before this commission that the bearers have to bring their complaints, which may sometimes occur, against the Interment Commissary, under whose immediate control they are placed, and the matter is there settled.

(31.) The Church and Cemetery Commission has to name from amongst the attendants of the Lutheran and Catholic funerals those who are to be cross-hearers. These, as well as the bearers, must fulfil most exactly and conscientiously the orders of the Commissioner of Interments, and must only attend when required by him.

Section IV.—*Of the Grave-diggers.*

(32.) The Church and Cemetery Commission appoints the sextons and their assistants, who are bound by oath to fulfil the regulations and necessary arrangements of the Commission.

(33.) The Church and Cemetery Commission appoints one of the sextons as chief, who must always live in the town, and to whom the Interment Commissioner must make known the event of a death, in order that it may be notified to the Church and Cemetery Inspector, who thereupon orders the preparation of a grave.

This chief sexton has a register, in which he enters all the notifications of interments that have been sent to him, and which, when asked for, he must lay before the Church and Cemetery Commission.

No grave can be prepared, unless the warrant for it has been signed by the Church and Cemetery Commission.

Every grave must be six feet deep, three feet and a-half wide, and seven feet long for an adult.

The measurement for children is regulated by the Church and Cemetery Inspector on each separate occasion. Between the graves in the ordinary course there must be an interval of one foot.

(34.) The whole of the sextons, in which is included their assistants, are under the inspection of the Church and Cemetery Inspector, who must keep them to their duty, and who is answerable for any misdemeanor, or offence or neglect of the sextons.

(35.) The sextons must always be respectably dressed in black during the interment, and those who go to the house of mourning must always appear in neat and clean attire, and must be studious at all times, whether engaged within or without the churchyard, to preserve a modest and proper behaviour. Drunkenness, neglect of duty, or abuse of their services, will be punished by the Church and Cemetery Commission, and on repetition of the offence the offender will be dismissed. The sextons are forbidden, on pain of dismissal, from making any alteration in any family vault, or grave, or in the ordinary graves, without especial orders. They shall, on the other hand, keep all the flowers, borders, and shrubs in the neatest order, and one of the sextons must be an excellent gardener, whose office it shall be to keep the plantations and borders in good condition.

Any assistant who has been guilty of any fault which has led to the dismissal of the sexton, shall not be able to be employed again as sexton.

(36.) The salary for the making of a grave is settled by the Church and Cemetery Commissioners, on the roll, and no more than this sum can either be demanded or received, under pain of dismissal.

An assistant who has to perform the work of a sexton on account of sickness, must give the sexton half the remuneration. In case the sexton allows the assistant to do his work, or, on occasion of increased work requiring the employment of an assistant, the assistant must receive the full pay.

That assistant who has signalized himself by the exact and excellent performance of his duties, shall be the first to be promoted when a vacancy occurs.

When the qualifications are equal, the assistant of the longest standing shall be promoted, and when this is equal, the oldest shall be made sexton.

The complaints of the sextons and assistants against the Inspector or amongst themselves are to be settled by the Church and Cemetery Commission.

Of the Cost of Interment.

The Church and Cemetery Commission undertake to conduct the interments at the price fixed by them in the tax roll.

The whole rates could only be made so moderate, by making all interments to depend on the Church and Cemetery Commission, therefore the solemnities of interment can be superintended by no one except the said Commission, under the regulation of the printed orders.

The Interment Commissioner, on the occasion of a death, must call the attention of the friends to these orders. It depends entirely on the choice of the friends to which of the four classes of prices the funeral shall belong.

(39.) The Commission of Interments has to receive the payment for the interment from the friends, and must immediately pay it over to the Church and Cemetery Commission.

(40.) Besides, or in addition to the authorized payment printed in the tax roll, and determined by the Church and Cemetery Commission as the sufficient remuneration of the Inspector, Commissioner of Interments, the bearers and sextons, no one is, on the occasion of a death, either to give money or to furnish food and drink.

The practice of furnishing crape, gloves, lemons, &c., by the friends of the dead, is also given up, and the persons engaged in conducting the interment, must take all the requisites with them, without asking or receiving any compensation, under pain of instant dismissal.

The time which these orders are to remain in force.

(41.) Experience will best show what alteration is necessary in these regulations, and they are therefore after some years to be laid by the mixed

Church and School Commission before the Senate for revision, and further regulation.

The rate of Interment for the Christian communities of the free town of Franckfort.

The following, by order of the Legislative Assembly, of the 31st May, 1836, is the table of the rate of interment, which is here made known for every one's observance and obedience.

The interments of adults are divided into four classes :—

				English Money.		
				£.	s.	d.
The 1st class costs	50 florins	=	4	7	6
The 2nd „	36 „	=	3	3	0
The 3rd „	22 „	=	1	18	6
The 4th „	15 „	=	1	6	3

The interment of children are also of four classes :—

First Class.

			English Money.		
			£.	s.	d.
Children from 10 to 15 . . .	22 florins	=	1	18	6
„ 5 to 10 . . .	16 florins	=	1	8	0
„ 0 to 5 . . .	12 florins	=	1	1	0

Second Class.

Children from 10 to 15 . . .	16 florins	=	1	8	0
„ 5 to 10 . . .	11 florins	=	0	19	3
„ 0 to 5 . . .	8 florins	=	0	14	0

Third Class.

Children from 10 to 15 . . .	10 florins	=	0	17	6
„ 5 to 10 . . .	8 florins	=	0	14	0
„ 0 to 5 . . .	4 florins	=	0	7	0

Fourth Class.

Children from 10 to 15 .	6 florins	=	0	10	6
„ 5 to 10 .	5 florins	=	0	8	9
„ 0 to 5 .	2 florins 30 kruitzers	=	0	4	4

For the funeral of all the city militia and officers of the line, twelve florins must be paid for the cross, the pall, and the making of the grave, inclusive of the carriage, by the friends of the dead.

The interment of a pauper will cost six florins, eight kruitzers.

The expenses of the interments of the institution for paupers are settled by the Church and Cemetery Commission, with the officers of that institution.

If the Interment Commissary be employed by the friends of the deceased, to announce the occurrence of the death, he is to receive three guilders per day.

SECTION V.—*The Regulations with regard to the House for the reception of the Dead.*

The following are the regulations regarding the use of the house for the reception and care of the dead, which are here made known for every one's observance.

P 2

(1.) The object of this institution is—

    a. To give perfect security against the danger of premature interment.

    b. To offer a respectable place for the reception of the dead, in order to remove the corpse from the confined dwellings of the survivors.

(2.) The use of the reception-house is quite voluntary, yet, in case the physician may consider it necessary for the safety of the survivors that the dead be removed, a notification to this effect must be forwarded to the younger burgermeister to obtain the necessary order.

(3.) Even, in case the house of reception is not used, the dead cannot be interred until after the lapse of three nights, without the proper certificate of the physician that the signs of decomposition have commenced. In order to prevent the indecency which has formerly occurred, of preparing too early the certificate of the death, the physician shall in future sign a preliminary announcement of the occurrence of death, for the sake of the previous arrangements necessary for an interment, but the certificate of death is only to be prepared when the corpse shows unequivocal signs of decomposition having commenced. For the dead which it is wished to place in the house of reception, the physician prepares a certificate of removal. This certificate of removal can only be given after the lapse of the different periods, of six hours; in sudden death, of twelve hours; and in other cases, twenty-four hours.

In case of the thermometer being below 10 degrees of Reaumur, (30 Fahrenheit), removal can only take place when there are unequivocal signs of death, and under the certificate of death from the physician.

(4.) The custody and treatment of the dead in the house of reception is the same for all ranks and conditions.

(5.) The superintendence of the house of reception is conferred upon the Inspector of the Church Yard. He must possess the requisite medical and surgical knowledge, and must be examined by the Sanitary Board with regard to his qualification for the office, and must be instructed according to their direction.

(6.) The guardians of the dead are under the control of the inspector, and must receive a special instruction with regard to their duties.

(7.) The dead which are placed in the house of reception must not be interred until unequivocal signs of decomposition have appeared.

The inspector determines the time of interment.

(8.) The dead, on arrival at the house of reception, are immediately placed in separate rooms, which are built for that purpose, and which are numbered, and there receive all the proper means of security.

(9.) In the house of reception, there are besides these rooms two other chambers; one is used as the animating chamber, the other, as a bath room.

The kitchen, which is also near at hand, is used to furnish hot water, or whatever may be required.

(10.) In case a body gives signs of re-animation, it must be brought immediately into the chamber used for that purpose, when all the means will b applied by the inspector, according to the instructions he has received

(11.) This chamber, in which there is a bed, must always be carefully locked, in order that it may never be used for any other purpose. The inspector alone has possession of the key of this chamber.

(12.) There must be in this chamber every necessary provision of medicines, and of means of resuscitation and proper ventilation of the air, according to the instruction of the Sanitary Board, and all these arrangements must be kept in most perfect order by the inspector.

(13.) If any particular case occurs in the house of reception, the Sanitary Board must immediately have information of it, and the Board must from time to time examine into the state of the house.

(14.) Permission to friends and relatives to enter the rooms of the dead is not granted unconditionally, on account of considerations of health, but it depends upon the consent of the inspector. Entrance into the waiting hall, from which the rooms in which the dead are deposited range, is at all times allowed to the relatives of the dead.

(15.) A register is kept in the house of reception, in which is entered the rank and name of the dead, the age, the last disease, the day and hour of the death, the placing in the house of reception, and the time of interment, and the name of the last physician. Every registration is signed by the inspector.

(16.) No payment is made for reception and guarding of the dead in the house of reception, nor for the services of the inspector or nurses, nor for the heating of the chambers. These expenses are defrayed from the Interment Fund.

(17.) The inspector and nurses are strictly forbidden to allow any persons to visit them in the buildings of the burial ground.

(18.) When the inspector has been examined by the Sanitary Board, as to his special qualifications, and has passed, the oath is administered to him by the younger burgermeister.

Instructions to the Inspector in regard to the House of Reception.

(1.) The inspector must be examined as to his medical and surgical knowledge, by the Sanitary Board, and as to his treatment of suspended animation, in which he is specially instructed by the Sanitary Board, and is then sworn in by the younger burgermeister.

(2.) The inspector has to instruct his assistants, and must see that his instructions are strictly followed.

(3.) He must answer for all that is out of order in the house of reception.

(4.) As long as there are corpses in the house, the inspector must not leave his house.

(5.) He has to keep a register, in a form which is prescribed, and must punctually and clearly fill up all the heads of the form.

(6.) As soon as a corpse is brought to the house, the inspector must determine in which of the rooms it is to be placed, and order all the necessary arrangements and means of security, and the attendance of guardians, and must not leave the dead until everything has been arranged for its proper protection and care.

(7.) The Cemetery Inspector must superintend the attendants night and day.

(8.) No corpse can be interred until unequivocal signs of decomposition have appeared. On this matter the inspector has to act according to the instructions of the Sanitary Board.

(9.) Should the case arise, that the dead sets in motion the alarum, or that the nurses perceive a slight colour in the cheek, or a slight breathing, or a movement in the eye-lid, the inspector must immediately arrange that the body be brought into the fresh air of the re-animating chamber, which is properly warmed, and he will there adopt all the other means, on which he has received instructions from the Sanitary Board.

(10.) When these signs of life have appeared, the inspector must immediately give information of the circumstance by a messenger to the physician who last attended the person, in order that a notification of the same may be made to the *Physikat.*

The tidings of the re-animation shall be conveyed to the house of mourning by the physician alone, and then only when there is no longer any doubt of the resuscitation.

(11.) One of the first essentials in the house is cleanliness. The Cemetery Inspector has therefore strictly to watch that everything which belongs to the house is kept most perfectly clean by the nurses.

In order to preserve the purity of the air, he must see that the arrangements for ventilation are kept in perfect order.

(12.) He must also see that the rooms are properly warmed during the cold weather.

(13.) The Cemetery Inspector is not specially paid for his services in the house of reception, but has a house free, besides the salary determined by the Cemetery Commission, and printed in the salary table.

Instructions in respect to the Watchers or Nurses.

(1.) The nurses, amongst which the sextons may be sometimes employed, are named and appointed by the Church and Cemetery Commission, on good behaviour.

(2.) They are under the superintendence of the Cemetery Inspector, and must obey his orders with the greatest exactitude and alacrity.

(3.) As soon as a corspe is brought to the house the nurses must convey it immediately into the room pointed out by the inspector, and afterwards do all that is required of them by him.

(4.) They must be instructed in all their duties by the inspector.

(5.) He, whose week it is to watch in the warder's chamber, must never leave the chamber when there are corpses in the rooms, on pain of instant dismissal; but if anything requires him to leave the chamber, he must first summon with a bell one of the other nurses to take his place.

(6.) The nurses must keep everything in the house in the greatest cleanliness. Any one who has frequently to be reminded of his duties through carelessness shall be dismissed from the situation.

(7.) If roughness be shown by a nurse to the dead, he must be punished with instant dismissal, and a notification of the same must be given by the Church and Cemetery Commission to the police, in order that proper inquiry and punishment be given.

(8.) In case the alarum is set in motion, or any other sign of life is perceived, the nurse must immediately inform the Inspector, and quietly and gently fulfil all his directions.

(9.) The nurses are forbidden to use tobacco in the house.

(10.) They are forbidden to receive any visits in the house, and more especially to allow any person to come during the night into the ward-chamber.

(11.) There shall be in the warder's chamber a clock, which, by a certain mechanism, can tell when, and how long a nurse may have slept during the night. Frequent negligence of this kind will be punished by dismissal.

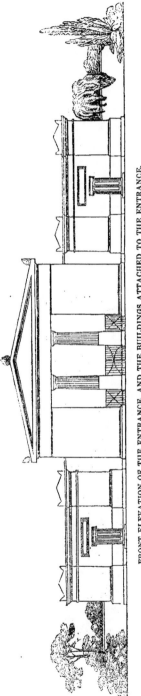

FRONT ELEVATION OF THE ENTRANCE, AND THE BUILDINGS ATTACHED TO THE ENTRANCE,
OF THE CHRISTIAN CEMETERY AT FRANCKFORT-ON-THE-MAINE.

A.—Hall.
B.—Room for the persons who
accompany the dead.
C.—Chambers for the dead.
D.—Warder's room.
E.—Chamber with a bed.
F.—Bath.
J.—Small kitchen.

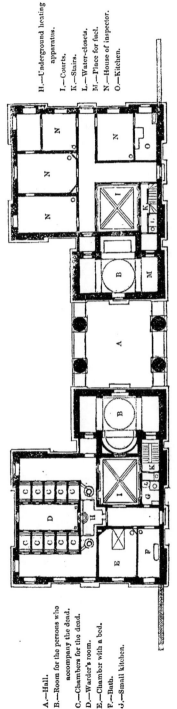

H.—Underground heating
apparatus.
I.—Courts.
K.—Stairs.
L.—Water-closets.
M.—Place for fuel.
N.—House of inspector.
O.—Kitchen.

GROUND PLAN OF THE ENTRANCE OF THE INSTITUTION FOR THE RECEPTION AND CARE OF THE DEAD, ATTACHED TO THE CEMETERY.

Scale of 150 Franckfort feet.

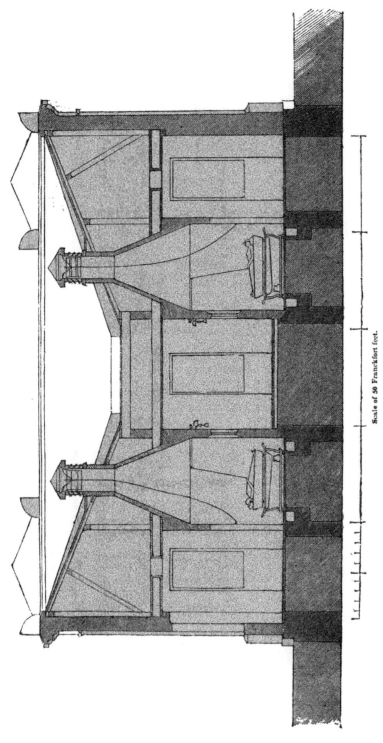

Scale of 50 Franckfort feet.

TRANSVERSE SECTION OF THE PROBATIONARY HOUSE OF RECEPTION AND CARE OF THE DEAD PREVIOUS TO INTERMENT AT THE CEMETERY.

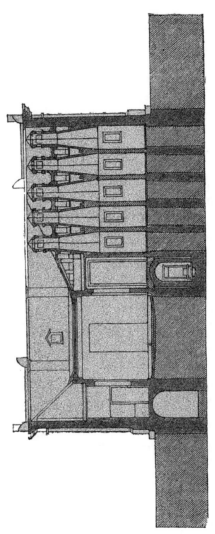

LONGITUDINAL SECTION OF THE PROBATIONARY HOUSE OF RECEPTION AND CARE OF THE DEAD
PREVIOUS TO INTERMENT AT THE CEMETERY.

No. 2.

REGULATIONS FOR THE EXAMINATION AND CARE OF THE DEAD, AND FOR RELIEVING THE APPREHENSIONS OF PREMATURE INTERMENTS, PROVIDED AT MUNICH.

Regulations for the Examination of the Dead.

Whereas it is of importance to all men to be peifectly assured that the beings who were dear to them in life are not torn from them so long as any, the remotest, hope exists of preserving them; so is death less dreadful in its shape when one is convinced of its actual occurrence, and no longer a danger exists of being buried alive.

In order to afford this satisfaction to mankind, and to preclude the possibility of any one being considered as dead who is not actually so ; that the spread of infectious disorders be avoided as much as possible ; that the quackeries so highly injurious to health may be suppressed; that murders committed by secret violence may be discovered, and the perpetrators delivered over to the hands of justice, is the imperative duty of every wise government; and in order to accomplish these objects, every one of which is of infinite importance, recourse must be had to the Safety Police as the most efficient means, by a strict medical examination into the deaths occurring, and a conformable view of the body.

In consideration of which, the orders already existing on this subject will undergo a strict examination, and, with the august consent of the government of the Isar-Circle, the following general regulations have been fixed upon :—

1. An examination of all dead bodies, at two different times, and this without exception to rank, is henceforth to take place in the metropolitan city of Munich, and the suburbs belonging thereto.

2. The first examination is to be held immediately after death has taken place, and the second shortly before the interment.

3. At the public hospitals, both examinations are intrusted to the acting physician, who has however strictly to observe those regulations relating to the certificates for the examination of the dead.

4. The first examination is to take place at the very spot where death has taken place, or where any dead body may be discovered, by the sworn surgeon of the district; the second examination, however, by the surgeon appointed by and belonging to the Police Establishment.

5. The city of Munich, with the suburbs, are to be divided into Eight Districts ; for each of these districts a separate surgeon is hereby appointed, viz. :—

[Here follow the eight districts, with the names and residences of the Surgeons appointed for each district.]

6. As soon as a death takes place, immediate notice must be given by the Soul-nuns, Midwife, &c., &c., or by any such person charged with the arrangements for the burial. This said notice must state the street, the number of the house, and of the floor where the dead body is lying; whereupon the said surgeon has immediately to go there, and conduct the investigation according to his instructions.

7. Previous to this, and before the first examination has taken place, it is neither permitted to undress nor to clean the dead body; nor is the body allowed (in cases of natural death) to be carried out of that room where death has taken place, or to be removed from the spot ; and it is not even permitted to remove the cushions from under the head of the dead body. Every violation of this decree will be punished with a fine of from 5 to 15 florins, or with imprisonment from one to three days.

8. Those regulations issued by the examining surgeon respecting the treatment of the dead body, or which relate to the clothes and other objects of the deceased, must be strictly obeyed.

9. After the examining surgeon has convinced himself that every hope of re-animation has disappeared, he fills up the certificate of examination ac-

cording to his instructions; but be it observed at the same time, that if a medical man has attended the deceased, such is bound to enter in the said certificate the description of the disease, and to certify it by his signature.

10. If the dead body remains in the dwelling-house until the burial takes place, the second examination by the surgeon from the Police must be held there; and for this reason the certificate must be forwarded into his hands as soon as possible.

11. But if the dead body after the first examination has been removed to the house for the reception of the dead, in order to remain there, this said certificate should previously, or at the delivery, be taken to the Inspector of his Institution, in order that no obstacle may arise to its reception.

12. The utmost cleanliness and greatest order is to prevail in this said house for the reception of the dead, where the dead bodies removed there are to be placed under a perpetual and proper watch; and the Police Surgeon is bound to call at the Institution twice every day, namely, in the morning and in the evening, to institute a very minute examination of the dead bodies there; and in case of any signs of re-animation, to render speedy and the most serviceable assistance.

13. If the medical man who conducts the second examination perceives those signs in a corpse which do not leave any doubt whatsoever that a death has taken place, he then enters the verification in the certificate, which thereupon is taken to the Directory of Police, who then grant the permission for the interment.

14. Without such a legal certificate permitting it, no body is allowed to be buried; and that Priest or Clergyman who will assist at any burial without having seen this certificate forfeits a sum from 15 to 30 florins.

15. Proper arrangements have been made that the Printed Forms for the decreed Certificates may always be obtained at the Directory of Police, and will be delivered gratis to the officiating medical men of the Public Hospitals, as well as to the Examining Surgeons; a receipt however must be given for them.

16. All those persons nominated for the execution of these measures, as the Soul-nuns, Midwives, attendants at the house for the reception of the dead; the Inspector of such House, the Examining Surgeons, the Surgeons of the Police, &c., &c., will be supplied with the printed regulations, as well as the most minute instructions, for which purpose they will be sworn, and be ever subject to a rigorous inspection.

Munich, Nov. 20, 1821.

[The regulations which follow this are chiefly as to the different prices of different degrees of the religious service.]

Regulations for the Guards or Watchers at the House for the reception of the Dead near the Burial Ground at Munich, with reference to the Inspection of Dead Bodies.

1. There must be at least two healthworthy and active men, as trusty as possible, appointed as Body Watchers, and specially sworn in by the Police.

2. When a body is intended to be placed in the house for the reception of the dead, it must be previously notified to the Inspector of the same, and the before-mentioned "Examination Ticket," or a special official order, be delivered over to him.

3. It is forbidden to the Body Watchers to place any body there without the previous knowledge and concurrence of the Inspector.

4. Should no obstacle arise, the corpse is then received by the Body Watchers, and deposited in the place appropriated to it.

5. The cover of the coffin must then be immediately withdrawn, the face of the deceased uncovered, and the hands and feet disengaged from the bandages attached to them.

6. The place where the bodies are watched must be kept warm day and night, and lighted during the night without interruption.

7. Great cleanliness is to be observed, and a supply of pure air to be kept up.

8. The Watchers must constantly remain in the watch-room, and frequently by day and night enter the room for the reception of the dead, in order carefully to observe the bodies lying there.

9. The Police Surgeons will particularly instruct the Body Watchers as to what signs or appearances they are especially to observe, and how they are to act with regard to them. On this point they are to take the greatest care.

10. Should any sign or appearances which may betoken re-animation proceed from any body, it must be immediately brought into the watch-room with every care and precaution, and placed on the bed provided with mattrasses and blankets for that purpose.

11. On such an event occurring, not only the Inspector must be informed of it, but the Police Surgeon must be called in without a moment's delay.

12. As to the treatment of the body until the arrival of the Surgeon, the Inspector and Body Watchers are informed by the Police Surgeon. In all cases must warm water be prepared, and the safety apparatus arranged.

13. The body, thus awakened from its sleep, must be treated with extreme care, and everything must be avoided likely to create any strong impression on it.

14. No coffin wherein a body is placed must be closed, nor must any preparation for the burial take place, until the distinct permission from the Police Surgeon is issued.

15. The entrance into the room for the reception of the dead is allowed to every one under proper restrictions, care being taken that the quiet and good order there are not disturbed.

16. Any Body Watcher who shall be convicted of any neglect in the performance of his duties, will be punished with a proportional fine and imprisonment, and dismissed on a repetition of the offence.

Munich, Nov. 20, 1821.   Royal Police Direction.

Regulations for the Proceedings at the Second Examination of the Corpses by the proper nominated Surgeon of the Police.

1. The second examination of the deceased must be performed by the appointed Police Surgeon, who must, however, take particular pains to satisfy himself that the first examination has been duly executed, that the certificates were properly drawn up, that the Soul-nuns have fulfilled their various duties, and that both the Inspector, as well as the appointed Watchmen belonging to the house for the reception of the dead, have duly discharged the duties with which they are intrusted, and that, moreover, nothing has been undertaken or omitted that should not be in accordance with the various intents and purposes of the decreed examination of the bodies.

2. This said Surgeon must be supplied with a copy of all the regulations relating to the examination of the bodies, as well as copies of all such regulations for the guidance of all others charged with the performance of any of these duties.

3. If the Surgeon who is appointed by the Police feels convinced that by one person or other any act has been performed contrary to the prescribed duties, or that any negligence in the execution of the service exists, he must, on pain of personal responsibility, give immediate notice to the Police.

4. The same (the Police Surgeon) is bound to issue proper instructions, more particularly to the Soul-nuns, to the Inspector of the house for the reception of the dead, and to the Watchers and attendants of the said institution, as well as to all individuals assisting at any of the examinations; which said instructions relate to the method of proceeding, and treatment of the dead bodies, especially in such a case where re-animation might again take place, and repeated caution must be given on this subject.

5. The second examination with which he is charged must either be undertaken in that house where death has taken place, or in the house for the reception of the dead. In the first case, when, for instance, the deceased

is kept at the house where death has taken place until the final interment, the Police Surgeon must receive the necessary information through the medium of the examining ticket. which has been issued and signed by the medical man of the district, and which ticket must be forwarded to him, either through the Soul-nun, or through any such person charged to attend the deceased.

6. The stated sickness, or the manner how death ensued, as also the time in which deceased is to be buried; all of which, having been entered on the ticket, must serve him for guidance whether the second examination must be more or less accelerated. In all cases, however, such must be undertaken as timely as possible, so that generally interment may take place after 48 hours.

7. He has, accordingly, to go to that place stated in the certificate of examination, examine the corpse with due minuteness, and, in case the burial may be proceeded with, he has to state it in the certificate; such is then to be forwarded to the Royal Police, where the permission for interment is granted.

8. If it is intended to remove the body to the house for the reception of the dead, such may take place without any hesitation after the proceedings of the first examination; and in this case the Police Surgeon must find both the body and certificate at that place.

9. The Police Surgeon is bound to attend twice every day at the house for the reception of the dead of the burial-ground, viz., every morning from 9 to 10 o'clock, and in the afternoon from 3 to 4 o'clock. On his arrival, such dead bodies, with their certificates, which have been examined. must be shown to him; he examines them, and signs those certificates which do not admit of any delay; which certificates are afterwards forwarded to the Royal Police authorities, in order to procure the certificate of permission for the burial.

10. Of all such dead bodies having undergone the second examination by the Police Surgeon, and which have been considered by him proper for burial, minute lists must be kept by him containing the consecutive numbers, as well as the statement of that day on which the interment has been ordered, and all such observations which have been entered in the certificate of examination.

11. Such corpses which from the manner of their death are subject to any judicial examination or dissection, will, after their previous dissection, be received by the proper judicial authorities, and the interment is to take place according to the existing orders.

12. Should information be forwarded to the Police Surgeon that signs of re-animation have been observed in any body, it is to be his first and most sacred duty to attend instantly at the place and spot, in order to conduct all attempts at restoration, and to issue orders about the mode of treatment of the re-animated body.

13. Attending minutely to his duties, it is certain that he may perceive divers symptoms which are not only important to him as Examining Surgeon, but also as surgeon to the Police; he has therefore to attend minutely to such observations, and, together with his own, communicate such to his superior authorities.

14. In case the Police Surgeon should be prevented, either by indisposition, absence, or any other cause, from conducting the examinations with which he is intrusted, he is forthwith to give immediate notice to the Royal Police, in order to provide for a proper substitute, whom he may himself propose.

15· It is fully expected from the Surgeon of the Police, that, impressed with the importance of the business he is charged with, he will do all in his power to attain the manifold important objects belonging to it. Any negligence of which he may be guilty will be rigorously punished, and on a repetition of the offence he will be discharged.

Royal Police Direction, Munich.

Instructions to the Soul-Nuns as to their Duties in regard to the Inspection of the Dead.

(1.) As soon as a person is dead, or appears to be so, the nurse or sister of charity in attendance is immediately to give information of the same to the medical man appointed to the district.

(2.) For this purpose she obtains the *form of notification* for conducting the inspection of the dead, which contains the divisions of the districts of inspection, and the names of the physicians appointed to each district.

(3.) In order that the physician may inspect *immediately, and without the slightest delay,* the case of death in his district, the name of the street, the number and floor of the house in which the death occurs is to be given with exactness, so that he may not in any way be hindered in going to the place and making the earliest possible inspection.

(4.) Before this inspection has taken place, it is expressly forbidden to undress the corpse, or wash it, or, if the death is a natural one, to remove it from the bed or room in which the death took place, or even to take away or alter the position of the pillow.

(5.) Any disobedience to this law will be punished by a fine of from 5 to 15 florins, or by a three days' imprisonment.

(6.) The physician will make a note of all the circumstances of the first inspection, according to his instructions. If he should consider that particular arrangements are necessary, they are to be adopted immediately.

(7.) His note of remarks shall be left at the house, in the charge of the soul-nun, and through them the signature of the physicians attending the person who had died, if such there has been, shall be procured.

(8.) If the dead is retained at the house till the time of interment, the note of inspection must be directly handed over to the public surgeon, in order that he may make the second inspection, and determine further what is necessary with regard to the interment.

(9.) If after a certain length of time he sees no reason to postpone the interment, he will make a note to that effect and give it to the police direction, and from them is procured the sanction for the interment.

This sanction will be given in to the clergyman's office belonging to the district, and thence handed over to the officer who has the care of the house for the reception of the dead previous to interment. Without this sanction no corpse can be interred.

(10.) The corpse must be retained until interment in an apartment where there is fresh and pure air. The coffin must not be closed, nor the face covered till after the second inspection, and the hands and feet must not be bound.

If any signs of life should be observed, the district physician is immediately to be called.

(11.) If the corpse is conveyed into the house for the reception of the dead, the second inspection must be made there. The district physician's note of inspection is to be given to the officer of the house for the reception of the dead at the time, or before the corpse being brought there, and that officer is to hand over the note to the public surgeon. Without this note of inspection, no corpse can be received into the house for the reception of the dead.

(12.) The soul-nuns, or midwives, or whoever is intrusted with this office, must wait for the second inspection; and for the time when the public surgeon shall pronounce that the interment is necessary. For this purpose the surgeon will make the requisite certificate, which must then be given to the proper officer, who immediately gives the sanction for the interment.

(13.) As the second inspection in the house for the reception of the dead must take place, according to the regulations, in the morning between 9 and 10, and in the afternoon between 3 and 4, the sanction for interment may be procured between 11 and 12 in the morning, and 4 and 5 in the afternoon.

No. 3.

DEFECTIVE ARRANGEMENTS FOR THE VERIFICATION OF THE CAUSES OF DEATH.

Thomas Abraham, Esq., Surgeon.

You are Registrar of Deaths in the City of London Union. Since you have been Registrar, have you had occasion to send notice to the coroner of cases where the causes of death stated appeared suspicious ?—Yes, in about half-a-dozen cases. One was of an old gentleman occupying apartments in Bell Alley. His servant went out to market, and on her return, in less than an hour, found him dead on the bed, with his legs lying over the side of it. He had been ailing some time, and was seized occasionally with difficulty of breathing, but able to get up, and when she left him she did not perceive anything unusual in his appearance. I went to the house myself, and made inquiries into the cause of death; and although I did not discover anything to lead to the suspicion of his having died from poison or other unfair means, I considered it involved in obscurity, and referred the case to the coroner for investigation. Another case was of a traveller who was found dead in his bed at an inn. The body was removed to a distance of forty miles before a certificate to authorize the burial was applied for. His usual medical attendant certified to his having been for several years the subject of aortic aneurism, which was the probable cause of his sudden death, although the evidence was imperfect and unsatisfactory, and could not be otherwise without an examination of the body, and I therefore refused to register it without notice to the coroner.

A third case occurred a few days ago. A medical certificate was presented to me of the death of a man from disease of the heart and aneurism of the aorta. He was driven in a cab to the door of a medical practitioner in this neighbourhood, and was found dead. He might have died from poison, and, without the questions put on the occasion of registering the cause of death, the case might have passed without notice. There was not in this case, as in others, any evidence to show that death was occasioned by unfair means, but the causes were obscure and unsatisfactory, and I felt it to be my duty to have them investigated by the coroner.

But for anything known, you may have passed cases of murder ?— Certainly; and there is at present no security against such cases. The personal inspection of the deceased would undoubtedly act as a great security.

In the course of your practice, have you had occasion to believe that evil is produced by the retention of the corpse ?—Yes; I can give an instance of a man, his wife, and six children, living in one room, in Draper's Buildings. The mother and all the children successively fell ill of typhus fever: the mother died; the body remained in the room. I wished it to be removed the next day, and I also wished the children to be removed, being afraid that the fever would extend. The children were apparently well at the time of the death of the mother. The recommendation was not attended to: the body was kept five days in the only room which this family of eight had to live and sleep in. The eldest daughter was attacked about a week after the mother had been removed, and, after three days' illness, that daughter died. The corpse of this child was only kept three days, as we determined that it should positively be removed. In about nine days after the death of the girl, the youngest child was attacked, and it died in about nine days. Then the second one was taken: he lay twenty-three days, and died. Then another boy died. The two other children recovered.

By the immediate removal of the corpse, and the use of proper preventive means, how many deaths do you beheve might have been prevented ?—I think it probable that the one took it from the other, and that if the corpse of the first had been removed the rest would have escaped;

although I, of course, admit that the same cause which produced the disease of the mother might also have produced it in the children. I believe that, in cases of typhus, scarlatina, and other infectious diseases, it frequently happens that the living are attacked by the same disease from the retention of the body.

Have you had occasion to observe the effects of cesspools in your district?—Yes, and that they are very injurious to the health. In the states of the weather when offensive emanations arise from the cesspools and drains, I have often heard people complain of headache, giddiness, nausea, languor, and an indisposition for exertion of any kind; and I have known a walk or a ride in the open air to remove those symptoms, but in an hour or two after their return home they have found themselves as bad as before. Their sleep brings them little or no refreshment; in truth, they have inhaled, during the whole of the night, the noxious atmosphere, which is very depressing, and will fully account for their rising, as they often say, as tired as when they went to bed. As an example, I may mention the case of a compositor, residing in Draper's Buildings—a narrow, confined, and filthy place, where there was always a disgusting stench in every house. He was the subject of disordered stomach and liver, which might have been induced by his night-work and intemperance: the stinking hole in which he resided contributed its share towards it, without doubt. This man remained at home for a week, when he was getting better, but had scarcely any appetite. I advised him to walk in Finsbury Circus two or three times a-day, as long as he could without fatigue; and on several occasions, when he returned to his dinner, he said, "Now, if I had had my dinner in Finsbury Circus I could have eaten a hearty one, but now I do not seem to care anything about it." I believe that if I had entered that man's house with a good appetite for a dinner, and had remained there for an hour, that I should have cared no more about eating than he did,—which I attribute to the nauseating and depressing effects of the effluvia from the cesspools, drains, and general filthiness of the place.

Are you aware whether this state of things arose from the cesspools or the state of the sewers?—I conceive the worst have been cesspools; but the drains, if they open, are just as bad. I was called upon to visit a patient living in a court in Whitecross Street, ill of typhus fever; in the centre of it was a gully-hole, which was untrapped and smelt horribly. The fever went through the whole of that court. I gave it as my opinion at the time, that the case I visited was occasioned by the gully-hole, and that the fever would go through the court, which it did.

Have you perceived the present state of the drains in the city of London?—At times they smell very strongly, which scarcely any one can fail to notice; but I have heard country-people complain of them at times when they have not attracted any particular notice from me.

Are you aware that decomposing matter is allowed to accumulate in them?—Yes; very recently they took up the refuse in our street, Old Broad Street; it smelt very badly, and it was black and horribly filthy.

How long before had the sewer been cleansed?—I do not know. I do not remember its having been cleansed, before the last September, since I have been there, which is about nine years.

Do you remember to have perceived the smell from the sewers before the last September?—Yes; there is a gully-hole near my own house from which there was constantly an offensive smell: it was much worse after a thaw in winter, or a shower of rain in summer. A neighbour living two doors from me being more annoyed by it than I, made great efforts, and at length succeeded in getting it trapped; and I have not since perceived any smell from it, though I observe it now in other places. The gully-holes are trapped now in most of the respectable streets, but in the bye and poor streets they are not trapped.

From the evidence which has come before you, have you any doubt that the existing state of sewers in the City are the latent cause of much disease and death?—I have not the least doubt of it in the world.—A great deal of active disease, which creeps on gradually and insidiously, may be traced to that cause.

In the poorer districts, in what state is the surface-cleansing of the streets?—Even the best streets are very badly cleansed, but in the poorer streets of the city the cleansing is very bad indeed—horribly bad! Take Duke's Place, for example; you will see cabbage-stalks and rotten oranges that have been thrown away, and they often remain there for several days. We do not get our streets swept oftener than once a-week.

If there were a perfect system of drainage and cleansing in the city, do you think that the health and the duration of life of the inhabitants would be extended?—I think there would be a considerable extension.

What is the physical condition of the children born in London of parents who are natives of the rural districts, as compared with the physical condition of children who are born in the country of parents of the same class?—The children born and bred up in London are more frequently of small stature and have slender limbs, are deficient in stamina and powers of endurance, are of irritable frames and prone to inflammatory attack, than children born and bred up in the country. An impure atmosphere is immeasurably more injurious to children than adults. Children also suffer more from want of opportunities of exercise in the open air. The beneficial effects of pure air and exercise on children who have been born and pent up in London are most marked: a weakly child, and which, if kept in London, would perhaps always continue weakly, would most likely become strong and healthy if sent into the country. I cannot doubt that children born of healthy parents, and bred up in the country, would be more robust and stronger than children born of the same class of parents and bred up in London, and that this difference may be justly ascribable to atmospheric influence.

When children are weakly, what is the effect on the temper and character?—The temper and character of weakly children are generally found to correspond with, and are most probably derived from, the character of their constitution: their temper is quick and irritable, their passions ardent, their perception keen, and their imagination predominant over their judgment.

You are speaking, of course, of the general characteristics of individuals as specimens of the population brought up under such circumstances?—Yes, of persons coming under my own observation.

Have you, as Registrar of Deaths, noticed the larger proportion of infant mortality in the city?—There is, I conceive, all over the kingdom, a large proportion of infant deaths; but I have no doubt that a considerable proportion of the excess of infant deaths in London is ascribable to atmospheric influences.

It appears, from the Mortuary Registration, that of deaths in the city of London, about one-half are deaths of children under ten years of age; whilst in a rural district, take the county of Hereford for example, only one-third of the deaths are deaths of children.

Do you conceive it probable that this different rate of infant mortality is to be traced chiefly to the difference of the atmospheric influence, the average age of all of the labouring classes being, in Herefordshire, 39 years, whilst in the City of London the average age of the deaths of all the labouring classes is only 22 years?—I am decidedly of opinion that a greater proportion of the excess of infant mortality in London, and the reduced duration of life, are ascribable to atmospheric impurity.

If all cesspools were removed, and water-closets substituted; if water were introduced into the houses of the poorest classes; if the sewers were regularly flushed weekly, or oftener, so as to prevent accumulations of deposit and the escape of miasma, such as you have described; if the carriage

Q

and foot pavements were more frequently and completely cleansed; if these several public duties were performed with practicable efficiency, can you express a confident opinion that decrease and premature deaths would be considerably diminished?—I am quite confident that the adoption of such measures would not only diminish disease of every kind, but greatly improve the moral as well as the physical condition of the inhabitants.

No. 4.

THE PROPORTIONS OF DEATHS AND FUNERALS PREVENTIBLE BY SANITARY MEANS.

Henry Blenkarne, Esq., South West District Surgeon of the City of London Union.

Have you in your district perceived any effects resulting from interments in the parochial burying places?—I have no cognizance of any bad effects resulting from those interments. The first twenty years of my life I lived close to a burial-ground, and never was aware or heard of any prejudicial consequences arising. I may observe, however, that when a relation of mine has attended the church she has been enabled to perceive whenever a vault underneath the church has been opened. She has said, " I feel they have opened a vault;" and on inquiry it has turned out to have been so.

Have you observed any evil effects following the practice of the long retention of the corpse in the house amidst the living?—Yes, I have observed effects follow, but I cannot say produced by them, though they were perhaps increased by them. In those cases which I have had where there has been a succession of cases of fever in the same family, after a death it has generally occurred that the parties affected have complained two or three days before that they felt very unwell. Generally this has been the case. I have, in such instances, ordered them medicine immediately. Since the Union has been established we have immediately removed all fever cases to the Fever Hospital.

The retention of the corpse amidst the living, under such circumstances, must aggravate the mortality, must it not?—There cannot be a moment's doubt about it.

What, from the observations in your district, has been the actual state of the sewerage, and cleansing dependent upon it, as the cleansing of the cesspools?—There has been great improvement in the city of London by the improvement of the sewerage, in so far as it has removed the cesspools. When you went into a respectable house formerly, you could, in the city, tell the state of the weather by the smell from the cesspools. Where water-closets are substituted, the health of the inhabitants has undoubtedly been improved. In the poorer neighbourhoods, where they have still cesspools, they are still very bad. I constantly tell them, if you get rid of that nasty cesspool you'll get well and keep well; it is of no use my giving you physic until that is done. Where there have been deposits accumulating in the sewers, and the drains have been choked up, the effect has been just the same as if there had been cesspools.

You are aware that in respect to sewerage it is the practice to allow deposits to accumulate in the sewers, and then, when the private drains are stopped up, to open the sewer and get out the deposit by means of buckets, and remove it in carts?—Yes, I am.

Have you seen any illness result from this practice?—I cannot state a case, though I have no doubt of its highly injurious effects; but can decidedly speak to illness arising from the accumulations. The illness is just the same as from cesspools: a low depressing nervous fever, most like that which is described to be the form of the jungle fever. In November or December last, they were taking up the deposits from the sewers near Broken Wharf, in Upper Thames-street :, the stench from it was quite sufficient to have produced any fever: it was not within my district, and I do not know what were the effects. Fortunately there was clear weather, and the wind blew towards the river.

Have you any doubt that the removal of such refuse, as well as the accumulation, must be attended with danger to life?—Yes; if any person in a state of mental or bodily depression were exposed to such an influence, it would produce low fever; it would be dangerous in proportion as it was stagnant.

In passing through the city, have you been assailed with smells from gully-holes?—Only yesterday, in passing through the city, the smells from many of the gully-holes were very offensive; and several medical friends agree with me in attributing extremely prejudicial consequences as arising from this cause.

The following case is related on the authority of Dr. Good, as having occurred within the city of London, and is mentioned by Mr. Fuller, in a letter from a surgeon who has paid great attention to the influence of sewerage, and who adduces the facts of the case in evidence that typhus may be produced by the miasma from sewers :—" Soon after the closing of the Parliamentary Committee, I learned, from the late Dr. Hope, the particulars of a case which, to my mind, has completely proved the production of typhus fever from it, and was so much in the character of an *experimentum crucis,* that I did not consider it necessary to prosecute the inquiry any further. The case is as follows :—" A family in the city of London, who had occupied the same house for many years, enjoying a good state of health, had a nursery-maid seized with typhus fever; the young woman was removed from the house and another substituted in her place. In a short time the new nurse-maid was attacked with typhus fever, and was also sent away. A few weeks after one of the children was seized with the same fever: an inquiry was now instituted by the medical man in attendance, in order to ascertain, if possible, the cause of this frequent recurrence of typhus fever, when the following facts were brought to light :— The nursery was situated on the upper floor but one of the house, and about a fortnight or three weeks before the first case of fever occurred, a sink was placed in the corner of the nursery for the purpose of saving the labour of the servants ; this was found to communicate with the common sewer, and to be quite open, or untrapped ; they ordered it immediately to be effectually trapped, and then no other case of fever occurred, although it continued to be occupied as before ; and, when I learned the case, more than a twelvemonth had passed."

Have you met with cases analogous to the one here stated?—I have met with several such cases. I know of an instance where a room in an old house had an offensive stench, and the health of the person living in it was always bad. A stench was perceived in the room, which it was guessed might arise from the decay of dead rats in the wainscot. The party went to much expense to pull down the wainscot, when it was found that there was an opening which communicated with the cesspool below. The hole was properly cemented and stopped up, and the room has since that time become quite habitable and healthy ; and where I have directed the cesspools to be emptied, as the predisposing cause, the general result has been that the sick have immediately got well. From my knowledge of the local causes I can predicate, with certainty, what will be the general effect on the health in the case of removal of the parties.

Besides the houses of the labouring classes, are there many houses of the middling classes in your district in the city of London that are provided with cesspools?—Many houses that I go into are provided with cesspools. I mentioned the other day to a lady that I should never be enabled to keep her well so long as there was a cesspool in the house ; I told her that the expense of continued medical attendance would pay for a communication with the common sewer and better cleansing.

Are you aware that a new practice has arisen of preventing the accumulation of deposits in the sewers, by flushes of water, which remove all deposits weekly, and so far prevent the year's accumulation and corruption of deposits in the sewers. If this system were enforced in the city, have you any doubt as to the extensive prevention of disease and mortality which would be thereby effected amongst all classes?—Certainly it would be a great boon, in a sanitary point of view, to the population of the city of London. I am so much convinced of this, that in my own house I put a stick under the handle of the water-closet, so as to have a continued flow or flush of water for some length of time; this I do to remove any accidental accumulation. Of course the flushing of the common sewers would have the same effects.

Besides the accumulations in the sewers, is there at this time no decomposing refuse from the defective cleansing of the courts and bye-streets, and poorer districts?—Yes; in the poorer districts there is accumulation. In one court, for example, called Harrow-court, Thames-street, where there is almost always low fever, there is always dirt and filth, and I am constantly exhorting the people to remove the filth; but the great difficulty with the poor people is commonly how to get the water. There is a court in Cornhill which a man was cleansing the other day by applying a hose to the water-cock (which is used in case of fire), in order to cleanse the pavement. An officer belonging to the water company coming by, said, "If I see you doing that again, I shall indict you."

Are you aware that the streets are swept oftener than weekly in the city of London?—My impression is—not oftener.

It has been proposed that water should be laid on, and kept at high pressure in the streets, so as to enable the courts and alleys, the foot and the carriage pavements, to be washed daily by means of a hose attached to the water-pipes. This, which has been proposed for protection against fire, as well as for cleansing the streets more completely, has, I am informed, been done in Philadelphia. If the system were carried out in the city of London, what do you conceive would be the effect on the health of the population in the poorer districts?—I should certainly say that it would tend greatly to prolong life amongst the population.

From the mortuary registries it appears that the average duration of life among the professional persons and gentry in the city of London, who live in better cleansed and ventilated houses, and better cleansed streets, is, on the average of the whole class, about 43 years, and 6 per cent. of the deaths are deaths from epidemic disease; whilst among the labouring classes the proportion of deaths from epidemic disease is 19 per cent., and the average age of all who die is only 22 years. With such sanitary regulations as are under the public control of the public authorities, to what extent do you think it probable the duration of life amongst the labouring classes may be extended?—So far as I can judge, without examination of the particular cases, I should say that the average might be extended one-half at the least.

The majority of the cases of epidemic diseases may decidedly be ascribed to the want of cleanliness and ventilation. On looking over the mortuary registry of the deaths occurring in Upper Thames-street and the district attached to it, I find the causes of death most frequently registered are "low fever," "low fever," occurring one after the other. This recurrence of low fever corresponds with my experience of sickness, which so often assumes the character of low typhoid nervous depression. The medicine I use in the greatest quantity is ammonia, as an active diffusive stimulus. For all classes this medicine is in constant use. In damp weather we have always much increase of this illness; the dampness produces a depression which lays them open to the atmospheric poison.

Have you had instances where better cleansing has taken place and illness diminished?—Yes; for example, in Ireland-yard, containing a large number of families of coal-beavers and others, a place which I never was out of from continued illnesses: the yard has been much better cleansed, the houses put in better order, and now there is very little illness there. I know for a fact, that in the neighbourhood of London-wall, where recently great improvements have taken place in the sewerage and ventilation, disease has greatly diminished, especially *low fever*. Formerly they had a sewer which used to be stopped up and overflowed; they have had of late a new sewer, which now works better; they have no stink or stench in the kitchens, as formerly, and they have nothing of the same kind of disease going on there that they used to have before.

Are the houses in Ireland-yard occupied by the same inhabitants?—Just by the same class. The habits of coal-beavers are reputed to be none of the best in respect to general cleanliness or temperance.

Have you observed any alteration in their habits?—Not in the least.

Have you observed what is the personal condition of the natives of London?—The real cockney is generally of stunted growth.

Have you observed whether the children born in London of parents who have come from the rural districts are as tall or as strong as the parents?—Generally shorter children, though some of them are as tall, but all are of comparatively weakly constitutions; they are particularly predisposed to strumous disease. I have been so impressed with the effect of children living in a London atmosphere, that I have been anxious to send them out of it when possible.

Does not defective cleansing, as causing atmospheric impurity, not only tend to produce disease and shorten the duration of life, but depress the physical condition of the population?—Decidedly.

No. 5.

Dr. Wray, Medical Officer of the West London Union.

You have read what is stated by Mr. Blencarne, and by Mr. Abrahams—do you generally agree with them as to the effects of defective cleansing, on the condition of the population?—I agree with the whole of what they state; it perfectly accords with my own experience, which has been about 25 years in this district. I have during that time observed a great falling off in the condition of the children; they are stunted, squalid, poor-looking things, and there is a great deal of deformity amongst them.

Have you observed moral effects attendant on the physical depression?—Yes; I have observed a great deal in our neighbourhood. I think the females of the poorer classes who are not strong for work, are more apt to take to courses of livelihood other than by work;—that very many of them go upon the town.

No. 6.

Mr. Thomas Porter, Surgeon to the St. Botolph's Bishopsgate District.

Have you observed any emanations from the sewers in your district?—In Liverpool-street there is now a cleansing of the sewers by opening the top, taking the soil out, and carting it away.

What is the effect of this process?—It vitiates the atmosphere to a considerable extent.

Have you observed any effects from it?—I have often found headache to result from it to myself, and parties have complained to me of the same effects.

What is the state of the drainage?—There are some districts, such as Halfmoon-street, which are imperfectly drained, where the cesspools are suffered to overflow and run along the kennels at the sides of the street, causing fœtid and deleterious exhalations; in this street and the alleys opening into it, especially Thompson's-court, Thompson'-rents, Baker's-court, Providence-place, and Campions-buildings, fever prevails nearly the whole year round. It also prevails very much in Bligh's-buildings, Lamb-alley, Dunning's-alley, Sweet Apple-court, Montague-court, Artillery-lane, Rose-alley, and Catherine-wheel-alley. These places, all of which are badly drained and not regularly cleansed, are seldom without fever for any length of time.

In these places are there any water-closets?—No; they have nothing but common necessaries, which are usually allowed to run over before they are emptied, and it is impossible to enter the tenements without being assailed by the disagreeable and unhealthy effluvia thence arising.

Have they water laid on in the rooms of the several tenements?—Seldom in the rooms; generally in some place in the court to which they all go. Many have not that even, and they resort to the common street pumps. I do not remember an instance where water is properly laid on in any house of the labouring classes.

What rents are paid for houses in this condition?—Rent for one room is from 1s. 6d. to 4s. 6d. per week. The rents are very high in proportion to the size and accommodation of the rooms.

You say you have observed emanations from the sewers within your district?—Yes; they are frequently very offensive in moist warm weather. You may, indeed, almost tell the condition of the weather from the smells from the public sewers. Recently in returning from Islington along the City-road from the Canal bridge to Finsbury-square, and along Sun-street, I noticed in passing near the gratings, as every person must have noticed, a peculiarly offensive effluvium.

Within the city itself have you perceived the same effluvium on passing the gratings of the sewers?—Frequently; it is so general that no particular place is distinguished by being free from it.

Suppose a tradesman or a merchant returning from Change in a state of depression from anxiety passing through a street, exposed to a succession of smells and breathing the effluvium from such sewers; what is likely to be the effect upon him?—A low nervous fever, with considerable gastric derangement. The greater part of fever cases which I have to treat are of this description.

Is that with every class of persons?—Yes, with every rank of life. They are mostly of the low or typhoid type, and do not bear depletion. In my ordinary course of treatment I generally begin by emptying the stomach and bowels, and by lowering the diet. I then use a moderately stimulating treatment with a perfect absence of solid food.

Is gross feeding or excess very common amongst the people of your district?—Not very common. Excess from drinking is more frequent than excess from eating.

In what proportion will there be of excess from eating or drinking in such cases?—Amongst the labouring classes perhaps there may be one case in ten from excess of drinking, and one case in thirty from excess of eating.

If these excesses had taken place in a purer atmosphere, do you conceive the results in disease would have followed?—In most instances the system in a pure atmosphere would have thrown off the inconvenience without fever.

Then excess or depression both predispose to the attacks of disease from atmospheric impurity, and especially to the direct influence of the effluvium in question?—Yes, certainly; excess of watching, want of rest, mental anxiety, every depressing cause predisposes to an attack.

Besides the defects in respect to the cleansing of the cesspools and the drains, are there not defects in respect to other portions of cleansing, such as dust-bins neglected?—Yes, in those places there is no person to regulate or to see that done which ought to be done; consequently the dustmen and scavengers duty is much neglected, and places are filled with decomposing remains, which remain there two or three weeks in summer and much longer in winter. The carelessness of the people themselves as to cleanliness is also deplorable, as it operates very injuriously on their health and comfort; the floors of their rooms, the passages, stairs, and landings are often suffered to remain unwashed for weeks and months, and the walls and ceilings are seldom cleansed or whitened, so that what with filthiness of one kind or other they present an appearance of wretchedness beyond all description.

What is the condition of the children born or kept in courts or places of the condition you describe, with badly cleansed drains, with privies, and without water or conveniences for cleansing introduced into their habitations?—The children are, for the most part, of delicate or weak frame, and subject to struma. The health of children depends partly whether they were born in such places or not, whether their parents on each side are Londoners, as there appears to be a gradual decline in physical power by a long continuance in a vitiated atmosphere, which passes from parent to progeny, and partly also in a family where one part of the children have been born and brought up in the country and the other in town; those born in the country, and not coming into London until they are five years of age, will have comparatively strong frames, and will resist such influences, whilst those born in town will be comparatively of delicate frame, weakly and strumous, liable to glandular disease, and diseased affections of the joints and the spine. Generally they are shorter in stature, sometimes they are taller, but then they are slender and very delicate, in which case they are likely to have bending of the limbs.

What is the condition of females born under such circumstances?—I have observed that the females are less depressed than the males, and are reared with less difficulty.

Why is this so?—I have not been able to determine. It may be that the male requires more extensive and powerful exercise, and that in pure air, than the female, and consequently that the female suffers less from the want of it.

What are the moral characteristics of the population brought up under these depressing physical circumstances?—They have decided unwillingness to labour. They are not so strenuous as the more healthy people from the country. They are more apt to resort to subterfuge to gain their ends without labour. Light employments they do not object to, and do comparatively well in. But it is difficult to keep a native of London, either male or female to heavy work; they will avoid it if they can. The cause is in most cases physical from the deficiency of ability to labour. The greatest part of them are mentally irritable and impatient under moral restraint.

Is any similar difference marked on the condition of the children of tradespeople between those children of tradespeople brought up in London and those born in the country?—Yes, there is a similar difference perceptible, but less in degree. Amongst tradesmen, too, it is the extensive practice of the parents to send their children out of town to school or on visits, which may powerfully affect them beneficially. In the tradesman's family they have better sleeping rooms, and greater cleanliness in person, and in bed and body linen, and also a better regulated dietary.

What is the effect of such atmospheric impurities as those described in the chances of recovery from attacks of disease?—It lessens the chances of recovery and greatly impedes convalescence. Indeed, in many instances, very little progress can be made until the patient is sent out into the country. In a case of fever which occurred to a strong healthy man, aged 24, a carman, in a close neighbourhood, the house being without drains and ill ventilated; no progress could be effected until he was removed into the country, although the fever had decidedly subsided. I believe that in this case something else would have supervened, had he not been removed. I frequently remove patients in a respectable condition, finding no chance of recovery without it. Many of the better conditioned houses being badly adapted for the treatment of fevers, having low ceilings and insufficient ventilation.

What will be the difference in respect to the time of cure or convalescence between a well and an ill-cleansed neighbourhood?—A difference of perhaps one-half.

Suppose the rooms of each house supplied with water, the privies and cesspools removed, drains from the houses to sewers, and the sewers so constructed as to be cleansed, and to convey away daily such refuse as that which is allowed to remain decomposing in the close courts during weeks. Supposing the surfaces of the streets cleansed as frequently after the manner in use in Philadelphia and other towns where they are cleansed with water daily, to what extent do you conceive disease would be reduced? —Of fevers two-thirds certainly, and other diseases would be considerably lessened.

No. 7.

Mr. John H. Paul, Surgeon, Medical Officer of the City of London Union.

In what condition in respect to cleanliness are the courts and other places within your district, chiefly inhabited by the labouring classes?—The cleansing of the courts and alleys in my district is defective. I agree with what Mr. Blenkarne says in respect to cesspools. For instance, in one room in a house in Sugar Loaf-court, Garlick-hill, next to their common cesspool, I have frequently attended patients, and before going, I surmise that whatever disease they are primarily affected with, it will generally run into one of low character with tendency to typhus. In the interval of little more than a twelvemonth, I have attended several occupants of the house, one after the other, who have all been, to a certain extent, similarly affected. I have generally improved their health by giving diffusive stimuli, and have occasionally prevailed on them to remove.

How many visits in the year may you have paid to this same house?—Upwards of forty visits. But there are other houses where there are similar evils, where I have had occasion to visit them still more frequently. In one house in Star-court, Bread Street-hill, which is similarly situated, where almost the whole of the inmates were laid up with fever, and where I had to visit it three times a day for upwards of three weeks. There were deaths on each floor of that house. Fever assumed, at one time, so malignant an aspect, that there appeared to be no possibility of saving them, except by removal. I do not remember one case of a removal in time where death ensued. The ward inquest had the inhabitants removed, and the house cleansed.

But was the cesspool removed?—Emptied but not removed.

Then in time you will have a recurrence of the same evils in the place in question?—Yes, certainly.

What is the condition of children brought up in such places?—Generally pale and emaciated, scrofulous, and apt to mesenteric disease.

You were medical attendant at the Norwood school, where the pauper children from the city of London are taken. Do you think, that on a view of the children, and without any positive knowledge of the sort of residences of the parents of the children, you could on the view select from the rest, the children who came from the courts and alleys, such as you have described in the city of London?—I have but little doubt of it, though generally speaking the children from the city were of rather a better description than those from more crowded localities. Indeed, the courts and alleys of my district are superior to those in other quarters of the metropolis. They are situated near the banks of the Thames with a considerable fall towards the river. Some parents also take their children much out into the open air, and in these the influence of the place would not be so visible, but with the majority there would be but very little mistake. Whilst at Norwood, my chief trouble arose from this sick and diseased class of children, who generally improved very much after being there some little time.

What was the moral condition of these physically depressed children, as compared with other pauper children, whose position had been less unfavourable?—The moral condition of this depressed class of children was generally worse also.

No. 8.

Effects observed of Dark, Ill-ventilated, and Ill-drained Localities on the Moral and Physical Condition of the Population of Paris.

Dr. la Chaise, in his Medical Topography of Paris, which is an early attempt to investigate the influence of localities on the moral and physical condition of a population, gives the following description of the physical condition of the short-lived population bred up in the narrow and dark streets, and ill-cleansed and badly ventilated houses of Paris, which description may serve for comparison with those given of the native population in the crowded and badly cleansed districts of London.

" The Parisian," he says, " in stature is often below what is commonly termed middle-size. His fair skin, soft to the touch, forms a striking contrast to that of the inhabitant of small towns, and, above all, to the countryman ,who is more exposed to the various changes of the weather, and to the action of the sun and light. The hair of the Parisian is generally fair or light brown, and his eyes blue. His muscular frame is little developed, so that the form has on the whole a feminine appearance. In the labouring class the muscles of the lower limbs are sometimes developed, but irregularly and incompletely, which is explained by the exercise given exclusively to certain muscles by their employment or handicraft ; these irregularities of development are much less frequent in the rural districts where the movements, and consequently muscular actions, are much more equally divided. The temperament, that is to say the physical constitution peculiar to the Parisian, differs, as is perceived, from each of the distinct and determined forms admitted by physiologists. He seems to partake of the union of many,—to be intermediate between those which are recognized under the names nervous, bilious, and lymphatic-sanguine; the first seems, however, to predominate.

" It is not, however, rare to meet in Paris with physical constitutions entirely in the extremes and contrasted with each other ; that is to say, there are here, as in other large towns, large numbers of weakly and debilitated, vulgarly called sickly, and others with hollow chest and tall slim figure.

" The women of Paris are rather pretty than handsome ; without regular features, they owe to the development of the cellular tissue, and to the fairness and fineness of the skin, a certain softness of form which is very graceful ; and a quick and spiritual eye makes one forget the paleness of their cheeks.

" Considered morally, the portrait of the Parisian presents colours which are not impossible to seize, notwithstanding their great variety. He may be said generally to be lively, spiritual, industrious, and deserving the name of frivolous. Much less perhaps is given him. He is inquisitive, and carries into his work a taste, an ardent imagination, and inventive mind, which he is willing to believe should compensate for sustained activity. There necessarily results from this a great nervous susceptibility, an *encaphalique* predominance, which it is important to the physician never to overlook.

"If a sound and firm organization allows a few to resist the effects of this premature exercise of the organ of thought, a rapid increase in its functions always shows itself in the injury done to the other organs, and generally to the muscular system, which bear the marks of feebleness and often of deplorable languor. In this life, too active morally and too indolent physically, the nervous system acquires not what is vulgarly called a feebleness or delicacy, but a susceptibility, or rather a predominance, which is affected by the least shock. Hence that fickleness, and that vivacity of desires, that changeableness in the tastes, in a word that coquetry, that unequal and whimsical moody character, those caprices and vapours. The character is not alone affected by this excess of susceptibility; all the organs, the whole of the economy of the body feels it in turn; the nervous system acts particularly on the uterus, developes it prematurely; thus the women generally arrive at puberty much earlier at Paris than in the provinces, and especially than in the country. It is not unfrequent to find young girls of 12 or 13 fully formed and capable of becoming mothers, whilst in the country, even in the south, they do not attain that period till the age of 15 or 16."

No. 9.

NOTE TO PAGE 128, ON SIR CHRISTOPHER WREN'S PLAN FOR EXTRA MURAL INTERMENTS, AND FOR EXCLUDING GRAVE-YARDS ON THE REBUILDING OF THE CITY OF LONDON.

Whosoever examines the various modern plans for the improvement of the metropolis, and compares them with the plan of the architect of St. Paul's, will see in them only small approximations to his conceptions, and that they only provide for a few large openings, without reference to any general sanitary considerations, and without providing for the mass of the population, whereas he was for " excluding all narrow dark alleys without thoroughfares, and courts," such as are commonly left untouched in the new lines of streets; and he had provided that not only " all church yards," but " all trades that use great fires, or yield noisome smells, be placed out of town." If, as is confidently maintained on such evidence as that before referred to, *ante* p.22 and 25, the proportions of death might even now be reduced by one-third in the city of London by better drainage and other sanitary measures (independently of the removal of those courts and alleys, &c., on the evidence of the proportions of mortality actually prevalent in districts such as he would have constructed, facilitating, and almost necessitating by regular lines an early and more systematic drainage below the streets, as well as a free and copious flow of fresh air from above, it may be as confidently maintained that the mortality and numbers of burials would have been reduced in like proportions from the period of the rebuilding of the city. The whole of the deformed area stands as a monument of the disasters incurred to the living generation, by a weak and careless yielding, not of the present to the future, but of the present itself, to blind and ignorant impulses, which have entailed immense demoralization, waste of health, and life and money, and a large proportion of the evil which now depresses the sanitary condition of the population of that particular district which his improvements would have covered. " The practicability of this whole scheme," says the Parentalia, "without loss to any man or infringement of any property, was at that time fully demonstrated, and all material objections fully weighed and answered; the only, and as it happened, in-

surmountable difficulty, was the obstinate averseness of great part of the citizens to alter their old properties, and to recede from building their houses again on the old ground and foundations, as also the distrust in many, and unwillingness to give up their properties, though for a time only, into the hands of public trustees or commissioners, till they might be dispensed to them again, with more advantages to themselves than otherwise was possible to be effected ; for such a method was proposed, that by an equal distribution of ground into buildings, leaving out church-yards, gardens, &c. (which are to be removed out of the town), there would have been sufficient room both for the augmentation of the streets, disposition of the churches, halls, and all public buildings, and to have given every proprietor full satisfaction ; and although few proprietors should happen to have been seated again directly upon the very same ground they had possessed before the fire, yet no man would have been thrust any considerable distance from it, but been placed, at least, as conveniently, and sometimes more so, to their own trades than before."
" By these means the opportunity, in a great degree, was lost of making the new city the most magnificent, as well as commodious, for health and trade of any upon earth, and the surveyor being thus confined and cramped in his designs, it required no small labour and skill to model the city in the manner it has since appeared." The plan was approved by the King and the Parliament, but opposed by the corporation, who, it is stated in a history of the city institutions, by one of its officers, conceived that they would have lost population and trade by the plan ; *i. e.*, they would have been spread beyond its jurisdiction. But on both points this policy was dreadfully mistaken. Only a burthensome population is obtained by overcrowding, that is to say, a larger than the natural proportions of the young and dependent, of widowhood, and early and destitute orphanage, and of sickly and dependent, and prematurely aged adults. As an example of the coincidence of pecuniary economy with enlarged sanitary measures, it may be mentioned, that it is shown in a report on a survey made for sanitary purposes by Mr. Butler Williams of the College of Civil Engineers, Putney, that a loss of not less than 80,000*l.* per annum is now incurred in carriage traffic alone on two main lines of street, namely, Holborn Hill to the Bank, and Ludgate Hill to the same point, being made crooked and with steep acclivities instead of straight and level, as Sir Christopher Wren designed them. It is to be regretted that the discussions on the rebuilding of Hamburg have presented an instance of a similar conflict of local interests, which, in a few instances, has been so far successful as to preserve several dense masses of crowded and unwholesome habitations for the poorer classes, in the face of the recent experience of the sort of population which, to the surprise of the better classes of inhabitants, issued out of them and made the city at the time of its destruction a scene of plunder and anarchy more terrible than the fire itself.

No. 10.

LETTER FROM THE TOWN CLERK OF STOCKPORT, ON IN-FANTICIDES COMMITTED PARTLY FOR THE SAKE OF BURIAL MONEY.

DEAR SIR, *Stockport, 25th January,* 1843.

I HAVE no doubt that infanticide to a considerable extent has been committed in the borough of Stockport ; and I have been professionally engaged in prosecuting two distinct charges of infanticide, of which I give you the following summary :—

The first case was against Robert Standring, by trade a hatter. He had a female child about sixteen years of age, who, from imbecility, was not very likely to obtain her own living. One morning, about five o'clock, he sent her to call up a labouring hatter, with whom he (the father) was going to work during the day; but, previous to his so sending her, he gave the child some coffee. After the child's return she was seized with vomiting, and all the usual symptoms of illness caused by mineral poison, and died during the course of that day. The coroner (the late Mr. Hollins) held an inquest on the body, but refused to allow any surgical examination; and charging the jury that the death was a natural one, such a verdict was returned. In about three months afterwards, the case, and some suspicious circumstances, came to the knowledge of the Stockport police; and I was consulted as town-clerk and clerk to the justices. The magistrates issuing a warrant for the exhumation of the body, I attended with a competent surgeon and chemist (Mr. John Rayner), and a large—very large quantity of arsenic was found in the stomach, and all parts of the body which could be affected by arsenic taken internally were remarkably preserved from putrefaction. Standring, being apprehended, was tried before Mr. Justice Coleridge at the Chester Assizes. The judge apparently summed up for a conviction; but the jury, after a long deliberation, returned a verdict of acquittal. The verdict was an extraordinary one, and can only be accounted for by the general feeling against capital punishments, which enables so many criminals (capitally indicted) to escape any punishment.

The inducement for this murder, so far as it could be ascertained, was of a twofold character; partly to obtain money from the burial friendly societies, in which Standring had entered his child as a member, and from which he received about 8*l.*, and partly to free himself from the future burthen of supporting the child. The judge, in summing up the case for the consideration of the jury, remarked upon the apparent inadequacy of the motives for the murder; but, with all due deference to his lordship, when it is known to be an established fact that Mr. Ashton, a manufacturer of Hyde, was murdered by two miscreants whose only inducement was 10*l.* divided between them, there can be no scale laid down to indicate the lowest price for murder.

The other case involved no less than three distinct cases of murder. Robert Sandys, and Ann his wife, and George Sandys, and Honor his wife, were brothers and sisters-in-law, living in Stockport, in two adjoining cellars. They were bear or mat makers. Robert had two sons and two daughters, all young children, and George had a female child also very young. Two of the female children of Robert Sandys were one morning taken very ill, and one of them died the same day, under very suspicious circumstances, the neighbours publicly declaring that the children must be poisoned. These two girls (along with their brother, a little boy about five years of age) having been in the morning of the illness in the company of Bridget Ryley (a girl of inoffensive but imbecile mind), their mother, Ann Sandys, after the neighbours said the children must have been poisoned, said, "Oh, Bridget Ryley must have given them something." Bridget Ryley had given them some cold cabbage, which Ann Sandys well knew, and the boy who had been with them was not at all unwell. Bridget Ryley was apprehended, and by accident I was present at the coroner's inquest. I came in just at its termination, Bridget Ryley being in custody, and Ann Sandys being about to close her examination. After she had concluded her examination, which was very strong against Bridget Ryley, she began to apologize for Bridget, saying, She did not think the poor girl (as she called her) intended any harm to the child; and she evidently wished to make it appear that the poisoning was all a matter of accident. Bridget Ryley was then asked to say what she knew about the business, and she earnestly protested her innocence, saying the child had died of the same complaint as another child of Ann Sandys had died of three weeks before. It appeared strange that the mother of the child should both criminate and exculpate Bridget Ryley, and I thought I could perceive a watchful restlessness in her eye, which ill accorded with the probable grief of a bereaved parent; I therefore communicated to the coroner my opinion that the mother of the children might be the murderess, and that if so, the child which had been buried three weeks before would also prove poisoned. The coroner thought it a very proper inquiry, and adjourned the inquest, directing this other child to be exhumed; and it proved to have been poisoned by arsenic. Whilst this exhumation was taking place, Honor Sandys met one of the constables, and she expressed a wish that they would not disturb her dear little infant. The constable told me this, and directions were consequently given for its immediate exhumation. Arsenic had also caused the death of this child. Ann Sandys then said that Bridget Ryley must have poisoned them all, and that a child which Bridget Ryley had nursed had died in a similar way. (This was after Ann Sandys was in custody and charged with this murder.) This last child so nursed by Bridget Ryley was exhumed, but it had died a natural death. Now all these three children so poisoned were in friendly burial societies, and their parents would receive for their funerals about 3*l.* for each child. The expense of the funeral would be about 1*l.*, and the profit on each murder 2*l.*, and the liberation from the future expense of keeping the child.

At the ensuing assizes for Chester Mr. Justice Coltman postponed the trial to enable the boy, the son of Ann Sandys, to be educated for examination. This boy would have proved some very material facts as to the mode in which the poison was administered, but as this did not come out in evidence, as the boy was not considered capable of being examined at the subsequent assizes, it is hardly fair now to state them.

Mr. Justice Erskine tried the cases, and Robert Sandys was convicted, but his wife Ann Sandys acquitted. I afterwards was told by one of the jury that they acquitted her because they thought she acted under the control of her husband, and they thought that justified her acquittal. The judge and counsel had been silent on this point, satisfied with their own knowledge, that in murder the wife, though acting with her husband, is guilty and punishable, and thinking the jury as wise as themselves.

In consequence of an objection to the admissability of a statement made by Ann Sandys before the coroner, and also to the form of the indictment, judgment was respited to the following assizes. The judges determined for the Crown on both points, and sentence of death was passed on Robert Sandys. Afterwards, and without any communication to the parties prosecuting, the sentence of death was commuted to transportation for life. George and Honor Sandys were not tried, as the evidence was not so conclusive against them, and Robert and Ann were believed to be the principals in these murders.

I know it to be the opinion of some of the respectable medical practitioners in Stockport that infanticides have been commonly influenced by various motives—to obtain the burial moneys from the societies in question, and to be relieved from the burthen of the child's support. The parties generally resort to a mineral poison, which, causing sickness, and sometimes purging, assumes the appearance of the diseases to which children are subject ; and as they then take the child to a surgeon who prescribes after a very cursory examination, they thus escape any suspicion on the part of their neighbours. Each child in Sandys' case was so treated, but they took care not to administer the physic obtained.

How to prevent these infanticides is a question of great difficulty. I think these societies are of great use if under proper regulation and inspection. These cases may be good arguments for requiring the due inspection, after death, of each child in a burial society by a surgical examiner, who might judge, in most cases, whether a *post-mortem* examination were advisable or not; but as these societies are very useful on the whole, the partial misuse of them cannot avail against their general use. Probably an application to these societies of the law applicable to life assurance companies might tend to prevent the crime of infanticide. The object of these burial societies is the decent interment of the deceased member. In life insurance companies no person is by law allowed to recover from an insurance company more money than the value of his interest in the life of the person whose life is insured : for instance, should his interest in a life lease be worth 500*l.* he may insure and recover 500*l.*, but not 600*l.* He therefore receives by the policy that which he loses by the death, and no more. If he has no interest the policy is void. Now, applying this principle to these burial societies would make it necessary that some officer of the society should prepare for and superintend the interment of the child, and that no further sum than requisite for the decent interment should be expended, and no money in any case should be paid to the friends of the deceased; also, no party should be insured in more than one society.

None of our registrars of births and deaths are medical men, and no case of infanticide has been discovered through the instrumentality of the Registration Act.

I shall be glad to furnish you with the briefs in these cases of murder, should you desire them, or with any further information in my power.

In all four deaths each child was in a burial society, and arsenic was indisputably the cause of death.

I may also mention that each death was of a female child. The male children, more likely to be useful to their parents, were in each case spared.

I have the honour to be,

Your most obedient servant,

HENRY COPPOCK,

Town Clerk of Stockport, and

Clerk to the Stockport Union.

[In answer to a subsequent inquiry, Mr. Coppock stated that at the time the offences detailed in the above letter were committed, both the parties were in employment. Standring was a hatter, in full work, and making with industry 20*s.* a-week; the Sandys, Robert and George, were mat-makers, not making more than from 7*s.* to 10*s.* per week each; the women contributing, it is presumed, to the earnings of the family.]

No. 11.

A RETURN OF THE AVERAGE AGES AT WHICH DEATHS AND FUNERALS OCCURRED DURING THE YEAR 1839 TO THE SEVERAL CLASSES OF SOCIETY IN THE SEVERAL SUPERINTENDENT REGISTRARS' DISTRICTS OF THE METROPOLIS;

Also of the PROPORTIONATE NUMBERS of DEATHS to the POPULATION of each such District : setting forth the excess in Numbers of Deaths and Funerals in each such District above the proportionate Numbers of Deaths and Funerals in healthy and well-conditioned Town Districts: setting forth also the amount of Reduction of the ordinary Duration of Life of each Class in the District, as compared with the standards of Longevity afforded by the Insurance Tables deduced from the experience of the Population of Carlisle, and of the County of Hereford.

The explanations given in respect to the totals inserted at § 37 are applicable to the annexed district returns, which are only submitted as the best approximations that can be obtained in the present state of the registration. The practical bearing of the consideration of the ages of deaths as well as the proportionate numbers of deaths on the subject of provision for funerals is shown in §§ 72, 75, 76, 78, 79, 80, 81, also §§ 160, 161, 163, 169, 173, and note to § 150, also § 205. For the sake of those who are engaged as members of committees in the investigation of the health of the populous towns and the causes of mortality, it may be of public use to give full explanations of the principles on which returns should be made to measure the relative pressure of those causes in different localities, or amongst different classes of the community : it may also be of use to show the necessity of careful provisions for the registration of facts which are of great importance to every community.

Dr. Price, in his work on Annuities and Reversionary Payments, states that in his time the proportion of deaths in London within the bills of mortality was rather more than 1 to 22 of the population annually, which he states as an equivalent proposition to saying that the average duration of life to all who died was 22 years. Again he observes that—

"One with another, then, they will have an expectation of life of $22\frac{1}{4}$ years; that is, one of $22\frac{1}{2}$ will die every year." p. 255.

In p. 274, that—

"In the dukedom of Wurtemberg, the inhabitants, Mr. Susmilch says, are numbered every year; and from the average of 5 years, ending in 1754, it appeared that taking the towns and country together, 1 in 32 died annually. In another province which he mentions, consisting of 635,998 inhabitants, 1 in 33 died annually. From these facts he concludes, that, taking a whole country in *gross*, including all cities and villages, mankind enjoy among them about 32 or 33 years each of existence. This very probably is below the truth ; from whence it will follow, that a child born in a country parish or village has at least an expectation of 36 or 37 years; supposing the proportion of *country* to *town* inhabitants, to be as $3\frac{1}{2}$ to 1, which, I think, this ingenious writer's observations prove to be nearly the case in Pomerania, Brandenburg, and some other kingdoms.

By Mr. Milne, in his work on Annuities, and in his article on Mortality in the last edition of the Encyclopedia Britannica, by Dr. Bissett Hawkins, and by nearly all statistical writers, the proportions of deaths to the population, and the average ages of death, are treated as equivalent. Dr. Southwood Smith has been misled to adopt the same view. He states in his work on the Philosophy of Health, p. 135, that "There is reason to believe that the mortality at present throughout Europe, taking all countries together, including towns and villages, and combining all classes into one aggregate, is 1 in 36. Susmilch, a celebrated German writer, who flourished about the middle of the last century, estimated it at this average at that period. The result of all Mr. Finlaison's investigations is, that the average for the whole of Europe does not materially differ at the present time." "It has been shown that the average mortality at present at Ostend is 1 in 36, which is the same thing as to assert that a new-born child at Ostend has an expectation of 35½ years of life."

Having of late had occasion to make rather extensive observations on this subject, it appears to be a public duty to state, that in no class of persons, in no district or country, and in no tract of time, has the fact hitherto appeared to be in coincidence with this hypothesis; and also that returns of the proportions of deaths to the population, when taken singly as the exponents of the average duration of life, are often mischievously misleading, exaggerating those chances of life sometimes to the extent of double the real amount. If Dr. Price, instead of resting satisfied with Susmilch's hypothesis, had taken the actual ages of the dying within the bills of mortality, he would have found only a casual approximation to the hypothesis for the whole metropolis; and if he had taken the worst conditioned districts, that,· as applied to them, it was in error full one-half. On Mr. Milne's own data it appears that the proportions of deaths to the population at Carlisle, instead of coinciding with the ascertained average ages of death, 38·72, were in the year 1780, 1 in 35; in 1787, they were 1 in 43; and in 1801, they were I in 44. Having caused an average to be deduced from the actual ages of 5,200,141 deaths which occurred in the Prussian States from 1820 to 1834, instead of 36 years, the actual average age of deaths was only 28 years and 10 months. The average ages of death n France, as deduced from Duvillard's table, founded on the experience of one million of deaths, instead of being 36 years, was 28 years and 5 months.

The public errors created and maintained by taking the proportions of deaths as exponents of the average ages of death, or of the chances of life to the population, may be illustrated by reference to the actual experience amongst nearly two millions of the population, or upwards of forty-five thousand deaths in thirty-two districts, equivalent to as many populous towns, which the Registrar-General has obligingly enabled me to examine for the year 1839.

The Carlisle table is taken as the standard for the duration of life, to measure the loss of life in the several districts, as it gives the probability of life from infancy, well ascertained for one town, and nearly coincides with the experience of the annuity offices on the select class of lives insured by them, and with the results which I have obtained from the mortuary registries showing the average age of death in the county of Hereford. Each of the recognized insurance tables may, however, be used. If the Carlisle table be taken, the chances of life at infancy would be 38·72; by the Chester table it would be 36·70; by the Northampton, 25·18; by the Montpellier table, 25·36; by the last Swedish table, 39·39; by the experience of Geneva, 40·18. After the attainment of twenty years of age these several tables give the chances of life as follows:—by the Carlisle table it would be 41·46; by the Chester table, 36·48; by the Northampton table, 33·43; by the Montpellier table, 37·99; by the Swedish table, 39·98; by the Geneva experience, 37·67; and by the experience of the Equitable Society, 41·67. For civic purposes in this country, the most important period for considering the chances of life is after coming of age, or after the attainment of twenty-one years; the average ages of all who die above that age in each district of the metropolis are therefore given to illustrate the extent of loss of life to each class of adults, which is the more important to be observed, as it has been hastily supposed that the pressure of the more common and removable causes of disease is almost exclusively upon the infant population.

In illustration of the errors occasioned by taking the proportions of deaths as the exponent of the duration of life; if we take the proportions of deaths in the district of Islington, with its population of

55,720, we find the deaths for the year only 1 to every 55 of the population, which would appear to be a highly healthy standard; whereas, when we examine the average age of death of all of that population who have died during that year, we find it to be only 29 years: in other words, we find that the average duration of the period of existence has even in that district been shortened by at least nine years to all, and to an extent of at least six years on the average to the class of adults. If we examine the pressure of the causes of death upon each class of the community, in the same district, we find that the class of artisans, instead of attaining 39 *years,* have, on the average, been cut off at 19 years; and hence that children and adults, and on the average all those of the labouring classes who have died, have been deprived of 20 years of the natural expectation of life; and that even the class of adults who have died have been deprived of 15 years of working ability, involving extensive orphanage and premature widowhood. If we take such a district as Bethnal Green, inhabited by weavers and a badly conditioned population, the returns of the proportionate number of deaths to the population (1 in 41) would lead to the supposition of an average vitality of nearly double the real amount, which appears from this year's return to be only 22 years for the whole population. For the working classes in that district it is no more than 18 years. If we carry investigations closer, and into the local causes of the mortality, we have them developed in such evidence as that given by Mr. T. Taylor, one of the registrars of that district;—or in other districts by such information as that given by Mr. Worrell, the registrar of St. Pancras, or by registrars of St. George's, Hanover Square, or by the registrar of a district of Marylebone, where we find the state of overcrowding (noted in § 26), combined with the insufficient supplies of water, the defective drainage and neglect of cleansing which is described in the answers—attended by a reduction of 12 years' duration of life to the adult artisans. In the opulent parish of St. George's, Hanover Square, it is attended by a loss of 16 years; in Marylebone and in St. Pancras, by a loss of 17 years. The external and internal circumstances of the labouring population, where such results have been obtained, vary widely, and the results are commonly the mean of extreme differences. For example, in the parish of St. Margaret's, Leicester, which has a population of 22,000, almost all of whom are artisans engaged in the manufacture of stockings, where the average age of death in the whole parish was, during the year 1840, 18 years, I succeeded in obtaining the ages of death in the different *streets,* when it appeared that this average was made up as follows:—Average age of deaths in the streets that were drained (and that by no means perfectly) 23½ years; in the streets that were partially drained, 17½ years; in the streets that were entirely undrained, 13½ years. Though the defective drainage and cleansing was the main cause, it was doubtless not the only cause of this variation. That, however, was a year of a heavy mortality, and the average age of death in that and another district during the years 1840, 1841, and 1842, was in the streets drained 25½ years; in those partly drained 21, and those not drained, 17 years. The general average was 21 years. The proportions of death to the population in Leicester were during the same period, 1 in 36½. The inquiries promoted in the districts of other towns have developed instances of large masses of population amongst whom even lower average duration of life than any noted in the first report is attendant on the circumstances described as causes.

So far as estimates of the number of the people before a census was taken may be depended upon, it appears that the proportionate numbers of deaths in the metropolis were, at the commencement of the last century, 1 to 20. At the time the first census was taken (1801) the proportion of deaths to the population within the bills of mortality appeared to be 1 to 39. At the present time it appears to be 1 to 40. Having had the average ages of death within the bills of mortality in the metropolis calculated from the earliest to the later returns published, they appear to be, as far as they can be made out from the returns, which are only given in quinquennial and decennial periods, as follows:—

Of all returned as having died during the

	The average Age was	
	Years.	Months.
22 years, from 1728 to 1749	25	1
25 years, from 1750 to 1774	25	6
25 years, from 1775 to 1799	26	0
25 years, from 1800 to 1825	29	0
6 years, from 1825 to 1830	29	10

Thus, whilst it would appear from the proportionate numbers of deaths to the population that the average duration of life in the metropolis has doubled during the last century, it appears from the returns of the average ages themselves that it has only increased four years and nine months, or about one-fifth. The district of the old bills of mortality comprehends little more than one-half of the metropolis. The average age of death for the year 1839 for the whole metropolis, it will have been seen, is only 27 years. So far as an average for that year for the old district can be made out from the several recent district returns, it would appear to be no more than 26 years. But the earlier mortuary registration was known to be extremely defective, especially in the registration of deaths in the poorer districts, and the recent lower averages are ascribable to the closer registration of the infantile mortality in those districts. The earlier returns are only to be regarded in so far as the errors from period to period are likely to have compensated each other; they are only adduced as indicating the degree of proportionate progression, correspondent with the general physical improvements of the population. But the slow general improvement, made up by the great improvements of particular classes, is consistent with the positive deterioration of others. The average age of death of the whole of the working classes we have seen is still no more than 22 years in the whole of the metropolis. In large sub-districts, if we could distinguish accurately the classes of deaths, the average would be found to be not more than half that period: a rate of mortality ascribable to increased over-crowding and stationary accommodation, greatly below anything that probably existed at the commencement of the century. The chief errors in the existing returns are errors which cause the extent of the evils which depress the sanitary condition of the population, and the mortality consequent on those evils to be under estimated.

The erroneous conclusions as to the ages of the populations from the proportions of deaths, have perhaps arisen from assumptions of the existence of states of things rarely, if ever, found, namely, perfectly stationary populations and perfectly stationary causes of death. I have been asked "If 1 out of 40 die yearly, must not the average age of all who die be 40 years?" The answer, by actual experience, as we have seen, is, that it is often not 30 years; and perhaps the reason why it is not so will be most conveniently illustrated by hypothetical cases. For example, let it be assumed that in any given year 40 persons die out of 1600, which is in the proportion of 1 to 40, and in consequence of an unusual prevalence of measles, or some disease to which children are subject, the greater number of deaths occur amongst the infant portion of the population, and hence, out of the 40 deaths, 20 occur at 5 years of age, 10 at 25, and 10 at 60. Then the total existence had, would have been $(20 \times 5) + (10 \times 25) + (10 \times 60 = 100 + 250 + 600 = 950$ years, and this divided by 40, the number who died would give $\frac{950}{40} = 24$ years nearly as the average duration of life to each of the 40 who died.

On the other hand, suppose a severe winter, in which the peculiar causes of mortality may have pressed unusually heavy upon the older lives, and let the numbers who died have been 20, at 60 years of age; 10 at 40; and 10 at 5; in such case, the total existence enjoyed would have been

$(20 \times 60) + (10 \times 40) + (10 \times 5) = 1200 + 400 + 50 = 1650$ years, which, divided by 40, would give $\frac{1650}{40} = 41\frac{1}{4}$ years as the average duration of life to each.

And again, where, in fact, the proportion of death in one year may be represented as 1 death out of 20 of the population; the average existence enjoyed may be greater than when 1 in 40 died for the reason given in the former case. As for example, in the year when 1 in 20 died, it may have happened that the deaths were among the older lives, and that, taking one with another, the average age of all who died might be 50; while in the other case the mortality might have been amongst the infant population, when the average age might have been 20. If the proportion of 1 in 40, or 1 in 20, were to obtain each year continuously, taking one life with another, the average duration to a population just born, of whom 1 in 40 died, and whose place should be supplied each year by a new birth, would be about 20 years to each life, or one-half; and of a similar population, of whom 1 out of 20 died annually, the average duration of life to each would be about 10 years, or one-half the period at the expiration of which all the lives would have expired.

When these examples are considered, it will be understood that the average age of death may remain stationary, or may go on increasing, whilst the proportions of death remain the same, or vary. The actual mortality of most districts is found to be coincident chiefly with its physical condition, and is most accurately measured by the years of vitality which have been enjoyed, *i. e.*, by the average age of death. The numbers of deaths increase or diminish considerably, and frequently create erroneous impressions, whilst the average ages of death are found to maintain a comparatively steady course, always nearest to the actual condition of the population, and give the most sure indications.

The chief test of the pressure of the causes of mortality is then the duration of life in years: and whatever age may be taken as the standard of the natural age or the average age of the individual in any community may be taken to correct the returns of the proportions of death in that same community. For example, in the returns of the St. George's, Hanover Square district, it appears that in 1839, the proportions of deaths was 1 to 50 of the population; but the average number of years which 1325 individuals who died during that year had lived, was only 31 years, or 8 years below the average period of life in Carlisle. There was then in that district during that year a total loss of 10,600 years of life, which at 39 years may be considered as equal to an excess of deaths of 272 persons, and in a healthy state the proportions of deaths should have been 1 in 63 instead of 1 in 50 of the population. The excess in numbers of deaths in the metropolis has been measured by this standard, the total number of years of life would in a healthy community have been divided in portions of not less than 39 years to every individual who died.

The effect of migration or of emigration, in disturbing the results of returns of the average ages of death in particular localities appears to be commonly much exaggerated.

As formerly, when navy surgeons, overlooking the filth of their ships, which has since been removed, and not perceiving the effects of the atmospheric impurities arising from the overcrowding, which have since been diminished by better ventilation, directed their whole attention to supposed distant causes and mysterious agencies, and were wont to ascribe the whole of the fever which ravaged a fleet to infection from some casual hand, who was found to have been received on board from some equally filthy and ill kept prison where the " gaol fever " had been prevalent; so now, in some of our towns, we find much ingenuity exercised to avoid the immediate force of the facts presented by such returns, by a search for collateral and incidental defects in them. Thus in Liverpool the whole of its vast excess of mortality has been charged upon the poorer passengers who pass through the port. In other towns also, all the excess of deaths from epidemic or infectious disease is charged upon the vagrant population. In New York and some of the American cities, where inquiries have been stimulated by the example of the sanitary inquiry in this country, a common observation made on the proved excess of mortality is, that a large proportion of " foreigners" frequent the city. An inquiry into the cases themselves would generally show that if, instead of the proportion of the immigrant population being a small per-centage, it formed a very large proportion of the population included; still the proportion per cent. of sickness and mortality, from consumption and other diseases, amongst the resident population, is the greatest ; and that even in lodging-houses the disease most frequently appears first in the occupants who are stationary, and last in the new comers. In some badly conditioned districts, where there is a very severe mortality observable on children, a less proportionate amount of mortality prevails amongst the adults who are migrant, than on other adults resident in somewhat less depressed districts, but who are more stationary. Of all classes (unless it be the higher classes who resort to watering-places) it is not the sickly and the weakly who travel for subsistence as handicraftsmen, or for subsistence in commerce, but the healthy and robust. In so far as the general results of mortuary registration of any district are disturbed by a population who are migrant (who are not only above the average strength, but who generally come with the additional advantage of health by travel in the open air and in a purer atmosphere), they are usually disturbed by unduly raising and giving the locality an appearance of an average of health, and the fatally deceptive chances of longevity that do not belong to it. Whilst therefore the localities gain by the average health and strength of the migrant population, other districts have the credit of a share of the excess of disease and mortality which really belong to unhealthy localities. In other words, the population migrating through such districts carry away more disease and mortality from the crowded districts than they take into them. If there had been a mortuary registration at Walcheren, or any pestilential stations productive of an excessive mortality in the army, the registries probably would not have given the localities credit for more than half the mortality which belonged to them. The real sickness and mortality of the more depressed town districts are often made to appear lower than they are by the number of cases treated in distant workhouses, hospitals, and dispensaries, for which no credit is given to the locality where the cause of death occurred.

It would doubtless proportionately enhance the value of such returns as those in question, if the rule were fully carried out that " the population enumerated must always be precisely that which produces the deaths registered ;" the grand desideratum being, as expressed by Mr. Milne, for insurance purposes, "to determine the number of annual deaths at each age which takes place among the living at the same age ;"[*] but the facts cited of the greater proportion of adults, and of health in those adults who are immigrant, will answer the objections to the superior applicability to local or class insurance tables, deduced from actual local observation of the local rate of mortality prevalent amongst that population, whether migrant or stationary, and without reference to the actual ages of the living (though that were desirable), compared with deductions from any general insurance table, *i. e.* the experience of a distant and wholly unconnected population. Deductions from tables, however correctly made from the experience of other towns, must be, and are proved, by such experience as that hereafter cited, to be merely " guess-work." Vide ' General Sanitary Report,' pp. 218, 219. For myself, I make it a general rule of precaution neither to receive nor adduce statistical returns as evidence without previous inquiry, wherever it is possible, into the particulars on which they are founded, or with which they are

---

[*] Art. ' Mortality,' Ency. Britan., last edit., p. 524.

connected. I adduce them less as principal evidence, proving anything by themselves, than as proximate measures, or as indications of the extent of the operation of causes substantiated by distinct investigations. The general conclusions which the facts that have come to my knowledge tend to establish on the subject of the experience of mortality are, that there is no general law of mortality yet established that is applicable to all countries or to all classes, or to all times, as commonly assumed; that every place, and class, and period has rather its own circumstances and its own law, varying with those circumstances; that the actual experience of any class or place, or period, even with the disturbance of any ordinary amount of migration, or immigration, or any ordinary influx of young lives from births, is a safer guide than any experience deduced from the experience of another people living at another time and place, or any assumed general law.

For many public purposes, I have submitted it as a desideratum that population returns should give not merely the *numbers* of each class, or of those engaged in each distinct occupation, which only enables us to resort to the fallacious standard of the proportionate numbers of deaths, to judge of the mortality incidental to the class, but the total ages of each class, which would serve as an index of alterations in the sanitary condition of that same class. Such returns of the total ages should, for the public use, be reduced to their simplest proportions. In the form in which they are usually given, only in intervals of quinquennial or decennial periods, they are extremely meagre, and involve so much inaccuracy in any attempts that might be made to use them, for the purpose of comparing district with district, as to be generally useless. Whereas, if the ages of any class, or of the general population living in any district, and the ages of those of them who die, were reduced to the simplest proportions—that is, if the total years of age, whether of the living or dying, were divided by the total number of individuals from which the returns were made, the public would be enabled to make comparisons between district and district, and to judge of the relative degrees of pressure, in each, of the causes of mortality. As the simple proportions of average ages of the living have not yet, that I am aware of, been used, or even calculated in any instance, I beg leave to exemplify them.

Mr. Griffith Davies is theoretically of opinion, on a formula of De Moivre, that in general the average age of death in any community is necessarily higher than the average age of those living in the same community: and that in a stationary population the average age of death will, under ordinary circumstances, be in the ratio of 3 to 2 higher than the average age of the living. I have had the average age of the living population, on which the experience embodied in the Carlisle Insurance table was founded, calculated: and if that may be considered to have been a stationary population, the proportion of the ages of the living to those of the dying was practically as about 3 to 4: for whilst the average age of the dying was $38\frac{3}{10}$, the average age of the living population was $32\frac{9}{10}$. The average age of the dying in Hereford, in which the increase of population had been very slight, was 39. But the average age of the living population, so far as it can be made out from quinquennial returns, was 28 years and 5 months. On this and all returns of the ages of the living, in the mode in which the returns have been collected, allowance must be made for understatements of ages by some of the adult members of the community. On the whole, the proportion of the ages of the living to the dying appears to be in an ordinarily healthy and stationary community, as about 3 to 4.

As yet the observations have not been on a sufficiently wide basis; but it appears that wherever there is any divergence between the average ages of the living and the average ages of the dying, the divergence beyond their natural proportions may be taken as indicating the proportionate operation of some disturbing cause upon either line, as by some extraordinary increase of births, or by immigration or emigration, on the average ages of the living, and on the line of the average ages of the dead.

So far as I have been enabled to observe or collect from the extremely imperfect data at present available to the public service, the line of the average ages of the living is comparatively steady; the disturbances by migration and immigration which often compensate each other, for the same place and period, being much the same at different periods, and seldom affect the results materially, whilst the variations in the pressure of the causes of death from year to year, are usually considerable, and warrant the assumption that in general the disturbances occasioning the divergence described, are from the operations of causes of death upon that line. Wherever the pressure of the causes of death has yet been observed to be very great, there the line of mortality, or the average age of death, is below, what may be called, the line of vitality constituted by the average age of the living; and wherever there is on the whole any diminution of those causes of death, as by better ventilation, or by widening streets, opening new thoroughfares, better supplies of water, sewering and cleansing, and improvements in the general habits of the population, there the line of mortality, the infantile mortality especially, diminishes, the average age of each adult class, up to sexagenarians or octogenarians, increases, and the average age of death ascends above the average age of the living. The means of observation are as yet too few to elicit more than indications for the guidance of sustained investigation, to determine whether the divergence of the two lines may be reduced to any rule.

In Liverpool,—where the investigations into the condition of the resident cellar population certainly show an increase of the causes of death,—overcrowding, defective ventilation, bad supplies of water, and increased filth,— the average age of death is, for the whole town, 17 or 18 years only, whilst the average age of the living population, so far as it can be made out from the mode in which the census is prepared, is 24 years. As far as can be ascertained by reference to previous registries of one large parish, where the ages of the dead were formerly entered, the average duration of life in that town has gradually fallen. The average ages of all who were buried in St. Nicholas parish between the years 1784 and 1809 was 25.

In Manchester, the average age of the living is 25 years, but the average age of the dying is only 18. In Leeds, the average age of the living is also 25 years, but the average age of the dying is only 21.

	Years.	Months.
The average age of all who *live* in the town parishes of Middlesex, so far as they can be made out from the only available materials,—the returns in quinquennial periods,—is only	26	2
But the average age of all who *die*, judging from one year's return, appears to be about	27	0

If, however, we allow for the understatement of ages, the two lines for the whole metropolis would be nearly coincident. On the experience of Carlisle and Hereford, the average age of death should be twelve years higher.

Arranging the several districts of the metropolis, in the order of the average age of deaths, we find the average age of the living decrease with the average age of the dying; and the proportion of births to the population increase with the decrease of the average age of death. The excess in the proportionate number of births beyond the proportions in such a county as Hereford (1 to 44), where the average age of death is much higher, and proportionate number of deaths to the population, afford important indicia.

Districts in which verage Age of Death of the whole Population is	Average Age of Death in the District, of all Classes.	Average Age of all who live in the District.	Proportions of Births to the Population.	Proportions of Deaths to the Population.	Excess above County of Hereford in the Number of	
					Deaths and Funerals.	Births.
ighest . . . . . omprising 2 Districts.) Population 120,678.	Years. 35	yrs. mon. 27 11	1 to 41	1 to 42	966	145
Intermediate . . . (6 Districts.) Population 311,022.	30	27 5	1 to 39	1 to 46	1,836	689
Intermediate . . (12 Districts.) Population 774,937.	27	26 11	1 to 33	1 to 40	7,457	5,718
owest . . . . . (12 Districts.) Population 663,290.	23	26 5	1 to 30	1 to 41	5,735	6,822

It will be observed that in the least healthy districts where the pressure of the causes of mortality is the most extensive, the average age of death falls nearly three years and a half *below* the average age of the living, whilst in the higher districts the line of mortality rises towards the natural position, or nearly four years above it. But it must still be borne in mind, in the inspection of the returns from the highest district, that the average is made up of districts which are probably retrograding, connected with others which are advancing,—of districts such as are developed by Mr. Worrell, registrar, in his note on one of the returns from St. Pancras, comprising streets, the connected courts and alleys from which are widely as separate and distinct in condition,—and, if I may use such an illustration, as little appropriate for any average that could be represented by numerals —as were the conditions of Lazarus and Dives.

Even the lowest proportion of deaths to the population presented in the district returns, that of Hackney, where it is only 1 to 56, appears to be a proportion in excess by nearly one-eighth, *i. e.* the deaths from epidemics, as well as the excess of more than one-third in the deaths of children under 10 years of age. The return, from the healthiest district in the returns, of the average age of deaths gives an average of 7 years' loss of life for the whole population; whilst for the *adults* of the middle classes it gives 10 years, and for the *adults* of the working classes 7 years' premature loss of life. Even in the county of Hereford where there is a proportion of deaths of 1 to 64 of the population, and the standard of the Carlisle table of insurance where an average age of 39 years of death is attained, it will be observed that even this average includes a large proportion (542), or nearly 1-third in the number of deaths under 10 years of age, and 123 or 1-14th deaths from epidemics, besides others involving deaths from preventible causes. Only 329, or 1 in 5 of the deaths in this very healthy county, were deaths registered as from old age. By the removal of this excess of deaths, the excess of births which replace them would even in these districts be of course still further diminished.

It may be conjectured that if there were the means of distinguishing accurately the various classes of the living amongst whom these deaths fall, the irregularity of the proportionate number of deaths which probably arise amongst the labouring classes would be accounted for. The present returns of the number of births do not distinguish the classes amongst whom the births occur. Taking the districts in the order of the average age in which deaths occur to the labouring classes, and comparing the proportions of the deaths and funerals with the proportions which occur in Hereford, the excess of deaths and funerals was in 1839 as follows:—

Districts in which average Age of Death of Artisans, &c., is	Average Age of Death of Artisans, &c. in the Districts.	Excess in Number of Deaths of Artisans, &c., in the District above the Deaths of Agricultural Labourers in Herefordshire.
1. Highest number of the class (comprising 2 Districts.)	38	483
2. Intermediate (1) number of the class (5 Districts.)	27	548
3. Intermediate (2) number of the class (10 Districts)	23	1,773
4. Lowest number of the class (15 Districts.)	20	4,121

The totals of the subjoined district returns for the metropolis are as follows:—

	Number of deaths of each class.			Number of deaths from Epidemic disease.	Average age at death of all who die above 21.	Average age at death of the whole class, including children.
	Adults.	Children under 10 years.	Total.			
Gentlemen . .	1724	529	2253	210	60	44
Tradesmen . .	3979	3703	7682	1428	51	25
Labourers . .	12045	13885	25930	5469	49	22
Paupers . .	3062	593	3655	557	60	49
Undescribed . .	2996	2761	5757	1051	56	28
Totals .	23806	21471	45277	8715	53	27

The following totals of the mortuary registration of the several registrars' districts in Hereford for the same year are given for comparison:—

	Number of deaths of each class.			Number of deaths from Epidemic disease.	Average age at death of all who die above 21.	Average age at death of the whole class, including children.
	Adults.	Children under 10 years.	Total.			
Gentlemen . .	49	19	68	2	65	45
Farmers, &c. . .	205	45	250	14	60	47
Labourers . .	833	324	1157	87	58	39
Paupers . .	26	11	37	1	71	51
Undescribed . .	124	143	267	19	68	30
Totals .	1237	542	1779	123	60	39

The total number of births registered in the several districts in the metropolis, where it is yet far from complete, in the year 1839, was 51,232, or 1 to 37 of the population. The total number of births registered in Hereford during the same year was 2379, or 1 to 44.

The positions advanced in the Sanitary Report of the greater proportion of births in the districts where the deaths are the most frequent, is confirmed in respect to the metropolis by a more recent return with which I have been obligingly favoured by the Registrar-General, in which he shows,—

	Proportion per cent.		Ratio of deaths to births.
	Deaths.	Births.	
" Unhealthiest sub-districts ·	3·14	3·66	1 to 1·17
Less unhealthy sub-districts · ·	2·68	3·18	1 to 1·19
Average sub-districts · · · ·	2·43	3·35	1 to 1·38
Healthier sub-districts · · ·	2·17	2·64	1 to 1·22
Healthiest sub-districts ". · ·	1·87	2·47	1 to 1·32

" The mortality is 68 per cent. higher in the unhealthy than in the healthy sub-districts : the proportion of births is 48 per cent. greater in the unhealthy than in the healthy sub-districts."

If the deaths in the metropolis during 1839 had been in the same proportion to the population as they were in Hereford, there would have been 8866 funerals less during that year.

If the proportion of births in the metropolis during that year had been the same as in Hereford, there would have been 16,053 births the less.

Or to vary the illustration :—

If the deaths in Hereford had been in the same proportion as the deaths in the metropolis, the community in that county would during that year have had 977 funerals the more.

If the births in Hereford had been in the same proportion as in the metropolis, there would during that year have been 540 births the more.

If the deaths in the whole of England and Wales had been in the proportions attained in some districts, and attainable in all, namely, 1 in 50, there would during the year have been 31,866 funerals less, and more than ten times that amount of cases of sickness the less.

If the proportions of births in the whole kingdom had been the same as those occurring in average healthy districts—such as that of the town district of Hackney, for example, of 1 to 42—there would have been 139,958 births the less to make up for the excess of deaths.

The importance of the subject will justify the reference to other examples.

The commissioners for taking the census of Ireland have bestowed considerable labour to effect various improvements, with a view to determine more accurately the actual condition and progress of the population. They have attempted, amongst other improvements, to ascertain not merely the total number of houses, but the number of each description of houses in each district. From the want of any system of mortuary or birth registration in Ireland their attempts to ascertain correctly the proportions of deaths and births to the population appear to have been to some degree frustrated; and the return of the average age of death must be received as an approximation, giving higher than the real chances of life in that country. From the mode which the commissioners adopted of collecting the ages of the living, by taking the actual age of each individual with precautions, it appears probable that their returns on this head are more trustworthy than those obtained in England.

The proportions of births to the population obtained by the Census Commissioners in Ireland are, I conceive, below the real amount; the proportions of deaths are confessedly so. The proportions of deaths and several other results may however serve for comparison between one province and another and between one county and another. I have taken the following results from several of their tables, or have had them calculated from their data. I submit them as indications of the momentous public truths that still lie open for investigation, of which truths the most important are the extent of the operation of the causes of mortality, which can only be correctly ascertained on the spot by inquiries for a mortuary registration, by responsible officers of superior qualifications and intelligence as officers of health. The fractional numbers are omitted in the returns from the provinces,

	LEINSTER.				MUNSTER.				ULSTER.				CONNAUGHT.				IRELAND.			
	RURAL.		TOWN.		RURAL.		TOWN.		RURAL.		TOWN.		RURAL.		TOWN.		RURAL.		TOWN.	
	Houses.	Families.	Houses.	Families.	Houses.	Families.	Houses.	Families.	Houses.	Families.	Houses.	Families.	Houses.	Families.	Houses.	Families.	Houses.	Families.	Houses.	Families.
First Class houses	2	2	24	33	1	1	12	14	1	1	10	9	·5	·6	7	10	1·3	1·4	15·9	21·
"Good farm-houses, or in towns houses in a small street, having from 5 to 9 rooms and windows"	21	21	37	39	13	13	44	49	21	21	56	60	8	8	30	33	16·8	17·2	43·6	46·6
"A better description of cottage, still built of mud, but varying from 2 to 4 rooms and windows"	17	46	23	16	34	34	30	25	45	45	23	21	39	39	36	33	41·9	41·7	26·8	21·7
"All mud cabins having only one room"	28	28	14	10	50	49	13	10	32	32	9	8	51	50	25	22	40·	39·7	13·7	10·7

	LEINSTER		MUNSTER		ULSTER		CONNAUGHT		IRELAND	
	Males.	Females.	Males.	Females.	Males.	Females.	Males.	Females.	Males.	Females.
verage age at death	32· 31·5	25· 25·4	28·2 27·	23·6 23·7	31·8 32·	23·8 23·6	26·1 24·3	22·6 22·4	29·6 28·9	24·1 24·
	32	25	28	24	32	24	25	23	29	24
Average term of premature loss of life as compared with the experience of Carlisle or the county of Hereford	30		27		31		24		28	
	7	14	11	15	7.	15	14	16	10	15
	9		12		8		15		11	
nnual proportion of births to the mean population	1 in 32·3		1 in 29·5		1 in 31·1		1 in 28		1 in 30·3	
verage age of all who lived in 1841	25		24		24		23		24	
roportion of widows to every 100 of the population above 17 years old	13	17	12	16	12	15	12	17	12	16
ate of increase on population since 1831	3·35		7·59		4·36		5·58		5·25	
xcess in number of births to every 10,000 of the population above the proportion of births in Hereford	73		95		84		117		90	
ositive numbers of births in excess above the proportion of births in Hereford	14,515		22,875		20,003		16,624		74,016	

The proportion of widowhood (which would generally be attended by its proportion of orphanage) to the short duration of life in the worst conditioned districts is submitted as confirmatory of the principles expounded in the General Sanitary Report on the condition of the labouring population in Great Britain. Vide p. 188, *et seq.*

Conformity of the rate of increase of population with the ages of the living and the dying was not to be expected in the returns where the emigration from the different provinces is (probably) variable; but in the two provinces where the household condition appears to be the worst, and the proportion of mud cabins the greatest, there we find the mortality is the highest.

Where the pressure of the causes of mortality is the greatest; where the average age of death is the lowest, and the duration of life is the shortest, there the increase of population is the greatest. The proportion of children is great because life is short and the generation transient; the middle aged and the aged are swept away in large proportions; and marriages are disproportionately early. But, says a political economist in an essay in support of Mr. Malthus's original view, " The effect of wars, plagues, and epidemic disorders, those terrible correctives, as they have been justly termed by Dr. Short, of the redundance of mankind on the principle of population, sets its operation in the most striking point of view. These scourges tend to place an old country in the situation of a colony. They lessen the number of inhabitants, without, in most cases, lessening the capital that is to feed and maintain them." What I apprehend the actual facts when examined, place in a striking point of view, is the danger of adopting conclusions deeply affecting the interests of communities, on hypothetical reasonings, and without a careful investigation whether the facts sustain them: the facts them-

selves, when examined, show that (be it as it may with war) epidemic disorders do *not* lessen the number of inhabitants ; and that they *do* in all cases
that have been examined lessen the capital that is to feed and maintain them.
They lessen the proportion of productive hands and increase the proportion
of the helpless and dependent hands. They place every community, new or
old, in respect to its productive economy in the position which the farmer will
understand by the like effects of epidemics upon his cattle, when in order to
raise one horse two colts must be reared, and the natural period of work of
the one reared is, by disease and premature death, reduced by one-third or
one-half.   The exposition already given, *vide* General Report p. 176, *et seq.*
p. 200, of the dreadful misery and disease-sustaining fallacy which erects
pestilence into a good, is further illustrated by the effects of the proportions
of the dependent populations of Ireland.   Thus in England, the population
above 15 and under 50 years of age in every ten thousand is 5025; and
this five thousand have 3600 children below 15 years of age dependent
upon them.   In Ireland, the population above 15 years of· age is 4900—
in other words, there are 125 less of adults in every ten thousand ; and
this smaller proportion of living adults, with eight or ten years' span less
of life or working ability, have 4050, or four hundred and fifty more
children dependent upon them.   In England there are 1,365 persons in
every ten thousand, or 13½ per cent. above 50 years old to exercise the
influence of their age and experience upon the community.   In Ireland
there are only 10 per cent., or 1050 in every ten thousand of the population
above 50 years of age.

It appears from a report which the Census Commissioners give on the
sanitary condition of Dublin, that the mortality in the different localities of
that city varies with their physical condition in the lower districts, and
coincides with the description already cited in the general report, from the
report of Dr. Speer, the physician to the Dublin Fever Hospital (*vide*
General Sanitary Report, p. 96).   The like consequences follow to the
lower Irish population settled in the English towns with the like habits,
which permit them to accumulate refuse round their dwellings, and live in
an atmosphere compounded of the miasma of a pigsty and a privy, and the
smoke of a chimney in a crowded room.   The Census Commissioners of
Ireland have endeavoured to obtain returns of the chief causes of the
mortality ; and it appears from the report upon them, that hitherto, notwithstanding all that has been said and written, that fever has returned
nearly decennially in periods, irrespective of any general distress in that
country, and has extended its ravages to classes who were exposed to the
miasma, but who suffered no distress.   "Cases of starvation," it is stated,
" have been registered from returns at almost every age; 79 of them took
place in the rural district, or 1 death in 11,539 of the general mortality of
the open country, and minor towns and villages; 18 in the civic, or 1 in
13,009 of the deaths in towns of or above 2000 people; and 20 occurred
in hospitals ; the patients having been admitted when suffering from want
of food, or in such a destitute condition as subsequently produced death
from exhaustion.   Including the deaths in hospitals with those in the
civic districts, to which they properly belong, it appears that the deaths
from want and destitution in the larger towns have been 1 in 7240 to the
total mortality of these places.   During the first 5-year period, these deaths
were on an average but 6 per annum, and in the last 5-year period (that
ending June, 1841) they had increased to the yearly average of 18."

The dependency of the duration of life upon the physical condition of the
population, and the connexion of several classes of moral and economical
facts, with the proportionate mortality, may be further exemplified.   Taking
the four counties in Ireland in which the proportions of mud hovels are
the greatest ; and the four counties in which the proportions of such tenements are the least ;* I have added the average ages of death as additional
proofs and exemplifications of the conclusions stated in pp. 128 and 129,
and other parts of the General Report.

* The county of Dublin is left out as having a disproportionate amount of

	The four Counties where the average proportion of mud hovels, as habitations, is the lowest.				The four Counties where the average proportion of mud hovels, as habitations, is the highest.			
	Down.	Wexford.	Kilkenny.	Monaghan.	Kerry.	Mayo.	Clare.	Cork.
Proportion per cent. of families occupying habitations which are mud cabins having only one room*	24·7	29·4	30·9	31·5	66·7	62·8	56·8	56·7
			29				61	
Proportion of deaths from epidemic disease to every 10,000 of the population	36	28·5	36·8	40·4	50·2	51·0	53·1	43·3
			35·5				47·8	
Average age of all who have died during the 10 years ended 6th June, 1841	33·6	34·10	33·2	31·4	24·10	23·2	24·5	28·8
			33·4				26·8	
Average age of all the living in 1841 . . .	24·10	25·10	24·8	24·2	23·1	23·0	22·9	24·0
			24·11				23·5	
Proportions of births to the population	1 in 33·4	1 in 34·3	1 in 33·6	1 in 32·5	1 in 28·8	1 in 28·	1 in 28·7	1 in 31·8
			1 in 33·4				1 in 29·9	
Increase per cent. of the population since 1831 .	2·7	10·6	7·9	2·5	11·7	6·2	10·9	9·9
			5·0				8·7	
Per cent. of the population, 15 years and under . .	39·7	35·6	37·8	40·9	42·4	43·1	42·4	39·7
			38·8				41·9	
Above 50 years. . . .	12·0	12·5	10·9	10·9	9·4	9·4	8·7	10·4
			11·6				9·5	
Proportion per cent. of male and female population, 17 years and upwards.								
Unmarried .	42	44⅓	45⅓	41	37	36	40½	42
			43¾				39	
Married . .	49	47	45½	49½	55	56	51½	50
			47¾				53	
Per cent. of the population, 5 years old and upwards, who can neither read nor write	27·5	41·3	51·2	51·3	70·4	79·0	63·1	65·6
			42·8				69·7	

Proportions of crimes† of violence or passion to each 10,000 of the population on an average of 8 years to 1842 :—

	Down.	Wexford.	Kilkenny.	Monaghan.	Kerry.	Mayo.	Clare.	Cork.
Murders and Manslaughters { Proportions	·11	·20	·44	·55	·71	·87	1·08	·52
{ Positive Numbers.	34	35	83	88	166	271	249	316
Proportions			·32				·72	
Rapes and Assaults, with intent to commit { Proportions	·66	·15	·22	·35	·71	·51	·46	·28
{ Positive Numbers.	15	22	31	58	166	159	108	178
Proportions			·17				·44	

* The census, which gives not only the description of the houses, but the different description of holdings or sizes of farms, shows that in both groups of counties they are nearly of the same size, but the farms are rather the largest in the best conditioned group. In both sets, 93 per cent. of the farms are under 30 acres ; upwards of 40 per cent. of them from 1 to 5 acres only ; 35 per cent. of them from 5 to 15 acres ; 13 per cent. from 15 to 30 acres ; and about 7 per cent. only above 30 acres ; so that the chief differences would apparently be in their houses.

† By my colleagues and myself, the uncertainty of the returns of commitments, or of convictions, as data to judge of the amount of crime committed in any district, was demonstrated in §1 to §4 of our Report as Commissioners of Inquiry into the condition of the Constabulary Force in England and Wales ; but that uncertainty attaches perhaps in the least degree to the higher classes of crimes.

The general sanitary condition of the population of Scotland and the pressure of the preventible causes of death appears to be lower than in England, and higher than in Ireland, and so it appears from the recent census is the average age of the living.

It may be conceived that the low average age of the living in these cases is ascribable mainly to an increasing proportion of children incidental to an increasing population. Not so, however: the average age of the living is more powerfully influenced by disturbing causes affecting the population of adults, each with accumulated years, than by causes affecting the infantile population. One adult of 50 years added to the living is equal to the addition of 50 infants, and so with the average ages of deaths. The average ages of the living appear to have increased and not diminished with the increasing population. Be the sanitary condition of the poorest classes and the amount of disease and death what it may, as compared with former periods (and there is direct evidence that it is in populous districts increasing), there has been some improvement in the residences of the middle and higher classes; household drainage and cleanliness has in some districts been improved; the quantity of town and land drainage and cultivation has of late increased in various proportions in each country; and the decrease in the causes of mortality appears to have been followed by an increase of the average age of the living, of particular classes at the least, sufficient to present an increase, though a dreadfully slow one, in the average age of the adults living. The increase of the proportion of adults may be represented as follows:—

	England.		Ireland.		Scotland.	
	1821	1841	1821	1841	1821	1841
Per centage of Population of 15 Years and under . . .	39·09	36·07	41·06	40·44	41·0	36·4
Over 15 Years . .	60·91	63·93	58·94	59·56	59·0	63·6
	Yrs. M.	Yrs. M.	Yrs. M.	Yrs. M.	Yrs. M.	Yrs. M.
Average age of each living individual .	25·3	26·7	2·37	24·0	25·1	25·9

In abundance of employment, in high wages, and the chief circumstances commonly reputed as elements of prosperity of the labouring classes, the city of New York is deemed pre-eminent. I have been favoured with a copy of "*The Annual Report of the Interments in the City and County of New York for the Year* 1842," presented to the Common Council by Dr. John Griscom, the city inspector, in which it may be seen how little those circumstances have hitherto preserved large masses of people from physical depression. He has stepped out of the routine to examine on the spot the circumstances attendant on the mortality which the figures represent. He finds that upwards of 33,000 of the population of that city live in cellars, courts, and alleys, of which 6618 are dwellers in cellars. "Many," he states, "of these back places are so constructed as to cut off all circulation of air, the line of houses being across the entrance, forming a *cul de sac*, while those in which the line is parallel with, and at one side of the entrance, are rather more favourably situated, but still excluded from any general visitation of air in currents. As to the influence of these localities upon the health and lives of the inmates, there is, and can be, no dispute; but few are aware of the dreadful extent of the disease and suffering to be found in them. In the damp, dark, and chilly cellars, fevers, rheumatism, contagious and inflammatory disorders, affections of the lungs, skin, and eyes, and numerous others, are rife, and too often successfully combat the skill of the physician and the benevolence of strangers.

"I speak now of the influence of the locality merely. The degraded habits of life, the filth, the degenerate morals, the confined and crowded apartments, and insufficient food, of those who live in more elevated rooms, comparatively beyond the reach of the exhalations of the soil, engender a different train of diseases, sufficiently distressing to contemplate, but the addition to all these causes of the foul influences of the incessant moisture and more confined air of under-ground rooms, is productive of evils which humanity cannot regard without shuddering."

He gives instances where the cellar population had been ravaged by fever whilst the population occupying the upper apartments of the same houses were untouched. In respect to the condition of these places, he cites the testimony of a physician, who states that, " frequently in searching for a patient living in the same cellar, my attention has been attracted to the place by a peculiar and nauseous effluvium issuing from the door indicative of the nature and condition of the inmates." A main cause of this is the filthy external state of the dwellings and defective street cleansing, and defective supplies of water, which, except that no provision is made for laying it on the houses of the poorer classes, is now about to be remedied by a superior public provision.

Years. Months.

The average age of the white population living in New York, according to the census, is 23 3
But the average age of all who die there is only . . 20 0

Or an excess of deaths over the ages of the living of more than three years and three months; denoting, if the like excess prevailed from year to year, an increasing pressure of the causes of mortality. If the mortality be the same from year to year the chances of life would appear to be lower in New York than in Dublin, where, according to the data given by the Census Commissioners, it would appear to be 25 years 6 months.

In America little attention and labour appear to have been bestowed in any of the rural districts on general land drainage. Yet nature inflicts terrible punishment for the neglect of the appointed and visible warnings and actual premonitory scourges, amongst which are the mosquitoes and the tribes of insects that only breed in stagnant water and live in its noxious exhalations. The cleansing and the general sanitary condition of the American towns appear to be lower than in England or Scotland, whilst the heat there at times is greater and decomposition more active; pestilence in the shape of yellow fever, ague, and influenza is there more rife, the deaths in proportion to the population more numerous, and the average age of death (so far as there is information) amongst the resident population much lower.

Years. Months.

The average age of the whole of the living population in America, so far as it can be deduced from the returns at the periods given in the census, is only . 22 2

Notwithstanding the earlier marriages, and the extent of emigration, and the general increase of the population, the whole circumstances appear to me to prove this to be the case of a population depressed to this low age chiefly by the greater proportionate pressure of the causes of disease and premature mortality. The proportionate numbers at each interval of age in every 10,000 of the two populations are as follows:—

	United States of America.	England and Wales.
Under 5 years	1744	1324
5 and under 10	1417	1197
10 ,, 15	1210	1089
15 ,, 20	1091	997
20 ,, 30	1816	1780
30 ,, 40	1160	1289
40 ,, 50	732	959
50 ,, 60	436	645
60 ,, 70	245	440
70 ,, 80	113	216
80 ,, 90	32	59
90 and upwards	4	5
	10,000	10,000
Average age of all the living.	22 years 2 months	26 years 7 months.

Here it may be observed, that whilst in England there are 5025 persons between 15 and 50 who have 3610 children or persons under 15; in America there are 4789 persons living between 15 and 50 years of age who have 4371 children dependent upon them. In England there are in every ten thousand persons 1365 who have obtained above 50 years' experience; in America there are are only 830:

The moral consequences of the predominance of the young and passionate in the American community are attested by observers to be such as have already been described in the General Sanitary Report as characteristic of those crowded, filthy, and badly administered districts in England where the average duration of life is short, the proportion of the very young great, and the adult generation transient.

The difference does not arise solely from the greater proportion of children arising from a greater increase of population, though that is to some extent consistent with what has been proved to be the effect of a severe general mortality; the effects of the common cause of depression is observable at each interval of age: the adult population in America is younger than in England, and if the causes of early death were to remain the same, it may be confidently predicted that the American population would remain young for centuries.

	Years.	Months.
The average age of all alive above 15 in America is	33	6
The average age of all alive above 15 years in England and Wales is	37	5
The average age of all above 20 years in America is	37	7
In the whole of England the average of all above 20 years is	41	1

The difference at the different stages of age, appear also to prevail in proportion to the different pressure of the causes of disease and mortality in different districts in England : *e. g.* In the town parishes of Middlesex the average age of the living above 15 years is 35 years and 10 months; but in Hereford it is 39 years and 2 months. In Middlesex the average age of the adult population, that is of all above 20 years, is 38 years and 8 months; whilst in Hereford it is 42 years and 1 month.

The comparative amount of disease and death elsewhere, it need scarcely be said, in no way affects the positive amount of evil in this country, or dispenses with the duty of adopting such practical measures as may be preventive of a single one of the cases of preventible deaths which abound in masses in the large districts having the least unfavourable averages.

The instances have been adduced to exemplify the suggestions of amendment in the mode of measuring the amount and influence of mortality, and more especially to show the importance of giving the average age as well as the numbers of deaths and the average age of the living in each class of the community.

The subsequent district returns and the notes extracted from the reports made by the local registrars to the Registrar-General, in corroboration of the General Sanitary Report, will show the immense importance to the community of the facts that require investigation. It cannot be too urgently repeated that it is only by examinations, case by case, and on the spot, that the facts from which sound principles may be correctly distinguished. They can only be well classed for general conclusions and public use by persons who have large numbers brought before their actual view and consideration, and who have thus brought before them impressively the common circumstances for discrimination, which no hearsay, no ordinary written information will present to their attention. The attainment of this immensely important public service might properly have been submitted as a principal instead of a collateral object, to the improvement of the practice of interment, for the appointment of such a small well qualified agency as that proposed, § 225, of some five or six trustworthy officers of public health for each million of a town population with the requisite powers and responsibilities for ascertaining the actual amount of the preventibl causes of death, and informing the local officers and the public of what is to b done for their removal.

The districts are placed in the order of the average age of death of the whol population during the year 1839, commencing with the highest average.

District	Class	Number of Deaths of each Class.			Deaths from Epidemic.	Average Age at Death of all who die above 21.	Average Age at Death, including Children.	Years' Average premature loss of Life by		Proportionate Number of Deaths to Population.	Exc in Num of Deat abov Healt stand
		Adults.	Children under 10.	Total.				Deaths above Age of 21.	Deaths of all Classes.		
		No.	No.	No.	No.	Years.	Years.	Years.	Years.	No.	No.
Greenwich. Population 80,811.	Gentry	62	18	80	9	62	48	..	..		
	Tradesmen	150	97	247	42	54	31	8	8		
	Artisans, &c.	947	414	1,361	227	56	36	6	3	} 1 in 39	159
	Undescribed	141	110	251	35	58	30	4	9		
	Paupers	109	21	130	17	62	52	..	..		
	Totals and Averages	1,409	660	2,069	330	..	..	..	..	..	
		..	..	..	..	57	36	5	3	..	
	No. of Births 1,780					Age of Living 28				Births 1 in 45	
Camberwell, Population 39,867.	Gentry	58	23	81	11	58	38	4	1		
	Tradesmen	111	86	197	35	54	28	8	11		
	Artisans, &c.	137	134	271	54	51	26	11	13	} 1 in 51	100
	Undescribed	98	37	135	13	61	42	1	..		
	Paupers	92	6	98	7	62	56	..	..		
	Totals and Averages	496	286	782	117	..	..	..	..	..	
		..	..	..	..	57	34	5	5	..	
	No. of Births 709					Age of Living 27·5				Births 1 in 44	
Hackney, Population 42,274.	Gentry	50	11	61	6	61	47	1	..		
	Tradesmen	134	94	228	21	52	29	10	10		
	Artisans, &c.	117	120	237	35	55	27	7	12	} 1 in 56	155
	Undescribed	80	102	182	36	60	25	2	14		
	Paupers	46	4	50	1	67	61	..	..		
	Totals and Averages	427	331	758	99	..	..	..	..	..	..
		..	..	..	..	57	31	5	8	..	..
	No. of Births 995					Age of Living 26·10				Births 1 in 42	
St. George, Hanover Square. Population 66,433.	Gentry	110	28	138	12	59	45	2	..		
	Tradesmen	112	79	191	23	50	29	12	10		
	Artisans, &c.	528	344	872	130	47	27	15	12	} 1 in 50	272
	Undescribed	18	17	35	3	61	32	1	7		
	Paupers	77	12	89	8	59	51	3	..		
	Totals and Averages	845	480	1,325	176	..	..	..	..	..	..
		..	..	..	..	50	31	12	8	..	..
	No of Births 1,260					Age of Living 28·3				Births 1 in 53	

* Mr W. B. Robinson, the Registrar for West Hackney District, describes the condition of the house where the greatest mortality prevails as " bad, with murky superficial gutters within a yard of the fron doors. Supply of water bad, quite insufficient for health, and that only three times a week; cleanliness no prevailing. Shacklewell is, beyond doubt, the most healthy village in the district, or, I may say (afte nearly 30 years' practice here), within the same distance from London (two miles). The only parts of th district that are particularly unhealthy are the streets I have named, together with Hartwell-street, Dalston but all these require three things only to render them not less healthy than the other parts of the neigh bourhood :—1, Proper and effectual drainage, and removal of superficial drains and gutters. 2, A constan supply of water, so as to wash away impurities in the drains, and enable the inhabitants to preserve greater degree of cleanliness, &c. 3, That the houses should be kept in better repair, and frequently lime washed; and the privies should be more frequently emptied, and not allowed to run over; and that an stagnant ditch, within a certain distance from houses, should be covered over."

† Mr. E. Jay, Registrar of Hanover-square District.—Name any particular streets, courts, or houses which from the number of deaths occurring therein, and the nature of the diseases, appear to you to be unhealthy —" I should therefore say that the most unhealthy streets, &c., in my district are Oxford-buildings, Brown.

District	Class	Number of Deaths of each Class.			Deaths from Epidemic.	Average Age at Death of all who die above 21.	Average Age at Death, including Children.	Years' Average premature loss of Life by		Proportionate Number of Deaths to Population.	Excess in Number of Deaths above a Healthy standard.
		Adults.	Children under 10.	Total.				Deaths above Age of 21.	Deaths of all Classes.		
		No.	No.	No.	No.	Years.	Years.	Years.	Years.	No.	No.
Rotherhithe. Population 13,916.	Gentry . .	6	..	6	1	57	49	5	..		
	Tradesmen .	12	2	14	2	50	40	12	..		
	Artisans, &c.	70	14	84	2	51	40	11	..	1 in 41	79*
	Undescribed	78	121	199	50	52	19	10	20		
	Paupers .	33	5	38	3	68	56	..	..		
	Totals and	199	142	341	58	..	..	..	..	..	..
	Averages .	..	..	..	..	54	30	8	9	..	..
		No. of Births	335		Age of Living 26·7			Births 1 in 36			
St. Olave's. Population 18,427.	Gentry . .	4	..	4	..	64	..	..	..		
	Tradesmen	55	46	101	24	48	25	14	14		
	Artisans, &c.	603	215	818	107	43	30	19	9	1 in 19	229†
	Undescribed	5	14	19	7	50	16	12	23		
	Paupers .	47	4	51	8	59	54	3	..		
	Totals and	714	279	993	146	..	..	..	..	..	..
	Averages .	..	..	..	..	45	30	17	9	..	..
		No. of Births	519		Age of Living 27·0			Births 1 in 36			

street, Toms-court, Thomas-street, Grosvenor-market, Grosvenor-mews, George-street, and Hart-street; and to these, perhaps, may be added North-row, and Dolphin-court, and Providence-court, also the north end of Davies-street, adjoining Oxford-street. I have observed small-pox always to exist, when prevalent anywhere, in No. 24, George-street (Grosvenor-square); and much sickness and mortality have occurred in No. 18, Oxford-buildings. Oxford-buildings consist of 18 inhabited houses, containing many wretched families, principally Irish labourers; it was improved lately, in consequence of the exertions of humane individuals, but is still the seat of great poverty and vice. The ventilation here is so bad, that even visiting the houses is a disagreeable duty, from the foul air breathed even for a short space of time. The supply of water is good, and the drainage is reported by those who attend to the subject to be perfect, as it is throughout the parish; but the bad effluvia show that there must be some defect in this point. Three families frequently live in one room, some of the houses containing upwards of 50 persons; many of them live almost entirely on potatoes and herrings, and beer when they can get it. Want of fuel in many cases in winter. Brown-street.—Occupied by the poor and working class; the rooms very small, badly ventilated, and cleansed; the damp kitchens, with frequently stone-floors, are lived and slept in. Living is bad, from the poverty which prevails here. Hart-street.—Many poor families reside here, often in great want. Tolerably well drained. Toms-court.—Contains eight houses; inhabitants in a wretched state in many cases, partly from want of employ, partly from intemperance. Small-pox and epidemics have raged here. George-street.—Some of the houses here are inhabited by working men of a better class, but it also contains others in a wretched condition, in point of cleanliness and ventilation, and much privation is suffered by the inhabitants. Grosvenor-market.—This spot is particularly close, being built almost in *cut de sac*; the houses are dark, badly ventilated, and most unhealthy; the food of some of the poorest principally potatoes; a large slaughter-house situated here adds to its unhealthiness; great want of fuel in winter. Grosvenor-mews.— Here the inhabitants are very thickly crowded, and among the children there is always much mortality; in one house, at the time of taking the census, there were 80 persons. The inhabitants consist of coachmen and their families, as do many of the mews in this district. This class is frequently intemperate; they live over stables, are ignorant of the necessity of free ventilation, and many appear to suffer in consequence. New comers from the country complain of the want of free air, to which they ascribe their deteriorated health. Thomas-street.—Some of the houses in bad condition, and inhabited by the poorest families. No attention to ventilation. Supply of butchers' meat casual and infrequent. Pneumonia and bronchitis are frequently fatal in these poorer districts; and he who enters the damp, dark, underground kitchen, in which all the occupants live and sleep, in which the room is made more close by a fire required for their cooking, the atmosphere is loaded with moisture from wet clothes hung across the narrow space to dry, and probably some child ill of disease, sees that such a state of surrounding circumstances shuts out all chance of recovery in at least the majority of cases."

* Mr. G. Pitt, the Registrar of the Rotherhithe District, states:—" Hanover-street contains about 35 or 40 houses, in a very old and dilapidated state. The houses have generally six or eight rooms each, and sometimes as many families of the poorest kind, chiefly Irish. As the street has no thoroughfare, and is on an incline of at least 10 feet, it is badly drained. The water and filth constantly remaining in the street, it is most unhealthy. The same remarks apply in all respects to Spread Eagle-court, except that the houses stand upon level ground. Norfolk-place and Kenning's-buildings are exposed to the most offensive exhalations of about 150 feet in length of open sewer, which receives the filth of the whole surrounding neighbourhood. Typhus prevailed here at one time to a most serious extent. The persons who occupy the houses above described are labourers, with uncertain employment, and their earnings of course irregular. Their food of the coarsest kind, with habits by no means temperate.

† Mr. W. Stainer, the Registrar of St. Olave District.—In what parts of your district has the number of deaths registered in the years 1838, 1839, 1840, 1841, and 1842 been the greatest, in proportion to the population?—" In the densely populated courts and alleys where there are open drains and sewers, and the inhabitants are living in dirt, stench, and a state of wretchedness to be conceived only by those who have

S

District.	Class.	Number of Deaths of each Class.			Deaths from Epidemic.	Average Age at Death of all who die above 21.	Average Age at Death, including Children.	Years' Average premature loss of Life by		Proportionate Number of Deaths to Population.	Excess in Number of Death above Health standard
		Adults.	Children under 10.	Total.				Deaths above Age of 21.	Deaths of all Classes.		
		No.	No.	No.	No.	Years.	Years.	Years.	Years.	No.	No.
Kensington, (including Chelsea). Population 114,952.	Gentry. .	193	50	243	17	60	45	2	..		
	Tradesmen	204	120	324	33	50	30	12	9		
	Artisans, &c.	559	619	1,178	223	53	24	9	15	1 in 51	58·
	Undescribed	202	181	383	47	58	30	4	9		
	Paupers .	106	36	142	24	61	44	1	..		
	Totals and Averages .	1,264	1,006	2,270	344	.. 55	.. 29	.. 7	.. 10	..	..
		No. of Births 2,782				Age of Living 27·5				Births 1 in 41	
Islington. Population 55,720.	Gentry. .	83	35	118	11	61	42	1	..		
	Tradesmen	151	121	272	43	50	26	12	13		
	Artisans, &c.	177	260	437	108	47	19	15	20	1 in 55	26
	Undescribed	106	27	133	9	61	46	1	..		
	Paupers .	49	10	59	3	60	49	2	..		
	Totals and Averages .	566	453	1,019	174	.. 54	.. 29	.. 8	.. 10	..	..
		No. of Births 1,177				Age of Living 26·11				Births 1 in 47	
St. Martin in the Fields. Population 25,195.	Gentry . .	23	4	27	2	57	46	3	..		
	Tradesmen	60	47	107	22	45	24	17	15		
	Artisans, &c.	165	137	302	82	48	26	14	13	1 in 36	20
	Undescribed	89	112	201	42	51	21	11	18		
	Paupers .	68	4	72	4	65	60	..	..		
	Totals and Averages .	405	304	709	152	.. 52	.. 28	.. 10	.. 11	..	..
		No. of Births 601				Age of Living 28·4				Births 1 in 42	
Poplar. Population 31,091.	Gentry .	16	7	23	2	61	43	1	..		
	Tradesmen	44	40	84	18	51	26	11	13		
	Artisans, &c.	235	240	475	80	53	25	9	14	1 in 47	18
	Undescribed	19	10	29	2	63	36	..	3		
	Paupers .	45	3	48	2	64	53	..	..		
	Totals and Averages .	359	300	659	104	.. 55	.. 28	.. 7	.. 11	..	..
		No. of Births 1,106				Age of Living 25·10				Births 1 in 28	

witnessed it. Prior to the year 1841 several very unhealthy courts existed, in which some of the earlie[r] cases of Asiatic cholera occurred on the first appearance of that disease in the metropolis, but these hav[e] been removed, and the ground now forms the site of the termini of the Brighton and other railways. Ther[e] are large open sewers completely stagnant through or near them, the smell from which in summer is s[o] dreadful that it is extraordinary how human beings can bear it. The supply of water is scanty. Th[e] inhabitants are not more dirty than might be expected from their circumstances."

* Mr. James Pursey, the Registrar of St. Mary, Paddington.—In what parts of your district has the greate[r] number of deaths occurred from small-pox, measles, scarlatina, hooping-cough, diarrhœa, dysentery, choler[a] influenza, or fever (typhus)?—" Kent's-place, Church-place, North-wharf-road, Dudley-street, Green-street. And state generally the condition of those unhealthy streets, courts, and houses, as to drainage, supplie[d] of water, cleanliness.—" There being no sewer, the drainage is bad. A good supply of water may be had proper receptacles were set up. Filthy condition ; Kent's-place particularly ; so much so, that the medic[al] officer stated to me that he intended to write to the guardians thereupon."

Mr. T. W. C. Perfect, the Registrar of St. Peter's, Hammersmith.—" All that part of the district calle[d] Mulberry-hall, consisting of various courts and alleys ; South-street, in an unfinished state ; High-bridge including New-street ; Foundry-yard ; Trafalgar-street and Henrietta-street ; the New-road, and all th[e] houses erected, and now building in Mr. Scott's park. Always damp and aguish."

Mr. W. Larner, the Registrar of the North-west District.—In what parts of your district has the greate[r] number of deaths occurred from small-pox, measles, scarlatina, hooping cough, diarrhœa, dysentery, choler[a] influenza, or fever (typhus)?—" Chelsea Workhouse, Leader-street, Oakham street, Little College-stree[t]

District	Class	Number of Deaths of each Class.			Deaths from Epidemic.	Average Age at Death of all who die above 21.	Average Age at Death, including Children	Years' Average premature loss of Life by		Proportionate Number of Deaths to Population.	Excess in Number of Deaths above a Healthy standard.
		Adults.	Children under 10.	Total.				Deaths above Age of 21.	Deaths of all Classes.		
		No.	No.	No.	No.	Years.	Years.	Years.	Years.	No.	No.
Marylebone. Population 137,955.	Gentry . .	156	40	196	20	59	46	3	..	} 1 in 45	857*
	Tradesmen	198	172	370	57	51	27	11	12		
	Artisans, &c.	682	759	1,441	251	48	23	14	16		
	Undescribed	347	324	671	104	54	27	8	12		
	Paupers .	288	73	361	61	54	42	8	..		
	Totals and Averages .	1,671	668	3,039	493	.. 52	.. 28	.. 10	.. 11	..	..
	No. of Births 3,511					Age of Living 27·9				Births 1 in 39	
Stepney. Population 90,657.	Gentry . .	64	9	73	3	65	56	..	..	} 1 in 41	620†
	Tradesmen	169	104	273	47	53	31	9	8		
	Artisans, &c.	568	591	1,159	247	48	23	14	16		
	Undescribed	203	274	477	101	56	22	6	17		
	Paupers .	189	28	217	28	63	54	..	..		
	Totals and Averages .	1,193	1,006	2,199	426	.. 53	.. 28	.. 9	.. 11	..	..
	No. of Births 2,502					Age of Living 26·6				Births 1 in 36	
St. Mary, Newington. Population 54,607.	Gentry . .	79	13	92	6	62	50	..	..	} 1 in 46	338
	Tradesmen	75	64	139	23	50	26	12	13		
	Artisans, &c.	325	420	745	162	52	22	10	17		
	Undescribed	75	76	151	31	59	30	3	9		
	Paupers .	64	6	70	1	60	55	2	..		
	Totals and Averages .	618	579	1,197	223	.. 55	.. 28	.. 7	.. 11	..	..
	No. of Births 1,620					Age of Living 26·8				Births 1 in 34	

Arthur-street, and Britton-street. The above streets are not supplied with sewers to drain the surface, and, consequently, the waste water of the houses is carried away by cesspools on the respective premises attached to each house. Generally supplied by water being laid on from the Chelsea Water-works Company. In general, a want of cleanliness. According to the returns on taking the census in 1841, it was found to be the case that very many of the houses in the above-mentioned streets (principal of which are only four-roomed houses) contained 10, 12, and in some cases more persons; therefore, it may be inferred from those returns it oftentimes occurs that three, four, and frequently more, sleep in the same rooms in these streets."

* Mr. Edward Joseph, the Registrar of the Rectory District, states :—" Calmell-buildings, to which I allude, is a narrow court, being about 22 feet in breadth; the houses are three stories high, surrounded and over-topped by the adjacent buildings; the drainage is carried on by a common sewer running down the centre of the court, the receptacle for slops, &c. from the houses on both sides; the lower apartments, especially the kitchens, which are under ground, are damp and badly ventilated, light and air being admitted through a grating on a level with the court. At all times, but especially so in warm weather, a most offensive effluvia is perceptible everywhere. The houses are 26 in number, and rented at about 20l. to 30l. per annum; each contains 10 rooms, which the renters of houses let out to families or individuals, who in their turn in many instances receive as lodgers those who are unable to bear the expenses of a room; by such means an immense per centage is added to the original rent. According to last year's census, the number of inhabitants in this court was 944, of whom 426 were males, 518 females; of this number, 178 were children under 7 years of age; 200 from 7 to 20 years; 459 from 20 to 45; and 189 from 45 years and upwards. The number of persons in one house varied from 2 to 70. Males employed, 261; females, 163. Total number of the working population 424, leaving 520 without occupation; the greater part of these were children and old persons, dependent upon parochial relief and the assistance of others. The following is a statement of the comparative mortality in different parts of the houses, as it occurred during the past year :—In the kitchens, 1 in 13; parlours, 1 in 37; first floor, 1 in 30; second floor, 1 in 33; attics, 1 in 12."

† Mr. A. Barnett, the Registrar of the Limehouse District.—In what parts of your district has the number of deaths registered in the years 1838, 1839, 1840, 1841, and 1842, been the greatest in proportion to the population?—" In those parts of my district in which there exists the greatest amount of distress, namely, the want of food, of firing, of water, also of cleanliness, both of person and habitation, and, I may add, of the district generally; as examples, may be mentioned the districts surrounding Jamaica-place, Salmon's-lane, Eastfield-street, Limehouse-causeway, Three-colt-street, and the Tile-yard." And state generally the condition of those unhealthy streets, courts, and houses, as to drainage, supplies of water, and cleanliness.—" The drainage is frequently altogether wanting, in most cases very imperfect; the supply of water insufficient, and want of cleanliness very apparent."

Mr. T. Barnes, the Registrar of the Shadwell District.—In what parts of your district has the number of

District	Class	Number of Deaths of each Class.			Deaths from Epidemic.	Average Age at Death of all who die above 21.	Average Age at Death, including Children.	Years' Average premature loss of Life by		Proportionate Number of Deaths to Population.	Excess in Number of Death above Health standard
		Adults.	Children under 10.	Total.				Deaths above Age of 21.	Deaths of all Classes.		
St. Pancras. Population 129,711.		No.	No.	No.	No.	Years.	Years.	Years.	Years.	No.	No.
	Gentry . .	151	49	200	15	61	45	1	..	⎫	
	Tradesmen	349	286	635	108	50	27	12	12	⎬ 1 in 43	93.
	Artisans, &c.	622	674	1,296	237	47	22	15	17	⎬	
	Undescribed	269	354	623	199	55	23	7	16	⎭	
	Paupers .	232	49	281	47	61	50	1	..		
	Totals and Averages .	1,623	1,412	3,035	656	..	..	..	..	..	..
		..	..	..	..	53	27	9	12	..	
	No. of Births 3,264			Age of Living 26·10					Births 1 in 40		
West London. Population 33,629.	Gentry . .	12	4	16	2	53	38	4	1	⎫	
	Tradesmen	83	103	186	41	49	22	13	17	⎬	
	Artisans. &c.	393	381	774	186	46	22	16	17	⎬ 1 in 27	387
	Undescribed	149	17	166	23	47	38	15	1	⎭	
	Paupers .	99	16	115	26	64	55	..	...		
	Totals and Averages .	736	521	1,257	278	..	..	..	..	..	..
		..	..	..	..	49	27	13	12	..	
	No. of Births 698			Age of Living 27·7					Births 1 in 48		

deaths registered in the years 1838, 1839, 1840, 1841, and 1842, been the greatest in proportion to th population?—" New Gravel-lane, and the several courts and alleys communicating therewith, Angel gardens, New-street, and Labour-in-vain-street, Shadwell; Red Lion-street (including the workhouse) Upper Well-alley, Cross-alley, and Upper Gun-alley, Wapping. The drainage is bad; the supplies o water are insufficient. In these parts of the district the density of population is great. In many cases whole family, consisting of seven or eight persons, sleep in the same room."

* Mr. Worrell, the Registrar of the Gray's Inn-lane District :—" To ascertain and compare the healthy with the unhealthy parts of my district, I have placed against each street the whole number of deaths from al causes during the last five years. I have taken the number of deaths from a population of 5000, resident in what I consider healthy streets ; and I have also taken the number of deaths from a population of 5000 resident in streets which I consider unhealthy. The 5000 occupying the best houses are composed of mer chants, professional gentlemen, and the richer class of tradesmen ; they occupy 728 houses, containing about 7800 good rooms ; the streets are wide, well drained, and have a plentiful supply of water. The 5000 occupying the unhealthy streets are composed of the lower class of tradesmen, journeymen mechanics, la hourers, and costermongers ; they occupy 434 houses, containing about 2800 rooms, the best of which are little better than the worst of the 7800 before mentioned ; the streets are .mostly confined, the drains in a bad state, and in many places the accumulation of filth renders the atmosphere foul, whilst the supply o water is not very good. The number of deaths which I find in the healthy streets during five years. amongst a population of 5000, amounts to 325 ; and, during the same period, amongst 5000 occupying the unhealthy streets I find 613. No doubt many of the residents in the best houses go into the country, with the view of benefiting their health, and there die ; but certain it is that many more of the poorer classes die in the workhouses and hospitals—so that, no doubt, amongst a certain number of poor, at least two deaths occur to one amongst the same number of rich. Having been a collector of rates upwards of 25 years, and, as a house agent, having had much to do with the letting of houses, I am thoroughly acquainted with the neighbourhood ; and, having taken an active part in collecting and distributing voluntary contri. butions in times of distress and severe weather, I have been enabled to judge of the condition of the poor and their habitations, and I have always observed that sickness prevails much more in places where sewers and drains are bad,than in other parts where the inhabitants are equally poor, but have more wholesome houses to live in. Any suggestion here as to remedy may, probably, be considered out of place, but, having had much experience as a Commissioner of Pavements, as well as in several offices of local manage. ment during the last 25 years, and having given much attention to the subject (an evil which, in my opinion, affects the metropolis to an extent little imagined), I have no doubt as to the means of remedy, and improvement in the local administration being perfectly easy and effectual."

" In another classification he arranges, from descriptions of streets with nearly equal population, the highest in each class ; the relative proportions, and average ages of deaths, are ascertained to be as fol. lows :—

	Population.	Deaths.	Average Age of Death.
Class 1	1432	97	35
Class 2	1165	119	32
Class 3	1448	157	25
Class 4	1386	200	21

" The above statement proves that, out of a population of 1432 occupying the best houses, 95 deaths oc. curred within five years, 29 of which, at and under five years of age ; and that out of a population of 1386, occupying the worst houses, the whole number of deaths are one hundred and eighty-nine, one hundred and four of which at and under five vears of age."

† Mr. F. Hutchinson, the Registrar of the South District :—State generally the condition of those un. healthy streets, courts, and houses, as to drainage, supplies of water, cleanliness,—" The drainage of all or

District	Class	Number of Deaths of each Class.			Deaths from Epidemic.	Average Age at Death of all who die above 21.	Average Age at Death, including Children.	Years' Average premature loss of Life by		Proportionate Number of Deaths to Population.	Excess in Number of Deaths above a Healthy standard
		Adults.	Children under 10.	Total.				Deaths above Age of 21.	Deaths of all Classes.		
		No.	No.	No.	No.	Years.	Years.	Years.	Years	No.	No.
Whitechapel. Population 71,753.	Gentry	17	4	21	..	58	47	4	..	} 1 in 31	768
	Tradesmen	142	130	272	42	50	26	12	13		
	Artisans, &c.	741	637	1,378	261	48	25	14	14		
	Undescribed	116	313	429	107	58	16	4	23		
	Paupers	166	37	203	38	63	51	..	..		
	Totals and Averages	1,182	1,121	2,303	448	..	..	..	..	..	..
		..	..	..	..	51	26	11	13	..	..
	No. of Births 2,103					Age of Living 26·2				Births 1 in 34	
St. James, West-minster. Population 37,407.	Gentry	27	9	36	1	57	42	5	..	} 1 in 50	251
	Tradesmen	68	66	134	23	51	26	11	13		
	Artisans, &c.	161	190	351	59	46	21	16	18		
	Undescribed	52	83	135	28	52	20	10	19		
	Paupers	81	15	96	7	58	49	4	..		
	Totals and Averages	389	363	752	118	..	..	..	..	..	..
		..	..	..	....	51	26	11	13	..	..
	No. of Births 844					Age of Living 28·2				Births 1 in 44	
East London. Population 39,655.	Gentry	14	3	17	..	63	50	..	..	} 1 in 36	372
	Tradesmen	134	164	298	76	53	23	9	16		
	Artisans, &c.	265	391	656	145	51	21	11	18		
	Undescribed	36	10	46	1	50	38	12	1		
	Paupers	87	11	98	18	65	57	..	..		
	Totals and Averages	536	579	1,115	240	..	..	..	..	..	..
		..	..	..	..	54	26	8	13	..	..
	No. of Births 1,235					Age of Living 27.0				Births 1 in 32	
Holborn. Population 39,720.	Gentry	36	9	45	3	58	47	4	..	} 1 in 36	367
	Tradesmen	144	164	308	75	52	24	10	15		
	Artisans, &c.	231	353	584	149	50	19	12	20		
	Undescribed	21	6	27	2	54	41	8	..		
	Paupers	105	32	137	35	60	46	2	..		
	Totals and Averages	537	564	1,101	264	..	..	..	..	..	..
		..	..	..	..	53	26	9	13	..	..
	No. of Births 969					Age of Living 27·2				Births 1 in 41	

most of these courts and houses is exceedingly defective. About a year ago, for instance, I thought it my duty to complain to the local authorities respecting a privy in Hanging-sword-alley, that had been full for a great length of time, and could not have been used, but for a hole just below the seat, by means of which the fluid contents flowed into the open gutter. The effluvia from these houses arising from the defective state of the drains is most offensive. In some houses there are only cesspools in the cellars, which are emptied only once in from six months to three years. Water is supplied from the New River three times a-week for about two hours. In many of the houses, water-pipes have never been laid down, and in others the Company have stopped the supplies, in consequence of non-payment. Some of these places, and in particular Plumtree-court, are in a most filthy state. Offal, accumulations of dirt, and the refuse of vegetables, &c. lying in the gutters. The houses are generally remarkable for their dirty and uncomfortable appearance, and are mostly without any proper receptacle for dirt and ashes. The population is very dense; 15 to 20, and, I am informed, sometimes 30 persons, inhabiting one house, consisting of six rooms. The general condition of the population is very bad, particularly as regards the women and children, who are more confined to these localities than the men, the latter being generally employed elsewhere during the day-time. Many of the persons renting these houses suffer in pocket by letting lodgings to parties who never pay; and in health, by thus crowding their families, so as to induce disease and infectious disorders."

* Mr. C. H. Rich, the Registrar of the Mile End New Town District, observes :—" With reference as to the healthy and unhealthy streets in my district, I have been carefully through my books, and I cannot particularize any one place more than another. The drainage is very bad; the hamlet is drained principally by surface drainage, which empties itself into a ditch which is uncovered. It runs along the north side of the

District	Class	Number of Deaths of each Class			Deaths from Epidemic	Average Age at Death of all who die above 21	Average Age at Death, including Children	Years' Average premature loss of Life by		Proportionate Number of Deaths to Population	Exce in Num of Deat above Healt stand:
		Adults	Children under 10	Total				Deaths above Age of 21	Deaths of all Classes		
		No.	No.	No.	No.	Years.	Years.	Years.	Years.	No.	No.
Shoreditch. Population 83,552.	Gentry. .	63	23	86	14	65	47	..	..		No.
	Tradesmen	153	150	303	63	47	23	15	16		
	Artisans, &c.	498	802	1,300	271	51	19	11	20	} 1 in 38	73
	Undescribed	150	75	225	34	57	37	5	2		
	Paupers .	234	49	283	56	57	46	5	..		
	Totals and Averages .	1,098	1,099	2,197	438	..	..	..	..	..	
		..	..	..	..	54	26	8	13	..	
	No. of Births 3,058					Age of Living	26			Births 1 in 27	
City of London. Population 55,967.	Gentry. .	32	12	44	3	63	43	..	..		
	Tradesmen	247	244	491	84	48	23	14	16		
	Artisans, &c.	213	270	483	94	50	22	12	17	} 1 in 50	40
	Undescribed	77	29	106	15	58	39	4	..		
	Paupers .	..	..	..	..	..	..	..	..		
	Totals and Averages .	569	555	1,124	196	..	..	..	..	..	
		..	..	..	..	51	25	11	14	..	
	No. of Births 1,210					Age of Living 27·7				Births 1 in 46	
St. John & St. Margaret, Westminster. Population 56,718.	Gentry. .	37	14	51	9	55	42	7	..		
	Tradesmen	82	102	184	47	46	20	16	19		
	Artisans, &c.	458	581	1039	264	48	21	14	18	} 1 in 39	52·
	Undescribed	38	24	62	9	56	49	6	..		
	Paupers .	97	19	116	17	57	46	5	..		
	Totals and Averages .	712	740	1,452	346	..	..	..	..	..	..
		..	..	..	..	50	25	12	14	..	..
	No. of Births 1,730					Age of Living 26·11				Births 1 in 33	

hamlet, which makes it very unwholesome; there has, within the last three years, been a sewer made (do\
High-street and Well-street), which has much improved that part of the district. The hamlet has been mu
improved within the last four years as regards the paving of several of the streets which were in a most filtl
state; they are now under the commission. If Luke-street and Underwood-street, which contain about
houses in each street, were paved, it would be a great improvement, and no doubt beneficial to health. F
want of proper sewerage, the health of the hamlet is generally bad."

* Mr. N. Bowring, the Registrar of the district Haggerstone West, specifies as the seats of the greatest mo
tality,—"Philips-street, Edward-street, Mill-row, Wilmer-gardens, and the upper part of Hoxton O
Town (east side), in which the principal diseases are typhus-fever, consumption, inflammation of th
lungs, and scarlatina. Two of those places mentioned above, namely, Mill-row and Wilmer-garden
are without drainage; but at the back of the west end of Philips-street, south side of Edward-street, and
the back of the upper end of Hoxton Old Town, is an open ditch, almost a dead level, in which filth
every description is thrown. I believe it is under the management of the Commissioners of Sewers, bi
is seldom cleaned out; the stench emitted, particularly in the summer months, is almost intolerabl
and is considered by the inhabitants as the sole cause of much illness and death. Drainage very deficien
Water supplied three times a-week. The people generally of cleanly habits."

† Mr. George Pearse, the Registrar for the St. John the Evangelist District, thus describes the condition
the places in the lower districts, where the greatest mortality occurs :—"Great Peter-street, Perkin's rent
Duck-lane, and Old Pye-street, are the most densely populated in the district. The houses in Great Pete
street, for the most part, are very old, irregular, and uncleanly. Occupied by tradesmen and small sho
keepers, together with labourers, mechanics, and others of uncertain earnings. The houses in the other thr
streets are often occupied by 10 or 12 persons in one room, most of them of the lowest grade in society, suc
as mendicants, hawkers, costermongers, lodging-house-keepers, thieves, and abandoned females of irregula
and intemperate habits. Their food chiefly consists of salt-fish and other scraps, collected by the mendican
and disposed of to the general dealers. The houses are, for the most part, very low, filthy, and dilapidate
badly drained, and indifferently supplied with water. There are other unwholesome nuisances arisin
from the collecting and boiling bones, soap, and tallow, &c. Holland-street, Medway-street, Marlboroug
place, New Peter-street, with several other avenues, surrounding an extensive waste (formerly the site
Marlborough-square) oftentimes nearly covered with stagnant water. The houses are small, very dirt
and dilapidated, low in situation, without any drainage, having stagnant waters back and front; some i
the occupation of the labouring class, and laundresses low in the scale, irregular in their earnings an
habits. Many cases of typhoid fever have occurred here, and several recently. Rochester-row, Strattor
ground, and Artillery-square, are thickly populated by tradesmen of all kinds and others; they are withou
sewerage or proper drainage; the first having an open ditch through the centre for the greater part; an

District	Class	Number of Deaths of each Class.			Deaths from Epidemic.	Average Age at Death of all who die above 21.	Average Age at Death, including Children.	Years' Average premature loss of Life by		Proportionate Number of Deaths to Population.	Excess in Number of Deaths above a Healthy standard
		Adults.	Children under 10.	Total.				Deaths above Age of 21.	Deaths of all Classes.		
		No.	No.	No.	No.	Years.	Years.	Years.	Years.	No.	No.
St. James, Clerkenwell. Population 56,709.	Gentry . .	52	15	67	8	60	46	2	..	} 1 in 43	474
	Tradesmen.	99	109	208	50	49	23	13	16		
	Artisans, &c.	324	533	857	183	50	19	12	20		
	Undescribed	82	17	99	6	59	44	3	..		
	Paupers .	76	14	90	2	60	50	2	..		
	Totals and Averages .	633	688	1,321	249	..	..	..	..	..	..
		..	..	..	..	53	25	9	14	..	..
	No. of Births 1,771					Age of Living 25·11				Births 1 in 32	
St. George in the East. Population 41,351.	Gentry . .	18	3	21	..	63	54	..	..	} 1 in 36	408
	Tradesmen	66	72	138	29	49	23	13	16		
	Artisans, &c.	313	481	794	158	. 46	18	16	12		
	Undescribed	62	14	76	3	60	46 .	2	..		
	Paupers .	93	14	107	14	61	52	1	..		
	Totals and Averages .	552	584	1,136	204	..	..	..	..	..	..
		..	..	..	..	51	25	11	14	..	..
	No. of Births 1,404					Age of Living 26·6				Births 1 in 29	
St. Giles and St. George. Population 54,250.	Gentry . .	66	32	98	15	60	40	2	..	} 1 in 36	528
	Tradesmen	119	114	233	44	52	26	10	13		
	Artisans, &c.	280	584	864	221	51	17	11	22		
	Undescribed	42	20	62	9	53	35	9	4		
	Paupers .	208	34	242	53	54	46	8	..		
	Totals and Averages .	715	784	1,499	342	..	..	..	..	..	..
		..	..	..	..	53	25 .	9	14	..	..
	No. of Births 1,622					Age of Living 27·9				Births 1 in 33	

the occupiers of the latter are under the necessity of pumping out into the open street (generally at night) the offensive water that collects in the cesspools within their dwellings. Part of Vauxhall-bridge-road, which is contiguous to Douglas-street, Bentinck-street and place, with sundry other small streets or places communicating with them on the one side, and Upper and Lower Garden-street, with Dean's-place, on the other. The houses are small and numerous; inhabited by labourers, laundresses, costermongers, and others; without proper drainage, having open ditches and stagnant waters in their vicinity. Typbus and scarlatina have been frequent here, and several deaths therefrom have occurred within the last few weeks. In Causton-street the houses are small, populous, with courts or places occupied by labourers generally, and an open ditch in front. Ship-court, with Cottage-place, is situated very low; composed of small, ill-ventilated, dirty, dilapidated houses; thickly inhabited by labourers and others of very low and irregular earnings and habits; adjoining several large dilapidated premises, with extensive wastes or yards used as pig and cow-yards, or for the purpose of collecting slop-soil and other filth, left evaporating in the open air, without sewerage or proper drainage. Vine-street, with Champion's-alley, York-buildings in Grub-street, on one side, and Scott's-rents on the other, for the most part are small old houses, peopled by the labouring classes, with bad drainage, and the wharfs in Millbank-street, for the deposit of slop-soil and other nuisance."

* Mr. J. Verrall, the Registrar of the St. John's District.—" The following places appear to me to be unhealthy from the absence of all habit of cleanliness in most of the inhabitants; the want of drainage; the ruinous condition of the houses; the number of lay-stalls, in which filth of all kinds is accumulated, and the number of pigs kept in the neighbourhood,—King-street, Queen-street, Gold-street, Ship-street, Hilliard's-court, and Pruson's island. In the following places (in addition to the foregoing) the houses appear unhealthily crowded and very dirty, with inadequate means of ventilation, namely, Church's-gardens, New-court, Crown-place, Miner-court, Macord's-rents, Ellis-court, Petrie-court, Hampton-court, Rycroft's-court, and Matthew's-court.

† Mr. George Lee, the Registrar of the St. Giles' South District reports generally, as to the condition of the worst parts of the district, that they are characterized by insufficient drainage, indifferent supply of water, cleanliness neglected.

Mr. John Yardley, Registrar of St. George, Bloomsbury District.—" They are places without a thorough-fare to (two of them are built many feet below the surface of the street adjoining), and surrounded with houses of much greater height." .

District.	Class.	Number of Deaths of each Class.			Deaths from Epidemic.	Average Age at Death of all who die above 21.	Average Age at Death, including Children.	Years' Average premature loss of Life by		Proportionate Number of Deaths to Population.	Excess in Numb[er] of Death above Health standa[rd]
		Adults.	Children under 10.	Total.				Deaths above Age of 21.	Deaths of all Classes.		
Strand. Population 43,894.		No.	No.	No.	No.	Years.	Years.	Years.	Years.	No.	No.
	Gentry . .	47	21	68	8	59	40	3	..		
	Tradesmen	129	132	261	58	51	25	11	14		
	Artisans, &c.	299	382	681	178	48	21	14	18	1 in 41	41.
	Undescribed	26	19	45	4	55	28	7	11		
	Paupers .	15	5	20	..	65	49	..	..		
	Totals and Averages .	516	559	1075	248	..	..	..	..	..	..
		..	..	..	..	51	24	11	15	..	..
	No. of Births 957				Age of Living 27·3			Births 1 in 46			
Lambeth. Population 115,833.	Gentry . .	141	64	205	19	58	37	4	2		
	Tradesmen	340	452	792	174	50	21	12	18		
	Artisans, &c.	452	704	1,156	245	49	19	13	20	1 in 46	97[?]
	Undescribed	113	68	181	27	59	35	3	4		
	Paupers .	173	38	211	37	56	44	6	..		
	Totals and Averages .	1,219	1,326	2,545	502	..	..	..	..	..	..
		..	..	..	..	52	24	10	15	..	..
	No. of Births 3,782				Age of Living 26·2			Births 1 in 31			
St. George, Southwark. Population 46,622.	Gentry . .	32	9	41	5	61	45	1	..		
	Tradesmen	66	53	119	18	54	30	8	9		
	Artisans, &c.	371	591	962	248	53	20	9	19	1 in 39	49[?]
	Undescribed	35	15	50	10	50	30	12	9		
	Paupers .	22	6	28	2	58	45	4	..		
	Totals and Averages .	526	674	1,200	283	..	..	..	..	..	..
		..	..	..	..	53	23	9	16	..	..
	No. of Births 1,574				Age of Living 26·5			Births 1 in 30			

* Mr. W. Fitch, the Registrar of the St. Clement Danes' District, describes the houses of the lower classe[s] as excessively crowded.—" The number of persons sleeping in the same rooms are generally the whol[e] family, from two to six persons, and often more. I beg to observe, that where persons occupy different room[s] in one house they are generally very particular in keeping the doors of their rooms closed for the purpos[e] of preventing others passing up and down stairs overlooking their abode, thereby causing a very great chec[k] to ventilation. Washing clothes, and placing them to dry in the rooms during the night, is another incon[-] venience the wretchedly poor are labouring under in many parts of my district, and this to a great extent.

† Mr. C. Mears, Registrar of Waterloo-road, No. 1 District.—In what parts of your district has the numbe[r] of deaths registered in the years 1838, 1839, 1840, 1841, and 1842 been the greatest in proportion to th[e] population ?—" In the undermentioned parts :— Whitehorse-street, Wootton-street, Windmill-stree[t] Windmill-row, Little Windmill-street, and courts, Isabella-place, Broadwall, Cornwall-road and plac[e] Cottage-place, Commercial-road, Bond-place and Commercial-buildings, Princes-court, Eaton-street, Brad[-] street, Roupell-street, New-street, Mitre-place, John-street, Salutation-place." And state generally th[e] condition of those unhealthy streets, courts, and houses, as to drainage, supplies of water, cleanliness. " In the above places there is very imperfect drainage ; very few have any communication with the sewer[s] The houses have cesspools, and the water runs to waste and settles on the surface, leaving the lower part of the houses damp. Supplies of water tolerably good ; cleanliness, indifferent."

Mr. J. Green, Registrar of Waterloo-road, No. 2.—In what parts of your district has the greatest number [of] deaths occurred from small-pox, measles, scarlatina, hooping-cough, diarrhœa, dysentery, cholera, influenz[a] or fever (typhus) ?—" Juston-street, Hooper-street, Whiting-street, Apollo-buildings, courts and street adjacent, Charles-street, Harriot-street, Frazier-street, Lucretia-street, James-street, Barnes-terrace, Granb[y] place and Granby gardens, Burdett-street, Francis-street." And state generally the condition of thos[e] unhealthy streets, courts, and houses, as to drainage, supplies of water, cleanliness.—" In the above-name[d] streets the drainage is very imperfect, and much filthy water is thrown often into the streets. A plentifu[l] supply of water. Many pay but little attention to cleanliness. Densely populated. In many houses fro[m] four to eight or nine in one room.

‡ Mr. R. Bell, the Registrar of the Kent-road District :—In what parts of your district has the number [of] deaths registered in the years 1838, 1839, 1840, 1841, and 1842 been the greatest in proportion to the popu[-] lation ?—" There are many close, filthy courts in this district ; in these, the deaths are uniformly the highest and the local registration does not correctly show this fact, for the people inhabiting them are very poor, an[d] in extreme illness are often removed either to the workhouse or the hospitals, and they die in those places. And state generally the condition of those unhealthy streets, courts, and houses as to drainage, supplies o[f] water, cleanliness ?—" Drainage,—open gutters choked, and pits of stagnant water. Supplies of water—goo[d]

District	Class	Number of Deaths of each Class.			Deaths from Epidemic.	Average Age at Death of all who die above 21.	Average Age at Death, including Children.	Years' Average premature loss of Life by		Proportionate Number of Deaths to Population.	Excess in Number of Deaths above a Healthy standard.
		Adults.	Children under 10.	Total.				Deaths above Age of 21.	Deaths of all Classes.		
		No.	No.	No.	No.	Years.	Years.	Years.	Years.	No.	No.
St. Luke. Population 49,982.	Gentry . .	21	6	27	3	56	38	6	1		
	Tradesmen .	62	52	114	17	49	25	13	14		
	Artisans. &c.	391	569	960	306	49	20	13	19	} 1 in 40	538
	Undescribed	85	49	134	17	58	35	4	4		
	Paupers .	..	..	..	..	..	..	..	..		
	Totals and Averages .	559	676	1,235	343	.. ..	.. 50	.. 12	.. 17	..	..
							22				

No. of Births 2,271   Age of Living 25·11   Births 1 in 22

Bermondsey. Population 34,847.	Gentry. .	3	5	8	...	51	20	11	19		
	Tradesmen	66	59	125	16	48	25	14	14		
	Artisans, &c.	202	373	575	144	51	18	11	21	} 1 in 42	364*
	Undescribed	24	26	50	6	45	21	17	18		
	Paupers .	62	14	76	15	57	47	5	..		
	Totals and Averages .	357	477	834	181	.. 51	.. 22	.. 11	.. 17	..	..

No. of Births 1,151   Age of Living 24·7   Births 1 in 30

Bethnal Green. Population 74,087.	Gentry. .	39	11	50	4	61	46	1	..		
	Tradesmen	110	136	246	56	53	24	9	15		
	Artisans, &c.	468	874	1,342	369	51	18	11	21	} 1 in 41	794†
	Undescribed	69	19	88	6	57	44	5	..		
	Paupers .	76	19	95	19	65	49	..	..		
	Totals and Averages .	762	1,059	1,821	454	.. 54	.. 22	.. 8	.. 17	..	..

No. of Births 2,674   Age of Living 25·2   Births 1 in 28.

supply from water-works. Cleanliness—as a general rule they seldom attend to this, unless they expect a visit from the medical or other officers: they excuse it by stating that they have to work for their living. The people live very close in small rooms; have often more than one bed in a room. Beds are made of straw and shavings to sleep on, and a great number sleep on the floor; from three to ten persons in a room; almost every room is a sleeping-room."

Mr. J. Bedwell, the Registrar of the Borough-road District :—In what parts of your district has the number of deaths registered in the years 1838, 1839, 1840, 1841, and 1842 been the greatest in proportion to the population ?—" My district, formerly nearly a square, bounded on the west by about 50 houses in Blackfriars-road ; on the south, by about 70, in the Borough road ; on the east, by about the same number in Blackman-street, and partly on the north by Wellington-street ; I find the greatest number of deaths in proportion to the population in the small streets within the above quadrangle. Drainage very deficient; supply of water plentiful ; cleanliness little attended to by a great number. The density of population extreme. Small houses with a family in each room. We have lodging-houses in the Mint where from 50 to 150 sleep nightly ; 10 large beds in one room in some of them."

* Mr. J. Paul, the Registrar of St. James's District.—In what parts of your district has the greatest number of deaths occurred from small-pox, measles, scarlatina, hooping-cough, diarrhœa, dysentery, cholera, influenza, or fever (typhus)? And in what parts have epidemic diseases been most fatal ?—" I do not know. Neither small-pox, scarlatina, measles, hooping-cough, diarrhœa, nor influenza has been peculiarly localized. My experience of a longer date as surgeon to the poor of the district leads me to believe that cholera, dysentery, and typhus fever have been more prevalent in London-street and its vicinity, and the Tar-yard In both these places drainage is bad ; and the inhabitants of the former locality obtain their supply of water from a running ditch—a common receptacle for everything, where a hundred cloacinæ empty themselves. Drainage is bad in many parts of the district ; lots of small houses are built ; streets of a better description unfinished ; their proprietors, who look only to the cash returns, pay little attention to the drainage or cleanliness. There appears to be no remedy for these calamities. The supply of water is now pretty good."

† Mr. George Reynolds, the Registrar of the Church District, in answer to the question, In what parts of your district has the number of deaths registered in the years 1838, 1839, 1840, 1841, and 1842 been the greatest in proportion to the population ? states. " In Beckford-row, Elliot-row, Alfred-place, Camden-gardens, Pitt-street, Pott-street, Camden-street, Wolverley-street, New York-street, and Punderson-gardens." And state generally the condition of those unhealthy streets, courts, and houses, as to drainage, supplies of water, cleanliness.—" The places I have named are entirely without drainage. Supply of water, one hand-cock to many houses. Cleanliness, great want of." Name any particular streets or parts which, according to the facts that have fallen under your notice, appear to you to be healthy, and with reference to the points adverted to in the preceding question, compare the healthy with the unhealthy portions of your district.—" My

District.	Class.	Number of Deaths of each Class.			Deaths from Epidemic.	Average Age at Death of all who die above 21.	Average Age at Death, including Children.	Years' Average premature loss of Life by		Proportionate Number of Deaths to Population.	Excess in Number of Deaths' above a Healthy standard.
		Adults.	Children under 10.	Total.				Deaths above Age of 21.	Deaths of all Classes.		
		No.	No.	No.	No.	Years.	Years.	Years.	Years.	No.	No.
St. Saviour's. Population 32,980.	Gentry . .	9	1	10	1	52	47	10	..		
	Tradesmen	45	43	88	17	52	26	10	13		
	Artisans, &c.	250	248	498	93	45	22	17	17	1 in 36	422
	Undescribed	89	198	287	65	51	15	11	24		
	Paupers .	23	9	32	4	59	40	3	..		
	Totals and Averages .	416	499	915	180	..	..	..	..	..	..
		..	..			48	21	14	18	..	..

No. of Births 1,145   Age of Living 27·3   Births 1 in 29

entire district, I think, would be in a much more healthy condition had we efficient drainage ; instead of which, even this, the main road of the parish, is without a sewer, notwithstanding the Commissioners of Sewers have been repeatedly memorialized, and the following fact brought under their notice, that the cellars of the houses do not extend to the depth of 3 feet 6 inches below the level of the carriage-road, and yet there is an average of 18 inches of water during the greater part of the winter season, that many persons are obliged to use the pump for many hours daily to preserve their property." He gives the following letter from a medical officer of great experience :—

"289, Bethnal-green-road, October 31st, 1842.

" Dear Reynolds,—As you are aware, I have attended many of the inhabitants of this road and its vicinity, and I do not hesitate to say that many of their diseases are to be attributed entirely to the want of drainage. They are—1st, febrile diseases ; 2nd, diseases of the respiratory organs ; 3rd, nervous diseases ; 4th, diseases of the digestive organs ; and lastly, cachectic diseases. Of the first kind, the very numerous cases of fever in the undrained districts that occur shortly after the autumnal. rains, I take in the light of cause and effect. Rheumatism (acute and chronic) are the result of sleeping in houses the walls of which absorb the surface water and elevate it by capillary attraction to the height of two or three feet. The diseases of the respiratory and digestive organs are above the average number, and are attributable to the same cause. The nervous diseases I attribute to the poisonous gases exhaled from putrifying matter. They are—1st, epilepsy. In two families this disease attacked every one of the younger branches of the family, and they were cured by removal to another district. Many cases of spasm of a particular muscle, as one or two of the muscles of the face, the large muscle in front of the neck, and even some of the muscles of the arm ; also frequent cases of the most inveterate hysteria, have been temporarily relieved by removal, and have returned again on their return home. Of the cachectic diseases, some are produced, others aggravated, by this cause. Scrofula is of this latter description. The cases of the children in your own family show that it is impossible to prevent suppuration when the patient is constantly breathing a humid atmosphere. This has also been the case with one of your immediate neighbours. That form of scrofula termed tabes mesenterica, I think, is, in many cases, brought on entirely by the same cause. Want of time prevents my extending the example of diseases attributable to this cause.

" I am, dear Reynolds, yours truly,   " T. TAYLOR."

Mr. James Murray, the Registrar of the Hackney-road District, in answer to the question, In what parts of your district has the number of deaths registered in the years 1838, 1839, 1840, 1841, and 1842 been the greatest, in proportion to the population ? states, " The greatest number of deaths registered, in proportion to the population, have occurred in all the streets leading into Old Cock-lane, especially the courts therein, and in all the streets leading into the Hackney-road as far as Strout's-place, viz., Old Nichol-street, New Nichol-street, Half Nichol-street, Vincent-street, Mead-street, Turville-street, and courts therein, Collingwood-street, Old Castle-street, Virginia-row, Austin-street, Gascoigne-place, and Weatherhead, Nova Scotia, Green Gate, and Cooper's-gardens, and Wellington-row." In what parts of your district has the greatest number of deaths occurred from small-pox, measles, scarlatina, hooping-cough, diarrhœa, dysentery, cholera, influenza, or fever (typhus) ?—" The greatest number of deaths from the diseases named have occurred in precisely the same parts of my district, especially in the courts and in those anomalous assemblages of small cabins built on low and undrained ground, called gardens." And in what parts have epidemic diseases been most fatal ? —" Epidemic diseases have been most fatal wherever the greatest number of people are congregated on the smallest space, which is again the identical spot mentioned above, with the exception of Wellington-row and the gardens, where the deaths appear to be chiefly caused by their low, damp, and almost swampy condition during winter. Pneumonia being there the prevailing cause of death, with occasional instances of putrid sore throat." And state generally the condition of those unhealthy streets, courts, and houses, as to drainage, supplies of water, cleanliness.—" These streets and courts have generally an imperfect drainage, suitable only to a former state. These drains are very near the surface ; and some of the houses are built over them, so as to communicate a dampness prejudicial to health. The gardens herein mentioned appear to be entirely without drainage. The supply of water in the streets is generally good, but in the courts and in the gardens is derived from a main, to the cock of which the inhabitants have common access while the water is on, and have to fetch it in pails to their houses, which mode of supply I consider to be insufficient for health or cleanliness. The population is very dense, in some cases amounting to nearly 30 persons in a single house. As an average, an enumeration district may be taken, 57 houses, 580 persons. On taking in a larger district, 30,000 people congregated on a spot about half a mile square. The houses are universally let out in rooms, a custom apparently introduced by the French refugees ; the houses built by whom are all on the Edinburgh Old Town or French fashion, with large rooms on each floor, intended for a family, with a common staircase. A single room now generally contains a family, with tools of trade, bed, and kitchen, which, coupled with uncleanly habits, occasions a constant effluvium, very oppressive, and, I doubt not, unhealthy. In the larger houses, the lowest grade live in damp under-ground kitchens."

No. 12.

EXAMPLES OF ORDINARY UNDERTAKERS' BILLS IN THE METROPOLIS.

No. 1.

	£.	s.	d.
Elm coffin, lined, ruffled, mattrass, sheet, and pillow. . .	3	11	0
Leaden coffin, plate of inscription, 5 men with ditto . . .	6	15	0
Outside case, brass engraved plate, 5 men with ditto, & making-up	9	9	6
Pall 7s. 6d., 2 porters, scarfs, staves, covers, bands, & gloves, 38s.	2	5	6
Four gentlemen's crape scarfs, bands, and gloves . . .	6	12	0
Seventeen silk ditto ' ditto · . .	41	5	0
Hearse, 4 horses, feathers and velvets for ditto . . .	5	16	0
Five coaches, pairs, ditto for ditto	9	15	0
Six coach cloaks, bands, and gloves, 60s., truncheons & wands 6s.	3	6	0
Eighteen pages and bearers, silk bands, and gloves . . .	11	14	0
Attending and assistance, 63s.; scarf, band, and gloves for minister, 55s.	5	18	0
Hatband and gloves for clerk and sexton, 30s.; grave-digger, &c., 3s. 6d.	1	13	6
Paid vault dues 4l. 12s. 6d.; letters 20s.; fetching company 4s.6d.	5	17	0
Two crape bands and gloves for servants 20s.; 8 silk do. do. 5s.	6	0	0
Thirty-four men's allowance 28s.	1	8	0
	£ 121	**5**	**0**

No. 2.

Elm shell, lined, ruffled, mattrass, sheet, and pillow . . .	3	8	0
Leaden coffin, plate of inscription, and 5 men with do., & making up	6	3	0
Outside case, engraved plate, 5 men with ditto . . .	8	13	0
Pall 7s.; 2 porters' scarfs, staves, bands, and gloves . .	2	7	0
Lid of feathers 21s.; 3 men with do., and bands and gloves 45s.	3	6	0
Hearse, 4 horses 2l. 14s.; feathers and velvets for ditto, 2l. 6s. .	5	0	0
Two coaches, pairs 2l. 14s.; ditto ditto 1l. 2s. . .	3	16	0
Three coachmen's cloaks, bands, and gloves	1	11	6
Ten pages and bearers 40s.; bands and gloves for ditto. 5l.; truncheons and wands 4s.	7	4	0
Eight gentlemen's cloaks 8s.; 4 crape bands, &c., 40s.; 6 silk ditto 6l. 6s.	8	14	0
Two bands and gloves for clerk and sexton 30s.; 2 ditto for private servants 17s.	2	7	0
Attending 21s.; 18 men's allowances 18s.; letters of invitation 4s.	2	4	0
Paid dues 7l. 14s. 6d.; pew-opener, &c. 2s.; fetching company 2s.	7	18	6
	£ 62	**11**	**0**

No. 3.

Covered coffin, lined, ruffled, plate of inscription, mattrass, sheet and pillow	4	19	0
Pall 7s.6d.; 2 porters. gowns, staves, and for bands & gloves 30s.	1	19	6
Four gentlemen's cloaks, crape bands and gloves 1l.18s.; attending ceremony 20s.	2	18	0
Hearse and coach, pairs 3l.12s.; velvets for ditto 21s.; 2 cloaks and bands 11s.	5	4	0
Six pages, bands, gloves, truncheons, wands, 62s.; fetching company 9s.	3	11	0
Paid 10 men's allowance 25s.; stone 10s.; turnpike, gravedigger 4s.	1	19	0
	£ 20	**10**	**6**

No. 4.

	£.	s.	d.
Smooth elm, polished nails, inscription, lined, mattrass, sheet, and pillow	4	10	0
Pall 7s.; 4 crape bands; 6 ladies' hoods and gloves. . .	2	17	0
Attending 5s.; dues at church 18s.; 5 men's allowance 6s.6d.	1	9	6
	£ 8	16	6

To the Executor of —— ——, Esq.

Dr to —— ——.

For the Funeral of —— ——, Esq., died 19th February, aged 80,
N. 5 and 84 B., Cemetery, All Souls.

	£	s.	d.
To a 6 ft. × 22 elm coffin, lined and ruffed with fine cotton .	2	10	0
Wool bed	0	10	6
Fine sheet and pillow	0	18	0
Lead coffin, solder, and workmanship	6	18	0
Lead plate of inscription	0	5	0
Inch and a half oak coffin, made to receive the above, covered with fine black cloth, 3 rows of brass nails, 4 pair of large handles, star and serpent, and finished with rays . . .	15	15	0
Brass plate of inscription	2	8	0
To the use of the best velvet pall	0	10	6
Three crape hatbands	0	12	0
Three crape scarfs	3	0	0
Silk scarf, hatbands, and gloves, the Rev. Mr. Lynarn . .	2	6	0
Seven silk scarfs	10	10	0
Seven silk hatbands	4	7	6
Five silk scarfs, hatbands, and gloves, Rev. Mr. Rue, Mr. Hawes Smith, Rule Field	11	10	0
Eleven pair of kid gloves	1	18	6
Two porters, with silk dressings	0	18	0
Two hatbands and gloves for ditto	0	15	0
The plume of ostrich feathers	1	1	0
Man carrying ditto	0	6	6
Silk hatbands and gloves for ditto	0	7	6
Hearse and four	3	10	0
Feathers and velvets for ditto	2	18	0
Three mourning coaches and four	10	10	0
Feathers and velvets for ditto	2	14	0
Four coachman's cloaks	0	4	0
Silk hatbands and gloves for ditto	1	10	0
Eight hearse pages, with truncheons	1	16	0
Silk hatbands and gloves for ditto	3	0	0
Six coach pages, with wands	1	7	0
Silk hatbands and gloves for ditto	2	5	0
Silk hatband and gloves for clerk at the ground . .	0	12	6
Four hatbands and gloves for servants of the two carriages .	2	10	0
One hatband and gloves for terrace beadle . . .	0	10	6
One hatband and gloves for man servant . . .	0	7	6
Four pair of habit gloves	0	12	0
Attending the funeral	1	1	0
Silk hatband and gloves	0	16	0
Twenty-six men's expenses as customary . . .	1	19	0
Turnpikes	0	6	6
Paid dues at the cemetery	22	7	6
Silk scarf, hatband, and gloves (Mr. Owen) . . .	2	6	0
Paid for the bell	0	6	6
	£ 130	16	0

The Funeral Expenses of Mary Maria ————— ————,

Performed by ————, ————.

Nov. 15, 1834. £. *s.* *d.*

	£.	s.	d.
5 ft. 9 inch. 17 elm, lined, ruffed super linen	2	5	0
Tufted mattrass	0	14	0
No. 10 shroud, sheet, cap, and pillow	2	5	0
Stout lead coffin, soldering up	7	7	0
Lead plate ditto	0	5	0
Six men with lead coffin	0	18	0
Two men attending on the surgeons	0	6	0
Making up—plumbers	0	5	0
Elm case, covered with fine black cloth, set 2 rows all round, No. 1 nails; 4 pair cherub tin handles, gripes and drops; 8 screws, black	7	7	0
Brass engraved plate, fine laquered	2	12	6
Six men in with case moving down stairs . . .	0	18	0

Nov. 21 :—

	£.	s.	d.
Best pall, lid of feathers	1	8	0
Four fine cloaks	0	6	0
Nine rich silk bands for gentlemen	6	6	0
Nine pair gentlemen's best kid gloves	1	16	0
Two porters and furniture 16s.	0	13	9
Featherman, 2 pages and wands	0	12	6
Hearse and 4 horses	2	12	0
Feathers and velvets for ditto	3	3	0
Six hearse pages and truncheons	1	5	0
Mourning coach and four horses	2	12	0
Feathers and velvets for ditto	1	1	0
Two coach pages and wands	0	8	6
Two coachmen's cloaks	0	2	0
Two velvet hammercloths	0	6	0
Attending funeral	0	7	6
Fifteen silk bands for 2 porters, 8 pages, 3 feathermen, and 2 coachmen	6	0	0
Fifteen pair gloves for ditto ditto	1	2	6

	£.	s.	d.
Paid dues at St. Margaret's	2	9	6
Lead fees ditto	0	16	7
Bell and searchers	0	8	0
Bearers	0	3	0
Sexton	0	3	0
Extra digging	0	15	0
Grave-maker	0	3	0
Men's allowance, coffin case and funeral . .	0	12	6
	5	10	7

£ 60 19 1

Exposition of the English Law in respect to Perpetuities in Public Burial Grounds.

[From the decision in the case of Gilbert *v.* Buzzard and Boyer, 2nd Haggard's Reports of Cases argued and determined in the Consistory Court of London, containing the Judgments of the Right Hon. Lord Stowell.]

In what way the mortal remains are to be conveyed to the grave, and there deposited, I do not find any positive rule of law, or of religion, that prescribes. The authority under which the received practices exist, is to be found in our manners, rather than in our laws : they have their origin in natural sentiments of public decency and private affection; they are ratified by common usage and consent; and being attached to a subject of the gravest and most impressive nature, remain unaltered by private caprice and fancy, amidst all the giddy revolutions that are perpetually varying the modes and fashions that belong to the lighter circumstances of human life. That bodies should be carried in a state of naked exposure to the grave, would be a real offence to the living, as well as an apparent indignity to the dead. Some *involucra*, or coverings, have been deemed necessary in all civilized and Christian countries; but chests or trunks containing the bodies, descending along with them into the grave, and remaining there till their own decay, cannot plead either the same necessity, or the same general use.

*   *   *   *   *

The rule of law which says, that a man has a right to be buried in his own church-yard, is to be found, most certainly, in many of our authoritative text-writers; but it is not quite so easy to find the rule which gives him the right of burying a large chest or trunk in company with himself. That is no part of his original and absolute right, nor is it necessarily involved in it. That right, strictly taken, is to be returned to his parent earth for dissolution, and to be carried thither in a decent and inoffensive manner. When these purposes are answered, his rights are, perhaps, fully satisfied in the strict sense in which any claim, in the nature of an absolute right, can be deemed to extend.

*   *   *   *   *

It has been argued, that the ground once given to the body is appropriated to it for ever; it is literally in mortmain unalienably; it is not only the *domus ultima*, but the *domus æterna*, of that tenant, who is never to be disturbed, be his condition what it may; the introduction of another body into that lodgment at any time, however distant, is an unwarrantable intrusion. If these positions be true, it certainly follows, that the question of comparative duration sinks into utter insignificance.

In support of them, it seems to be assumed, that the tenant himself is imperishable; for, surely, there can be no inextinguishable title, no perpetuity of possession, belonging to a subject which itself is perishable. But the fact is, that "man" and "for ever" are terms quite incompatible in any state of his existence, dead or living, in this world. The time must come when "*ipsæ periere ruinæ*," when the posthumous remains must mingle with, and compose a part of, that soil in which they have been deposited. Precious embalments, and costly monuments may preserve for a long time the remains of those who have filled the more commanding stations of human life; but the common lot of mankind furnishes no such means of conservation. With reference to them, the *domus æterna* is a mere flourish of rhetoric; the process of nature will speedily resolve them into an intimate mixture with their kindred dust; and their dust will help to furnish a place of repose for other occupants in succession. It is objected, that no precise time can be fixed at which the mortal remains, and the chest which contains them, shall undergo the complete process of dissolution, and it certainly cannot; being dependent upon circumstances that vary, upon difference of soils, and exposures of seasons and climates; but observation can ascertain them sufficiently for practical use. The experience of not many years is required to furnish a sufficient certainty for such a purpose.

Founded on such facts and considerations, the legal doctrine certainly is, and has remained, unaffected; that the common cemetery is not *res unius ætatis*, the property of one generation now departed, but is, likewise, the common property of the living, and of generations yet unborn, and is subject only to temporary appropriations. There exists in the whole a right of succession, which can be lawfully obstructed only in a portion of it, by public authority, that of the ecclesiastical magistrate, who gives occasionally an exclusive title, in such portion, to the succession of some family, or to an individual, who has a fair claim to be favoured by such a distinction; and this, not without a just consideration of its expedience, and a due attention to the objections of those who oppose such an alienation from the common property. Even a bricked grave, granted without such an authority, is an aggression upon the common freehold interests, and carries the pretensions of the dead to an extent that violates the rights of the living.

If this view of the matter be just, all contrivances that, whether intentionally or not, prolong the time of dissolution beyond the period at which the common local understanding and usage have fixed it, is an act of injustice, unless compensated in some way or other. In country parishes, where the population is small, and the cemetery is large, it is a matter less worthy of consideration; more ground can be spared, and less is wanted; but, in populous parishes, in large and crowded cities, the indulgence of an exclusive possession is unavoidably limited; for, unless limited, evils of most formidable magnitude take place. Churchyards cannot be made commensurate to the demands of a large and increasing population; the period of decay and dissolution does not arrive fast enough in the accustomed mode of depositing bodies in the earth, to evacuate the ground for the use of succeeding claimants: new cemeteries must be purchased at an enormous expense to the parish, and to be used at an increased expense to families, and at the inconvenience of their being compelled to resort to very incommodious distances for attending on the offices of interment.

In this very parish three additional burial-grounds are alleged to have been purchased, and to be now nearly filled. This is the progress of things in their ordinary course; and if to this is to be added the general introduction of a new mode of interment, which is to ensure to bodies a much longer possession, the evil will become intolerable, and a comparatively small portion of the dead will shoulder out the living and their posterity. The whole environs of this metropolis will be surrounded with a circumvallation of church-yards, perpetually increasing, by becoming themselves surcharged with bodies, if indeed land-owners can be found who will be willing to divert their ground from the beneficial uses of the living to the barren preservation of the dead, contrary to the humane maxim quoted by Tully from Plato's Republic:—" Quæ terra fruges ferre, et, ut mater, cibos, suppeditare possit, eam ne quis nobis minuat, *neve vivus neve mortuus.*"

No. 13.

OF THE EXTENT OF INTRA-MURAL BURIAL GROUND PROVIDED, AS COMPARED WITH THE QUANTITY REQUIRED FOR THE METROPOLIS, AT THE STANDARD OF 110 PER ACRE.—Vide Report, § 139, § 160, § 161, § 171.   The plan represents the statistical facts and proportions of space after the mode used by Mr. Sopwith, the engineer. Each square of the subjoined plate represents an acre. The extent of squares coloured shows the extent of ground occupied by each religious denomination. The blank spaces show the extent of deficiency of public ground for the burial of the population in single graves.

CHURCH OF ENGLAND PAROCHIAL BURIAL GROUNDS. Burials 191 per acre.

PROTESTANT DISSENTERS' BURIAL GROUNDS. Burials 246 per acre.

PRIVATE OR TRADING BURIAL GROUNDS. Burials 403 per acre.

JEWS' BURIAL GROUNDS. Burials 23 per acre.

ROMAN CATHOLICS' BURIAL GROUNDS. Burials 1043 per acre.

BURIAL FEES.—*A Return of the Amount of the Burial Fees received by the Clergymen of several of the Parishes of the Metropolis was given in to the Committee of the House of Commons by the Bishop of London. The following Table gives the same Amount of Fees divided by the Returns of the Number of Burials, in the Years 1830, 1831, and 1832, returned from the several Parishes, to an order of the House of Commons made in the Year 1834.*

PARISHES.	No. of Burials in 1830.	No. of Burials in 1831.	No. of Burials in 1832.	Average of the three Years.	Amount of Burial Fees in 1838.			Amount of Burial Fees in 1839.			Amount of Burial Fees in 1840.			Average Burial Fees, 1838-9-40.			Average Fee per Burial.		
					£.	s.	d.	£.	s.	d.	£.	s.	d.	£.	s.	d.	£.	s.	d.
St. James, Westminster	1,063	1,168	1,087	1,106	329	0	0	298	0	0	246	0	0	291	0	0*	0	5	3*
St. Botolph, Bishopsgate	248	300	319	289	36	1	2	42	7	2	23	9	10	33	19	4	0	2	3
St. George the Martyr	158	218	147	174	70	12	6	59	5	10	59	0	8	62	19	8	0	7	3
St. John, Westminster	815	893	984	897	123	7	0	93	19	8	105	13	7	107	13	5	0	2	5
St. George in the East	705	681	802	729	101	15	0	101	8	0	74	8	6	92	10	8	0	2	6
St. Bride	162	223	175	187	51	6	8	51	2	0	81	2	4†	61	3	8	0	6	7
St. Giles and St. George, Bloomsbury	1,296	1,669	1,934	1,633	1,038	4	0	768	4	0	870	15	0	892	7	8	0	10	11
St. Dunstan, Westminster	115	113	122	117	39	9	2	24	0	8	35	5	10	32	18	7	0	5	8
St. Clement Danes	395	524	494	471	121	14	0	112	19	10	86	3	4	106	19	4	0	4	6
Bethnal Green	617	951	1,064	877	71	4	0	67	4	0	62	3	6	66	17	2	0	1	6
St. Botolph, Aldersgate	140	168	160	156	60	8	4	58	2	8	45	10	0	54	13	8	0	7	0
St. George, Hanover Sq.	1,224	1,389	1,389	1,334	597	17	0	423	8	2	488	11	2	503	5	5	0	7	6
St. Giles, Cripplegate	231	225	307	254	87	9	6	66	6	10	56	14	10	70	3	9	0	5	6
St. Andrew, Holborn	587	586	847	673	306	0	1	324	14	1	223	15	2	284	16	5	0	8	6
St. Catherine Cree	36	33	40	36	75	3	6	43	16	6	56	13	6	58	11	2	1	12	6
St. Olave, Hart Street	22	19	28	23	60	8	0	37	4	0	32	2	0	43	4	8	1	17	7
Allhallows Barking	50	64	66	60	31	19	6	7	19	0	15	16	6	18	11	8	0	6	2
Total	7,864	9,224	9,965	9,016	3,202	0	2	2,580	2	11	2,563	5	9	2,781	16	3	0	6	2

* The Average for the previous six Years was £405.

† Increase of 1840, from two tablets.

N.B.—This List specifies only the Clergyman's Fees, not those paid to the Churchwardens, Clerk, or Sexton.

PAROCHIAL BURIAL-GROUNDS IN THE METROPOLIS.

PLACES OF BURIAL.	Population in 1841.	Estimated Extent in Square Yards.	Annual Number of Burials.	No. of Burials per Acre.
Allhallows Barking, Great Tower Street	1,924	825	50	293
Allhallows, Bread Street . . .	263	100	'Scarcely any'	..
Allhallows, Lombard Street . . .	516	350	'Seldom used.'	..
Allhallows, London Wall . . .	1,620	615	24	189
Allhallows, Staining Lane . . .	502	619	20	156
Allhallows-the-Great, Thames Street	672	346	50	319
Allhallows-the-Less, ditto . . .	181	412		
Alphage, St. London Wall . . .	976	388	50	624
Andrew's, St.	35,301	4,840	250	250
Andrew's, St. Burial-ground, Gray's Inn Lane	..	9,258	312	163
Andrew's, St. Undershaft . . .	1,163	265	70	1,278
Andrew's, St. Wardrobe, and St. Ann, Blackfriars	3,596	657	100	737
Anne, St. and St. Agnes within Aldersgate	513	1,650	70	205
Ann's, St. Limehouse.	19,337	24,500	150	30
Anne's, St. Soho	16,480	2,732	200	354
Augustine's, St. and St. Faith's. .	1,070	3,700	30	39
Bartholomew, St. the Great . . .	3,414	783	100	618
Bartholomew, St. the Less . . .	744	183	8	212
Benet, St. Fink	383	277	6	105
Benet, St. Paul's Wharf	588	297	36	587
Bennet, St. Sherehog.	145	145	'Seldom used.'	..
Botolph, St. Aldersgate	5,906	1,918	250	631
Botolph, St. Aldgate	9,525	1,545	250	783
Botolph, St. Bishopsgate . . .	10,969	3,034	250	399
Botolph, St. by Billingsgate . .	278	266	3	55
Bride's, St. Fleet Street . . . . Ditto, Ground in Farringdon Street	6,126	1,472	130	427
*Bridewell Chapel	529	2,400	10	20
Broadway Chapel of Ease to St. Margaret's and St. John . . .	..	7,220	500	335
Catherine, St. Coleman Street . .	322	388	36	449
Catherine, St. Cree, or Christchurch	1,740	1,100	100	440
Chapel Royal, Tower.	..	525	4	37
Charlton Church	..	2,150	30	68
Chelsea Hospital Burial-ground . .	Vide St. Luke.	6,696	55	40
Chelsea Old Church		1,210	6	24
Christ Church, Blackfriars Road .	..	8,448	520	298
Christ Church, Newgate Street . .	2,446	1,934	30	75
Christ Church, Spitalfields . . .	20,436	6,413	350	264
Clement, St. Danes	15,459	1,736	100	279
Clement, St. Danes, 2nd Ground, Portugal Street.	..	1,422	300	1,021
Cripplegate Poor-ground, Warwick-place, St. Luke's	..	1,400	100	346
Dionis, St. Backchurch	806	132	20	733
Dunstan, St. Fleet Street . . .	3,266	851	208	1,182
Dunstan, St. in the East. . . .	1,010	600	150	1,210
Dunstan, St. Stepney	63,723	21,795	200	44
East India Company's Chapel Yard, High Street Poplar . . .	..	6,447	60	45
Edmund, St. the King	391	164	'Seldom used.'	..
Ethelburga, St.	669	240	30	605

* Extra-Parochial.

PLACES OF BURIAL.	Population in 1841.	Estimated Extent in Square Yards.	Annual Number of Burials.	No. of Burials per Acre.
Fulham Church	9,319	12,000	200	81
George's, St. Bloomsbury . . .	16,981	12,100	300	120
George, St. Botolph Lane . . .	235	76	2	127
George's, St. District Church, Camberwell	39,868	11,640	100	42
George, St. Hanover Square, Burial-ground, Uxbridge Road . .	66,453	24,200	1,200	240
George, St. in the East	41,350	15,000	500	161
George, St. the Martyr	Vide St. Andrew's.	12,100	200	80
George, St. Burial-ground, Old Kent Road	46,644	1,368	130	460
George, St. the Martyr, Southwark .		4,050	470	562
Giles, St. Camberwell	39,868	16,000	500	151
Giles, St. Cripplegate	13,255	4,700	200	206
Giles, St. in the Fields	37,311	4,958	400	390
Ditto, Burial-ground, St. Pancras	..	24,200	1,560	312
Greenwich Church	29,755	2,740	700	1,236
*Greenwich Hospital Burial-ground .	..	22,480	300	65
Gregory, St. by St. Paul's . . .	1,444	1,095	100	442
Grosvenor Chapel, South Audley Street	..	6,000	36	29
*Guy's Hospital Ground, Snow's Fields	..	3,120	85	132
Hackney, South	Vide St. John	3,300	100	145
Hackney, West		6,534	200	148
Helen, St. Great	659	779	30	186
Holy Trinity, Brompton	9,515	26,524	100	18
Islington Chapel of Ease . . .	..	17,659	416	114
James, St. Chapel of Ease, Clerkenwell		3,500	350	484
James, St. Clerkenwell	56,756	2,000	400	968
James, St. Burial-ground, Ray Street, Clerkenwell	..	800	150	907
James, St. Clerkenwell, 2nd Ground	..	1,000	300	1,452
James, St. Duke's Place	964	338	15	215
James, St. Garlickhithe	520	162	20	598
James, St. New Church	..	8,100	260	155
James, St. Piccadilly	..	4,840	60	60
Ditto, Burial-ground, Hampstead Road	..	26,620	624	113
John, St. Baptist, Savoy	414	600	50	403
John's, St. Chapel of Ease . . .	..	26,000	1,560	290
John's, St. Chapel, Walworth .	..	6,400	150	113
John's, St. Church, Waltham Green	..	3,600	15	20
John's, St. Clerkenwell	Vide St. James	315	200	3,073
Ditto, Burial-ground, Benjamin Street	..	1,079	12	54
John, St. the Evangelist	108	7,260	500	333
John, St. the Evangelist, Horslydown	..	9,740	250	124
John, St. the Evangelist, Great Waterloo Street	..	5,924	400	327
John's, St. Hackney	37,771	31,000	700	108
John, St. the Baptist	367	363	12	160
John, St. High Street, Wapping .	4,108	6,600	250	183
John's, St. Hoxton	..	6,050	600	480
John, St. Zachary	183	905	6	32

* Private.

PLACES OF BURIAL.	Population in 1841.	Estimated Extent in Sq. Yards.	Annual Number of Burials.	No. of Burials per Acre.
King's Road, Chelsea	..	4,840	130	130
Lawrence, St. Jewry	625	200	35	847
Leonard's, St. Ground, Hackney Road	..	2,000	225	544
Leonard's, St. Shoreditch . . .	83,432	8,000	300	181
Luke's, St. Burial-ground, Bath Street	..	1,240	200	781
Luke, St. Chelsea, New Church .	40,179	19,360	468	117
Luke's, St. Old Street	49,829	9,287	500	261
Magnus, St.	239	44	6	660
Margaret's. St.	..	5,000	50	48
Margaret, St. Lothbury	189	291	12	300
Margaret, St. Pattens, with ⎱ St. Gabriel, Fenchurch Street. ⎰	553	81	'Closed'	..
	..	473	4	41
Mark's, St. Kennington	..	8,960	500	270
Martin, St. in the Fields, Burial-⎱ ground, Camden Town . . ⎰	..	19,360	832	208
Ditto, Burial-ground, Drury Lane	..	1,269	40	153
Martin, St. Orgars	353	99	'Seldom used'	..
Martin, St. Outwich	135	123	12	472
Martin, St. Vintry	288	450	3	32
Mary, St. Abbotts, Kensington . .	26,834	6,620	330	241
Mary, St. Abchurch, with St. Law-⎱ rence Pountney . . . . . ⎰	907	566	6	51
Mary, St. Aldermanbury. . . .	751	313	30	464
Mary's, St. Burial-ground . . .	..	2,776	200	349
Mary, St. Aldermary	494	173	8	224
Mary, St. at Hill	987	167	40	1,159
Mary, St. at Bow	..	2,716	52	93
Mary, St. Chapel, Hammersmith .	..	8,960	20	11
Mary, St. Haggerstone	..	7,260	100	67
Mary, St. Lambeth	115,888	2,400	250	504
Mary, St. Islington	55,690	7,450	750	487
Mary, St. le-Strand, Burial-ground,⎱ Russell Court . . . . . . ⎰	..	473	90	921
Mary, St. le-Strand	2,520	200	12	290
Mary, St. Love Lane	..	100	'Seldom used'	..
Mary Magdalen, St.	..	288	12	202
Mary Magdalen, St. Bermondsey .	34,947	9,184	600	316
Mary's, St. Newington	54,606	8,160	350	208
Mary's, St. Paddington	25,173	20,116	936	222
Mary's, St. Rotherhithe, and . .	13,917	11,800 ⎱	345	139
Trinity District Church . . .	..	200 ⎰		
Mary, St. Somerset	375	389	'Seldom used'	..
Mary, St. Staining	268	423	..	..
Mary's, St. Stoke Newington . .	..	3,000	50	81
Mary's, St. Whitechapel . . .	34,053	4,219	150	172
Ditto, Workhouse-ground . . .	..	2,776	200	349
Mary, St. Woolnoth	317	33	'Very few'	..
Mary, St. Woolwich	25,785	12,800	600	227
Mary-le-boue, St..	138,164	13,500	520	186
Mary-le-bone, St. Old Church,⎱ High Street . . . . . . ⎰	138,164	2,000	36	87
Mary-le-Bow, St..	346	250	30	581
Matthew, St. Bethnal Green . .	74,088	12,100	600	240
Matthew, St. Friday Street . . .	160	208	21	489
Michael, St. Bassishaw	687	222	30	654
Michael, St. Cornhill	454	240	6	121
Michael, St. Queenhithe. . . .	647	266 ⎱	30	342
Ditto, Burial-ground, Trinity Lane	..	158 ⎰		
Mildred, St. Bread Street . . .	351	242	'Seldom used'	..

PLACES OF BURIAL.	Population in 1841.	Estimated Extent in Square Yards.	Annual Number of Burials.	No. of Burials per Acre.
Mildred, St. Poultry	280	84	..	..
Nicholas, St. Acon	194	287	..	..
Nicholas, St. Cole Abbey . . .	254	67	' Never used'	..
Nicholas, St. Olave	431	334	20	290
Pancras, St. Old Church	129,763	24,200	400	80
Paradise Row Burying-ground . .	..	8,532	1,040	590
*Paul's, St. Cathedral	..	3,745	'Seldom used'	..
Paul's, St. Covent Garden . . .	5,718	4,064	200	129
Ditto, Burial-ground contiguous to Workhouse	..	3,455		
Paul's, St. Deptford	..	12,000	360	145
Paul's, St. Hammersmith . . .	9,888	6,888	200	141
Paul's, St. Shadwell	10,060	3,000	250	403
†Penitentiary Burial Ground . . .	..	432	10	112
Peter, St. Cheap, corner of Wood St.	227	96	' Never used'	..
Peter, St. Cornhill	656	287	40	674
Peter, St. District Church, Walworth	..	7,800	300	186
Peter-le-Poor, St..	559	48	'Seldom used'	..
Peter's, St. New Church, Hammersmith	3,565	1,210	50	200
Peter, St. Paul's Wharf	341	292	'Seldom used'	..
Poplar New Church	20,342	14,686	300	99
Olave, St. Hart Street	816	462	36	377
Olave, St. Jewry	168	306	'Seldom used'	..
Olave, St. Silver Street	972	335	' Never used '	..
Olave's, St. Tooley Street . . .	6,745	770	200	1,257
Saviour's, St..	18,219	2,700		
Ditto, Cross Bones Ground, Red Cross Street	..	4,500	244	143
Ditto. College Park Street . . .	..	1,040		
Sepulchre, St..	..	1,746		
Ditto, in Church Lane	12,325	1,785	256	293
Ditto, in Durham Yard . . .	..	702		
Stephen, St. Walbrook	322	306	50	791
Swithin's, St. Cannon Street . .	389	241	20	402
Ditto, 2nd Ground	..	66	24	1,760
Temple Church, St. Mary's. . .	..	400	' Very few '	..
Thomas Apostle, St.	648	340	'Seldom used'	..
†Thomas, St. Hospital Ground, Snow's Fields	..	1,449	84	282
Trinity Church, Minories . . .	579	302	7	112
Vedast, St.	427	108		179

* Collegiate.   † Privat

PROTESTANT DISSENTERS' BURIAL-GROUNDS AND OTHERS.

PLACES OF BURIAL.	Estimated Extent in Sq. Yards.	Annual Number of Burials.	No. of Burials per Acre.
EPISCOPALIANS.			
St. Leonard's, Chapel, Bromley	270	52	932
St. George's, Chapel, New Road	3,250	125	186
PRESBYTERIANS.		.	
Gravel Pit Chapel, Hackney	3,300	100	147
St. Andrew's, Scotch Church	900	100	538
CONGREGATIONALISTS OR INDEPENDENTS.			
Independent Chapel, Greenwich	1,000	100	484
Pulling's Chapel, Deptford	400	50	605
Wickliffe Chapel, Stepney	600	150	1,210
Ebenezer Chapel, Shadwell	680	120	854
Dr. Burder's, Hackney	3,168	100	153
Meeting House, Old Gravel Lane	60	4	323
Esher Street, Lambeth	1,210	72	288
Brunswick Chapel, Three Colts Street . . .	480	52	524
Collier's Rents, Borough	970	50	249
Abney Chapel, Stoke Newington	780	36	223
Mile End Chapel	2,420	52	104
Trinity Chapel, Poplar	1,200	36	145
Stockwell Green	725	' Very few '	..
BAPTISTS.			
Enon Chapel, Woolwich	112	25	1,080
Worship Street Chapel	720	30	202
Regent Street, Lambeth	320	12	181
Cox's, Dr., Chapel, Hackney	824	26	153
Maze Pond	650	10	74
East Street Chapel	140	2	69
Hammersmith	2,420	30	60
WESLEYAN METHODISTS.			
Methodist Chapel, Woolwich	1,226	100	395
City Road Chapel	2,148	150	338
Stafford Street, Peckham	336	16	230
Wesleyan Chapel, Hammersmith . . .	2,430	18	36
Southwark Chapel, Long Lane, Borough . .	780	' Very few '	..
ROMAN CATHOLICS.			
Parker Row, Dockhead	300	100	1,613
Moorfields	120	30	1,210
Poplar	833	140	813
QUAKERS.			
Long Lane, Bermondsey	2,728	60	106
Coleman Street	4,759	35	35
Hammersmith	1,210	1 or 2	6

PLACES OF BURIAL.	Estimated Extent in Sq. Yards.	Annual Number of Burials.	No of Burials per Acre.
JEWS.			
Mile End Road	4,840	52	52
North Street, Mile End Road	24,200	200	40
Chelsea	4,800	22	22
Grove Street	10,890	30	13
FOREIGN.			
Swedish Chapel	450	10	108
UNDESCRIBED.			
Union Chapel, Woolwich	1,500	100	323
Cannon Street Road	2,400	550	1,109
Paradise Row, Lambeth	8,532	1,040	590
New Bunhill Fields, Islington	4,300	520	585
Ebenezer Chapel, Long Lane	265	20	365
Bunhill Fields	18,150	600	160
Zion Chapel, High Street, Borough . . .	210	2	46
Poplar Chapel	8,000	52	31
Maberly Chapel	270	3	54
Brook Street, Ratcliffe Highway. . . .	700	2 or 3	21
Millyard Chapel	960	1	5
Whitfield's Chapel, St. Pancras	4,650	300	312
York Street Chapel, Lock's Fields . . .	1,860	'Very few'	..
Denmark Row, Cold Harbour Lane . . .	400	..	..
Salem Chapel, Woolwich	360	'Seldom any'	..
Little Alie Street, Goodman's Fields . . .	'Small'	6	..

GENERAL BURIAL-GROUNDS.

PLACES OF BURIAL.	Estimated Extent in Sq. Yards.	Annual Number of Burials.	No. of Burials per Acre.
*Bunhill Fields, City	8,000	1,000	605
*Bunhill Fields, New	3,250	1,560	2,323
*John's, St. Borough	1,440	142	477
*London, North East	24,200	250	50
*Sheen's New Ground.	9,680	600	300
*Spa Fields.	14,520	1,560	520

* Private.

CEMETERIES.

PLACES OF BURIAL.	Estimated Extent in Sq. Yards.	Annual Number of Burials.	No. of Burials per Acre.
Highgate Cemetery	101,640	220	10
Nunhead ditto	242,000	208	4
East London ditto, Beaumont Square, Mile End	26,620	850	154
City of London and Tower Hamlets ditto, Mile End	135,520	624	22
West of London and Westminster ditto, Earls Court, Brompton	193,600	254	6
South Metropolitan ditto, Norwood	193,600	180	5
Kensal Green, All Souls' Cemetery	222,640	800	17
Abney Park Cemetery	145,200	200	7

LONDON:
Printed by WILLIAM CLOWES and SONS, Stamford-street.
For Her Majesty's Stationery Office.

I

RETURN TO the circulation desk of any
University of California Library
or to the
NORTHERN REGIONAL LIBRARY FACILITY
Bldg. 400, Richmond Field Station
University of California
Richmond, CA 94804-4698

ALL BOOKS MAY BE RECALLED AFTER 7 DAYS
- 2-month loans may be renewed by calling
  (510) 642-6753
- 1-year loans may be recharged by bringing
  books to NRLF
- Renewals and recharges may be made 4
  days prior to due date.

DUE AS STAMPED BELOW

12,000 (11/95)

Y

Ps